Toxic Diversity

Toxic Diversity

*Race, Gender, and
Law Talk in America*

Dan Subotnik

NEW YORK UNIVERSITY PRESS
New York and London

NEW YORK UNIVERSITY PRESS
New York and London
www.nyupress.org

Library of Congress Cataloging-in-Publication Data
Subotnik, Dan.
Toxic diversity : race, gender, and law talk in America /
Dan Subotnik.
p.   cm.
Includes bibliographical references and index.
ISBN 0-8147-4000-6 (cloth : alk. paper)
1. Race discrimination—Law and legislation—United States. 2. Sex
and law—United States. 3. Critical legal studies—United States.
4. United States—Race relations—Philosophy.   I. Title.
KF4755.S23 2005
342.7308'73—dc22   2005001781

New York University Press books are printed on acid-free paper,
and their binding materials are chosen for strength and durability.

Manufactured in the United States of America

10 9 8 7 6 5 4 3 2 1

Qu'est-ce que je dois écrire, Maman?

Contents

Preface
Doubt Everything

"[I]n most things my philosophy is that of doubt,"[1] Cicero wrote more than two thousand years ago, and, for much of the time since, doubt has enjoyed a position of honor at the philosopher's table. For Jacob Bronowski, a distinguished scientist in our own time, academic work is an adventure in doubting: "It is important that students bring a certain ragamuffin, barefoot irreverence to their studies; they are not here to worship what is known, but to question it."[2]

Why should we face our world with skepticism? Because exercising doubt offers the best evidence available that we are alive? Indeed, many scholars understand Descartes's "*Cogito ergo sum*" as "I doubt therefore I am."[3] So as not to be misled by language that is too unrefined to convey the complexity of a speaker's or writer's thoughts? Because authors may not withstand the temptation to conceal the truth in order to ingratiate themselves with intended audiences? Because there may be no other antidote to the the vanity of authors when self-interest overwhelms their analytical skills? Finally, is foundational skepticism necessary because authors tend to overstate their positions out of terror that for all the intensity of effort, they will be found to be bores?

All of the above, I suggest—and more. Asked for his favorite epigram, Karl Marx responded, "*de omnibus disputandum,*" i.e., "doubt everything."[4] We must approach the world skeptically, Marx suggests, because, in ways that are often extremely difficult to detect, all cultural phenomena—texts no less than anything else—are the conscious or unconscious products of power relationships. This view has been so highly developed in our own time by French thinker Michel Foucault—with specific regard to language—that it is now next to impossible for a reader to ignore the relationship between power and culture.

Doubt Everyone but the Doubters

Which brings me to the central questions of this book: Are contemporary gender and race texts too quick to cast suspicion on everything that white males do and say, while refusing to subject women and minorities to similar scrutiny? If so, does such selective skepticism warrant a skeptical reading of its own—especially at a time when gender and race issues play such a large role in American culture and politics?

Assuming "yes" as to the first question at this point, I begin a response to the second. One could argue that Marxist and Foucauldian skepticism are not necessary when interpreting the work of race and gender critics on the premise that, being minorities and women, they have no appreciable power to exercise. Even accepting the premise, however, the conclusion does not follow. To open the discussion, I call on a leading feminist scholar and America's most prominent student of discourse. Having eavesdropped on hundreds, if not thousands, of conversations, best-selling author Deborah Tannen (*You Just Don't Understand: Women and Men in Conversation*) holds that conversation often has a subtle purpose that goes unrecognized and that, if we are to learn to get along with one another, that other purpose needs to be understood. To put it bluntly, men engage in discourse, according to Tannen, to establish superiority or power over their conversational partners. The implications are not hard to extract. The only way to protect oneself from being abused or played for a fool is to listen to male voices with skepticism.

Is Tannen right? To probe more deeply into the matter, we need to assess the power of the instinct to subordinate and unsettle others. We are learning more and more about this intriguing and disturbing psychological impulse every day, and some day soon someone will immortalize him- or herself for putting the pieces together. For now, consider that we begin in early life with teasing. As we grow up we "rattle," "jerk around," "signify," "get over on," "bait," "get others' goats," "push others' buttons," "yank their chains," "get the best of," "jive," "stick it to," "roast," "play the dozens," "talk trash" or "s—t."

We need not invoke here Hobbes's vision of life as "a perpetual and restless desire of power after power, which ceaseth only in death."[5] The foregoing range of expression, derived from both general American popular culture and black popular culture, suggests not only that the drive to needle others for advantage is so fundamental a part of human nature that it is not worth railing at but also that it is by no means limited to groups in power. One can reasonably surmise, indeed, that it is tied to the instinct to play and to release aggression and that members of "subordinate" populations "twit" even more than do those at the top, precisely because twitting is the only source of power available to them.

Are men's *writings* more trustworthy than their conversations? The answer, painful to admit, seems obvious. Books and articles are a part of the social conversation. As such, they are no more reliable than oral communication: whatever a male author may explicitly say, he is most likely announcing to his readers, "I am smarter than you." Writings of black men, in this view, should elicit no less in the way of skepticism or occasional cynicism.

All the World's a Stage?

As suggested, Tannen's finding fifteen years ago was that the instinct to one-up others was more characteristic of males than of females. But is it not possible, even likely, that women have wrested success from men, in the intervening years, precisely by adopting men's styles? And if this is the case, shall we not also conclude that authorship *generally* may be less an act of communication than of performance? That even serious writing can be a game, a show, and sometimes a con?

I need to make an admission. Literary theorists—and especially race and gender critics—deserve our abiding gratitude for insisting that, no matter how scrupulously trained or well intended, writers are never neutral on the subjects they describe or analyze. To allow text to be properly evaluated, responsible readers today demand to know authors' personal connections to their projects. Responsible writers must accommodate this need, however intimate or embarrassing the revelations may be and however it may affect their credibility with readers. Aware of these responsibilities and anxious to earn readers' trust, I make the following disclosures about the origin of this book, which resulted from a series of "clicks."

I heard the first one in the late 1980s, when my school was in its formative years and an important issue came up: on a thirty-plus-person faculty, seven of whom were tenured—six white men, one white woman, and no minorities—how to establish a fair tenure process for future applicants? On the theory that, lacking a critical awareness of their own power, white men could not understand the work of women and persons of color, the faculty voted overwhelmingly to include one untenured woman on the tenure committee to "represent the interests" of women and one untenured person of color to "represent the interests" of minorities.

Untenured faculty are rarely, if ever, allowed to make decisions about permanent faculty because they have not yet proved to be worthy themselves of such positions. How then could the new rule be understood? Was it largely a power play pushed through by my school's women and minorities because they could? Not a word of argument was offered to support a theory that unbridgeable intellectual gaps separated men and women, whites and minorities. In fact, I knew the white men on the faculty to be more than fair-minded in approaching race and gender matters, a conclusion supported by their overwhelming support for the proposal, which passed easily.

Even if different groups have difficulty understanding each other, however, were there not better ways of addressing the problem? The school could send the academic work of its women and minority faculty for a fair review to outsiders, themselves (tenured) women and minorities. Or the untenured representatives could have participated in the appropriate discussions but not voted. By pushing identity buttons so as to help tip the scales for women and minorities, the school seemed to be setting a crude and even dangerous precedent.

Of course, the enthusiasm of women and minorities for the measure was understandable. The issue of (shameless) self-interest aside, we live in a competitive world. It might be asking too much of anyone to reject the increased prospect of lifetime economic security through one or two additional votes in their favor. But how to explain allegedly hegemonic white males proving so effete? For all the cant to the contrary, power is a zero-sum game.

A second "click" came several years later when a colleague wrote a book, *Cultivating Intelligence,* in which she presented this troubling finding: "our students have abandoned logic as an ideal. . . . White men seem disproportionately affected with this particular form of incapacity. The white men who contract this disease can't think. Perhaps they never could."[6] What was disconcerting about this passage was not just that the writer, a black woman, would make such a sweeping statement or even that the white students I knew were no less bright than anyone else. I, at least, was used to racial grandstanding. Rather, it was the realization that a white man—at least on a law faculty—would never be allowed to draw such a conclusion about black women, much less promote it as a scholarly achievement. Something again seemed out of balance.

The Big "Click"

Five years ago came the final "click." At the time I told one of my (then) deans that what was being taught in our universities about race and law was silly and destructive. On a personal level, I added, it was becoming hard for me to bear the burden of my own faults, let alone to accept responsibility for the failings of others, which even cursory study would reveal. Hoping for a chance to open debate on the subject, I asked the dean for permission to teach the course "Racism and American Law," previously the province of black female teachers. I pointed out that I had written extensively on race, that teaching a course is a time-honored way of helping scholars work out the inevitable kinks in their thinking, and that such engagement was especially important in an area where people have such firm ideas of what is important and acceptable. Finally, I must admit, I played the diversity card. Giving African Americans total and permanent control over a course on race and law, I argued, would just invite pedagogical problems; a course that did not address racial understandings with skepticism and "barefoot irreverence" would likely amount only to propaganda or therapy.

All for naught. My former dean, who is white and female, somehow believed she knew what students needed to hear and summarily rejected my proposal in a committee meeting, charging that my message to minorities would be reduced to "Get over it."

Getting Over It

To work through the pain and shock of the peremptory and public dismissal, and of having the decision upheld on appeal, I began putting together this book. The political had become the personal. Was the dean right? Would it have been better for all concerned if I had swallowed my pride and my doubt? Can a white male steeped in the tradition of skepticism be trusted to teach and (now) write on race and gender? Or, will he be even more inclined to psych out his students and readers? I cannot, of course, be a fair judge; readers will have to decide for themselves.

Readers, however, should be aware of how my marginalization may affect our relationship. As authors abjectly and almost ritually proclaim when making their acknowledgments, they and they alone are responsible for shortcomings in their work. If on account of omission, overreaching, or insensitivity, however, this project sometimes seems off-key or incomplete, can responsibility fairly be pinned on me? Must this not be laid to the dean who would not let me teach the course?

It took a village to write this book and I am deeply grateful to the villagers. Ken Rosenblum read drafts of the entire book. His firm control of the mother tongue, sly sense of humor, and general omniscience have affected every page of this book. Almost all the above can be said of our reference librarian, Hon. Gerard Giannattasio, who, while not omniscient—yet—is an indefatigable researcher who allows himself to be transported by grand projects and always ends up going far beyond the call of duty.

Tom Maligno fought me tooth and nail. But, on the theory that the arguments I presented needed to be heard, he was always willing to help. The book is far better as a result of his thinking. I hope he will take pride in our achievement.

Jen Zobel deserves thanks for reading the manuscript in its inchoate form, before I dared show it to outsiders. Her patience, persistence, detailed comments, and encouragement were invaluable.

Nichoel Forrett, my research assistant, did a first-class editing job and was a splendidly organized and meticulous source checker. I could never have met the publishing deadline without the investment of her heart and mind. I hope I did not do her grades too much damage.

Other research assistants who reviewed drafts of the manuscript with care include Brooke Lupinacci, Shafeek Seddiq, and Nzengha Waseme.

All the folks from Zobel to Waseme gave me hope not only for the future of my book but also for the future of our nation. They confirmed, as I had suspected, that women and minorities are far more resilient than the literature represents them to be and that they are eager for real talk. They also taught me that a (more or less) Euro-American male had not only the right but also the obligation to tell the race and gender story as he understood it.

My daughter, Eva, an attorney and legal scholar, and my friend Henry Ramer read and provided helpful commentary on a number of parts of the manuscript, and suffered through its progress with me. Hon. Richard Posner also commented on parts of the manuscript and offered moral support, as did Hon. Stanley Bernstein, who also tried to help me find an agent. Colleagues who read and commented on one or more chapters along the way include Tom Schweitzer, Marianne Artusio, Ted Silver, Rena Seplowitz, and Lew Silverman. Reference librarian Fred Kelsey performed yeomanly. My sister, Rena, an educational consultant, kept me up-to-date on developments in that field. My son, Joseph, provided incisive insights from the frontier of the natural sciences.

The issues discussed here were chewed over again and again with my ever-patient dinner companions, Rochelle Silfen, William Carmel, and Ted and Elsa Burtness. My old friend Nancy Fox and I, by contrast, rarely talked about specifics, mostly because she lives far away, but she followed the development of this book over five years with great interest and perhaps with some awe. I hope she forgives me for not always responding to her letters and lets me make it up to her.

Darren Johnson and Sharon Biddle worked with me as I struggled with my biggest challenge: finding a good title. My copyeditor, Andrew Katz, and NYU Press managing editor Despina Papazoglou Gimbel were superb.

Other colleagues, students, and friends were helpful in all kinds of crucially important ways but, for reasons that may already be imagined, preferred that their efforts not be acknowledged here. I chide them and thank them.

My experience teaching at Seton Hall School of Law and at the University of Chicago Graduate School of Business helped inspire this work. I thank all involved.

Dean Howard Glickstein merits thanks for providing financial sustenance all along the way. Ross Zirpoli provided food not only when he was supposed to but also when the cafeteria was closed.

Richard Delgado, NYU Press's outside consultant, was a prince. While recognizing in its early stages that the manuscript needed work, he never wavered in his support for ultimate publication. Whatever his take on the issues raised—and I fear the worst but nevertheless hope he will make it his business to commit it to print—I am deeply appreciative and recommend him wholeheartedly to anyone who writes on race and gender. I thank him also for his detailed comments.

NYU Press's acquisitions editor Deborah Gershenowitz did waver. She did, however, also keep an open mind long enough to let herself be persuaded by the various reviewers through whose hands the manuscript passed. Because of her determination to keep me sensible, the tough love shown in her extensive comments has been invaluable. I recommend her unequivocally too and hasten to emphasize that she is the ideal editor. She is smart and well-informed; she will tell you what she thinks, but she is *always* willing to listen.

Above all, I thank my wife, Rose Rosengard Subotnik, Professor of Music at Brown University, who, never doubting the value of the project, hung in all the way. Her touch is on just about everything in this book. Rose helped not only through discussion and editing but also by saving articles from her voluminous reading in literary theory, politics, and popular culture and by applying her highly refined sense of humor. When I faltered by failing to come up with the right word, she found the *bon mot juste*. When colleagues and students started running the other way as they saw me coming, I always had the security of knowing that I could turn to her—and I did.

Some of the material in this book has been modified from previously published essays. Grateful acknowledgment is made to the following publications for granting permission to use this material:

Dan Subotnik, "Goodbye to the SAT, LSAT? Hello to Equity by Lottery? Evaluating Lani Guinier's Plan for Ending Race Consciousness," 43 *Howard Law Journal* #2 (2000): 141, © 2000 by Howard University School of Law.

Dan Subotnik, "Bah, Humbug to the Bleak Story of Women Law Faculty: A Response to Professor Newman," 51 *Journal of Legal Education* #1 (March 2001): 141–50, © 2001 by Association of American Law Schools.

Dan Subotnik, "The Cult of Hostile Gender Climate: A Male Voice Preaches Diversity to the Choir," 8 *University of Chicago Law School Roundtable* #1 (2001): 37, © 2001 by The University of Chicago.

Dan Subotnik, "Critical Race Theory—The Last Voyage," 15 *Touro Law Review* #2 (Winter 1999): 657–84, © 1999 by Touro Law Review.

Dan Subotnik, "The Joke in Critical Race Theory: De Gustibus Disputandum Est?" 15 *Touro Law Review* #2 (Fall 1998): 105–22, © 1998 by Touro Law Review.

Dan Subotnik, "What's Wrong with Critical Race Theory: Reopening the Case for Middle Class Values," 7 *Cornell Journal of Law and Public Policy* #3 (1998): 681–756, © 1998 by Cornell University.

Dan Subotnik and Glen Lazar, "Affiliating the Rejection Letter," in *Affiliations: Identity in Academic Culture* (Lincoln: University of Nebraska Press, 2003), 54–72, © 2003 by the Board of Regents of the University of Nebraska.

PART I

The Signifying Monkey

Deep down in the jungle so they say
There's a signifying monkey down the way
There hadn't been no disturbin' in the jungle for quite a bit,
For up jumped the monkey in the tree one day and laughed
"I guess I'll start some s––t."   —Classic African American toast

1

Learning to Think about Race and Gender

Show 'em the first-rate sorcerer that you are
Long as you keep 'em way off balance
How can they spot you got no talents?
Razzle dazzle 'em, Razzle dazzle 'em
Razzle dazzle 'em
And they'll make you a star!   —Fred Ebb, lyricist, *Chicago*

On April 4, 1991, a professor at the New England School of Law was murdered not far from her home in Cambridge, Massachusetts. Mary Jo Frug's death, which was a result of a night-time street knifing, horrified friends—and acquaintances such as myself—and shook the community at large for months. That *Good Morning America* saw fit to report this item at 7:30 the next day highlighted the problem for Americans: if we were vulnerable in the ivory tower just steps from Harvard Yard, were we and our loved ones safe anywhere?

The crime, which has never been solved, raised other painful questions. Was Frug victimized for being a woman and, as some claimed, for being a fierce and well-known feminist? Did her feminism compel her to resist her presumably male attacker and thus help bring about her death? Answers to these questions have been hard to come by. We may, however, be able to clear up a related mystery, which would allow us to better understand Frug's work and, central to our purpose here, to test the sincerity and serious-mindedness of gender and race talk today.

Ten months after Frug's murder and after much debate, the *Harvard Law Review* published Frug's last article, "A Postmodern Feminist Legal

Manifesto (An Unfinished Draft)," a wide-ranging feminist attack on male power in the legal profession. Two months later, at the annual banquet of the *Harvard Law Review* (the *Law Revue*), some students lampooned Frug in a short piece entitled "He-Manifesto of Postmodern Legal Feminism" by "Mary Doe, Rigor-Mortis Professor of Law."[1] In this piece, a sex-obsessed feminist with "no sense of humor" seeks admission to heaven. Initially rebuffed, she is allowed to enter only when the Admissions Committee abandons all standards: "Heaven should be open to everybody. White, Black, Male, Female, Short, Bald, Talented, Untalented." The piece further suggested that Frug's article was accepted only under pressure exerted by her well-placed husband, a professor at Harvard Law.

Rush to Judgment

The law school community was scandalized. How could students be so lacking in feeling following a brutal murder? Would the offending students have mocked a male who had met a similar fate? Was Frug's death the symbolic fate of all feminists who take a hammer to the glass ceiling? Fifteen Harvard Law professors signed a letter charging that institution —then (as we shall see) in the middle of a gender war—with maintaining an environment of "sexism and misogyny." For Professor Elizabeth Bartholet, the "incident showed that something very scary about male anger towards women" was manifesting itself at Harvard. Some of Harvard Law's males weighed in. According to David Kennedy, female *Law Review* members could take it as a "direct threat of personal violence," and he strongly urged, along with a number of others, that the offending students be disciplined. For Professor Laurence Tribe, the grotesque thesis of the piece was that "hatred of women is a hoax perpetrated by paranoid feminists," and he likened the authors to Ku Klux Klan members and Holocaust deniers. The *Law Revue* satirists, he continued, "might as well have danced on Mary Jo's grave for what they did. They made a decision to desecrate her memory with verbal knife-stabs" and thus were guilty of "rape in all but biological reality."

In the end, a few new female law professors were hired. The students escaped discipline. Harvard effected no additional change other than to cancel the *Law Revue* banquets indefinitely.

However disturbing the parody, a conscientious cultural analyst has to wonder about the hype in the foregoing reactions. Does a "rape in all but biological reality" have any content? Or is it merely academic razzle-dazzle, Sturm und Drang without the "storm and turmoil"? If we are to learn something from the parody beyond the highly questionable taste of its creators, must we not ignore Tribe's seductive imagery and ask: Was the parody a symbolic crime against Frug and against women in general? Should readers take the protests against the *Law Revue* parody at face value?

A short detour can help begin the discussion. Called to the stand by Johnnie Cochran in the 1994 O. J. Simpson trial, Robert Heidstra testified that he was walking his dogs on the night of the Nicole Brown Simpson and Ron Goldman murders when he heard someone say, "Hey, hey, hey!" Black prosecutor Christopher Darden then cross-examined Heidstra by asking him about a report that at the time of the murders he had heard "the voice of a black man." When Cochran strongly objected to the question, Darden explained to the judge that an acquaintance of Heidstra's, Patricia Baret, had earlier reported to Detective Lange that Heidstra had "heard the very angry screaming of an older man who sounded black," so he, Darden, had the right to ask the question.[2]

"I resent that statement," Cochran shot back. "You can't tell by someone's voice when they're black. I don't know who's made that statement, Baret or Lange. That's racist." Cochran continued in this vein: "This statement about whether somebody sounds black or white is racist, and I resent it . . . I think it's totally improper in America . . . just to hear this and endure this." Apparently allowing himself to be silenced by the charge of racism, Darden moved on to other matters. Thus ended what could well have been a breakthrough line of inquiry in a trial that polarized the nation along racial lines.

Another exchange during that trial may be equally revealing. After Cochran had argued for the importance of allowing testimony of Detective Mark Fuhrman's habits of speech, prosecutor Chris Darden objected, claiming that the n-word is "the filthiest, dirtiest, nastiest word in the English language [and] will blind the jury. It will blind them to the truth [and] impair their ability to be fair and impartial." With the evidence allowed in, "the entire complexion of the case changes. It is a race case then. It is white versus black, African American versus Caucasian, us versus them, us versus the system."[3]

This potent argument threatened to knock the underpinnings out from Cochran's case. Speaking about the n-word, the distinguished scholar on race Andrew Hacker has explained that "[t]his word has the power to pierce, to wound, to penetrate, as no other has." Conscious of the word's history and power, a number of African Americans launched an effort a few years back to get the Merriam-Webster's Collegiate Dictionary to excise it.[4] Cochran, however, was too skilled to let himself be silenced. He responded by calling Darden's plea "the most incredible remarks I've heard in the thirty-two years I've been practicing," and he went on to "apologize to African Americans across the country." It was downright "demeaning" to suggest that African American jurors could not deliberate fairly after hearing Fuhrman's views, when their forebears had "lived under oppression for two hundred-plus years in this country," and they themselves had lived with "offensive words, offensive looks, [and] offensive treatment every day of their lives."[5] Judge Ito allowed inquiry into Furman's use of the n-word.

"I'm Madder Than Hell"

Was Cochran really too resentful to endure the discussion of voices? Did he feel demeaned? Was he playacting for litigation advantage? Or was he simply signifying?

It is time to define "sigging," which Harvard's Henry Louis Gates says is "so fundamentally black . . . [a] rhetorical practice" that it is hard to talk about.[6] Signifying, Gates reports in his landmark book, *The Signifying Monkey* (the source of this part's opening epigraph)[7] refers

> to the trickster's ability to talk with great innuendo, to carp, cajole, needle and lie. . . . to talk around the subject, never quite coming to the point. It can mean making fun of a person or situation. . . . [I]t is signifying to stir up a fight between neighbors by telling stories.[8]

Sigging is related to the African American practice of "turning it out," that is, deliberately "losing control, unleashing anger, acting obstinate or unreasonable"—sometimes also called "acting colored"[9] and manifesting itself as "talking s—t" or "trash." "Trash talk," meanwhile, is "disparaging, often insulting or vulgar speech about another person or group."[10]

So, again, how should readers evaluate Cochran's behavior? For this purpose, we need to decide first whether Darden's line of inquiry on the issue of racial profiling was improper as a matter of etiquette. A comment that a person "sounds black" should be no more offensive than a comment that he sounds Californian or French. Especially so, given that Darden was himself black, that race critics themselves are so quick to emphasize differences between majority culture and black culture, and that the comment was obviously not meant as a putdown of blacks. In this view, what is objectionable is not Darden's question but Cochran's discussion-ending outburst.

Sound, Fury, and Signifying

Of further help in evaluating Cochran's outburst on the black speech matter is a conversation that began just as the courtroom exchange ended. Pulling Cochran aside, Carl Douglas, his black assistant, who was in the best position to evaluate Cochran's argument, had a brief interchange with his boss: "If you said that to rattle Darden, it was brilliant," he told Cochran, perhaps bearing in mind research showing that 80–90 percent of African Americans are identifiable as such by their speech.[11] "[I]f you said it because you believe it, I disagree." Cochran, whose courtroom voice easily identified him as black, brushed him off. But Douglas refused to let the matter drop. "It was both," Cochran finally said. "Of course, I wanted to rattle him. But I also think it was racist to say that about how a voice sounds." "Johnnie," Douglas retorted, "that's bulls––t."[12]

Cochran's n-word argument also militates against taking it and him at face value. If African American jurors, calloused by a lifetime of exposure to offensive words, looks, and treatment, could easily adjust to the use of such a loaded word, is it conceivable that someone both as worldly and confident as Johnnie Cochran could not "endure" a frank discussion of black speech? Putting Cochran's two arguments together yields an even keener insight. What Cochran was urging upon the court was that a discussion of black speech would unhinge black jurors but that these jurors could stay focused and balanced after hearing a witness use a word whose power is so awesome that it can be referred to only through indirection. In sum, Judge Ito, the jurors, and other Americans had good reason to understand Cochran's performance in the same way as *Seinfeld* creators referred to their work product: "The Show About Nothing."

The connection between the Frug parody and the Cochran outbursts for a society fractured by gender and race tensions is the subject of *Toxic Diversity.* For the irrepressible Alan Dershowitz, Douglas's response to Cochran would seem to capture the histrionics and humbug of contemporary gender and race dialogue. As part of the Simpson Dream Team, Dershowitz could not properly contradict Johnnie Cochran on the subject of black speech. His position on interracial and intergender dialogue, however, was made unmistakably clear in the Frug case, where he spoke up for academic freedom while complaining of a McCarthyite witch hunt: "Women and blacks are entirely free to attack white men (even 'dead white men' . . .) in the most offensive of terms. Radical feminists can accuse all men of being rapists, and radical African Americans can accuse all whites of being racists, without fear of discipline or rebuke."[13] The best law school brains, he lamented, were devoted to "figuring out ways of constructing freedom of speech and the First Amendment just so as not to include [a] particular genre" of speech found offensive to women and minorities. "How many times," he asked, "have we heard that? 'I'm offended, it must be wrong.'"

So, rephrasing the *Law Revue* question: (a) Were the Harvard Law professors for real? (b) Were they, like the signifying monkey in the opening epigraph to this part, entertaining themselves in a down period? (c) Was theirs just a ploy to get more women hired? Or, perhaps, (d) all of the above?

"If You Prick Us"

It seems amazing that the critics of the *Law Revue* parody, who were so intent on identifying pain, could not imagine the pain that Frug's "A Postmodern Legal Manifesto" would have inflicted on the new male, who did not dismiss women's opinions out of hand but who listened carefully to what they were saying. If the article was designed to bring men down, would those with any male pride left not rise to "revenge"?

Frug's in-your-face misandry, indeed, cries for a response: "We are raped at work or on route to work," she writes, "because of our sex, because we are cunts [*sic*]." Women do not make love to their lovers out of admiration, fondness, or just animal attraction but because they need the physical security males provide and because "financial pressures arising from sex discrimination induce unmarried women to yield to the sexual demands of escorts and companions." These pressures continue after marriage. Because "refusal to have sex within marriage constitutes grounds for divorce, legal rules inhibit women who marry because of economic or safety incentives from practicing celibacy within marriage."[14] Under Frug's rules, a man whose wife refuses sex on the wedding night— and thereafter—would be stuck with her forever.

A *Law Revue* parody, however tough-minded, would thus seem to be fair academic game, particularly for someone who had never himself raped nor knew anyone who had. Words have consequences, a point that race and gender theorists regularly advance.[15] This view is especially compelling because women's attacks on men in the academy have been no less brutal. In the *Law Revue* tradition at Harvard, no one and nothing was off limits; the tastelessness of the "rigor-mortis" image aside (a matter we will come to), the *Law Revue*'s focus was on Frug's work, not her death or her personal life. There were no references to her appearance, her family, her religious beliefs, sexual practices, eating habits, or taste in art.

Actually, challenging Frug, as the *Law Revue* creators did and as I do here, honors Frug. At least one prominent feminist scholar explicitly asks for critical response: "To be taken seriously in the law and legal scholarship," says Harvard Law's Martha Minow, "means becoming the object of sustained criticism."[16] Before criticism can be sustained it has to be started, which is precisely what I am doing here.

When Minow's words were printed in 1989, it was impossible to identify the cutting-edge writers who were drawing the most attention. Today, with the development of giant databases, academic influence is, in at least one way, much easier to measure. Scores of citation studies rank scholars in all fields.[17] In a world drowning in text, readers easily determine who should be "taken seriously" as a leading "object of sustained criticism." A book such as this one, which cites Frug a dozen times, can only help solidify her standing in her field.

Nil Nisi Malum

Should the fact of Frug's death have made a difference? I suggest not. Dead white European males are primary targets for feminists in the culture wars and, indeed, are stock villains for many of them. The injury from such attacks to living men, moreover, is not mitigated by Frug's tragic death. The publication of her article and the posthumous rally on her behalf attest to the continuing influence of her work. As for what Frug herself would have wanted, consider that the impulse to write is said to arise from the fear of death and thus to answer the need for immortality.[18] Refusing to fully confront Frug's work precisely because of her death would compound the injury to Frug by thwarting her in the pursuit of perhaps her life's most important goal.

Undoubtedly, the parodic aspect of "He-Manifesto" had much to do with the academic community's response. But why necessarily presume that human beings make fun of people out of hatred or contempt rather than out of annoyance? Those who want to hear words of hate should listen to people who supposedly love one another.

He Jests Who Feels the Wound

The "He Manifesto" may indeed have allowed the editors to live with the horror of Frug's death and with the guilt of reliving it once they decided that a response was required. "To become conscious of what is horrifying and to laugh at it," noted the playwright Eugene Ionesco, "is to become master of that which is horrifying."[19] Humor at Auschwitz and Dachau was described by an inmate, who later became a distinguished neurologist and psychologist, as "among the soul's weapons in the fight for self-preservation."[20]

Ionesco is right, of course, at least for males. Reflecting an adolescent sensibility, the "sick" jokes first told in the fifties, usually by boys, were not psychotic products, born out of hatred for one group or another. In one of the early jokes, when Johnny's friends come over to ask him to come out and play ball, his father tearfully tells them that his son has been stricken with polio and has no use of his hands and legs. "That's OK," they say, "we can use him as second base." Such jokes fail the test of high-mindedness, but no one was taking pleasure in the new quadriplegic's condition. A case can be made that the joke bespeaks the group's need to maintain its stricken member as a continuing part of the community or to minimize the seriousness of a then epidemic.

Similarly, jokes about the Kennedy assassination, O. J. Simpson, the John Kennedy Jr. accident, the Timothy McVeigh execution, and the

Challenger disaster are better understood as self-prescribed therapies of release than as expressions of joy in the suffering of others—much less in that of "subordinated groups" (a term I will use for women and minorities generally). The effectiveness of this kind of therapy was demonstrated three weeks after 9/11 when an aspiring young Muslim comic got up on a London stage and introduced herself: "I am Shazia Mirza. At least that is what it says on my pilot's license."[21] After a moment of pin-drop silence, the crowd went wild. Mirza has since become a star. While not aiming for Mirza's success, nurses, doctors, police, and EMTs practice comedy medicine on themselves when they refer to those killed in fires as "Crispy Critters" and to those who die in traffic accidents as "Road Pizza."[22]

In fact, since a 1976 landmark article by Norman Cousins in the prestigious *New England Journal of Medicine*,[23] humor therapy has become big business. Today around the country, hospitals are setting up Laughmobiles and Laughrooms for pain and illness. Physiologists are studying the medical benefits of humor, and the Association for Therapeutic Humor promotes this research. In one protocol, women who have undergone mastectomies are shown a cartoon of a woman having her breasts flattened by a steamroller. "Yes, I've had my mastectomy," the woman is saying, "Why do you ask?"[24]

The handful of *Law Revue* participants, then, were guilty of nothing more than bad taste for ignoring likely reactions; they were not celebrating Frug's murder. What this means is that the *Law Revue* highlighted nothing "very scary about male anger towards women" and carried no "direct threat of personal violence against women" by symbolic Ku Klux Klan members in Cambridge. The parody gave women no reason to feel one bit more or less secure on campuses and streets.

Another part of the logic of the posthumous attack on Frug's article needs some elaboration. First, the staid *Harvard Law Review* was publishing an unfinished work, apparently for the first time. Frug, moreover, did not teach at Harvard or Yale. It seems fair to say that if she had taught at one of those schools rather than at the New England School of Law, there would have been nothing incongruous in the *Law Review*'s publication decision; such a happening would have been routine and unworthy of comment. What made the publication decision noteworthy was the idea, well captured by the parodists in the "Heaven should be open to everybody" shtick, that owing to the strong bias shown by law reviews against authors at low-status law schools,[25] the *Harvard Law Review* would not have found Frug's article up to its traditional standards if she had neither died nor been well connected. She thus acquired her "rigor-mortis" (the only kind of rigor available to her), and beat the system, by getting killed.

Insult and Injury

That the *Harvard Law Review* had never previously published any articles by New England School of Law professors—or since, one might add—may explain why, under question, the parodists themselves failed to explain the logic of the parody. To suggest that Frug was merely a professor at an unranked school was a no-win proposition for them; such a tactic would have multiplied their troubles with those devastated by Frug's murder by adding further insult to Frug's name.

On another level, it can be argued, the parody should have come as no shock to, and maybe should even have been welcomed by, Frug's highly sophisticated academic supporters. Philosopher Jacob Bronowski urges students to come to the university with "barefoot irreverence." For the distinguished nineteenth-century philosopher of knowledge Arthur Schopenhauer, "All truth passes through three stages. First, it is ridiculed. Second, it is violently opposed. Third, it is accepted as self-evident."[26] The philosopher's truth could have served as a motto for Mohandas Gandhi, man of action and, like gender and race critics, archenemy of white male imperialism: "First they ignore you, then they laugh at you, then they fight you, then you win."[27] If Schopenhauer and Gandhi were right, whatever the *Law Revue* creators' actual objectives, ridiculing Frug was an essential step in Frug's canonization as a feminist writer.

And who can deny the need for additional truth in social and political life? Among the first things the post-Apartheid government in South Africa did to bring social harmony was to establish a Truth and Reconciliation Commission. The premise, implicit in the title, is that the former is a prerequisite for the latter. Can this notion have any less currency in America?

But feminists should not have had to rely on dead males or on an appeal for reconciliation to welcome the attack on Frug's work; feminism has a rich tradition of mockery. Frug, after all, employed humor in her own work and enthusiastically advocated it for others. To be sure, she claimed membership in a "historically subordinated" group, which she (and others) argued should never be ridiculed: "'the circumstances of women's lives [are] unbearable,' . . . [h]ardly appropriate material for irony and play."[28] This asymmetric rule of fair dealings, founded on a theory of women's fragility, will be examined in depth later. For now, consider that through the use of humor the *Law Revue* was performing the valuable service of calling her grim views of women's lives into question.

Finally, if Frug had taken her cue from an impeccably credentialed white woman, as I happily and unreservedly do for my work, she might have thanked the parodists for satisfying her deepest existential longings for a meaningful life. The feminist hero I have in mind would not have written the *Law Revue* parody. But the author of *Sense and Sensibility* set the stage for the "He-Manifesto of Postmodern Legal Feminism" by advancing no demand for a sober response to her work nor by holding women out as social quadriplegics in need of special handling. "For what do we live," Jane Austen has asked millions of her readers, "but to make sport for our neighbours, and laugh at them in our turn?"[29]

Because participants in the foregoing stories are speaking off-the-cuff, not *ex cathedra*, their opinions cannot reach the deepest strata of gender and race consciousness. This book applies questions raised by the Frug and Cochran (melo)dramas to formal writing so as to promote the high-level discussion needed to address our deep-seated gender and race problems. Can groups properly evaluate the environments in which they find themselves without outside help? More particularly, in seeing themselves as ever-oppressed, do women and minorities not rush to judgment when issues come up? And if so, will this not impede realization of their stated dreams?

To begin the process of detecting and then clearing obstacles, Part I, beginning with this introductory chapter, provides a general survey of the gender and race literature. The next chapter sketches and then questions the major charges brought by minorities and women against white males. Chapter 3 offers an introduction to a radical school of inquiry known as critical race theory, traces its development, describes its methods, and explains how it has drawn minority academics in while keeping others at bay. Chapter 4 examines whether race and gender talk should be shaped by the same rules that apply to general social and political discourse, and particularly whether satire directed at subordinated groups is appropriate. Chapters 5 and 6 expand on the race and gender critiques surveyed in the first three chapters.

Part II explores in detail some of the challenges to the legal/political system brought in the name of women, giving particular attention to the question of whether the feminist critique furthers the cause of women or undermines it. It selects three such areas for discussion—the first two because they have elicited an especially large amount of feminist commentary, the third because it is arguably tied to a fundamental social problem. Chapter 7 evaluates the feminist claim that law schools oppress women students, and chapter 8 extends this discussion to a related claim concerning abuse of women faculty in the academy. Chapter 9 examines the issue of whether and how the law unfairly penalizes unwed parenthood.

Part III deals with a few critical challenges to the existing order brought in the name of minorities. Chapter 10 evaluates challenges by race theorists to prevailing conceptions of merit, and chapter 11 explores the relationship between race and crime. The conclusion summarizes the book and offers a few thoughts on where we go from here, while the Final Exam allows readers to determine whether they got out of the book what the author intended.

Playing with Fire

One issue to be faced throughout this book: Does the gender or race critic consider whether "it is water or gasoline he is tossing on the . . . fire [or only] whether it is a well-intended act"?[30] The reader may be puzzled by the notion that people would fail to consider the obvious consequences of their actions. An incident that took place in 1995 can help sharpen our focus. It involved the Reverend Al Sharpton and Fred Harrari, white owner of a Harlem-based clothing store. Wanting to expand operations, Harrari had refused to renew the sublease of a black-owned record store next door. Rev. Sharpton stated his position at one of the early protest rallies in September: "We will not stand by and allow them to move this brother so that some white interloper can expand his business on 125th Street." Two months later, in the wake of cries of "Kill the Jew Bastards" and "They're sucking the lifeblood out of the community," a black street vendor entered Harrari's place, shot four people, and torched the store, killing seven workers in the blaze.

When later asked about the tragedy, Sharpton defended himself against charges of inciting racial violence: "Yes, he [Harrari] was a white interloper. What they are trying to do is act like we can't say anything wrong about an individual white. Otherwise, that's racist. That's baloney."[31]

Readers—particularly those sensitive to charges of racism—are asked to remember this defense as black writers are challenged here and to consider that Harrari had been on 125th Street. for three years, long enough, arguably, to be disqualified as an "interloper." Readers should also imagine how Sharpton would likely have reacted if a black man had tried to set up shop at 5th Avenue and 44th Street and had met with a comparable reception.

The objective here is not to assess Sharpton's intentions or to suggest that all our social problems can be resolved through a simple test of symmetry. It is, rather, to launch a discussion of the hearts and minds of gender and race scholars from the heart and mind of a white scholar. To this end, consider "firefighter syndrome," the well-documented practice of a firefighter starting a blaze so that his unit will be called in and he can make himself a hero. In shouting "fire" in a flammable social and political setting, are gender and race critics laying the foundation for a permanent call on their diversity squads?

2

Smelling the Sewers but Not the Flowers

Take specific arguments very seriously in their own terms; discover that they are actually foolish.   —Professor Mark Kelman

"One of the ironies of the creative process," writes Pulitzer Prize–winning author Ernest Becker, is that "usually, in order to turn out a piece of work the author has to exaggerate the emphasis of it, to oppose it forcefully in a competitive way to other versions of the truth; and he gets carried away by his own exaggeration, as his distinctive image is built on it." If Becker is right about this phenomenon, which he ascribes to the author's fear of death-induced oblivion and the resulting need to leave a mark, readers should be tempted not only to doubt but also to dismiss and even laugh off scholarly work. But Becker, perhaps concerned with undermining the market for his own work, refuses to let readers off the hook so easily. "[E]ach honest thinker who is basically an empiricist," he insists, "has to have some truth in his position, no matter how extremely he has formulated it. The [reader's] problem is to find the truth underneath the exaggeration, to cut away the excess elaboration or distortion."[1] What about those who write about gender and race? Are they—we—"honest" thinkers who are entitled in Becker's system to the reader's deference?

Morality Play

Consider the facts of a 1967 case decided by the Wisconsin Supreme Court.[2] Shortly after Aleta Jones, a young nursing-home orderly, had borrowed $200 from her employer to get new dentures, she quit for a better job. Failing to talk her into staying, the employer, Fisher, demanded immediate repayment or deposit of the dentures as security. When Jones tried to run, Fisher pinned her down, ripping out the dentures. Distraught and suffering pain from the incident, Jones went to the police, who got the dentures back for her. In the subsequent suit against Fisher, a jury awarded Jones compensatory and punitive damages for the outrageous behavior, of $1,000 and $5,000, respectively. On appeal for lack of proof of physical damages, the State Supreme Court reduced the awards to $500 and $2,000.

The high court erred in reducing damages, according to Regina Austin, William Swader Professor of Law at the University of Pennsylvania, for not fitting the Jones claim into a larger context of the abusive relationship between "black domestics and their white employers."[3] The following fuller exposition of Austin's critique of the Wisconsin Supreme Court's opinion affords readers a rich opportunity to match their analytical powers and cultural understandings against those of a certified race and gender expert:

1. "The personal kindness and generosity the Fishers showed Mrs. Jones were at least as instrumental and manipulative as they may have been selfless and philanthropic." Knowing that women attach special significance to "personal feelings and the quality of their relationships," the Fishers "pulled the emotional strings by attempting to persuade Mrs. Jones to return to work."

   But are feelings of altruism and self-interest independent of one another? We normally make gifts to those who are good to us, or those from whom we want love or material benefits in the future. We do not bestow our largesse on total strangers. In any event, if the kind of manipulation exercised by the Fishers were criminalized, we would surely all be in jail.

2. "Fisher's use of force and violence should not have been viewed as a response to acts of provocation and betrayal on the part of Mrs. Jones, but to the frustration of the Fishers' sense of mastery and domination over her person."

   But would Austin feel a little betrayed if her secretary had borrowed $1,000 from her for a used car and had quit immediately thereafter, thereby raising doubt that the debt would be repaid?

3. "Instead of looking at the loan as charity . . . the court might have considered it as being in lieu of a raise."

So how could the Fishers possibly be upset with her for taking a hike? By Austin's reasoning, the money really belonged to Jones, so she was justified in taking it.

4. "The failure to seek medical attention and the consequent absence of medical testimony to substantiate her claim of distress may also be attributed to her limited income."

That may be so, but does a court not need evidence?

5. "If the Fishers were truly concerned about her, they would have been happy that she had obtained a better job."

By this reasoning, if she had truly loved Eddie Fisher, Debbie Reynolds would have exulted at being dumped for the still greater prize, Elizabeth Taylor; the Oakland Athletics would have rejoiced when Jason Giambi left them for the perennial-contending Yankees; and George III would have declared a holiday to honor the maturity and self-reliance of his American subjects evident in their march to independence.

Keeping Up with Jones

How should we understand the Jones case today? Citing research on the abuses in relationships between black domestics and white employers, Austin reads *Fisher v. Jones* as presenting "another example of gender and possibly race bias [through undervaluation] of pain and suffering experienced by female and/or minority plaintiffs."

There is a side to the story, however, that Austin does not bring out. It seems indispensable, however, for evaluating the relevance of the abusive relationship between "black domestics and their white employers" and thus the good name of the Wisconsin Supreme Court and, for that matter, that of Regina Austin herself: *De coloribus disputandum est* (You *can* argue about color); Aleta Jones was white.[4]

By attacking the Wisconsin high court without checking into Jones's ethnicity—or, conceivably worse, by ignoring what she knew to be Jones's actual ethnicity—Austin shows that she is not "basically an empiricist" and, accordingly, does not deserve Becker's presumption. Which leads to the seven-part thesis of this book: (1) Contemporary race and gender discourse (even in its highest reaches) follows the model of Austin's rush to judgment; (2) The purpose of such discourse is too often, like that of the Signifying Monkey and Johnnie Cochran, to signify, to rag on the white man, to rattle his cage, to break his chops; (3) Describing American society in terms of malevolent and powerful white males, on the one hand, and innocent and weak minorities and women, on the other, is not only inaccurate and highly offensive but, more important, poisons our race and gender climate; (4) Race and gender critics cannot be relied on to discipline themselves because the absence of sustained criticism wreaths them in a halo of self-righteousness that blinds them; (5) To overcome an eclectic culture of manipulation, self-delusion, baby talk, and bombast— that is, of wolf-crying, scapegoating, and getting up on high horses—all Americans must be ready to meet race and gender morality play with a forceful and unapologetic "NOT SO FAST" or "PROVE IT"; (6) We must test the fast-talkers on race and gender without fear; and (7) We can have the most frank discussions on these subjects without im- or exploding.

Engaging distinguished race and gender scholars is a daunting prospect, but readers must not fear entering the fray for lack of a formal credential. Paradoxically, a credential in this field may be less an advantage than a handicap: "so much 'race' speech has become ritualized and rhetorical," complains black Harvard sociologist Orlando Patterson.[5] "Much of what is written and spoken about race in our current debates is dishonest, confused, ill-informed, unhelpful," says Princeton Professor of Philosophy Anthony Appiah.[6] To the extent that race and gender critics believe in their own impotence, famed black sociologist W. E. B. Du Bois may explain why the discourse takes its current form: "Deception is the natural defence of the weak against the strong."[7]

The gender and race critics considered here are for the most part law school professors. There are two reasons for this. First, law professors as a group have the most keenly developed ideas about the intersections of race and gender with concepts of justice. Second, law professors have set an agenda for gender and race debate exciting and extensive enough to occupy anyone for years; that is to say, going beyond the legal academy would have made this project unmanageable.

BS, MS, PhD

What cannot be proved in a work of this size—but is certainly suggested here—is that corrupt gender and race talk infects the entire academy, which is only part of a still larger problem of the copious and pious non-sense produced at even our highest-ranking universities in the name of research. To the extent that, as is claimed, the A students run the academy while the B and C students run the world, the reader might want to think about whether, in the race and gender areas at least, the B and C students should take control of the academy as well.

Two very brief observations will have to suffice. The first, by Judge Richard Posner, is that Americans cannot rely any more on their public intellectuals, whose major public role is to produce sound and print bites for the entertainment industry.[8] The second comes from the late Nobelist Merton Miller in a remarkable 1992 article entitled "The Value of 'Useless' Research.'"[9] According to Miller, foolish research is the inevitable byproduct of good research and thus needs to be tolerated. Because bad research is often not only useless but also injurious, and because the billions invested in research fuel asphyxiating law school tuition levels for our children, Miller's position is rejected here. Law students have a right to know what is being sold to them for $30,000 per year, partially under the diversity label, and whether stratospheric tuition levels are going to their professors' heads.

He Who Lives by the Word . . .

A few words about method: Proving the foregoing multipart thesis requires that the closest attention be given to gender and race texts. The reasons should be obvious. Gender and race critics produce words and can be understood only through those words. They complain, moreover, of being muted. Speaking about women, for example, NYU Law professor Carol Gilligan says that the dominant culture has taken away their "voice."[10] A white male satisfies his scholarly obligation only by listening to the critics as they fervently entreat and as they have never been listened to before—though, perhaps also, as they may never wish to be listened to again.

Honoring the integrity of gender and race theory texts achieves still other objectives. If it is difficult for different groups to understand one another because they start from different premises, grounding discussion in the original text ensures at least that nothing is lost in paraphrasing. Gender and race issues, moreover, are treacherous because of people's natural loyalty toward their own group and antipathy toward others'. Offense can be avoided, and empirical good faith demonstrated, by allowing misguided gender and race critics to be hoist by their own petards rather than by those of a white man.

Sticking to the text on race and gender matters, however, is not likely to be enough to protect speakers and listeners from the fear and hurt of race and gender talk. Consider that, despairing of its students' ability to converse on the subject of race and gender, Harvard Law School—which at the time of this writing is considering a speech code—has just introduced a new course called "Managing Difficult Conversations" to teach the best and the brightest how to do so.

Because the Harvard materials are not available to the rest of us, two tacks are used here. First, a carefully balanced defense to charges against white males is employed. The thought is that if no group of critics is disproportionately targeted, intergroup dialogue will not be hobbled by feelings of particular ethnic or gender animus. Second, a strategy has been borrowed from a nineteenth-century poet who offered a tantalizing idea for expressing hard truths:

> When they're offered to the world in merry guise
> Unpleasant truths are swallowed with a will.
> For he who'd make his fellow-creatures wise
> Should always gild the philosophic pill.[11]

Comics such as Lenny Bruce, Richard Pryor, George Carlin, and Jackie Mason always understood this. The dry, academic treatise may be particularly off-putting for African American critics, a major audience for this book. All "great educators," but "especially those in minority American traditions," says University of Pennsylvania professor and Martin Luther King Jr. biographer Michael Dyson, "learn sooner or later that you better put some entertainment in your education."[12]

To come back to the Aleta Jones matter, empirical shakiness is not the only problem. It may not even be the major one. For even if Jones had been black, Austin's case would still be problematic, because from the get-go she goes out of her way to interpret every event and conversation against the white employers and in favor of Jones. How have we gotten to this point?

Naming Our Problem

"Whatever their differences," writes Professor Martha Chamallas, "feminists tend to start with the assumption that the law's treatment of women has not been fair or equal and that change is desirable."[13] Here is a major problem in a nutshell: injury does not have to be proved because it is assumed. What counts is the change effected by the charges made. Professor Joan Williams, a prominent gender critic, makes this explicit: "my goal is not to deliver the truth but to inspire social change."[14]

A similar ethic often characterizes race talk as well. Yale Law professor Stephen Carter tells what happened after he had written that the scholar's job is not to lead a cause but "to follow the truth wherever it leads." A "very respected scholar" responded in print, he recalls, "something like, 'That's a twelve-year-old nerd's vision of intellectual endeavor.'"[15] To the extent that truth-seeking and truth-telling are rejected as the standard for engagement, a price must be paid. "The first thing a man will do for his ideals," says renowned economist Joseph Schumpeter, "is lie."[16]

Joan Williams and the "very respected scholar" pose a serious problem for readers: how to deal with people who admit that truth is not their primary goal. If they do not even seek truth, they cannot earn the benefit of Becker's presumption. Should they therefore be dismissed for lack of credibility? There is no good solution. The only thing to be done is to ignore their confessions and take gender and race critics at their words.

I Feel, Therefore I Am Right

What follows from abandonment of truth-telling as a goal could be predicted. Women's feelings have become truths unto themselves, and overriding ones at that. Trained and presumably paid to be guided by reason, a feminist law professor claims to have learned an important lesson about life: "I no longer think about whether I should be offended. Instead, I am able to know that I am offended. The result," she exults, "is a feeling of wholeness."[17] This of course leads to the very syllogism that Dershowitz railed against in the prior chapter: "I am offended, [so what you say] must be wrong."

The emotional responses of racial minorities are no less true. Consider one of Ice-T's lyrics: "I'm 'bout to dust some shots off. I'm 'bout to dust some cops . . . die pig die."[18] Are these the destructive ravings of a mad-man who must be destroyed before he kills? Does Ice-T's message at least have to be countered? Is it important, at the least, to know if some particular act triggered the murderous rage, or if the wildly successful poet is displacing his anger on, say, an innocent cop (of unspecified race) with three young children who is far less advantaged than he is? Apparently no —on all counts. While making no reference to any particular piece of poetry, Georgetown University law professor Mari Matsuda assures her readers, "I would interpret an angry, hateful poem by a person from a historically subjugated group as a victim's struggle for self-identity in response to racism."[19]

The notion that feeling predominates over thinking feeds into destructive stereotypes of women and minorities, to wit, that they subordinate reason to emotions.[20] If self-expression trumps social etiquette, moreover, progress will be measured by emotion released, not by emotion controlled. In this view, the function of discourse is therapy, and truth becomes, in Norman Mailer's words, "no more nor less than what one feels at each instant in the perpetual climax of the present."[21]

Doing unto Others

Extending the range of therapeutic responses allowed to minorities for such problems, *New York Times* columnist Lena Williams tells of a well-dressed, middle-aged black man in Manhattan who was on a collision course with a group of young white youths on the sidewalk. Engrossed with themselves, as Williams describes the situation, the youths did not see the black man coming their way. At the point of contact, the man pushed his way through so forcefully that he nearly knocked one of the young women into the gutter. Was the black man acting savagely or just rudely? No. The black man was "striking a blow for his ancestors" for the times "they were forced into oncoming traffic [and] threatened with beatings . . . for failing to step aside with haste for white folks. I saw a brother fed up with eating crow," Williams concludes, "as in *Jim*."[22]

We need to—as gender and race critics like to say—"interrogate" this view. If the black man's conduct is affirmed, then whites seeking to amuse themselves may avoid social settings in which black people are likely to be present. Alternatively, whites will be tempted to reciprocate in kind with distracted black youths. It is hard to see how either response would help the cause of race relations.

Undoubtedly, Williams would object to the behavior of whites in this last case. Historically, it was whites, not blacks, who asserted dominion over America's sidewalks. Williams's intentions are, however, irrelevant; what counts now is the likely consequence when we rush to the defense of boors, when the golden rule is blithely defenestrated.

The argument for asymmetry in race relations, for disparate treatment, needs elaboration. Williams is not suggesting that whites are immune to emotional injury. Or that the white youngsters in the prior case were actually toying with the black man in some replay of a Jim Crow pas de deux. It is just that centuries of oppression have led black people to develop special responses to the outside world and that this rich mix of sensibilities, often reflected in the arts and in many other aspects of American life, is unattainable for whites. Again, those unique sensibilities were fashioned in the crucible of the white man's misdeeds. Consequently when the needs of whites and blacks are in tension, those of whites must take a back seat.

There is, however, another way to evaluate the Lena Williams story. Human beings in their formative stages are sent to school, among other reasons, to learn that they—and their group—are not the center of the universe. Learning how to analyze and tame their emotions is essential not only for a safe life but also for an educated one. Indeed, the well-named Objectivist school holds as an axiom that "emotions are not a means of cognition."[23] In giving themselves dispensation to shoot first and ask questions only later, race and gender critics like Mari Matsuda and Lena Williams are undermining fundamental civilizing norms. In this kind of setting, expressions of gender or race sensibility will come to sound like temper tantrums.

Playing the Rage Card

Consider a story provided by bell hooks, professor at City College in New York. She and a woman friend, who is black, had just taken their seats in the first-class section of an airplane when white flight attendants approached the friend and asked her to move to coach. Apparently, the friend "had been assigned the seat" but lacked the appropriate boarding pass. The friend tried to explain, but the flight attendants did not want to hear about the airline's mistake. "They wanted only to ensure that the white man who has the appropriate boarding card will have a seat in first class." The white man sat down and apologized for the inconvenience but, like the flight attendants, hooks was not mollified. She started shouting at him, as if he were responsible for the mix-up: "It was not a question of your giving up the seat, it was an occasion for you to intervene in the harassment of a black woman and you chose your own comfort and tried to deflect away from your complicity by offering an insincere, face-saving apology."[24]

Can hooks really believe this herself? In racializing the story and providing only minimal data, she does not allow us to test her response. How would hooks have reacted if her friend had been white? Given hooks's denial, isn't she admitting that her real agenda was to induce the flight attendants to publicly eject her neighbor from his seat? On a different plane, is hooks making a case for affirmative action in airline seating? Interestingly, hooks did not know whether the man had purchased a first-class ticket, which would have given him a right to the first-class seat—without apology—or whether there were other first-class seats open to her friend, who wanted to use an upgrade coupon. Indeed, it would have been hard for hooks to find out without talking to the white man or the flight attendants, which, apparently, she was not willing to do. This did not stop her, however, from expressing "killing rage" over the incident, the apt title of her book.

Is the problem not clear now? How can we have healthy interracial relations when critics are continuously reminding us of our strained and sometimes murderous past; when, like Lena Williams, critics see their principal function as whitewashing the thoughtless and ugly things that minorities do; when the claim of injury is nondebatable because offense is in the mind of the offense-taker; when unintended interracial contact is unavoidable in an integrated and crowded society; and when no matter how carefully we try to control our language, we cannot safely discuss our differences because, as French novelist Gustave Flaubert put it (in *Madame Bovary*), "[H]uman speech is [but] a cracked kettle we bang on for the bears to dance to"? With our fingers on a hair trigger, will the slightest contretemps not naturally morph into *casus belli*? And can any good come from this?

The academic world, says a member of the Academic Discrimination Advisory Board at the National Women's Studies Association, "is not a merit parkway." It is "more like a big male gang grope."[25] "At almost every campus I have ever been on as a student and faculty member," says Asian American law professor Sumi Cho, "I have encountered appalling cases of sexual harassment against Asian Pacific and Asian Pacific American women."[26] The condition of African Americans evokes even wilder charges. "Black bitch hunts," trumpets Regina Austin, "are alive and well in the territory where minority female law faculty labor."[27] Are Cho and Austin saying that conditions for the groups they speak for are worse than for other women? It would seem so; "black bitch hunts are alive" would, without more, seem to imply that white bitch hunts are not. Yet it is hard to test Cho and Austin on their pronouncements when they offer no evidence whatever that Asian American and black women should come to campus in terror. *RACE ipsa loquitur.*

Once a Slave, Always a Slave

Race critics are equally attracted to catastrophizing. "[W]hile slavery is over," declares Derrick Bell, a founder of critical race theory (about which more later), "a racist society continues to exert dominion over black men and their maleness in ways more subtle but hardly less castrating than during slavery."[28]

Images like these pervade race literature. The African American law-teaching community, Bell suggests, is on the verge of extinction. On what ostensible evidence? "[T]he numbers of those who are to replace us are much smaller than we had hoped."[29] Without knowing about Bell's expectations in this regard, it is not easy to solace him. But 178 more African Americans worked full-time in law teaching in 1998, when he wrote those words, than in 1988, which represents an increase from 4.8 percent to 7.8 percent of total law faculty.[30] Since African Americans represent 5.1 percent of lawyers, it seems fair to conclude that although the situation is not paradise, neither is it a wasteland. Nevertheless, Bell devalues racial discourse by ending his essay with an end-of-the-world vision of black life in academia. Citing the lost colony at Roanoke Island, he tells readers that the only "reminder of our endeavors [may be] the academic equivalent of the 'CROATOAN' carved on one tree."[31]

Another of Bell's stories, "Space Traders," a full-blown doomsday classic, is a tale of the arrival of visitors to this country from another planet. After a preliminary evaluation of American life, they realize that to complete their mission they will have to bring Americans back home with them for further study. But how and who? They are not strong enough to force the issue; they will need the cooperation of the American government and people. Quickly noting both America's contempt for minorities and its greed, they offer enough gold to bail out federal, state, and local governments in exchange for the African Americans. A great debate on the subject ensues, but in the end, blacks are marched off toward the spaceship in chains. The circle is now complete; "black people leave the New World as their forebears had arrived."[32]

Let It Rain, Let It Pour, All We Want Is Color War

Richard Delgado, the Derrick Bell Professor of Law at the University of Pittsburgh School of Law, has one of his characters point to the likely demographic prospect that "Caucasians will cease being a majority about midway in the next [i.e., current] century. At that point in the ordinary course of events they would lose power." So what is going on? "[T]hey're gearing up for a fight. It's one of the oldest tricks in the world—provoke your enemy until he responds, then slap him down decisively. . . . Right-wing fundamentalists have always had a morbid fascination with apocalypse," Delgado's character warns. "Formerly, they defined it in terms of H-bombs and nuclear Armageddon. . . . Now," the author of more than fifteen books predicts, "it is race war."[33]

But there is another old trick, one used frequently by trouble makers. Tell your followers that their enemy has weapons of mass destruction that are about to be unleashed against them. One has to wonder, in other words: Is Delgado's character merely anticipating civil war, or does he want to start one?

Delgado, and even more so Bell, are hardened veterans of the civil rights movement. During those dangerous earlier years, paranoia might, arguably, have been seen not as a problem but as a solution. As black psychiatrists William Grier and Price Cobbs put it in their classic work, *Black Rage*:

> We submit that it is necessary for a black man in America to develop a distrust of his fellow white citizens. . . . He must cushion himself against cheating, slander, humiliation. . . . if he does not so protect himself, he will live a life of such pain and shock as to find life itself unbearable. For his own survival, then, he must develop a *cultural paranoia* in which

every white man is a potential enemy . . . and every social system is set against him unless he personally finds out differently.[34]

But times change and yesterday's cures become today's diseases. Yet the younger generation of race critics shows no fewer paranoid symptoms. Reference here is not only to African Americans. "I cannot remember when I was not 'the enemy,'" writes Asian American law professor Chris Iijima, reviving notions of "Yellow Peril" days. "[W]hen I was born, the 'Japs' still were the enemy. Then it was the Red (Communist) 'Chinks,' and the North Korean 'gooks,' and then the Southeast Asian 'gooks.' At one point," he concludes, "Americans were afraid that the Japanese would take over the United States, and now it's the 'Chinks' campaign contributions that pose a national threat."[35]

An Excremental Vision

"What do the souls of black folks look like," asks African American law professor Anthony Farley of his white readers, "after you have been digesting them for 500 years . . . [and they are] vomited back onto their auction blocks?"[36] The question, he insists, shows Americans "what they have been masticating for the last half millennium." And herein, he carries on, lies the strength of critical race theory. "Like vomit," it cannot be ignored; for one "is lured by objects of loathing . . . [such as] a piece of filth, waste or dung."[37]

If minorities feel defined and defiled by this vile, feculent imagery, will they not also rage? What is the effect of that anger? "My rage burns . . . in my psyche with an intensity that creates clarity," writes bell hooks. "It is a constructive healing rage."[38] If rage clarifies and heals, it has to be cultivated.

Gang-grope, appalling sexual harassment, genocide, slavery, genital mutilation, vomit, and dung—and killing rage. To these images can be added "spirit-murder," a term apparently coined by Columbia Law professor and *Nation* columnist Patricia Williams and spread by a score of other critics. It refers to psychic injury done by white people to African Americans. What is the end product of portraying our environment as "an evil city, an evil city on a hill, an evil city that manufactures plague . . . a city of death"?[39] Orlando Patterson spells out the implications for white people: "no European-American person, except one insensitive to the charge of racism, dares say what he or she really means."[40] At the same time, the only sensible response for women and minorities to such senseless conditions is to retreat to their plastic bubbles, to insurrection, and even to suicide and murder.

Race and gender theorists nevertheless proclaim the value of inter-group dialogue. Patricia Williams wants to "relegitimate the national discussion of racial, ethnic and gender tensions so that we can get past the Catch-22 in which merely talking about it is considered an act of war, in which not talking about it is complete capitulation to the status quo."[41] "If engagement is the first step in healing," says Yale Law professor Harlon Dalton, "then the second is pure, unadulterated struggle. . . . We will never achieve racial healing if we do not confront one another, take risks . . . say all the things we are not supposed to say in mixed company."[42]

But how welcome will whites feel to participate in the debate when, calling racism a "crime and a disease," a leading race theorist famously announces that the "inability to know racial discrimination when one sees it . . . [is the product of] a reluctance to admit that the illness of racism infects almost everyone"?[43] Pleas for frank intergender and inter-race dialogue, moreover, can hardly be taken seriously when, while stressing the benefits of real interracial dialogue with one voice, gender and race theorists dismiss its value with another.

It Takes One to Know One

What, after all, can white males offer? "[W]omen's experience [is] a necessary prerequisite for doing feminism," argues one law professor, and "men who wanted to use the label 'feminist' would have to spend a significant number of years living as women to qualify."[44] Others generously allow white men to speak through their own experience, but "I would . . . give special credence to the perspective of the subordinated," says Mari Matsuda.[45] Well-known University of Chicago political scientist Iris Young holds that oppressed groups should have special representation and "group veto power regarding specific policies that affect a group directly."[46]

Why? Minority status, says Delgado, "brings with it a presumed competence to speak about race and racism."[47] The implication, of course, is that white status does not. Whites, says Michael Dyson, "may believe that their opinions and judgments are as fully informed and cogent as those of victims of racism. In this circumstance something approximating a lack of standing to speak exists because the insight gained by personal experience cannot be duplicated—certainly not without careful study of the oppression under scrutiny."[48] We must assume, adds Patricia Williams, "that the best insight and inspiration for . . . the amelioration [of social oppression] will come from those immediately and negatively affected."[49]

The issue is not only competence but also morality. Speaking about the O. J. Simpson case, Dyson asks that whites "who have benefited, whether explicitly or unconsciously, from racial inequality . . . now be courageous in rejecting a belief in the moral equivalency of black and white views about race": white "skepticism about black juries' ability to convict black criminals doesn't have the same moral gravity as the claims of blacks victimized by a legacy of racial injustice."[50] In sum, whites have no say as to whether the mostly black jury should have found Simpson guilty of the murder of Nicole Brown and Ron Goldman; in race debates with black people, white folks, like the youths in Lena Williams's story, must give way.

Presumptions in favor of subordinated populations, Derrick Bell suggests, should have legislative and judicial, as well as salon and barroom, applications.[51] In a landmark case, *Washington v. Davis,*[52] the U.S. Supreme Court held that in order to establish an Equal Protection violation of the Fourteenth Amendment, a plaintiff had to show that a challenged governmental action was taken with a "racially discriminatory" purpose—that demonstrating discriminatory effect was not sufficient. Bell argues that this limitation is too restrictive because much racism is subconscious and, even when conscious, can be easily concealed. Maybe so. But look what happens if the threshold for violation is "discriminatory effect."

Consider the case of the movie theater in which patrons interact exuberantly with actors on the screen. Showing pleasure or displeasure in this manner is apparently common in black communities and might even be expected from a culture in which expressivity is reputedly more valued than it is in the more formal, repressed majority culture. Distinctions between audience and performer may actually reflect Eurocentrist aesthetics. For Afrocentrist scholar and Temple University professor Molefi Asante, "The reactions and responses of the audience might be better understood . . . as the collective actions of the participants."[53]

Now suppose that talking back to the screen in New York City movie theaters generates complaints by whites (if not blacks), and the city responds with a no-talking ordinance at least for those theaters having a no-talking policy. Under *Washington v. Davis,* the ordinance would stand. Under the Bell rule, however, if blacks objected to the ordinance because separate is not equal, it would fail; the black community would have veto power over movie theater policies.

Anything You Can See I Can See Better

The notion that the nation's subordinated groups should be privileged in the political and legal debates of the age has reportedly received support from cognitive theory. To understand the point, we must go back to one of Du Bois's most cited observations, that blacks have had to develop a "double consciousness," a "second sight," to survive. Fair enough. But, perhaps inevitably, this intriguing hundred-year-old expression of stereoscopy as a survival mechanism has morphed into a claim of superiority; blacks not only see differently, but they also see better. Professor Deborah Post (a fellow at a high-prestige research center at Stanford as these words are written) has publicized a four-step scale of human cognitive development, apparently first developed by psychologist William Perry and later refined by Lee Knefelkamp.[54] Under this construct, cognitive development begins with step one—duality—where the world appears in black and white, that is, right and wrong; questions have answers. It proceeds to early multiplicity and then, third, to (full) multiplicity, where truth and meaning are understood to come in many shades. The process ends with contextual relativism, a term not adequately defined. According to Post —and here is the point of this little riff—women and minorities understand the world better than do white men because the former begin at step three. When you're black, you think you really know. Or, in street talk, "If you're white, you're none too bright; if you're black, you're in front of the pack."

Black women are even more cognitively privileged. Race critics frequently lament the "multiple oppressions" or "triple jeopardy" of black women. We see now that this cloud has a silver lining, for it suggests that black women have not double but triple consciousness. Through the power of synergy, Post—not incidentally, an African American woman—could begin beyond step three, at step four. If they preserve their early leads, African American women remain far ahead of everyone else. At what stage, it seems fair to ask, do African American women learn about the vulgarity of such talk or, at least, about the dangers of stereotyping?

Truth and beauty being interdependent, at least in Anglo culture, the cognitive deficiencies of whites cannot help but have profound aesthetic implications. "[T]he introduction of love, truth, beauty into the world has never been the preoccupation of white leaders and bosses of the West," whose goals have been "power, money, and lordship over subject peoples," says Houston Baker, the black former president of the Modern Language Association, who credits poet Amiri Baraka for the insight. It is "the newly emergent peoples" who are "attempting to show the hierarchical superiority of their beauty."[55]

What role can a white male scholar conceivably be given in race dialogue, suffering as he does from moral, cognitive, and aesthetic handicaps? What role can he have when race critics hold, in the bold words of prolific author and Columbia University's Teacher's College professor of psychology Derald Wing Sue, that people of color have a "clarity of vision and truth" so that "we can understand Whites better than they can understand us"? Assuming for the moment that Sue is right—his theory is tested throughout this book—even if whites did have something important to say to minorities, there would be no point in listening. "As people of color," says Sue, the former president of the Society for the Psychological Study of Ethnic Minority Issues, "we must rely on our intuitive and experiential reality. Never allow White folks to make us doubt our perceptual wisdom!"[56]

Chris Iijima highlights the role of white folks in race discourse: "Until [whites] understand that conversations about race are ones they engage to learn rather than to teach (which is their historical and customary position)," he says, "real and meaningful conversations cannot happen."[57] One young, white legal scholar has learned his multicultural lesson well: the white academic is welcome to evaluate social and political subordination, provided that he responds to minority critics and that he observes "the cautions of the diminished stature of his scholarship." He can earn a "limited, contingent legitimacy [only] by the approval of the groups whose subordination" he is interpreting.[58]

What a feeble vision of the modern-day academic. Consider that professors are given a system of economic security that those who must earn their keep every day look on with unmitigated envy—tenure. Notwithstanding the inevitable abuses that follow the establishment of such a sheltered class, this protection is thought necessary to encourage the freest, most heated debate on the fullest range of issues. The tenured academic is not, of course, obligated to engage the contemporary furies. But if the academic's job is to swallow whole what others dish out, he or she does not "deserve" tenure. Nor, perhaps, a job. "It's important for writers to generate . . . hostility," says Nobelist V. S. Naipaul, spelling out a creed that race and gender theorists would seem to have adopted for themselves. "If a writer doesn't generate hostility, he is dead."[59]

What then are our interracial obligations to one another? "In our face-to-face interactions," says Orlando Patterson, "Afro-American and Euro-American people should treat one another exactly alike: as responsible moral agents. We do not need any special sets of sensitivities," he goes on. "Any attempt to observe such sensitivities would be folly, for it will lead one down a path of either patronizing contempt or relativistic moral and social chaos."[60] To preclude patronizing contempt and social chaos Patterson's model for interracial discourse is adopted here.

A Texas Kerfuffle

Is it not yet clear that what is needed now on the part of white male scholars is *mano a mano, hermano/a a hermano/a* engagement on the subject of race? However much a group has suffered, there can be no presumptions in its favor; a constant state of pain, one might add, hinders a complete diagnosis of one's own condition. But, then again, what happens to those who take their academic duties seriously? Consider the case of Lino Graglia, a professor of law at the University of Texas. In a public statement made in the aftermath of the 1995 Hopwood case, which held unconstitutional the use of racial preferences in higher education, Graglia suggested that, as a group, Hispanics and blacks could not compete against whites in higher education institutions because in their cultures "academic failure is not looked upon with disgrace."[61] A strong statement to be sure, but one not lacking in support.[62] A major study showed that black and Hispanic students were left alone by parents if they kept grades in the C range; by contrast, white students had to earn Bs and Asian Americans had to come home with As.

It is important to note what Graglia was *not* saying: that minorities lack the intelligence to compete. The distinction is important because a few minority commentators have said the same thing as Graglia. John McWhorter's recent *Losing the Race: Self-Sabotage in Black America* contains by no means the first charge against African Americans for a "Cult of Anti-Intellectualism." And yet, Graglia's remarks ignited a firestorm. Jesse Jackson urged that Graglia be treated as a "moral and social pariah" for his "racist" and "immoral" remarks. Turning Graglia into an unperson, the dean of the University of Texas Law School announced that while the principle of academic freedom precluded any sanction, the law school administration would "sympathetically consider" student requests to transfer from Graglia's otherwise required class.

If white men are discouraged from participating in gender and race discourse because women and minorities know best, and if, when they do attempt to participate, they are ostracized and abused for having divergent views, what is the likely consequence? For Vanderbilt Law School professor Carol Swain, the stifling of white voices fuels a dangerous "new white nationalism," the title of her recent book.[63]

Worse yet, like living organisms, ideas tend to spread until resisted by an equally powerful force. Uncountered, like employees under the well-known Peter Principle, race and gender theory has been promoted far beyond its level of competence. The acute reader will understand that even the most highly trained race and gender theorists require discipline no less than their most free-spirited students.

Absent discipline, says Hoover Fellow and Stanford professor Thomas Sowell, who is black, race and gender commentators have come to see themselves as the anointed class or, one might say, the prophets in our society.[64] Their felt "state of grace," in turn, fuels their efforts to roil American social and political life. The late Berkeley African American studies professor June Jordan connects black virtue, anger, and power: "I do not believe that we can restore and expand the freedoms that our lives require unless and until we embrace the . . . unabashed moral certitude, and the purity—the incredible outgoing energy—of righteous rage."[65]

Who can talk to race critics under these circumstances? The prophet's function, after all, is not to listen but to teach. The prophet is normally celebrated not for subtlety of analysis but for clarity. The prophet says, "Give to the poor," but does not add, "Be careful not to create dependency." It should not be surprising, then, that black godliness has exacted a heavy earthly price, which functions as a tragic consequence of the civil rights movement. Shame, says Shelby Steele, "gave the United States a 'good' that was transcendent and beautiful, and in so doing, left us with a virtuousness that is the enemy of both freedom and black self-determination."[66]

The Odor of Sanctity

Might the claimed state of grace of subordinated populations be covering up baser motives? Shelby Steele says that when stigmatized as racists, "whites can be easily extorted by blacks for countless concessions."[67] How so? Consider again Iijima, who sees himself and other Asians suffering as the perpetual villains in American society, or Farley, for whom African Americans have always symbolized the white man's waste product. When presenting themselves as the crucified and excrementalized embodiments of hundreds of years of racial history, these authors were junior faculty members, soon to come up for a tenure vote, which would determine whether they could keep their jobs or whether they would have to uproot themselves and their loved ones and start again somewhere else. At times like these, academics, being human, might be especially concerned about their jobs. Job security may be even more important to African Americans and other minorities if they fear racism or internalize a conception of racial inferiority.

Here is the point. Normally a reader is free to disagree with a writer, the writer's fate being of rather little significance to anyone but him- or herself. A tenure vote against Iijima, however, supports the vitality of his claim to being an endangered species, worthy of all the protections that the status confers. It is an attack on his very self-conception and thus can be expected to be met with all the legal and political firepower that he can muster. Beyond that, it is a rejection of the combined traditions of Japan, China, the Philippines, Korea, etc., an act of war in this globalist, multicultural age. Similarly, to deny Farley tenure would be to perpetuate African Americans as a class of Untouchables. By wrapping themselves in race and gender flags, race and gender critics can rise above their own disposable selves to become institutions, indeed sacred ones. Endangering such institutions might give even a senior professor pause. In any event, Farley and Iijima are now tenured.

Again, it is not suggested here that Farley and Iijima—and perhaps other critics—are consciously or unconsciously motivated by self-interest; there is no way of knowing with sufficient certainty. But on the old theory that "all interest is self-interest," that motivation cannot be dismissed out of hand, especially since affirmative action, we now understand, helps minority professors get their own children rather than those of truck drivers into Harvard and Columbia. As a *New York Times* columnist recently put it, "When students and faculty activists struggle for cultural diversity, they are largely battling over what skin color the rich kids should have."[68]

A specific illustration of how race theory plays out in the academy on the employment side was highlighted in the preface. That tie was made even more explicit by the late professor Trina Grillo in a year in which she was being evaluated for promotion and tenure: "Maybe . . . we should hire all minority women with tenure," she mused. "While this is not exactly a likely development, it does make a fair amount of sense—the experience of minority women faculty is so different from that of other faculty that it is hard for other faculty to make realistic evaluations."[69] This is what we are left with. When a person complains that "my spouse doesn't understand me," we are primed to laugh; but when an academic thinks that she is entitled to a lifetime job without passing a probationary period because her colleagues don't understand her, she expects to be taken seriously.

Sincerity and Verity

Examining the motivations of seemingly heartfelt appeals by distinguished men and women professors is vulgar and uncharitable. But our obligations to our students and communities would seem to demand no less. Benjamin Disraeli poked fun at the bishop who "sympathizes with everything that is earnest," because "what is earnest is not always true. On the contrary," Disraeli held, "error is often more earnest than truth."[70] Readers might be well advised, accordingly, to place their faith in authors who approach their subject with irony and skepticism.

Raising the issue of sincerity and self-interest in the present context seems especially appropriate for several reasons. First, critical theory itself argues for the importance of examining motivation in the interpretation of texts. Law "[t]eachers teach nonsense," says Harvard Law's Duncan Kennedy, when they "seek to persuade students that legal reasoning is distinct, *as a method of reaching correct results,* from ethical and political discourse in general."[71] And ethics and politics are the prototype subjects for debate. Put another way, a body of work that defines itself as hermeneutical is fair game for hermeneutical analysis. Sauce for the goose and the duckling, in this view, would be sauce for the gander and swan as well.

Second, questioning the sincerity of black writers may be particularly useful if Swarthmore sociologist and Chair of Black Studies Sarah Willie is right. In her new study of black graduates of Howard and Northwestern, *Acting Black,* she found that her interviewees, far from being programmed by their race, subtly manipulated it by treating "*race as sets of behaviors that they could choose to act out* . . . as ethnicity and subculture. Consciously negotiating their identities, . . . the men and women in this study were *performing.*"[72]

Third, Delgado teaches his readers that ideology is a distraction in race discourse and that "attending to the material side of race" is most productive.[73] There is no interest more material than protecting jobs. Last, and perhaps most important in justifying a careful examination of the bona fides of race critics, is a view of human nature. Would America be a better place if Derrick Bell catapulted himself to power in a *coup d'état?* Would minorities' experiences with subordination induce them to monitor and then rein in any inclination toward excess when they were decision-makers? Not, it would appear, according to Harvard Law professor Randall Kennedy:

> [U]nless inhibited, every person and group will tend toward beliefs and practices that are self-aggrandizing. This is [not only] true of those who inherit a dominant status. . . . Surely one of the most striking features of human dynamics is the alacrity with which those who have been oppressed will oppress whomever they can once the opportunity presents itself. [Thus] it is not premature to worry about the possibility that blacks or other historically subordinated groups will abuse power to the detriment of others.[74]

In like manner, the great anti-imperialist Franz Fanon defines the "native" as "an oppressed person whose permanent dream is to become an oppressor."[75] Crowning death-penalty critic Derrick Bell Philosopher King would, in this view, ensure restoration of the guillotine for the *ancien régime.*

For Professor Judith Baer, Kennedy and Fanon would seem to be taking a hopelessly male perspective; women, because they are nurturers, can be different.[76] We shall come back to this matter later. For now, consider what bell hooks has to say: "We must challenge the simplistic notion that man is the enemy, woman the victim. We all have the capacity to act in ways that oppress, dominate, wound." It is important to keep in mind, she adds, "that it is first the potential oppressor within that we must resist."[77] Not to be aware of the human tendency to oppress makes us pigeons for would-be oppressors.

Be Careful What You Wish For

If we are to stem self-aggrandizing tendencies, a deeper look at race theory is required than has been given heretofore. What is fundamentally missing in the views of the race and gender theorists, says Sowell, is a sense of the tragic—that "there are no 'solutions' in the tragic vision, but only trade-offs."[78] Since costs of regulation "are generally not explicitly modeled" writes Professor Lloyd Cohen, using more formal language, discussion of various types of reform "is often carried on with the implicit assumption that costs are negligible and may be ignored."[79] Critics who believe that "good ends can be achieved without unpleasantness" have been labeled "sentimentalists."[80] We can fairly extend the characterization by calling them childish.

For conservative tragedians, rules of law are the results of hard balances struck. "Thou Shalt Not Steal" tells the hungry that no matter their suffering, theft cannot be the remedy. Tragedians understand that an argument in favor of theft can be constructed under these circumstances but that this is not the appropriate test. Instead, it is whether the argument is ultimately compelling under all the social as well as personal circumstances. The naive idealism of critical race theorists is reflected in a proposal to sabotage the jury system. In a famous *Yale Law Journal* article, Professor Paul Butler argues that our legal institutions are so biased against African Americans that for "nonviolent *malum in se* crimes such as theft or perjury, nullification is an option the [black] juror should consider."[81] The illustrative case he offers is of a poor black woman who steals from a rich employer (color unspecified).

Butler's proposal has received searing criticism from whites and blacks who are worried about the survival of the jury system under such a plan, and nothing valuable can be added here on the subject. It is on the economic side that the matter requires attention. From Butler's perspective, the proposal will benefit employees, whom he sees as forced by a cruel system into theft in order to make ends meet. But anyone familiar with labor markets understands that the most important qualification for a job, far more than skill and punctuality, is honesty. Incompetent and lazy employees will ordinarily be found out before they can do too much damage. A disloyal employee can sink the ship. In a dynamic system, therefore, "rich" employers will simply avoid hiring risky (i.e., dishonest) employees in the first place. And when black thieves are beyond criminal prosecution, we know exactly who will be excluded.

Offering another dubious suggestion, Iijima denies not just that "there is a 'pure' African-American or Latino race that is 'unmixed' by other races" but also that "individuals are free to choose a racial designation unaffected by how they are perceived in the larger society."[82] With these words Iijima was apparently registering his displeasure with the proposal made several years ago that census forms for 2000 allow individuals to check a multiracial box for the first time, a proposal condemned by many identity promoters on the understandable theory that it would dilute minority political power.[83] Congress capitulated to these latter critics by rejecting the idea of a multiple identity box, though it allowed individuals to check off multiple *separate* identities on the form. The problem is that it was the fast-growing multiracial population itself that claimed the right to so identify itself through a box of its own, and it did so presumably in the hope that other Americans would respect that claim.

Breaking the White Man's Chops

Even more troubling are the conscious race games that many writers play. James Baldwin wrote of his practice of "uttering stupidities and maintaining absurd theses" at conventions of white writers.[84] "I lives to harass white folks," says one of Derrick Bell's own heroes.[85] For Shelby Steele, much race discourse is a game, symbolized by his having taken a "delinquent's delight" during the days of "flagellatory white guilt [when] it was such great fun to pinion some professor or housewife, or best of all, a large group of remorseful whites, with the knowledge of both their racism and their denial of it. The adolescent impulse to sneer at convention, to startle the middle-aged with doubt," he continues, "could be indulged under the guise of indignation. And how could I lose? My victims," he concludes, "earnest liberals for the most part could no more crawl out from under my accusation than Joseph K. in Kafka's *Trial*."[86]

Black culture critic Stanley Crouch tells of a related game. The test for success used to be, "Can you as a minority group, live up to . . . bourgeois standards. But *now,*" he says, the test is, "can you, faceless America, put up with me acting obnoxious and not get irritated? Because if you do get irritated, then you're the racist pig I always knew you were."[87]

To the extent that Baldwin, Steele, and Crouch are right about games race critics play, the moral onus for the current state of affairs cannot in fairness be placed entirely on them. Of course, if race writers have manipulated gender and race to their advantage, they bear some moral burden for doing so. The only responsible course for self-respecting thinkers, the renowned philosopher Theodor Adorno once wrote, "is to deny oneself the ideological misuse of one's own existence."[88] Under a more familiar standard, white men are no less morally culpable: Fool me once, shame on you; fool me twice, shame on me.

A White Man's Burden

If gender and race critics are out of control on the subject of gender and race; if some of the smartest people in America are deliberately or unconsciously saying the dumbest things; if they are teaching African Americans that the white man has trapped them in an excremental hell; if they are teaching women that "male domination," while not destroying "the longing that men and women have to love one another, . . . has made fulfilling that longing almost impossible to realize";[89] if they are, as they concede, "pimping white guilt,"[90] then a white male patriot can no longer allow himself to remain silent.

But how to deal with thinking that is so entrenched that conflicting evidence is regularly ignored? The problem is illustrated in Hans Christian Andersen's well-known story of the emperor who, surrounding himself with yes-men and charlatans, is shocked when the child cries out that the emperor has no clothes. For many people, it seems, the story ends explicitly or implicitly with the humiliated emperor scurrying for cover. But they are wrong. The story is about overweening pride more than ignorance. In Andersen's last-minute text change, readers are told that the emperor knew that the child was right. Nevertheless, "he thought to himself: 'I must go through with the procession now.'"[91] The only workable solution to the problem of righteous pride is ridicule, something that the respectful and perhaps fearful crowd was, understandably, not prepared to offer. But this is precisely what Harvard Law professor Mark Kelman recommends for use in academic life in our own time. "Take specific arguments very *seriously* in their own terms," he writes in his seminal article, "Trashing," and "discover that they are actually *foolish*."[92] Kelman serves as a model for us here as we scrutinize gender and race opinion for willful self-delusion, among other things.

Hate the Sin, Love the Sinner

Let there be no mistake, however, as to the central purpose of responding to gender and race critics: to raise women and minorities from the refuse heap of their imaginings. It is *not* to bring therapeutic justice to white men by defrocking the high priests of race and gender, to wash away the original sin of white maleness, or to answer the feminist bumper sticker "Men have feelings too, but who really gives a damn?" Unlike the works examined here, *Toxic Diversity* is born of love. *Qui bene amat bene castigat,* the old Latin epigram goes, "those who love well chastise well."

The reader should understand that speaking frankly on the delicate subject of race and gender hurts me more than it does you. But, if a necessary step for social healing is, again, in Patricia Williams's words, "pure unadulterated struggle," if we must "relegitimate the national discussion of racial, ethnic and gender tensions," then in our debates with Professor Bell, whites must not hesitate to take inspiration from Carl Douglas's response to his friend Johnnie Cochran, "Derrick, that's bulls—t."

Prompting whites to speak frankly on the subject of race and gender may be the best way of unearthing their truest sentiments about race and improving race relations. Why did James Baldwin develop a practice of "uttering stupidities and maintaining absurd theses"? "If they listen respectfully and, at the end, overwhelm me with applause," he explained, "there isn't the slightest doubt: they are filthy racists."[93]

Pain and Gain

To be sure, undermining filthy racism by giving voice to honest white male opinion can be painful to those who listen. But in our society we believe that such pain is outweighed by the benefits of hearing what others have to say. This principle is most clearly reflected in our criminal law, where a vigorous defense is readily, if not always happily, given to accused perpetrators of even the vilest crimes. If the world is somehow a better place for giving serial killers a voice, then surely we need to hear voices coming from law-abiding, if misguided, white males.

Perhaps the best place to start is the central gender and race theory message that gender, race, and myriad other categories are nothing but social constructs. That is to say, the many distinctions that we draw between the races and genders in our culture have no foundational reality; they are ultimately fictions that we are taught to live by. In repeating this news over and over, gender and race critics ask white males to junk all their accumulated knowledge and instincts and take instruction from them. But is the belief system of critics any less of a social construct than that of white men? If not, maybe the pain that critics so consistently and bitterly complain of has also been created from nothing. A deconstruction of pain, then, should prove invaluable in understanding and assuaging gender and race hurt.

A brief discussion of the matter will have to suffice here. Some contemporary research has yielded a finding which, even if somewhat extravagant, is immensely useful: the report of pain has "no inherent relationship to events inside the body."[94] It is, furthermore, highly suggestive, so that what we are conditioned to expect will frequently affect our experience of physical events. In an intriguing experiment, one group of subjects was told that touching a vibrating piece of sandpaper would be painful, while another group was told that it would be pleasurable. The first group indeed found the experience painful; the second, pleasurable.

In another experiment, people reporting back pain were divided into two groups, "A" and "B." Group A was told that the cure would require medication and activity limits that would last as long as patients felt necessary: "Let pain be your guide." For group B, the regimens would be needed only for a short period of time. After a year, group A reported significantly higher "sick scores." Summing up this experiment, a prominent psychologist concluded that if the termination of a problem is not narrowly demarcated, "a suffering component to the pain problem may be promoted."[95]

Purely psychic pain is likely even more suggestible. The *Talking Cure*, for example, may cause more pain than it relieves. In numerous experiments involving the experience of sexual abuse or the death of a spouse, subjects who had been encouraged to feel their pain showed results inferior, and in some cases far inferior, to those who repressed it.[96] So, if people are taught that "You sound black" is a blow to their solar plexus, they may well double over in pain; if they are taught that it is no more significant than "You sound Irish," they will continue to stand tall. In characterizing sexism and racism as brutal and permanent, then, gender and race theory may be provoking self-induced pain and an expanding universe of highly questionable judgments.

Consider how Robert Allen, a senior editor of the *Black Scholar,* judges the 2000 presidential election. Of course "it was, first and foremost, about race, this stolen election. And then Gore didn't want to touch it because Gore didn't want to break with white supremacy. . . . That's how much white supremacy means to him. Can you imagine? He'd rather lose the presidency than stand with black folks."[97]

The only thing that matters is black power. That Al Gore, who has devoted most of his adult life to public service, undoubtedly sacrificed his own ambition not to white supremacy but to the nation, by saving it from chaos, or civil war, is unimaginable.

Consider at another level the executive director of Asian Americans for Equality, who recently spoke about the vast numbers of foreign-born New Yorkers who "use cash, don't own a phone, are uncomfortable sharing their identity and don't have a lot of belongings." He went on to argue that the law needs to protect such vulnerable folks from landlords who discriminate against them.[98] But what conclusion should right-minded Americans draw? That a widow must accept a prospective tenant who appears on her doorstep with a month's rent in cash and only one suitcase, and no identification or bank account? Is she forbidden to protect herself, by insisting on identification and perhaps references, not only against nonpayment of future rent but also against possible assault, rape, and perhaps premature detonation of a bomb? And while we are at it, would an Asian American landlord be allowed to screen out a WASP applicant under these same circumstances? The Asian Americans for Equality director does not say. Only someone who has never walked a mile in a landlord's Pradas, nor aspires to do so, could stake out the executive director's position. Sowell again nicely explains: The judgment of the anointed is "third-party decision making by people who pay no cost for being wrong."[99]

Little League Thinking

Consider, finally, that a few days before these words were written, Danny Almonte was unmasked as being over the age limit to play Little League baseball. His team's record was declared a nullity. Commenting on the sad situation, a Little League player opined that if Almonte had not been from Santo Domingo, he would not have been caught.[100] You don't have to be eleven years old to believe this. For a recent columnist, Almonte's team made the "critical mistake of speaking with accents or in Spanish while playing America's pastime" against a "lily-white" Florida team. According to this writer, since *Sports Illustrated*, which broke the story, presumably did not verify the birth dates of all players in the Little League World Series, the whole story "is nothing more than a case of racial profiling."[101]

We must try to understand these charges. Towering over his teammates at five foot eight, while claiming to be twelve years old, Danny Almonte had previously won all four games he pitched in the Little League World Series tournament, striking out sixty-two of the seventy-two batters he faced; one of those games was the first perfect game in World Series tournament play in forty-four years; Almonte's coach had earlier been banned from coaching in the Latin American Little League for using overage players; America has a journalistic tradition in which the media are charged with keeping America's institutions honest. Americans were then told that neither Danny Almonte's noteworthy achievements nor his physical characteristics might have drawn a reporter's attention, only his and his team's Hispanic character.

"In order to get beyond racism, we must first take account of race," Justice Blackmun famously wrote in *Bakke*.[102] When it is important to prove how downtrodden a group is, "We must first take account of race" morphs so easily and insidiously into "we must consider *only* race."

What is the impact of the stories told by minority critics? Can Latino kids function, much less thrive, when they think that they are hated for playing baseball against a lily-white American team? Can black people remain unscathed by the self-mutilating, self-excrementalizing imagery? Not according to historian Daryl Scott, who claims that "[d]amage imagery . . . has [always] served the cause of hegemonic political ideology," a point he illustrates with a view of black males as both psychologically impotent and castrated.[103] Surely, few will entertain dreams of glory if they imagine that, hovering overhead, a white man lusts to push them back down into the muck.

For all the practical and psychological benefits it provides, moreover, conjuring up anger is ultimately debilitating. "[N]o matter the headiness of our slogans," wrote Ralph Ellison, "an unthinking indulgence in anger can lead to a socially meaningless self-immolation and to intellectual suicide."[104] Seventeenth-century preacher Caleb Cotton explains why: "The intoxication of anger, like that of the grape, shows us to others, but hides us from ourselves."[105]

. . . And They Are Us

What, in particular, is being hidden that is so destructive? Where should African Americans be concentrating their energies? Black critic Shelby Steele spells it out for us: 70 percent of all black children are born to unwed mothers; 68 percent of all violent crime is committed by blacks, mostly against other blacks; 60 percent of black fourth-graders cannot read at grade level, thus creating an educational gap between African Americans and others—a gap, one might add, that never gets closed.[106]

Confronting these problems will not be pleasant, particularly for black people. But it is a necessary, if not sufficient, condition for their resolution. "Not everything that is faced can be changed," James Baldwin wrote, "but nothing can be changed until it is faced."[107]

What about the white man? Whatever their original sin, Steele says, whites should not be blamed for current conditions. These "statistics come far more from [the] crippling sense of [aggrievement and] entitlement," he writes. "The worst enemy black America faces today is not white racism but white guilt."[108] Former University of California–Berkeley linguistics professor John McWhorter has written an article, "Toward a Usable Black History," designed to overcome the pernicious effects of black-victimization theory by showing the richness and vibrancy of black cultural life before the age of black victimhood.

Hurt People Hurt People

Some will claim that no one listens to what the nation's race critics are saying, so those critics are not at fault for undermining the faith of women and minorities in America, and thereby generating destructive race and gender rage. But is that likely? Where else is the rage coming from? No one can pinpoint the origin of this wrath, but a reasonable inference is that Ice-T's opinions as well as those of Al Sharpton, Lena Williams, Robert Allen, Danny Almonte's supporters, and Asian Americans for Equality—and worse yet, those of Long Island Rail Road mass murderer Colin Ferguson—are prefigured in, shaped by, or legitimated by the paranoid fantasies of race theorists like Derrick Bell and by bell hooks's blind, albeit killing, rage.

Is this theory of criminality far-fetched? Not according to at least one sociological theory. UCLA professor Jack Katz explored the liberal hypothesis that a feeling of humiliation leads mechanically to crimes like Ferguson's, a notion that mitigates the moral offense. But, says Katz, this is not exactly right. The proof is that most of those suffering powerlessness and humiliation find other ways of dealing with it. "As with emotions in general," Katz writes, "people who become enraged must create the sensuality that makes them its vehicle." Like football players before the big play, they have to work themselves up into a heightened state.[109] Ferguson's act, in this view, was not automatic but contingent. And the environment for his "personal construction" of rage may well have been fashioned by Bell and hooks and their ilk.

Chilling

Assuming that rage has a volitional element and that, bearing little relationship to reality, it has done much harm, some anger management is useful now. Fortunately, there is hope of bringing down America's racial temperature, and the equally good news is that the cure is well within African American tradition. For African Americans are the inventors of *cool*. Born in the brutal atmosphere of slavery, *cool* meant remaining impassive, masking emotions, internalizing anger, says Marlene Connor, author of *What Is Cool?* "An open display of hatred or even anger meant certain punishment. An open demonstration of happiness might mean the removal or destruction of whatever made you happy." If, as the author herself emphasizes, cool *"is perhaps the most important force in the life of a Black man in America"* (emphasis in original),[110] are African Americans and the rest of us not well served to call upon this blessing of diversity to offset the reckless catastrophizing and race-blaming?

Staying cool can help us to see the distraction that race is. "Race functions as an explanation for why Gratz didn't realize her dream," Harvard Law professor Lani Guinier explains. "Race is much more convenient than individual failure."[111] That is to say that notwithstanding her higher level of preparation, Jennifer Gratz, one of the white plaintiffs in the recent Supreme Court affirmative action case,[112] had no valid claim. She should have known that her rejection by the University of Michigan had nothing to do with race, that she is just a loser.

It is one thing to give that painful message to Gratz, another to give it to a minority student. "What blacks in perilous circumstances need," says Derrick Bell, is "reassurance that others, not they, are the cause of the wretched circumstances in which they live."[113] But even Afrocentrists see the peril of teaching black people that they have no control over their own destinies. When a writer "ignores the African's agency," writes Molefi Asante, "he or she allows for the default position—white supremacy—to operate without challenge, and thus participates in the [destruction of] human personality." If African Americans are not allowed to be subjects, "we remain objects without agency, intellectual beggars without a place to stand."[114]

"It is so easy to put it all on the white man," writes Louis Farrakhan, drawing out the larger implications. "As long as we beat up on white people and make the world think that everything that went wrong in the world is due to them and we had nothing to do with this," he adds, "then we rob ourselves of the impetus, the motivation, the inspiration for personal change and for accepting responsibility. . . . There was a time when you could blame the white man," Farrakhan concludes, but "with the way we're raising hell today . . . you can't say that any more."[115] Expanding on this view, Orlando Patterson provides a global perspective on the contemporary racial climate. "The sociological truths are that America, while still flawed in its race relations," he says, "is now the least racist white-majority society in the world; has a better record of legal protection of minorities than any other society, white or black; offers more opportunities to a greater number of black persons than any other society, including all those of Africa."[116] Patterson is not saying that ours is the best of all possible worlds for African Americans, only that it is the best of all actual worlds to date.

Where a black man can be master of his fate, dumping on the white man is counterproductive, as are the continual calls by our universities and other institutions for diversity and affirmative action. These latter doctrines suggest to too many minority students that, privileged through their privilegelessness, they have no further obligation to themselves and to the rest of society.[117] Booker T. Washington was keenly aware of the destructive power of this halo effect one hundred years ago. "No greater injury can be done to any youth," he wrote, "than to let him feel that because he belongs to this or that race he will be advanced regardless of his own merits or efforts."[118]

Whether or not one agrees with Patterson, Farrakhan, Washington, Du Bois, or with McWhorter, who testifies to "the stupendous progress the race has made,"[119] one thing should be clear: race critics who cannot smell the flowers have no claim to higher sensibility—to Soul.

3

The Critical Race Theory Show

We must "flood the market with our stories." . . . Only as these rich
and varied stories are increasingly heard will we begin to shape a
new public discourse.
—Professor Charles Lawrence (quoting Robin West in part)

Hoping to tighten the screws on men, and despairing of discursive prose to do the job because it tends to "depoliticize, decharge and
dampen," Professor Nancy Cook strongly urges use of the narrative form
of discourse.[1] Richard Delgado echoes this message. "Stories, parables,
chronicles, and narratives," he says, "are powerful means for destroying
mindset—the bundle of presuppositions, received wisdoms, and shared
understandings [in our] legal and political discourse. They can show that
what we believe is ridiculous, self-serving or cruel."[2] As a consequence of
Delgado's "Storytelling for Oppositionists and Others: A Plea for Narrative," as well as of Charles Lawrence's plea above,[3] the personal epic has
become a central feature of American race and gender talk; indeed, since
1989, when Delgado's piece was written, a thousand morality plays have
bloomed. To convey a sense of their form and function, a few stories from
the life of Patricia Williams are provided below.

Williams is our model storyteller here because of an unmatched repu-
tation among race theorists. Cornel West has lauded the Harvard-edu-
cated law professor as "a towering public intellectual of our time [who]
articulates a synoptic vision, synthetic analysis, and moral courage with
great power."[4] Meanwhile, *The Rooster's Egg,* the source of the stories
that follow, has been called "a stunning achievement . . . a prophetic tes-
tament. . . . It bears much the same relation to the Civil Rights movement
of the 1960s which 'The Souls of Black Folk' does to the era of Recon-

49

struction. . . . It deserves national attention."[5] There is "no better writer in American legal education today," concludes yet another leading scholar.[6] Using any other writer as our model under the circumstances would elicit charges of selection bias.

If the foregoing commentators are right about Williams's work, engaging Williams's *The Rooster's Egg* should offer great rewards. If they are not—if even the talented tenth (W. E. B. Du Bois's term) of the talented tenth can lose their balance on race terrain—how much more likely are the rest of us to fall on our faces?

An Epic at the Five-and-Dime

While perusing the shelves of a variety store a few years ago, Williams noted that there were some dolls that were marked for sale at $3.99 each, while others, originally priced at $2.99, were marked down to the "must sacrifice" price of $1.99. Since price differentials for similar goods are common, Williams at first made nothing of this observation. But then she noticed that the dolls were identical in every respect but one: the cheaper dolls were black. Williams became distraught. Racism was "being made 'rational' . . . by market forces." For Patricia Williams this story "captures" the "devalued condition" of blacks in America and the "absolute necessity of a corrective response."[7]

The cruel power of the market for Williams extends not only over the inanimate world but also, and most painfully, over flesh and blood. She tells of how she came to adopt a child. Asked about ethnic preference, she is offended; she tells the agency that color does not matter. When the time comes to pay, she learns that the fee for "older, black, and other handicapped" children is half of what it is for other children. A frightening world looms for Williams. How will her son's "'price' at birth relate to what value doctors put on his various parts if he ever stubs his toe and shows up in a hospital? Will he be valued more as a series of parts in the marketplace of bodies or more as a whole, as a precious social being with not just a body or a will but a soul?" (ibid., 224).

Borrowing a term from Harriet Beecher Stowe, Williams asks, Who will rule the fate of this most precious bit of "living property"? Unable to "conspire in putting a [lesser] price on my child's head," Williams insists on paying full price for a black infant (ibid., 225).

Is Williams's interpretation of the five-and-dime and adoption stories sound? Is she using the oppositionist's craft to reveal fault lines in the already dangerous terrain of race relations? Or are her stories narrative high-jinks used to racially bait both the agency and the store which, for all we know, are run by blacks, as well as white readers for allowing these marketing and adoption procedures to continue?

Racing to Judgment

Specifically, as to the dolls, is Patricia Williams showing herself too ready to extract a global message from what she gives no reason to suppose is not a single experience? Are white dolls marked down or even sold in black neighborhoods? Is it racist for a child to want a doll that looks like herself or sexist when she favors a female doll over a male one? If it is the doll story—among all available evidence— that highlights "the absolute necessity" for change, should the store owner be presumed more interested in making a statement than a profit on her merchandise? Might the price differential for the dolls not reflect the impact of the harsher economic circumstances for blacks in our society, a condition that Williams never allows her readers to forget? If so, what relevance would this have? Would Williams have experienced less distress if the $1.99 dolls were of distinctly inferior quality or if the store owner did not stock black dolls at all because of their lower turnover? Finally, let us suppose that the black dolls regularly sold not for $3.99 but for $5.99. Would Williams conclude that the prices reflect the skyrocketing status of blacks? In sum, and in the absence of more information from Williams, is it more likely that the store owner or Williams herself is being "ridiculous"?

The adoption story elicits similar responses. If there are more black babies available for adoption, whatever the reason, is it more "cruel" to recognize that there are not enough black adoptive parents for the job and to let the market solve the problem? Or, in order to satisfy Williams's moral and aesthetic demands by creating hobgoblinal equalities in "price," are black babies to be damned to institutionalization or foster care? Other, more subtle, questions arise as well. Is it ethical to have, let alone express, preferences for gender and race in adoption matters? Is Williams, the critical race theorist and storyteller, credible when she claims indifference to the race of an adopted child?

How should we understand Williams's failure to deal with the complexity of the issues she raises? For this purpose, we return to Sowell's insight about social policy offering trade-offs, not solutions; fantasies of the best of all possible worlds, in this view, preclude any progress to a better world. But what fuels this willful ignorance of elementary economics and this rage at white men? One might reasonably, if at this point only tentatively, conclude that it is largely the terrible frustration and even humiliation felt by most sensitive people over an intractable and unacceptable racial status quo—one in which black people are so often at the bottom.

Consider a remark former senator George Mitchell offered at a graduation several years ago: For most of us, "life, when reduced to its essence, is a never-ending search for respect. First and most important, self-respect, then the respect of others."[8] Mitchell's observation will resonate most strongly with those who understand the risk in black street culture of "dissing" someone. In a setting where self-respect is perceived as fragile, solutions requiring adjustment on the part of black people will be resisted. A bogeyman must then be found.

Is this theory too facile, too conveniently exculpating of white people? Not according to Stanley Crouch, whose work supplies rich counterpoint to white-male bashing. Our "flagellation rituals," writes Crouch, are tied to a "refusal to accept the tragic fundamentals of human life" and result in a "politics of blame in which all evil can be traced to the devil's address, which is . . . the address of the privileged and the successful."[9]

Which leads to a final question about Williams: What caused the dramatic transformation from her high school years? Consider that Boston's Girls' Latin School, her prestigious alma mater, asked graduating students to select a guiding motto for inclusion in the yearbook. Williams's choice was from Robert Browning, a white man: "Look thou not down but up."[10] Fifteen years later Williams had abandoned all hope.

It would be easy to agree with black writer Carter Woodson's famous diagnosis that in undermining the well-being of black students "Harvard has ruined more Negroes than bad whiskey."[11] But unlike Williams, most of the people who are the subjects of this book did not study at Harvard. How did Williams and the others end up taking the slightest opportunity to find a slight?

An answer to this question requires a discussion of critical race theory, a more forceful version of what has simply been called "race theory" here. What is it and where did it come from? Since the critical race theory success story has been told elsewhere, a summary will have to suffice.[12] Derrick Bell, one of the movement's two founders along with Richard Delgado, reports that critical race theory embraces "an experientially grounded, oppositionally expressed, and transformatively aspirational concern with race and other socially constructed hierarchies."[13] An important text fleshes out the definition:

> Critical race theory recognizes that racism is endemic to American life. . . . [W]e ask how . . . federalism, privacy, traditional values or established property interests . . . serve as vessels of racial subordination. . . . Critical race theory expresses skepticism toward dominant legal claims of neutrality, objectivity, color blindedness, and meritocracy. These claims are central to an ideology of equal opportunity that . . . tells an ahistorical, abstracted story of racial inequality as a series of randomly occurring, intentional, and individualized acts. . . . Critical race theory insists on recognition of the experiential knowledge of people of color. [For this purpose, we use] personal histories, parables, chronicles, dreams, stories, poetry, fiction and revisionist histories.[14]

From this viewpoint, in order to overcome the illusion of race neutrality, scholars must respond by giving more, rather than less, attention to race. Indeed, it is fair to say that the critical race theory motto is Justice Blackmun's previously cited observation in *Bakke* about the need to "first take account of race."

What is the effect of this ideology of color consciousness which holds today's whites responsible for the ills suffered by racial minorities, and which has been tied by black commentators to the fear that, in an era of integration, African Americans could not compete through universal measures of character and achievement? If race is central because racial supremacy is central to American culture, then all features of American culture are presumed tainted. In such an environment racism can be presumed and need not be proved. Similarly, if racist behavior is understood as part of a pattern, and not as one or more individualized acts, then more than being on perpetual guard, minority groups must take the offensive. Finally, if the "experiential knowledge" of minorities is central, and if whites are precluded from this knowledge, then the role for whites is peripheral. The way in which critical race theorists have experienced race, the manner in which they convey this experience—particularly their oppositional stance—and the place for whites in race talk are all, of course, critically important to our purpose here.

Bottoms Up

Richard Delgado will be our guide to the history of critical race theory. When he took his first faculty position in the early 1970s, he tells us, a white male elite dominated civil rights discourse in our law schools.[15] A few black academics were around, some of whom were writing in this area, but establishment authors made little, if any, effort to welcome them into the conversation. Bell and Delgado, however, needed no invitation. Full of passionate intensity, they argued that whites did not—and probably could not—adequately represent minorities in these discussions. This argument helped crack the white civil rights cartel and induced law schools to hire not only black but also Hispanic and Asian law professors.

As a consequence of Bell's and Delgado's efforts, a new school took root in the mid-1980s. In a few short years, this school, which came to call itself critical race theory, came to dominate race scholarship. It achieved this result in part with a potent weapon: guilt. White males attempting to participate in the conversation were condemned, by Delgado, as imperialists.

> The time has come for white liberal authors who write in the field of civil rights to redirect their efforts and to encourage their colleagues to do so as well. . . . There are many other important subjects that could, and should, engage their formidable talents. As these scholars stand aside, nature will take its course [through] talented and innovative minority writers and commentators. The dominant scholars should affirmatively encourage their minority colleagues to move in this direction.[16]

In effect, "It's a black—or race—thing; you wouldn't understand." Heady with the prospect of complete victory, critical race theorists lost interest in conversation, collaboration, or compromise. The old guard had to go; and, lacking conviction, it largely did.

The Diversity Trap

The result of such an easy victory—and many new jobs—was predictable. In a setting where "diversity" came to be embraced in law school mission statements and credentializing organizations' standards, blackness could not help but become a credential, a condition lamented by black Harvard Law professor Randall Kennedy.[17] And where diversity began to trump "excellence," race discourse was inevitably corrupted.

Give a man a hammer, the old saw goes, and all problems start looking like nails. The critical race theory agenda, says Delgado, is "to move methodically from one area of the law to the next[,] showing how doctrine in each area is contingent, mystifying, and calculated to advance the interests of the powerful."[18] Taking control of race discourse by pounding down white law academics in a campaign of shock and awe, critical race theorists next turned their attention toward American culture in general. Scouring the broad landscape of American life, they have found race and racism implicated in a terrifying array of institutions and practices, in both high and popular culture, in the judicial system, and on the streets. Americans will never fare well in America, in this view, until the spirit behind such cultural phenomena, largely blocked from the view of whites, is destroyed. This spirit is characterized as white middle-class values.

Notwithstanding these successes, the dozen conferences that critical race theorists have organized, and the scores of books and hundreds of articles they have produced, there is one important respect in which critical race theory has not yet been taken seriously. Over the course of the last ten years, the period of its greatest flowering, critical race theory advocates have mounted their relentless attack on American culture. But while their charges have elicited occasional responses, there has been, until the past few years, no broad-based evaluation of critical race theory from outside the movement. Professors Daniel Farber and Suzanna Sherry tried to fill this void in their 1997 book, *Beyond All Reason: The Radical Assault on Truth in American Law.*

While a powerful work, several features have prevented *Beyond All Reason* from stalling the gender and race theory assault. First, Farber and Sherry's charge that multiculturalism and critical race theory are undergirded by anti-Semitism distracted attention from the more fundamental problems the authors identified. Second, Farber and Sherry were too quick to attack race and gender theorists' storytelling, when they should have noted the profound contribution that such narratives as the Bible and Greek myths make to our self-understanding. Third, they failed to develop the relationship of race and crime and dealt only in passing with race and academic performance, topics that race theorists have explored at some length and are crucial for understanding majority-minority relations. Fourth, and more generally, analyzing race and gender theory in the abstract, they provided little if any supporting data for their critique. Finally, they ignored the impact of contemporary gender and race dialogue on the nation. Whatever the reasons for the book's failure to galvanize an opposition, eight years have passed since its publication, and critical race theory is thriving. At UCLA Law School, to take but one example, a student can now concentrate in critical race theory.

Some important questions are in order here. Is critical race theory sound? To the extent that it is, it needs to be absorbed rather than evaded. To the extent that it is not, it needs to be challenged. Whites have not seen these issues clearly. But if the vision of whites is constrained, to what extent is it because of the fingers critical race theorists keep sticking in their eyes? To what extent do logs in their own eyes preclude a useful self-assessment by critical race theorists? What responsibility, if any, can be assigned to minority groups for racial conditions and relations? Is the function of critical race theorists to validate anything and everything that African Americans and some other minorities do? If so, what is the effect of that validation? Finally, are race theorists getting off on opposition for opposition's sake? All Americans, regardless of gender or color, need to address these questions.

White Men Can't Think

Critical race theory was never designed as a discipline for ascetics content to produce incremental truths through the suppression of personal preference and the painstaking weighing of evidence. Rather, critical race theory is a movement whose objective is to shake notions of knowing and being. If white men cannot feel the way minorities can, they are no better at thinking. Their thought processes, Patricia Williams says, exhibit some fundamental flaws, among them (1) the "hypostatization [i.e., treating the unreal as real] of exclusive categories and definitional polarities, the drawing of bright lines and clear taxonomies that purport to make life simpler in the face of life's complication"; and (2) a belief in the "existence of objective, 'unmediated' voices," such as those of judges, lawyers, and logicians, through which "transcendent, universal truths find their expression."[19] Williams's claim, indeed boast, about women's and minorities' subtlety of mind and their ability to transcend dualisms underlying the white man's truth (e.g., good/bad, insightful/inane, always/never) will receive considerable attention here.

We can now better understand the partiality of Williams, and of race and gender critics generally, to stories: stories neither classify nor appeal to authority; they cannot mislead. It follows that stories can bring us closer to the "truth" than can traditional methods of engagement.

If critical race theorists (and their associates) have the vision to see the world holistically, their mission should be clear. They must endeavor to break down categories. It will be hard work to deconstruct the white man's thinking, says Williams, but there is a reward:

> [B]oundary crossing, from safe circle into wilderness . . . [i]s the willing-
> ness to spoil a good party and break an encompassing circle. . . . The
> transition is dizzyingly intense, a reminder of what it is to be alive. It is a
> sinful pleasure, this willing transgression of a line, which takes one into
> a new awareness, a secret, lonely and tabooed world—to survive the
> transgression is terrifying and addictive.[20]

How right she is.

Hysterical Female

Regina Austin offers stereotypically repressed academics even giddier pleasures. "I grew up thinking that 'Sapphire' was merely a character on the *Amos 'n' Andy* program, a figment of a white man's racist/sexist comic imagination," she writes. Sapphire, who is known more for the size of her mouth than of her brain, "is the sort of person you look at and wonder how she can possibly stand herself. All she does is complain." After pondering the issue of whether Sapphire should be renounced or embraced, Austin concludes that "the time has come for us to get truly hysterical, to take on the role of 'professional Sapphires' in a forthright way . . . to testify on her own behalf, *in writing*, complete with foot-notes."[21]

What, according to Austin, should the mission of race and gender critics be? "[O]ur jurisprudence should create enough static to interfere with the transmission of the dominant ideology and jam the messages that re-duce our indignation, limit our activism, misdirect our energies, and oth-erwise make us the (re)producers of our own subordination."[22]

Sweet are the uses of adversity. Purified in the crucible of victimization, could gender and race theory develop free from cloying and stultifying self-righteousness? When rhetoric of this sort is combined with that of transgression, provocation, and transcendence—especially in the absence of fully elaborated critiques to provide discipline—would it be surprising if critical race theory proves attractive to those champing at the bit of traditional professorial rigor and self-restraint? Indeed, could critical theory avoid evolving into How Dost Thou Offend Me: Let Me Count the Ways?

Beyond the Pale

Perhaps nothing is as painful as being invisible in a white society like America. "I might as well be a stage prop," laments Frank Wu, a critical race theorist, an Asian American law professor, and the author of *Yellow: Race in America beyond Black and White.* He tells, through a story told by an Asian American Berkeley professor, about a white friend who claimed that she had come to understand the professor only through a novel about the Asian American experience. Wu is traumatized by the thought. "The fictional character becomes more believable than a real person, as though it is easier to know Asian Americans through representation than through the reality."[23]

But again, NOT SO FAST. If the deepest truths about the world are provided by stories, by what logic—besides that of white-beating—can Wu complain? You don't, of course, have to be a critical race theorist to believe in the power of narrative to illuminate. Hundreds of thousands of readers have looked to Amy Tan, Philip Roth, and Frank McCourt for insights into the ethnic communities they write about.

Wu claims invisibility in another way. When he goes to the supermarket and an Asian American family is either behind or in front of him, the clerk assumes they are all together. Wu's conclusion is ominous. The experience "means that I can disregard other Asian Americans only at my peril. I may pride myself on being an independent American, but I am inextricably bound to people with whom I have nothing in common except skin color."[24]

But is that the lesson Wu should be drawing from this second story? There are a few important things he does not report. Do other Asian Americans reside in his neighborhood? If they do, are they perhaps racially similar? Or are they Vietnamese or Filipino? In either case, do they shop as families? If there is a reason for the merchant's confusion, Wu is overreaching. In any case, if, as Wu strongly suggests, there is no cultural content to Asian Americanness, he has knocked an important support out from under an entire movement.

Invisible in these respects, Wu is too visible in another. He registers displeasure with those who ask him where he is from. He wisely recognizes that "where are you from?" is the American way of breaking the ice. But in his case, he complains, there is often a follow-up question when he answers "Detroit": "Where are you really from?" For Wu, the question marks the alienness of the Asian American, an observation he prominently records in his chapter "The Perpetual Foreigner: Yellow Peril in a Pacific Century."

But, once more, Wu is wilding. He concedes that Asian Americans are a small but growing minority and that 50 percent of Asian Americans are foreign-born. This suggests that there is still something exotic about Asian Americans as a group. But must not exoticism be distinguished from xenophobia? Of all Asian Americans under thirty-five who are married, Wu himself reports, half have non-Asian spouses.[25] To conclude, as Wu does, that America has consigned him and his co-ethnics to a perpetual condition of otherness would require a theory that whites marry the people they hate. Maybe. But if this theory is sound, the fact that only about 6 percent of whites and blacks intermarry could be taken to mean that those two groups do not hate each other, a notion that fatally controverts race theory.

Perhaps the question is born out of a natural curiosity that is probably both embedded in human nature and intensified in a highly mobile country like ours where so many of us are from somewhere else. Everything different from the norm is marked in some way for attention; man bites dog is news and dog bites man is not. Lots of folks are marked in our demographically heterogeneous society by name, accent, style of dress, as well as color. "Where are you really from?" is probably designed to elicit nationality of origin, as opposed to birthplace, where the answer is likely to be other than the prosaic Brooklyn or Dubuque. In a similar manner, never having met anyone with my name, new acquaintances often ask me, "What kind of name is Subotnik?" In any event, Wu's latter complaint is not one of underexposure but of overexposure. Perhaps the invisibility and salience balance themselves out on a scale of rough justice.

Another Chinese American law professor provides the most elaborate critique of the Asian American image. What offends him is the notion that Asian Americans are a "model minority." His indignation is fueled by a variety of studies, including one showing that, in 1980, Japanese

Americans had 5 percent more years of education and worked 2 percent more hours than whites, yet they earned the same. The professor, who says nothing about possible language gaps, further objects because

> the model minority myth works a dual harm by hurting other racial mi-
> norities and poor whites who are blamed for not being successful like
> Asian Americans. African-Americans and Latinos and poor whites are
> told, "look at those Asians—anyone can make it in this country if they
> really try." This blame is justified by the meritocratic thesis supposedly
> proven by the example of Asian Americans. . . . To the extent that Asian
> Americans accept the model minority myth, we are complicitous in the
> oppression of other racial minorities and poor whites. . . . This blame
> and its consequences create resentment against Asian Americans among
> African Americans, Latinos, and poor whites.[26]

By this account, highlighting the staggeringly successful adaptation of so many Asians to American conditions is offensive. This seems to mean that the assimilation of so many Asian Americans in terms of language and customs should go unmentioned and unexamined—and henceforth be unreplicated by other Asian Americans or other groups—not because the premise is false, or because even if true it is not flattering, or because even if in a way flattering it also suggests a willing rejection of indigenous culture. The problem is that the very mention of success creates tensions with other Americans and thus leaves successful minority groups in a bind. In this view, it would have been better for the social and economic health of Asian Americans (and for America generally) if they had not cracked open America's finest institutions of learning and helped keep the nation technologically competitive.

What gives? "In today's coded conversations about race," essayist Eric Liu says, rumors of inherent Asian superiority feed rumors of inherent African inferiority.[27] "This," he adds, "helps explain why some Asian American activists go to great lengths to remind people how troubled their community actually is, how riddled with shortcomings and pathology. They treat praise as damnation," he concludes, "commendation as calumny." Only in the inverted logic of our culture wars is success failure and failure success.

I Am Woman, Hear Me Cry

Having traced the development of critical race theory, we turn now to that strand's effect on the relationships of critical race theorists with each other and with outsiders.

The foregoing material offers this clear suggestion: the central critical race theory message is not simply that minorities are being treated unfairly, or even that individuals out there are in pain—assertions for which there are, after all, empirical data to serve as grist for the academic mill —but that the minority scholar herself hurts from injury both to herself and to those who have no voice.

Patricia Williams recalls a painful moment in her life when, after telling a blond-haired, blue-eyed woman that she did not "look Chicano [*sic*]," the woman gave Williams an earful. Remembering how it felt to be told "You don't talk like a black person," Williams tells us that she cried.[28] A knotty problem comes into view. Johnnie Cochran complained bitterly when a possible murderer was described as sounding black. Patricia Williams cried when recalling being told that she did not sound black. Just what is a student of black American speech allowed to say?

This matter needs to be put into a larger frame. What should a white academic, or anyone else who is trained to doubt, say to Patricia Williams when she says "I hurt"? "Don't worry, everything is going to be OK" (as a parent might say to her children)? "No, you don't hurt" (i.e., I don't believe you)? "You shouldn't hurt" (You have no persuasive case)? "Other people hurt too, and frankly, I am sorry to tell you, taking away your hurt will cause even more hurt to others"? Or, most dangerously, "What do you expect when you keep shooting yourself in the foot?" If the majority were perceived as having the well-being of minority groups in mind, these responses might be accepted, even welcomed. They might even lead to real conversation. But, writes Williams, the failure by those "cushioned within the invisible privileges of racial and other hierarchies of power . . . to incorporate a sense of precarious connection as a part of our lives is . . . ultimately obliterating."[29]

Fools Rush In

How are white people supposed to speak to black people? Not long after his installation as the president of Harvard, Lawrence Summers came to have a frank discussion with the vaunted "Dream Team" of the African American Studies Department. His agenda items included affirmative action and grading policies. After the meeting, some department members complained bitterly. Summers, they told the *New York Times* and other media, had come in like a "bull in a china shop." China shop? Is this characterization of vulnerability accurate or useful when applied to a group of some of the most powerful and brilliant academics in America? Was Summers's job, one wonders, to affirm department policies? More generally, consider the implication of some of the foregoing terms—"precarious connection," "ultimately obliterating." Whatever the terms may precisely mean, will such characterizations of the fragility of African Americans in American society serve to invite discourse from anyone other than fools and sociopaths?

We live, after all, in a society where a person's social obligation is to "feel your pain." In this respect, the transformation over the years could not be greater. Fifty years ago, it was a source of shame to be the first person to cry "Uncle"; you were a loser. Today, you win. In the new environment, "I hurt" establishes rights. First of all, it demands priority. It is for this reason that publishers regularly waive usual standards and privilege the undisciplined—even silly—and, above all, self-destructive writings witnessed here.

Second, by emphasizing a group solidarity born of pain, "I hurt" talk makes it harder for fellow group members to assess group behavior. Georgetown Law professors Charles Lawrence and Mari Matsuda help explain how "I hurt" talk works. "The pain expressed by the young people who looted and burned in L.A. [in 1992] is the pain of all of us."[30] But how can the authors know that the expression of pain was not a mask for hooliganism? Is it not human nature to make excuses for indefensible behavior? And what do the authors mean by "all of us"? Do they suppose that the Korean grocers share the looters' pain when their own pain from loss of their livelihoods is so much greater? If these scholars cannot feel the Korean grocers' pain, how can they expect black youths to do so?

Vision of the Anointed

Expressing pain has another effect, according to Lawrence and Matsuda. "The public expression of pain summons God into our presence," they write, quoting an unnamed theologian. "When we acknowledge the suffering that comes from oppression or racism or alienation or violence, there is a moment of epiphany when we can see that our pain is shared. In this moment," they continue, "we have a chance to breach the barriers that divide us."[31] In fact, the connection between race theory and the Divine Presence is still tighter. In a Christian society, suffering does not merely invoke the divine; it is itself a quality of the divine.

Who, under the circumstances, will challenge a comrade's expression of pain and risk banishing the Divine Presence from the scene? How will race theorists avoid feeling like holy men and women, the anointed?

Another risk inheres in associating suffering with the divine and allowing the apotheosis of race and race theory. Whatever Lawrence and Matsuda might have intended, their readers will be motivated not to avoid their own suffering but to wallow in it and then to inflict it on others. The rest of the book develops these themes. Suffice for now to note that "I hurt," as in *Mein Kampf* (i.e., "my struggle"), has fueled some of the greatest collective crimes the world has ever seen.

Enemy of the People

One who challenges a colleague's sense of injustice is not only an Enemy of God but also an Enemy of the People. Deborah Post spells it out. Two things are forbidden to black people, she says: (1) "The public criticism of those who have chosen to confront the majority, to condemn cultural domination and the more coercive elements of the politics of assimilation," and (2) "conduct which offers apologies for injustice, belittles members of the group . . . or aids and abets acts of oppression." Each of these "is an act of betrayal tantamount to treason."[32] The choice of language is crucial. By in effect characterizing all proponents of critical race theory as moral heroes and all opponents as immoral, Post allows no room for internal debate of critical race theory.

Less heavy-handed than Post, but no less determined to keep critical race theorists' attention directed outward, Richard Delgado suggests that it is "too early" to evaluate critical race theory, "if it is ever a good idea [to do it, and that] critical race theory should devote its efforts to critiquing social institutions, legal doctrine, and the culture of racism—not itself or its own members."[33] Can critical race theory produce a useful product if theorists are not free to challenge established doctrine?

It is not hard to conclude from these protectionist pleas that Post's and Delgado's goal is less sound critique than group unity. Indeed, this can be said to be the goal of all critical race theory. Consider the title of a new scholarly book: *Mexican Americans and the Law: ¡El Pueblo Unido Jamás Será Vencido!* (A United People Will Never Be Defeated!).

But do we not understand that all kinds of dangers follow when the academic comes to see his or her function as strengthening ethnic identities instead of challenging them? That for worldly success, a group needs reliable data and honest judgment more than it does unity? A current unifying myth can drive the point home. A story long circulating in the Middle East is that the CIA and Mossad planned the 9/11 devastation as a way of justifying war on Islam. Many are reported to believe this story. But ascribing murderous malice to another group in this manner is a trap. It may help achieve a much longed for unity, but any cultural institutions built on such a fiction must crumble more readily than did the Twin Towers.

Given prevailing rules of engagement (or nonengagement), few dissenting black law professor voices have been recorded. At least arguably, however, the job of the black writer has never been merely to venerate black people for their virtue. "We have criminals and prostitutes, ignorant and debased elements, just as all folk have," Du Bois wrote a century ago. "The black Shakespeare must portray his black Iagos as well as his white Othellos."[34]

Lord knows, there are plenty of Iagos around today who are poisoning the minds of the very people whose interests they are supposed to serve. And few are confronting them. As Stanley Crouch says, so many blacks "are afraid of being called self-hating or neo-conservative that we function too often like espionage operatives who cannot be expected to tell the truth publicly for fear of being castigated into unemployment or ostracized as traitors."[35] "Were a Black Balzac writing material about, say, Washington, D.C.," Crouch continues, "the charge of self-hatred would quiver with rage from the pages of reviewers." "If we are to rise above the mud of racial limitation," Crouch concludes, "we have to go far beyond . . . the overstated racial paranoia and insecurity[;] we must be willing to let the dogs bark as our caravan moves by."[36]

Let My People Go

"Now that blacks are free from . . . the societal understanding of blacks as a caste that can be oppressed and exploited at will," says black author Debra Dickerson, "the time has come for black people to free one another."[37] Among the first who should be released, I would suggest, is Clarence Thomas, whom some theorists have isolated in chambers. Crouch and Dickerson nevertheless pull punches; for in evaluating the work of race theorists they fail to name names. Hence their work has not generated the engagement that they themselves call for.

Economist Glenn Loury in effect identifies a third major purpose of "I hurt" talk in the race area: to protect insider groups from outsiders. "We would never tell the antagonists in a society divided by religion that the way to move forward is for the group in the minority to desist from worshiping their false god," he says. "But this, in effect, is what many critics are saying to black Americans."[38] Once again, a black writer ties race talk to the divine rather than to the empirical realm in order to silence would-be critics.

Veil of Tears

Is expressing pain a refuge for scoundrels? Recall Johnnie Cochran's use of the "I hurt" card to prevent full examination of a witness at the Simpson-Goldman murder scene. Consider also Clarence Thomas's opening statement in his confirmation hearings, which focused not on his behavior vis-à-vis Anita Hill but on his emotional state. He was shocked, surprised, and enormously saddened by developments. He had "suffered immensely." "I have never, in all my life, felt such hurt, such pain, such agony."[39]

It is because of the conversation-stopping effect of what they somewhat insensitively call the "first-person agony narrative" that Sherry and Farber deplore its use. "The norms of academic civility hamper readers from challenging the accuracy of the researcher's account; it would be rather difficult, for example, to criticize a law review article by questioning the author's emotional stability or veracity."[40]

How do we understand the patent contradiction between Patricia Williams's plea for full and honest discussion on race and gender, on the one hand, and the attempt by race and gender theorists to squelch discourse, on the other? In Jerry Sterner's powerful play *Other People's Money,* the president of Acme Tool & Die shows up on the doorstep of investment banker Larry Garfinkel, who has been trying to buy the company for some time. "Can we speak frankly?" he asks. "I hate when people say that," responds Garfinkel. "It means that they have been bullshitting me up to now."

No one sees the humbug of race discourse more clearly in this country than Shelby Steele. For Steele, what passes for race discourse is but a dance of dissimulation. Instead of giving rein to the full range of thoughts and feelings, both whites and blacks tend to scale back their discourse to avoid feelings of vulnerability. For whites, according to Steele, that vulnerability is that they are racist; for blacks it is that they are inferior. So a bargain is struck. Individual whites will defer to black claims of victimization in return for which they will not be branded racists. "At the center of our national social conscience," Steele argues, "is the idea that virtue is served more by helping people hide from their vulnerabilities than by helping them to overcome them." But this accomplishes little. "An activism of deference will not affirm that whites are not racists (uncritical deference to the black 'victim' is a form of racism). And the insistence that black difficulty is still the result of racism will not affirm blacks against the stereotype of inferiority."[41]

If, through the foregoing rhetorical strategies and bargains, race theorists have succeeded in limiting academic debate, why have they not had greater influence on public policy? Columnist William Raspberry asks his black readers to imagine that they are confronted by a homeless person who says, "it's people like you who are responsible for my homelessness in the first place. You got any spare change?" "When the homeless person insists on making me the enemy, I find it easy to just keep walking. I think white America is walking past black America's manifest problems . . . for much of the same reason. . . . We insist that all white people play the villain's role and we seem endlessly surprised when they just keep walking."[42]

Losing touch with white allies is, for Stanley Crouch, "one of the greatest tragedies of African American history." Martin Luther King Jr. himself knew that whatever the white man's sins, his good will was essential: "Our aim must never be to defeat or humiliate the white man, but to win his friendship and understanding."[43] This message is regularly forgotten by race critics.

In the absence of rejoinders from white males, it is difficult to know the reasons they have failed to rally behind critical race theory. One thing is certain. We need what Patricia Williams has called that "long-overdue national dialogue about race, gender, homophobia, and all the other divisive issues that block the full possibility of American community."[44] We need to confront what Debra Dickerson calls "civic terrorism."[45] Who knows? Criticizing critical race theory, as Judge Richard Posner writes, may "oddly . . . save [it]. White scholars," he adds, "have largely ignored this movement. This has been no favor to it. Criticism is the oxygen of a scholarly movement."[46] Patricia Williams recognizes, as many others surely will, that such discourse will be painful. But, "we must get beyond the stage of halting conversations filled with the superficialities of hurt feelings."[47]

The Last Shall Be the First

How do we do that? A classic story can help cut the link between God and the expression of alienation, and get the discussion off the ground. It is the Jewish Day of Atonement, Yom Kippur. In a three-thousand-year-old tradition, the congregation is occupied in mortifying its spirit and purging its vanity so as to be ready for the hour of judgment at sundown. No one has eaten or drunk anything for twenty-one hours and the atmosphere is surreal. In the middle of the service, the rabbi leaps to his feet and announces, "Lord, I am a nothing in your eyes." Transfixed by the rabbi's piety, the congregation redoubles its efforts at prayer. Twenty minutes later, the cantor, or service leader, leaps up, declaiming, "Lord, I am unworthy to sing your praises." The holy community is again stunned by the deep devotion before it returns to prayer. Twenty minutes later, the lowly sexton (the caretaker) arises from the back of the room, announcing, "Lord, I am a nothing." At this point the rabbi pokes the cantor, "Look who thinks he is a nothing."

You don't have to be Jewish to get it. "I am a nothing" in this case is not, as it purports to be, a statement of powerlessness. Rather, exemplifying marginal chic, the story shows how you have to be something to be a nothing. Professor Henry Louis Gates Jr., head of Harvard's African American Studies Department, mines black I-am-powerless talk for laughs when he suggests that academia should consider recognizing the minority faculty member who is "most oppressed; at the end of the year, we could have the 'Oppression Emmy' Awards."[48]

If race theorists insist that blacks are nothing in American society, others have an obligation to counter that blacks are people too. But white men with a heightened sense of responsibility have been made to internalize such distrust of their own feelings on gender and race matters that unbottling these feelings will require extensive treatment. What this book uses to break the logjam is play therapy.

Through this treatment, whites can crack the "hermetic bravado celebrating victimization and stylized marginality,"[49] a bravado that leads to the dominance on race and gender relations that the academic community and many of the media have ceded to the race theorists. Like kings of old, who also lived hermetically, critical race theorists need their fools.

It would be wrong to deny the tangle of pathology that underlies celebration of a flag that memorializes a criminal slave culture, precludes commemoration in a national museum on the Washington Mall the lives of millions who had no chance to make themselves remembered, and blinds us to the indignities that African Americans still suffer. Nevertheless, good citizenship requires a response from whites if it is honestly felt. "I hurt" should not end the conversation but, rather, begin it.

In particular, America needs to hear a rejoinder to eminent professor John Hope Franklin's manipulative characterization of African Americans who question the victim status of blacks as "Judases"[50] and to Harlon Dalton's no less manipulative declaration that "[t]he idea that affirmative action is bad because it stigmatizes those it seeks to benefit, is not just benighted, it is an example of 'soft racism.'"[51] We can no longer tolerate author Peter Brimelow's definition of a racist as "[s]omeone who wins an argument with a liberal."[52] Above all, wake-up serum needs to be administered to Derrick Bell to keep him from teaching that "[r]acial discrimination in the workplace is as vicious—if less obvious—than it was when employers posted signs 'no negras [*sic*] need apply.'"[53] Those who cannot forget the past are condemned to replicate it.

Scatter the Pigeons

Toward the end of *The Rooster's Egg*, Williams recounts a story first told by black *New York Times* columnist Brent Staples about his student days at the University of Chicago. Staples liked to take walks at night near the lake on the south side of the city. He realized early on that these strolls, which gave him much pleasure, terrified the whites he would encounter. Being basically a man of peace, he was much distressed. He tried first to be "innocuous" in his gait. Then he began whistling Vivaldi so people would hear him coming and take him for the student he was. All this solicitude for the sensibilities of others came at a price. For then,

> I changed. . . . The man and the woman walking toward me were laughing and talking but clammed up when they saw me. . . . I veered toward them and aimed myself so that they'd have to part to avoid walking into me. The man stiffened, threw back his head and assumed the stare: eyes ahead, mouth open. I suppressed the urge to scream into his face. Instead, I glided between them, my shoulder nearly brushing his. A few steps beyond them I stopped and howled with laughter. I came to call this game "Scatter the Pigeons."

"The gentle journalist who stands on a street corner and howls," Williams laments. "What upside-down craziness, this paradoxical logic of having to debase oneself in order to retrieve one's sanity."[54] Whose heart will not want to go out to Staples and to the critical race theorists who call our attention to his anguish?

And yet, a healthy climate for racial discourse would evoke a couple of questions. For in describing their lives as one extended "I hurt," critical race theorists disconcert and disjoin their alleged victimizers. Never mind that such a posture stifles the give-and-take of conversation and thus precludes much-needed intergroup engagement. Do critical race theorists really seek such engagement? Given all we have witnessed here, is it not conceivable at this very moment that in a convention hall somewhere Williams and her friends are doubled over, convulsed with laughter, sharing their own versions of "Scatter the Pigeons"?

4

Race, Gender, Jokes, Thinking, and Feeling

If we laugh at each other, we won't kill each other. —Ralph Ellison

In turning the "Scatter the Pigeons" story into a morality play with Brent Staples as its protagonist, is Patricia Williams not, once again, rushing to judgment? Put otherwise, was Staples right to tar the unidentified couple with bad motives and then to displace his pain onto them? Are Staples's needs the only ones that count?

Answers for many readers will depend on responses to a number of follow-up questions. Who had the upper hand in the situation? That is, who was weak and who strong, relatively speaking? How old and big is Staples? Was the couple old or frail? How were they dressed? How was he dressed? What time of night did the incident take place? How good was the street lighting? Were other people in the immediate vicinity? Had the couple recently been mugged—perhaps even by someone also whistling Vivaldi? What was the crime rate by the lakefront and what did the criminals look like? Had the couple just been terrorized by a black man who, as Lena Williams put it (in chapter 2), was "striking a blow for his ancestors" by "failing to step aside with haste for white folks"?

Staples provides no information to help resolve these questions. For what it's worth, I know something about conditions on the South Side lakefront, having lived in the integrated neighborhood of Hyde Park and having taught at the University of Chicago more or less during the period when Staples was a student. At that time, at least, the well-tended lakefront, which offers glorious vistas and swimming opportunities, closed down at night because of fear of crime. Among my most vivid memories is the night of August 16, 1989, when, at 10:00 p.m., hundreds of Hyde Parkers of all colors flocked into the lakeshore park and took back the night. The park, however, returned to its desolate state immediately upon conclusion of the once-in-a-lifetime total lunar eclipse.

Urban crime and the fear it should or should not generate are the subjects of a later chapter. For now, although critics have argued for the primacy of feeling over thinking—"I no longer think about whether I should be offended. Instead, I am able to know that I am offended"—it is assumed here either that the couple had no right to fear Staples or that being feared is an even greater burden than living in fear. It follows, then, that Staples was right; the couple deserved to be humiliated.

Foolish Consistency?

Which brings us to the issue addressed in this chapter: If the emperor can and should be ridiculed, what about others in his dominion? More specifically, does Delgado's previously mentioned plea to "show that what we believe is ridiculous" apply also to the beliefs of race and gender theorists? Of course, this is precisely the issue raised by the *Law Revue* incident.

An answer to these questions begins with a brief reminder that the operating jurisprudential principle for race critics is not symmetry but asymmetry. Justice Blackmun supports this view with another dictum in *Bakke*: "in order to treat some persons equally, we must treat them differently."[1] The notion also finds expression in the definition of racism frequently advanced by race critics: prejudice plus institutional power.[2] Thus, whites can be racists but blacks cannot. Molefi Asante, surely the best-known Afrocentrist, endorses this position on the theory that "[t]here is no such thing as black racism against whites; racism is based on fantasy; black views of whites are based on fact."[3] In this view, scholars are not needed as disinterested analysts in culture matters. Rather, as late Columbia University professor Edward Said taught, the intellectual's job "is to speak truth to power . . . to side with the weaker, the less well represented, the forgotten or ignored."[4]

But is Said right? Scripture enjoins judges not once but twice to refrain from being "partial" to the poor.[5] Indeed, as *New York Times* columnist Judith Shulevitz has observed, Said's prescription "is a recipe for becoming history's fool."[6] That social weakness does not immunize against mental frailty—that the weak are at least as ridiculous as everyone else—

is a proposition for which, surely, ample evidence has already been provided here. Telling truth to powerlessness, then, may be no less important than telling it to power. Shulevitz illustrates the point by noting that Said's prescription would have required intellectuals during our Civil War to side with the Slaveocracy—or, as it often called itself, the "Slave States." In our own time, it would require supporting Osama bin Laden.

You don't have to be white to argue for symmetry in political discourse. We have already heard Orlando Patterson urge whites and blacks to talk to each other as freely as they do among themselves; any other approach, he understood, was infantilizing. According to the distinguished black psychologist Kenneth Clark, both whites and blacks must face honestly all the ambivalence both feel for each other without "sentimentality." Whites must, in particular, "resist the tendency to attribute all virtue to the underdog."[7]

Treating race and gender critics as equals and not attributing all virtue to them is precisely my plan here. Patterson and Clark undoubtedly realized that asymmetry is a Pandora's box because there is no natural boundary to it. If affirmative action can be taken off the table on a theory that challenges to it exemplify "soft racism," other discomfiting issues will quickly be added to the list. Little, if anything, will then be left to talk about—and resolve.

The Importance of Being Earnest

Even if race and gender critics need to hear honestly felt responses from whites, it does not necessarily follow that satire should be allowed. For Frug, the dominant feminist position is that, as members of a historically subordinated group, women should never be ridiculed.[8] "Satire, sarcasm, scorn and similar tools should only be deployed upward," say Delgado and Jean Stefancic;[9] "it is never justifiable to use destructive humor at the expense of someone weaker, of a lower station than oneself."[10]

Delgado and Stefancic, in short, encourage black scholars to ridicule whites, but white scholars may not reciprocate. How should one respond to what could be taken as paradigmatic chutzpah? How can one group ever hope to find comfort with another or respect for another if it is obliged, in mixed company, to operate with one rhetorical hand tied behind its back? Is the answer to both questions that humor, and jokes in particular, are so dangerous that the need for open and full debate simply cannot be accommodated?

Fortunately, the destructive power of humor is a matter that can be readily tested. So, God was visiting Adam one day to bring him up-to-date. "I've got some good news and some bad news," God announced. Adam looked at God and asked for the good news first. "I've got two new organs for you," God told him, "a brain and a penis. The first will help you create new things; the second will help you build intimacy and re-produce. Eve will be especially happy with this one." Adam became ex-cited. "These are such wonderful gifts," he exclaimed, "what could the bad news be?" God looked upon Adam with sorrow, saying, "The bad news is that I gave you only enough blood supply for one of these organs at a time."

It is not likely that anyone, let alone Delgado and Stefancic, would re-sist the impulse to chuckle at a misandrous (i.e., anti-male) story which implies, on no empirical grounds, that a male president could not make national policy while having sex. But now let us turn things around a lit-tle. Here is a Whoopi Goldberg joke as recounted by Patricia Williams. What is the recipe for "Jewish American Princess Fried Chicken"? The answer: "Send your chauffeur . . . for the chicken," "Watch your nails when you shake the chicken," and "Have Cook prepare the rest of meal while you touch up your make-up."[11]

The Princess and the Pea

Supporting the Frug-Delgado-Stefancic view, Williams condemns the story, which she heard on the *Donahue* show. She would, presumably, feel the same way about the rabbi story from the last chapter. "[T]here is a real risk of destructive impact of jokes that make fun of supposed char-acteristics of historically oppressed and shunned people." According to Williams, the Jewish American woman is not the only one who needs pro-tection from brutish jokesters. So does the redneck—who "drinks beer, drives a pick-up, [is] low-class, talks bad"—and, Williams even suggests, the blonde.[12]

Similarly, Randall Robinson tells of how, while he was on the Letter-man show, Don Rickles quipped that were it not for the Mexicans, his bed would never be made at his Las Vegas hotel. For Robinson, author of

The Debt, which calls for reparations for African Americans, Rickles's simple statement was not only racist, it was "nakedly racist." Through such behavior, Robinson goes on, Rickles was casting a "vote not just for racism towards Mexicans, but"—note the escalation—"for religious, ethnic, and racial intolerance towards blacks, Asians, gentiles and Jews as well."[13]

The stories told by Williams and Robinson would no doubt repel Delgado and Stefancic and, very likely, others as well. But these reactions do not necessarily lead to the conclusion that ethnic jokes are evil. Professor Christie Davies, perhaps the leading authority on ethnic humor, complains about scholars who view ethnic jokes "in terms of their supposed consequences." The attempt to give great importance to jokes, Davies writes, "paradoxically results in the trivialization of humor, for in general jokes neither have consequences nor are intended to have consequences." Nor, Davies asserts, are ethnic jokes "a good indicator of . . . joke-tellers' feelings towards the butts of their jokes, which may range from dislike and hostility to amity and affection." "Those who seek to use ethnic jokes as a predictor of conflict," Davies advises, should "study more immediate indices of political tension."[14]

Davies goes on to talk about the "implicit (and, indeed, sometimes explicit) messages that lurk in English jokes about the Welsh eating cheese, the Scots eating porridge, or the Irish eating potatoes . . . blacks eating watermelon, or Mexicans eating beans, Canadian jokes about Newfies eating cod, Australian jokes about Italians eating spaghetti." The function of these jokes, Davies adds, "is to allow joke-tellers to mockingly announce: 'We are meat-eaters. You are not. We are wealthier and stronger than you.'"[15] How much serious disrespect, let alone antagonism, can be embodied in this culinary expression of power difference? It is not what goes into a man's mouth that makes him ridiculous, Davies is saying, but what comes out of it.

Regarding the fact that most of the employees in the Las Vegas hotel industry are of Mexican origin, Rickles may not have been making a politically important point, but neither was he saying that making his bed is all that Mexican Americans are qualified to do. Nor, along the same lines, was Whoopi Goldberg suggesting that most young Jewish women were princesses.

My Daughter, the Princess

The princess jokes, Davies continues, are of "indisputably Jewish origin and . . . the non-Jews who enjoy them are far more likely to be philo-Semitic devotees of Jewish humor in general than anti-Semites in disguise."[16] Is it even conceivable that a non-Jew conceived the rabbi joke? Or the following one?

Upon meeting Mrs. Levine on the street, an old acquaintance asks her about her health. Receiving a satisfactory reply, she asks Mrs. Levine about her daughter: "God bless her, she's fine. What a wonderful husband she has! He doesn't let her put her hand in cold water all day long! She lies in bed until twelve and then her maid serves her breakfast in bed. At three she goes shopping in Saks Fifth Avenue and at five she has cocktails at the Ritz. And dresses like a movie star! What do you say to such mazel [good fortune]?"

"And how's your son, Mrs. Levine? I hear he's married."

"Yes, he's married. Poor boy—he has no mazel. He's married to one of those fancy-schmancy girls. What do you think she does all day long? She doesn't do a thing. That good-for-nothing. She sleeps until noon. Then she has her breakfast brought to her in bed. . . ."[17]

"I do not know," wrote Freud about Jews, "whether there are many other instances of a people making fun of its own character."[18] Self-denigration, however, would seem to play a comparable role in African American humor. Lawrence Levine explains that the self-critical side of black and Jewish jokes is ambiguous, not a masochistic perversion. "Consciously or unconsciously, blacks [and Jews] used the majority's stereotypes in their humor in order to rob them of their power to hurt and humiliate. . . . Marginal groups often embraced the stereotype of themselves in a manner designed not to assimilate the stereotype but to smother it."[19]

"The Negro," writes the famed black author Zora Neale Hurston, "is determined to laugh even if he has to laugh at his own expense." "By the same token," Hurston continues, "he spares nobody else. . . . His 'bossman,' his woman, his preacher, his jailer, his God and himself, all must be baptized in the stream of laughter."[20] That humor allowed the safest mode for bearing up under the strain of white supremacy should be evident. "Given the persistence of racial violence and the unavailability of legal protections," Ralph Ellison asks, "what else was there to sustain our will to persevere but laughter?"[21]

The Signifying Monkey

We can now more fully appreciate the cultural impulse to one-up the world, to signify, which Henry Louis Gates defines as "language behavior that makes direct or indirect implications of baiting or boasting, the essence of which is making fun of another's appearance, relatives or situation," and which Gates has placed at or near the heart of the African American literary tradition.[22] The practical purpose is "to win, to persuade . . . scoring."[23] Those on the bottom of the social scale understand clearly that shaking things up and maybe, just maybe, coming out on top next time is precisely what the Signifying Monkey is after when, without any immediate provocation, he sets out to "start some shit." And it is precisely why he laughs.

The glory of the following classics of signification lies precisely in challenging the existing order. A slave is caught by his master appropriating a piece of turkey. "You scoundrel, you ate my turkey," the master admonishes. Fearing the worst, the slave points to the silver lining. "Yes, suh, Massa, you got less turkey," he acknowledges, "but you sho' nuff got mo' N————r."

In the wake of *Brown v. Board of Education,* two wealthy South Carolina blacks are in the Willard Hotel in Washington, D.C. They order several bottles of whiskey and ask the bell captain to send up some women. When two white women appear at the door, one of the Negroes cries out, "We sure are in trouble now." "Oh, shut your mouth, man," his friend rebukes him, "we ain't trying to go to school with them."

Assuming, as we have done, that these are jokes that Jews and blacks tell about themselves, it does not necessarily follow that they would like others to tell jokes about them. If race and gender theorists are right, moreover, as Oxford professor Alan Ryan puts it, that "racial and sexual minorities . . . live in constant fear of humiliation [and] so great is this fear that the sufferer will hardly be able to work at all unless everyone else exercises the utmost sensitivity to his anxieties,"[24] then the world needs to go all out to protect them in their fragility. And, by extension to a different kind of minority, perhaps Boeing is right to ban blonde jokes.[25]

But is the view of race and gender fragility, regularly advanced by critics, racist and sexist itself? Remember Johnnie Cochran's argument in the Simpson case (chapter 1): Blacks had "lived with oppression for two hundred-plus years in this country . . . every day of their lives," so Darden's argument that they could not handle testimony about Fuhrman's use of the n-word was "demeaning." Having to develop toughness in response to "offensive words, offensive looks, [and] offensive treatment," black people, he was arguing, became stronger, not weaker.

The Wheel Turns

There is certainly no consensus in the black community that blacks are made vulnerable by humor in which they are the targets of others. Take the case of *Amos 'n' Andy*, the show starring Sapphire, discussed in the previous chapter. It was an enormously successful radio and then television show that ran from 1928 to 1953, whose radio creators and actors were white. Under protest from civil rights organizations, the television show was driven off the air and the performers lost their jobs. Two decades later, Redd Foxx and even Jesse Jackson were lamenting the show's disappearance. Black comedian Flip Wilson's remarks on the subject are noteworthy. "Black self-consciousness has diminished enough," he suggests, "so black people are able to laugh at themselves and not be offended. I liked *Amos 'n' Andy*. If blacks can see the beauty in it," he continues, "then they should be able to see the shows."[26] Two decades after that, grande dame Bessie Delany was testifying in print that she "just loved 'Amos 'n' Andy' on the radio" and that "I have enough confidence in myself that [the stereotypes] did not bother me. I could laugh."[27] Henry Louis Gates supports this reading when he acknowledges that he is a big fan of the show.[28]

A spirit of revisionism has also blown across the Hispanic community. One of the most popular television programs of the 1960s was the *Bill Dana Show*. Born William Szathmary, Dana played José Jimenez, a not-too-clever bellhop with an overpowering Puerto Rican accent. Pressure from the Hispanic community drove him off the air in 1970. A generation later, Dana was receiving the Image Award from the National Hispanic Media Coalition.

That the great verities of yesteryear are the dubious propositions of today is also evident in the Little Black Sambo story. Sambo is a black-skinned boy who outwits several tigers by tying their tails together and making them run around a post at ever-increasing speed until they melt and turn into ghee (butter). A 1986 study by (white) humorologist Joseph Boskin concluded that at least up until two generations ago, Sambo had a profoundly negative effect not only on the image of blacks in the eyes of whites but, more important, on the self-estimate of blacks themselves.[29] For Drs. William Grier and Price Cobbs, however, Sambo may have been the first black revolutionary.[30] Mel Watkins, author of the most comprehensive text on African American humor, concludes that the negative impact of Sambo has been greatly overblown.[31]

If the fragile African American is a dubious model for constructing a racial etiquette, is the tragic vision of womanhood used to construct a gender etiquette equally inapposite? Jane Austen's notion that our function in this world is to serve as butts for others' jokes hardly supports the idea that women need special handling.[32] In our time, Katie Roiphe answers the question more fully, having in mind the image of the delicate and defenseless woman who falls apart upon hearing an off-color story. "The image that emerges from feminist preoccupations with . . . a professor's dirty joke," says Roiphe, "bears a striking resemblance to that fifties ideal my mother and the other women of her generation fought so hard to get away from." But, adds Roiphe, "here she is again, with her pure intentions and her wide eyes. Only this time it is the feminists themselves who are breathing new life into her."[33] Using Patricia Williams's bad reaction to jokes as the basis for a no-joke rule will, in this view, only undermine the cause of women.

Big Girls Don't Cry

Assuming that women and minorities are made of stronger stuff than the critic imagines, jokes about them are not injurious per se. To be sure, jokes will badly bruise individuals with eggshell sensibilities. But it is no more reasonable to design an etiquette around them than it is to ban sales of cars because some people are injured by them. The more important point is that gender theorists have long complained that they are not taken seriously. But who will open up to Patricia Williams if she starts to cry over a passing comment about her manner of speaking? Who will trust Chris Darden to try a case if he gets so rattled on the subject of black people's speech that he fails to pursue a central line of inquiry? Under these circumstances, it seems appropriate to continue the investigation into whether gender and race jokes should be tolerated.

So, back to the Garden of Eden. Adam is lonely, bored, and restless. He complains bitterly to the Almighty about his lack of companionship. After considering the matter, God tells Adam that he can have a suitable companion, only it will be expensive. Asked what He has in mind, God responds that it will cost Adam an eye, an arm, and a leg. Shocked by the price, Adam struggles to regain his composure. "What," he whimpers, "can I get for a rib?" The story's message is clear: women are less than ideal companions for men. The story may have been inspired by one of Sigmund Freud's classics about wives: "A wife is like an umbrella," he recounted, "sooner or later one takes a cab."[34] Don't get it? Not to worry. Freud, one of history's great authorities on the joke, decided to undertake his study of the joke only after being rebuked for telling so many bad ones[35] and, like other unsuccessful comedians, felt obliged to explain his own joke. Here is how he puts it: "Marriage does not allow . . . the satisfaction of needs that are stronger than usual. Yet, [o]ne does not venture to declare [it] aloud and openly . . . unless one is driven to do so perhaps by a *love of truth*." That satisfaction, for Freud, can come only from a "woman who is accessible in return for money. . . . The strength of the joke," Freud explains, "lies in the fact that nevertheless—in all kinds of roundabout ways—it has declared it."[36]

Still don't get it? OK, what needs to be said then—while staying within the rules of etiquette—is that Freud's pithy, hundred-year-old joke about the wife and the other woman may explain more about the kinds of practices that were and, equally important, were not taking place in different parts of the White House in the Clinton years than did all the columns in all the respectable newspapers.

Names Black People Play

Now a story from the modern age. The captain of a jet gets on the loudspeaker to announce that the oil tank has sprung a leak and that all the cargo and luggage will have to be jettisoned. A little later, the captain solemnly announces that some passengers will have to go too. There being no perfect way of making the difficult decision, he tells the terrified passengers that they will have to deplane in alphabetical order—by group. "African Americans," he announces. No one takes the cue. "OK, then," the captain continues, "Blacks." Again, no takers. "Colored people." At this point an eleven-year-old black boy tugs at his father's sleeve and asks, "Aren't we colored?" "No, son," says his father, "we're Negro."

The airplane joke neatly captures the lowly status of African Americans and the purportedly neutral rules they have had to live with. But it can also be said to highlight both the difficulty that African Americans have had over the past twenty-five years in naming themselves and their constant shifting of group name—from Negroes to Afro-Americans to African Americans to colored people—for the pleasure of juking (jerking around) others.

Which brings us back to the question of whether race and gender jokes should be allowed. For Freud, arising out of the "love of truth," the joke offers a valuable and concentrated social critique that would not have the same punch in normal discursive form. Truth-telling was no less important to America's feminist hero, Emily Dickinson. "Tell all the truth," our best female poet taught, "but," she cautioned, "tell it slant"; the straight truth can blind the listener to its value.[37]

Are wives not better off learning about where their husbands' minds are? Are black people not better off knowing that whites are on to them? Should rabbis not learn that their congregants may not be as sheeplike as they suppose? If we do not hear about our limitations and deficiencies, what chance do we have of curing them? "Better to listen to a wise man's rebuke," Scripture says, "than to the praise of fools."[38]

To be sure, some stories may be appropriate only in some settings and by some narrators. But why not courageously apply our intelligence, as we do in so many other areas of our lives, to working out the problems of this particular slippery slope?

Consider: after someone had advertised a puppy for adoption at one of the offices of the major international law firm Dewey Ballantine, a partner responded, "Don't let these puppies go to a Chinese restaurant." Unfortunately, this e-mail went out not just to the sender but to all Dewey Ballantine employees, at which point all hell broke loose. The managing partners felt compelled to apologize abjectly: "Comments of this nature are inconsistent with the values of this firm and will not be tolerated." They went on to stress that Asian American lawyers "were tremendously well-regarded and highly valued at the firm."[39]

This, however, did not settle the matter. The executive director of the National Asian Pacific Bar Association, for one, was not appeased. The e-mail reinforced the idea that Asians were "perpetual foreigners," who "were not within the norm of acceptability in American society." "What scares the rest of us," asked the president of the Asian American Bar Association of New York, is whether "it is pervasive at law firms generally or corporations generally that Asians can be mocked with impunity."[40]

The comment, however, was not about Asians or Asians in America generally. It was, moreover, a single comment by one individual who may not even have intended to send the message to all firm employees. Most important for our purposes is that the *New York Law Journal* reporter who wrote an article about the incident did not consider it relevant whether Asians did in fact eat dogs. His sole observation was that the joke derived from "stereotypes about Asian predilections for consuming animals Westerners consider pets" (Lin, 1). The offense taken, apparently, spoke for itself.

A *New York Times* reporter went deeper into the matter: "It is rare but not unheard-of for dogs to appear on the menu in a restaurant in China" (Glater, C1). The issue, however, is not whether dog is a menu item but whether it is served. It is, and though consumption is down from the old days, it may be increasing.[41] To the extent that consumption today is below the high, is not the likely reason—in addition to increasing prosperity—that the Chinese have been rebuked for the practice? In Chinese restaurants what goes into a customer's mouth can also make him or her ridiculous. Not commenting on a Chinese dietary practice would be, in Patricia Williams's words, "complete capitulation to the status quo."

Comedy and Comity

Giving up group jokes would exact an even higher price than not learning about ourselves. To identify a group is to differentiate it. Consciousness of difference will, by definition, always create tension between groups. Gender disequilibrium will be especially acute; men and women can try to feel each other's pain, to be caring, but we are fighting a losing battle.[42] How could it be otherwise when, to take but one example, most males want to sleep with ten times as many women as want to sleep with them? World historian Will Durant offered a particularly cogent image of marriage. "Love, which has always been a combat and a chase," he wrote, "becomes a war, in which the night's embrace is but a passing armistice."[43]

Not only in this world, but presumably in the next as well, for even Scripture offers no vision of a golden age of gender. The "leopard shall lie down with the kid" in peace,[44] but no such repose is in the cards for Mr. and Ms. Leopard and Mr. and Ms. Kid, much less for the successors of Adam and Eve.

What better consolation can men find in this world for the ravages of male-female combat than through expression of the sweet and joyful bond they share with the vast majority of men who have ever lived, whether Christian, Carthaginian, black, tall, fat, Hispanic, architect, jock, Muslim, pantheist, conservative, Taoist, orchestra conductor, stamp collector? We are all members of many groups. The consolation that comes from acknowledging our sundry and sometimes shifting bonds may well make it easier, rather than harder, for us to coexist with one another. Make fun not war, Ralph Ellison teaches us. "If we laugh at each other, we won't kill each other."[45]

A recent incident illustrative of what is happening at campuses today helps clarify these issues. At a University of New Hampshire dorm a student posted a flier:

> 9 out of 10 freshman girls gain 10–15 pounds. But there is something you can do about it. If u live below the sixth floor take the stairs. . . . Not only will you feel better about yourselves, but you will also be saving us time and wont be sore on the eyes [*sic*].[46]

For his offense, Timothy Garneau was charged with violating affirmative action policies, harassment, and disorderly conduct. After pleading guilty, Garneau was thrown out of his dorm (and started living in his car) and was put on probation. As if that were not enough, he was also required to meet with a counselor to discuss his "actions" and compose a three-thousand-word essay about his therapy.

Leave aside the specter of transforming America's "free speech" traditions into a Communist China–type re-education program. What price should Garneau pay for his signifying? Garneau did not direct his message to any individual. Nor, in addressing himself to women students, was he suggesting that women were unqualified or otherwise unworthy to be at the school. In fact, Garneau stated in his own defense that his satirical remark arose out of concern about congestion on dorm elevators during rush hours.

Undoubtedly, some women were made uncomfortable by the flier. But Garneau did not make up the "Freshman 15" weight-gain data. And it is hard to believe that if women had posted a notice announcing that too many men on campus were balding and needed toupees, it would have even registered with the university administration. Most important, I suggest, publicly breaking Mr. Garneau's chops is the kind of move that produces the opposite effect of the one intended; by making men self-conscious about speaking their minds, it aggravates gender tensions on campus. Admittedly, Garneau's punishment (which was eventually reversed) might satisfy retributive feminist sensibilities. But would it solve the elevator problem?

We Is Me

If group jokes provide a safety valve for social tension, why have we allowed them to fall into such disrepute? The answer, it should now be clear, is that race and gender theorists have so loaded down categories of race and gender, they have labored so hard to get the rest of us to feel the pain of women and minorities, rather than relieve it, that a fair assessment of the joke is almost impossible. Happily, if jokes have gotten us into the analytical dilemma we are facing here, they can also get us out. For a fuller evaluation of the joke reveals that gender and race are not the only axes on which the world turns; indeed, they are not even the primary ones. It is important to understand that group superiority is just an expanded version of a more basic strategy of self-superiority; "My group is smarter and more powerful than yours" is a more polite way of saying, "I am smarter and more powerful than you."

Consider the vacationer who, digging a hole on the beach, spots a lamp. Rubbing it produces a genie who offers to grant the vacationer the wish of his choice. As he is about to respond, the genie interjects a catch: anything the man asks for himself will be given doubly to his business partner. The excited vacationer is suddenly nonplused. After some reflection, he asks the genie, "Does it hurt to have one testicle removed?" It is not only our romantic helpmates with whom we are in mortal and immortal conflict.

This joke reminds us that notwithstanding all the posturings, in the beginning of life, and at the end, is an individual, not a group. A final story, which appears regularly on television these days in various forms, drives the point home. George goes to his doctor, an old and dear friend, complaining about various and increasing pains over a six-week period. After trying to reassure him, the doctor prescribes a battery of tests, just in case, and tells him to come back in three weeks time. Upon his return, George sees the doctor in the hall: "Any news to tell me?" "Well, I have some good news and some bad news to tell you," says the doctor. "Which would you like to hear first?" "Tell me the bad news," says George. "OK," responds the doctor. "You have a galloping cancer and there is nothing I can do for you. You have at most four weeks to live and they are going to be rough. I am so terribly sorry." Crestfallen, George exclaims, "What possible good news can you have to tell me after that?" "You see that beautiful blond nurse standing in the corridor?" asks the doctor, pointing, as George nods. "I'm f——g her."

Feeling and Thinking

Race and gender theorists will condemn the story because it commodifies the nurse and distracts us from the pain that George is feeling. But feeling the world's pain leads too often to paralysis. "Where one can't actually 'do' anything," as French philosopher Vladimir Jankelevitch has noted, there is a natural tendency to compensate, to "at least feel, inexhaustibly,"[47] to drown in Soul.

Thinking is far more productive. Thinking about our problems can produce solutions. When we hear stories about ourselves—whether or not they are told in "good fun"—we can begin to conquer our destructive and self-destructive inclinations. And we can drive out our demons. "If you can laugh at me, you don't have to kill me," says Dick Gregory. "If I can laugh at you, I don't have to kill you."[48] By thinking, we learn quickly that the nurse, qua nurse, is not important to the joke. No one is laughing at her, a point highlighted by the fact that George could just as easily have been crowing about winning the lottery.

As for George's pathetic need to triumph over the anticipated death of his friend, his aloneness, and his failure, we learn that we are all individuals who have to fend for ourselves and find victories wherever they may be, a valuable survival lesson when, as often happens, our lives seem meaningless. We may be at the very source and purpose of the joke here. Humor, suggests humorologist Stephen Leacock, arises in the gap between our earnest efforts and stark reality, or what he calls "the incongruous contrast between the eager fret of our lives and its final nothingness."[49]

Given the multiple benefits of thinking, wouldn't critics, who claim to have the well-being of racial minorities and women in mind, be wiser to urge their constituencies to think rather than to feel? The whole quality of our short life hinges on our choice here. As the renowned eighteenth-century man of letters Horace Walpole tells us—and the Harvard *Law Revue* story and all the *Challenger* Shuttle jokes bear out—the world is "a comedy to those that think [but] a tragedy to those that feel."[50]

5

The Unbearable Burden
of Being Black

> "Integration" [has] come to mean a form of assimilation that de-
> mands self-erasure rather than engagement of black contributions
> and experience.   —Patricia Williams

On the assumption that ridiculing opponents in social discourse is to be encouraged—both because it keeps them honest and because not to do so is patronizing and maybe even racist and sexist—
we can turn to antiblack-conspiracy theories, where satire has a particularly useful role to play. Not surprisingly, paranoia and strategies of
victimization have combined to produce a spectacular array of such
theories.

"We live in conspiratorial times," says Regina Austin,[1] who lists O. J.
Simpson, Clarence Thomas, Malcolm X, Marion Barry, Coors Brewing
Company, and Church's Chicken as subjects or perpetrators of antiblack
conspiracies. But it is the broader, more amorphous and thus insidious
conspiracies that primarily capture her attention, such as the one holding
that the AIDS virus was either designed to ravage Africans or resulted
from government-sponsored biological experiments that got out of hand,
and the one holding that whites introduced guns and drugs into the black
community in order to destroy it.

Is there any truth to these stories? Austin does not say. She does, however, admit that, in general, antiblack-conspiracy theories, which can
"generate individual and collective paranoia . . . are not uniformly accepted by black people, not the least because the theories often rest on the

slenderest of factual foundations" (ibid., 1022). One would think that a law professor at a top school would want to test such theories and to demolish those that are destructive.

The Power of Negative Thinking

Far from it. Antiblack-conspiracy theorizing, Austin says, "generates a counter-response to exclusion and discrimination by mobilizing collective black self-interest in a way that contributes to the growth and strength of the black public sphere. . . . if properly understood and responded to, [it] can lead to a genuine public criticism and the creation of a decent social space for blacks and others dissatisfied with contemporary conditions." These theories can be "energizing." Conspiracy theories, Austin explains, can enable people to focus their ideas and feelings. Evoking names of historic adversaries, like the Ku Klux Klan and the U.S. government, puts "limits on the forgetting and forgiving." The AIDS conspiracy theory, for example, recalls the infamous Tuskegee experiment in which the government prevented blacks with syphilis from getting treatment and teaches that the "solution to the scourge of AIDS, like the solution to the problem of syphilis, lies not in the cause, but in the cure, and that is in the government's hands." Indeed, for the conspiracy theorist, "[t]he absence of large-scale efforts to cure AIDS in the so-called 'Third World' is tantamount to the government's causing the disease."[2] In sum, while they are perhaps not always sound, Austin believes these theories are valuable for their *symbolic* truths. What a world. Though they contain at least a kernel of truth, good jokes are out; but theories which may be made out of whole cloth, on the other hand, are in.

Austin is hardly alone in embracing conspiracy theories. Rumor, says Michael Dyson, "allows black people to take back the power they lost, to reclaim a sense of authority over the forces that have taken over their lives. . . . So often," he continues, "reason obscures basics of reality and truth. [But r]eason is often the handmaiden of evil. Black folks know this."[3] Similarly, University of California–Davis professor Patricia Turner holds that, like "a scab that forms over a sore, . . . rumors are an unattractive but vital mechanism by which the cultural body attempts to protect itself from subsequent infection."[4] Dyson recommends that black people treat rumors as if true, in accordance with Pascal's famous Wager.[5]

Lies and Consequences

Does rallying black people under a false banner do them any good? If black people follow Austin, Dyson, and Turner and pursue a higher-order truth than facts will support, are they prepared to accept the consequences? Some, like Austin, may well understand that antiblack-conspiracy theories often stand on thin ice and function as rhetorical devices. But what of those even less secure about their place in the world and thus more easily influenced? Will cynicism help them when the government sets out to do some good, like literally staving off "subsequent infection"? It is worth testing the value of antiblack-conspiracy theorizing on government-sponsored campaigns against sexually transmitted diseases.

AIDS is ravaging the black community. One-half of all AIDS patients now are black; black people are nine times as likely to get AIDS as nonblacks; more blacks may be dying from AIDS than from homicide in the twenty-five to forty-four age cohort; and more black children have AIDS than do those of all other races and ethnic groups combined.[6] Teaching American youngsters that our government is no more interested in controlling AIDS in the black community than it was in controlling syphilis, then, is perverse. Explicitly refusing to aid in the propagation of AIDS to make a conspiratorial point, Henry Louis Gates says that AIDS is a "tragedy of monstrous proportions which could have been, and could be avoided" (ibid., quoting Gates).

Abandoning truth as a standard raises all kinds of other interesting questions. If O. J. Simpson is a wife-batterer, should he have been convicted of murder because of the symbolic truth of the charge? Is this what Patricia Williams has in mind when she promotes the benefits of "reconceptualizing from 'objective truth' to rhetorical event [so as to develop] a more nuanced sense of legal and social responsibility"?

In other words, even if conspiracy theories are energizing, is that enough to justify them? Wrong-way Riegels, the famous football player, surely galvanized the crowd—and even more so the opposition—when he ran the ball toward the wrong goal line, but he delivered a harsh blow to his own team, which lost the 1929 Rose Bowl game by one point. If the problem were simply energizing black people, moreover, America could solve it by pinning them down and shooting them full of methamphetamines. To put it still another way, lots of theories are energizing. Consider the rampaging white mobs of Klanners in *Birth of a Nation*. Are white supremacy theories to be promoted too, on the grounds that they energize reactions? In that case, Hitler, a master promoter of conspiracy theories, should be rehabilitated. For, whatever else can be said about Hitler, as Thomas Sowell says, he "made a difference." More important than having energy, it would seem, is channeling it wisely.

In the last analysis, race theory and antiblack-conspiracy theorizing may rest on a more slender foundation than even Austin recognizes. For all the talk about how white men draw "exclusive categories and definitional polarities . . . that purport to make life simpler in the face of life's complication,"[7] the charge better fits race theorists themselves. "Conspiracy," Gates complains, "is a nearly irresistible labor-saving device in the face of recalcitrant complexity [because it] posits a bright line between victims and victimizers." He illustrates with "those terrible myths about the extraordinary sexual prowess of the black man: How badly they serve us!"[8]

It is not difficult to imagine what Gates has in mind. If black men are better endowed than whites, if both black men and women are more sexually responsive, whites will not be able to compete for the attention of their mates. Whites, and especially white men, will thus have to keep blacks at a distance. At the same time, the supposed heightened sexuality of blacks will get in the way of their mental development. We are back to the joke about the inadequate blood supply for both mental and sexual function. Those who spread myths about black sexuality are, thus, antiblack themselves.

Authentically Black

Perhaps no conspiracy theory has served more to open up "social space" for race and gender critics—no charge has been used more for rhetorical advantage—than the one holding that white men are keeping minorities and women from living "authentically" in America. Patricia Williams's equation of integration and self-erasure has already been noted.[9] For Georgetown law professor Gary Peller, the threat posed by integration is cultural "genocide." Why? Because, says Peller, it is "itself a function of the powerful to impose their own views, to differentiate between knowledge and myth, reason and emotion, and objectivity and subjectivity. . . . Understanding what society deems worthy of calling 'knowledge' depends on a prior inquiry into a social situation. . . . Culture precedes epistemology [i.e., the science of knowledge]."[10]

Out of the classic theory of knowledge, continues Peller, who is white, the notion arose that "merit itself is neutral, impersonal and somehow developed outside the economy of social power—with its significant currency of race, class, gender—that marks American social life" (ibid., 132). Merit, says Delgado, "is that which I, the preexisting and presituated self, use to judge you, the Other. The criteria I use sound suspiciously like a description of me and the place where I stand." Blacks can hardly live authentically, we are told, when they are measured by standards created "to help justify racial domination."[11]

The public schools have played no small role in perpetuating this state of affairs, Peller claims. "Liberal integrationism," he explains, "entailed a trade-off of white 'redneck culture' with African-American culture: in consideration for the suppression of white, Southern, working-class culture in schools, blacks were expected to accede to the suppression of African-American culture as well."[12]

How have the schools achieved this transformation?

> The advanced degrees of administrators . . . the implementation of standardized tests on a widespread basis, the exclusion of religion from the schools, and the . . . replacement of corporal punishment . . . with therapeutic . . . counseling—these all reflect the attempt to substitute a standardized national culture of public school administration. . . . The formerly maternal relationship between student and teacher has been replaced by the cool of professional distance; graduate schools teaching expertly tested methods of instruction replaced traditional training of teachers through contact with older faculty. . . . The standardized test and the cultural commitment to the No. 2 pencil are the lived, institutional rituals that reflect the commitment to impersonality and objectivity.[13]

More fundamentally, the problem for Peller is the "immense resources and effort expended on integrating not only white schools, but also workplaces, neighborhoods and attitudes." "One gets the sense," he concludes, "that if at any point in American history, a nationalist program of race reform had been adopted, African Americans in virtually every urban center would not be concentrated in disintegrating housing, would not be sending their children to learn a nationally prescribed curriculum in underfunded, overcrowded schools and to play in parks and on streets alongside drug dealers and gang warriors."[14] *Brown v. Board of Educa-*

tion, in this view, was not a blessing but a curse. We will come back to the issue of schools shortly.

My Way

For Henry Louis Gates, by contrast, the claimed need to do things our way is one of the "founding lies of the modern age." "There is a certain way of living," he elaborates, "that is my way. I am called to live my life in this way. If I do not, I miss what being human is for me." The "Romantic fallacy of authenticity," he adds, "is only compounded when it is collectivized."[15]

The very question of whether blacks can live authentically in America is, for Stanley Crouch, premised on a gross fallacy. "In order to be 'authentic,' Negro Americans, so goes the politics of perpetual alienation, aren't supposed to identify with the ideals of the country at large. We are supposed to enlist all of our energies in pretending that we are part of some other tradition. . . . All that is just so much more hogwash."[16]

The truth of the matter, Crouch insists, is that "American culture, even in its most rigidly segregated precincts, is patently composite. It is," he explains, quoting black critic Albert Murray, *"regardless of all the hysterical protestations of those who would have it otherwise, incontestably mulatto.* Indeed for all their traditional antagonisms and obvious differences," Murray/Crouch conclude, "the so-called black and so-called white people of the United States resemble nobody else in the world so much as they resemble each other."[17] Also seeing no point to the authenticity debate, Princeton professor K. Anthony Appiah wants the racial agenda moved beyond cultural difference. "It is not black culture that the racist disdains," he says, "but blacks. There is no conflict of visions between white and black cultures that is the source of racial discord," he continues. "Culture is not the problem and it is not the solution. So maybe," he concludes, "we should conduct our discussions of education and citizenship, toleration and social peace without talk of cultures."[18]

On the subject of the cultural bias of standards, Crouch is particularly contemptuous. Now separatist self-esteem, he says, "is said to be the high road. We aren't supposed to have standards because standards were all developed as forms of exclusion and oppression." We deny "that tradition whenever our conciliatory cowardice gets the better of us and we treat black people like spoiled children who shouldn't be asked to meet the standards that the best of all Americans have met."[19] Rejecting the notion that blacks will never have the SAT scores of whites or Asians, Shelby Steele insists that blacks "will not overcome history until [they] are competitive with all others."[20] Being black, Steele is saying, is no excuse for ignorance.

Lowering the Bar

The question of standards can be raised more simply. If there is no knowledge that exists independently of culture, no universal knowledge, should, as a number of race critics seem to suggest, everyone be let into America's law and medical schools?[21] Or out of them?

The largest membership organization of law professors in the country now proposes downgrading the importance of—if not eliminating—the state bar exam both because the test does not measure the skills needed for professional success such as empathy for a client, the ability to perform legal research or communicate orally, and the commitment to public service work and because the test has a disproportionate effect on minorities.[22] On the same theories, two New York State Bar Association committees now propose a public service alternative to the current bar examination.[23] By claiming multiple purposes for these changes, the public cannot be sure which is paramount. The Society of American Law Teachers, however, makes clear in its "Statement on the Bar Exam" (July 2002) that ensuring a high standard of knowledge is not the central goal. "Even if the bar examination were a valid screening device," the report concludes, "one would have to ask whether its disproportionate impact on people of color could be justified." Here again, counter to *Washington v. Davis*,[24] intent (in this case that of the Bar Examiners) should not be controlling. The only thing that matters is how a decision affects black people, black people, that is, who want to be lawyers, not their future clients.

As for the public schools, one can hardly conceive of a more reactionary message than Peller's. In the South alone, over the past fifty years, social, economic, and educational development for blacks as well as whites has been nothing short of miraculous. That growth is hard to imagine without the changes in public education that have taken place. Shall the nation head back in the direction of the rod and the one-room schoolhouse out of empty sentimentalism and the terror of a No. 2 pencil?

No one will dispute that black culture today lacks the autonomy and vitality it had before the age of mass communications and the advent of a national and subsequently global economy. But surely this has little to do with racism, for the same observation can certainly be made about Irish, Italian, and especially German American cultures. Still another problem is that Peller and other critics fail to provide even an outline for an alternative, nonstandardized culture. What would be taught? What standards of performance would be adopted? How would students of different backgrounds learn to engage one another? "Being black," an old saying goes, "is not a program."[25] Without answers to the foregoing questions, must we not, at least tentatively, incline toward skepticism?

Bourgeois Crude

For Patricia Williams, the villain in the story of cultural oppression is, more broadly, white middle-class values. Middle class, for her, means variously, and somewhat contradictorily, "thrifty, greedy, smug, conventional, commonplace, respectable, hard-working, and shallow." While not without redeeming aspects, she concedes, this group of features which seems especially characteristic of the "amalgamated" white middle class, has led to a general "demand for conformity to what keeps being called the 'larger' American way, a coerced rather than willing assimilation." That is to say, she argues, that "some 'successfully assimilated' ethnics have become so only by paying the high cost of burying forever languages, customs and cultures."[26]

Williams lays down her challenge to white American middle-class values through a story of a hypothetical Russian immigrant girl who loses her Russian accent, goes to college, and, when she comes home, not wanting to be taken as "too ethnic" or too ignorant, starts holding herself out as a Citizen of the World. While recognizing that this is not necessarily bad, Williams warns that it can also "signal a lost balance, a sacrifice of appreciation for the bonds, the links, the ties that bind, that make family, connection, identity."[27] In sum, the desire to bond with her new country or with the world is a threat to her authenticity. What to do about a despotic, deracinating culture? If we are

> to be anything more than a loose society of mercenaries—of suppliers and demanders, of vendors and consumers—then we must recognize

that other forms of group culture and identity exist. We must respect the dynamic power of these groups and cherish their contributions to our civil lives, rather than pretend they do not exist as a way of avoiding arguments about their accommodation. And in our law we must be on guard against either privileging a supposedly neutral "mass" culture that is in fact highly specific and historically contingent or legitimating a supposedly neutral ethic of individualism that is really a corporate group identity, radically constraining any sense of individuality, and silently advancing the claims of that group identity.[28]

But, again, Pat Williams, not so fast. Courses and majors in Russian language, literature, and culture and study-abroad programs are available at many colleges. Perhaps more significant, the student is merely using her early college years to experiment with different identities to see which fits best. To make sense on an individual level of the young woman's college experience, it would seem, we must wait until she is thirty, or even forty. And beyond that we must try to ascertain, as carefully as possible, the nature and the value of the trade-off between allegiance to her original group and broader social intercourse.

On the other side of the equation, our government would seem to have a stake in binding the nation. We are a country of immigrants, a country of diverse races, a country with no national religion. If language is not emphasized, what will keep us together? But this emphasis, Williams suggests, is the Jim Crow position, with standard English now being foisted upon millions of what used to be called hyphenated Americans who are otherwise perfectly well-adjusted in their own cultures for the purpose of keeping them down. Mastery of a hegemonic language, however, serves as a determinant of social standing in all complex societies. It was, for example, through oral mastery of the King's English that Eliza Doolittle could be taken for a princess.[29] As English becomes the first of the world's second languages in this, the information age, we can hardly insist on anything but fluency in our own country.

Addressing the issue of cultural imperialism in relation to African Americans, University of Minnesota Law School dean Alex Johnson rejects "assimilationism," further holding "that integration is not a cultural one-way street in which African-Americans must absorb white norms in order to be assimilated into American society. Rather," Johnson says, "when integration does occur, African-Americans should have as much influence on whites as whites have on African-Americans."[30]

What this would mean as a practical matter Johnson does not say. Nationally known black educational expert Asa Hilliard supplies a possible answer with an observation about black culture. Black children show "a tendency to approximate space, number and time, instead of aiming for complete accuracy."[31] A similar observation about Hispanic culture has been proffered in relation to Rosa Lopez, a witness in the O. J. Simpson case:

> Many Western cultures, including the United States, consider time to be objective—something true and mathematical that can and must be precisely measured. Other cultures approach time differently—they see it as a general reference for coordinating activity, not a set schedule. . . . In [such] polychronic cultures, set time schedules are not as important as forming and nurturing human relationships, even if that requires "taking" more time or being "late." Thus, many Latinos [for example] naturally view information about time more generally and simply cannot see the judicial system's need for specificity and exactitude.[32]

Is Johnson suggesting that all children should be taught to be satisfied with approximating time and space or that America should set its clocks to what black people call CPT (colored people's time)? Is the second commentator suggesting that the judicial system must worry about the issue of cultural imperialism when it requires Rosa Lopez to adopt an "Anglo" mode of time when testifying about what she was doing at 10:00 p.m. on the night of Nicole Simpson's murder? Or that an American employer would have to accommodate Rosa Lopez's diversity needs if she regularly ambles into work two hours late? Absent a picture of how our already "composite" world would be different under an equal-influence regime, the culture complaint serves no purpose other than to create racial and ethnic division.

If we seek a deeper understanding of the issue of whose cultural standards ought to control, the subject of Peller's, Williams's and Johnson's work, we must look to our schools, for that is where the multicultural message has been taken most closely to heart. In the name of inclusion, over the past ten years, textbooks have been purged, gender-neutralized, and reconstructed. A wide array of new authors now grace reading lists. Schools celebrate all kinds of ethnic holidays in the classroom. A more diverse group of teachers and administrators populate our schools than ever before. But what do schools have to show for their efforts? Have comfort levels or test scores for minorities gone up?

The Wages of Diversity

A story of life at Berkeley (California) High School, told through a recent video, shows what happens when multiculturalism becomes the school's principal mission.[33] Made during the 1993–94 school year, "School Colors" deals with one of the first high schools to voluntarily integrate, a school that is about 38 percent white, 35 percent African American, 11 percent Asian-Pacific Islander, 9 percent Hispanic, and 7 percent mixed race; a school that has an Afro-American Studies department that sponsors fifteen courses ranging from black economics to Swahili. One cannot be sure of the extent to which the film accurately represents the school, or the extent to which the school represents urban America, but to the extent that these are representative, "School Colors" gives its viewers pause about Williams's and Peller's prescriptions.

Here are some vignettes from the video. A Hispanic student says it is an insult to be called an American. A black teacher tells his African American students that "America denotes the nation you live in . . . but the African part is your essence." A Chinese American boy is labeled "whitewashed" because he has white friends. A Hispanic girl breaks down when she is accused of betraying her group by dating a white boy. A white boy describes himself as "white, real white" and goes on to say he "likes to promote whiteness." A Hispanic boy complains of the Greek statue overlooking the campus, while the narrator explains that owing to concerns about ethnocentrism, "Toga Day" is now "Ethnicity Day." These sentiments, as could be expected, are reflected in Berkeley High geography. A student, pointing, says, "This is Africa. That's Europe. I don't care to go over there. I stay here, maybe [at the] snack bar, something like that, but, that's about it." "Berkeley High is like the real world," says another. "And the real world is totally segregated. No such thing as integration when it comes to America. We all want to be with our own kind and that's the way humans are." "I mean you come here and it's nothing in the middle; it's just black, white, Asian," says a white girl. "[I]t's really hard." It is not surprising that several students complained about being attacked by members of other groups.

Interethnic harmony, to be sure, may be less socially productive than an ethnic fix. So we turn to the academic side; how is integration going at Berkeley High? How are the kids doing? The answer is not reassuring. Of the advanced placement kids, we learn, 85 percent are white and Asian, while 85 percent of those in the lowest levels are black and Hispanic; in fact, at Berkeley High the D and F rate for the latter groups is three times higher than for the former.

One must consider, of course, both the possibility that white teachers are grading minority students more harshly and the fact that placement of students in classes is through tracking, a policy which, here as in other schools, is strongly attacked by some teachers. No teacher interviewed, however, suggests that any individual student was graded unfairly or placed in what educators might call an inappropriate "ability group." The conclusion is inescapable, at least for those at the top and the bottom of the academic scale at Berkeley High, that adopting a policy of hetero-geneous classes would be absurd.

This is not the place to discuss grading—or tracking. Our subject is what pursuing an authentic lifestyle might actually mean for young blacks—and for the rest of our community. Researching the issue of why black students in the Oakland high school system were not preparing themselves for college with math courses, as were the Chinese American students, late Nigerian-born anthropologist John Ogbu says that "they think it's white. Or it's hard."[34] Consider that in the period 1993–2002 black citizens or residents earned only 1.4 percent, .8 percent and 1.9 per-cent of PhDs in physics, astronomy, and mathematics, respectively.[35] If, as a result, science is seen as a white thing, what will induce our brightest black students to enter these professions? It is not just that to stay com-petitive we Americans need all the highly trained scientists we can get. It's that we rank "scientist" as the profession having the most prestige.[36] Un-less we take the position that that ranking itself bespeaks a kind of racism, if minorities are not well represented in science, what will counter the destructive conclusion that their absence reflects poorly on the group and evidences a lack of ability? This country can hardly afford a defini-tion of authenticity that amounts to a sociological reification of the racial status quo.

Here Come da Judge

A drive for authenticity will come at no smaller cost in the humanities. Here is Judge, a young black student at Berkeley High, talking back to Tiaye, who has just argued for the importance of knowing and using standard grammar: "Elijah Mohammed, Martin Luther King, Malcolm X, Huey Newton—they didn't speak what you wanna call functioning grammar—they, they function in this world. You ain't gotta speak the cracker language to live in a cracker world." After class, the black teacher explains why he did not respond to Judge: "I try to have people who are self-thinkers, who are confident to express their own ideas and their own concepts without feeling as if they're constantly under the gun so to speak, or they're constantly under threat of having to shut up because what they're saying is quote unquote wrong."

The accuracy of Judge's premise aside, his conclusion cannot be one that our students should be drawing in school. Would any professor at Columbia want Judge as her student? Here is the "authenticity" model at its worst. Judge must not be corrected, or even questioned, because to do so would cramp his self-esteem and then silence him. Is it not likely that his increased self-esteem will come at the cost of his learning standard English and of educational development more generally? Glenn Loury draws what seems to be the only logical conclusion from a story such as this one. "Anything that either incites other Americans to look upon inner-city blacks as different from themselves, or suggests to the inner-city blacks that their future is in any place other than the mainstream, is a dangerous thing."[37]

A Berkeley High student who rejects his education and the path it can put him on may be tempted by a career in hip-hop. Glorifying drugs, machismo, guns, and even murder, hip-hop is the authentic culture of opposition. "Either you identify with white society," says a recent Harvard Law graduate who started a hip-hop magazine, "and that's disgustingly empty—not to mention you'll be rejected or go insane—or you look to something that's rich and real."[38]

But is there a dark side to rich and real? Stanley Crouch offers an answer:

> In U.S. popular culture, we now see "the adored and feared terrible father" replaced within "the exalted tribe" by the naively admired black sociopath, the "alternately angry and orgiastic" gangster whose "street

knowledge" supposedly expresses the truest, least miscegenated, version of black culture—"the real deal." This is the ultimate extension of the romantic love of the outlaw, the bad boy, the nihilist, he who lives at the fantasy center of rock-and-roll anger.[39]

Crouch is on to something important. How can folks who believe that women are bitches and ho's, and that white people are out to snuff them out, survive, let alone make it, in middle-class society? That is not the issue for Dyson. The value of hip-hop is in providing a "critique of a society that produces the need for the thug persona."[40] What an idea! The way to critique a "society that produces the need for the thug persona" is to help create more thugs.

The implication of this discussion should be obvious to anyone who cares about race relations in America. If blacks are indeed serious about getting rid of racial hierarchy, says Harlon Dalton, they need to have "a better handle on which parts of our culture we want to preserve in more or less their present form and which parts we are willing to toss into the American stew. Fear of cultural loss is one of the hidden reasons that many of us are apprehensive about making peace with White America."[41] Unfortunately, a cult of authenticity hinders the necessary discussion.

Uncle Tung and Uncle Tom

If Berkeley High is not the model for promoting the educational well-being of our minority students, what is? In the spirit of diversity, let us listen to Art Yee's immigrant uncle. Art, an Asian American at Berkeley High is attending a family feast with his (unnamed) uncle. The uncle turns philosophical as the issue shifts from the symbolism of the fat choy and dried fish to the issue of whether the high school should create an Asian American studies program. "I don't think high school . . . should specially set aside a department [to] study just . . . Asians. We would rather have the kids learn more . . . general knowledge, like basic mathematics, basic English, how [to] compose a good English . . . paragraph. A culture is [to] pass from generation to generation. Basically, culture is directly [best] related in a small family unit instead of . . . in school." Art Yee and his uncle might bristle at the appellation "model minority," but Art Yee is going to go a lot further than Judge.

. . .

A conspiracy against people of color reportedly affects immigration policy no less completely than it does education. Patricia Williams laments that the rich are gaining entrance to the United States while "the Statue of Liberty's great motto [is being] retired just at the point when the homeless, huddled masses of the world are mostly brown and black."[42] This observation requires a range of responses. First, the rich receive an immigration preference only when they invest a substantial sum in an American business, thus presumably creating jobs for some of those same huddled masses that Williams seeks to protect.[43] Second, while the door to white immigration was open for most of our history, access to America for immigrants, including whites, has been substantially restricted for the past eighty years.

Finally, the fact of the matter is that all the hand-wringing notwithstanding, in each year for the latest ten-year period for which data are available, the number of immigrants into this country has exceeded the number in each of the previous seventy years, and a large number of these have been brown, black, and yellow. The face of immigration can be determined by looking to country of origin. According to the data for 1981–96, Mexico produced the most immigrants to the United States, 25 percent of the total.[44] The next nine countries in order were the Philippines, Vietnam, China, Dominican Republic, India, Korea, El Salvador, Jamaica, and Cuba. Charging that European Americans are trying to perpetuate their racial power through immigration is deeply blushworthy.

Any lingering concern about racism in immigration policy should be dispelled by data showing that minority-group opinion on immigration does not vary significantly from that of whites.[45] Carol Swain probably reflects majority opinion for minorities when she calls on Washington to "*Dramatically reduce the scale of current immigration and enforce more vigorously laws against hiring illegal aliens.*"[46] What sustains this opinion, presumably, is fear of competition by hard-working immigrants, not racism.

How to explain the seeming willful indifference to the racial facts of immigration? Nonhispanic whites, we have seen, are expected to constitute a minority of our population by the middle of this century. Anticipating this seemingly inevitable change, a theorist could suggest, nonwhites will feel a sense of exhilaration, a reaction the rest of us would have to be awfully dense not to understand. But in an important way, the change undermines the urgency of the critical race theory message. Critical race theorists solve the problem of their own coming irrelevance by warning that the prospect of the end of white male hegemony will soon lead whites to come down on minorities in an Armageddon-level effort to preserve their power. This, it is suggested, is what has precluded understanding of the reality of immigration and race and, in any event, is the explicit rationale offered by Delgado for "The Coming Race War."

However inspiring, and understandable, the hope of a culture change for people of color, who have been at the bottom, it is a silly distraction. First, if whites anticipate a culture change, they will undoubtedly put up stiff resistance, which will include stopping immigration cold while giving green cards to fifty million people from the former Soviet Union (many real Caucasians) and from eastern Europe. Such a response would not likely provoke a single ethical qualm. If, as race theorists suggest, preserving minority cultures is a function of government, how much greater is the obligation to preserve the national culture? The distinguished historian Samuel Huntington is already warning American citizens about the dangers posed by unassimilated Mexican Americans residing in areas considered by many Mexicans as *terra irredenta,* unredeemed land.[47]

Second—and this is not an issue of white supremacy—people of color delude themselves into thinking that a community of interests will last for more than five minutes following the imagined downfall of whites. Discussion will degenerate into whether instruction should be in Gullah, Thai, Tagalog, Spanish, Swahili, or Mandarin and whether a Taiwanese American Supreme Court justice can speak for Mainland Chinese Americans. In short, however quickening the prospects of racial and cultural transformation, minorities are surely better off living with, contributing to, and taking from the America of today than losing themselves in triumphalist fantasies. Returning to the real world of American immigration, a very large number of immigrants of color have achieved a measure of social and economic success that is nothing short of stunning. They have done so precisely because, given the opportunity to assimilate, they have, like many immigrants before them, willingly distanced themselves from their old cultures to some extent in order to devote their energies to the new one. Who is to say that they are wrong?

These considerations seem to apply to native-born blacks in America as well. According to Jennifer Hochschild, a professor of political science at Princeton, 20 percent of employed blacks worked as managers in 1990, up from 5 percent in 1950.[48] Identical numbers describe the increase in black employment rates in clerical and sales positions. Thus, Hochschild concludes, up to 40 percent of black workers can now be counted as mid-

102 I The Unbearable Burden of Being Black

dle class. This extraordinary transformation cannot have taken place without some degree of assimilation. Does the black middle class consider its birthright sold, as Williams implies? Would members of this class happily send their teenagers to Berkeley High for a different kind of education than they had?

No one would dispute that greater social and economic gains would be registered in the absence of the widespread racism that works to wear down black body and spirit. And surely no reasonable person will deny that this problem still requires the nation's wholehearted attention. But what follows from this? Pursuing an authentic lifestyle, and withdrawing from middle-class culture like the Amish or the Hasidim, makes sense only if blacks are willing to forgo the benefits of participating in such a culture. Ambitious and competitive African Americans will clearly not subject themselves to this level of self-denial.

No Good Deed Goes Unmocked

Critical of American culture generally, race theorists have found conspiracies even in those aspects of culture ostensibly designed to help the very populations that they themselves claim to want to benefit. Bell sets the stage for our discussion here with his work on *Brown v. Board of Education,* from which he developed the principle, lauded by race theorists, of interest convergence. According to this principle, the *Brown* decision was not motivated by a fair reading of the Constitution or by a sense of debt to black Americans for slavery and racism. For Bell, it is better understood as the consequence of Cold War politics—more precisely America's need to secure the cooperation of the emerging nations, many of whose populations were brown and black.[49] Bell's baleful message to the black community is that it should have no great expectations of America, since a convergence of its interests with those of white counterparts occurs so infrequently.

No argument here about Bell's specific finding of a white self-interest in *Brown* or his conclusion that the Cold War was a dominant factor in the decision, which was the product of extensive research on his part. What deserves comment is that interest convergence is presented as a conceptual breakthrough. Most, if not all, behavior is multiply motivated. A person chooses to eat ice cream because she is hungry, she needs a pick-me-up, she likes the taste, it cools her off, it reminds her of her childhood, and, much more likely, because it represents a subtle combination of these factors. A father may help his child with her homework not only because he wants to see his daughter succeed, but also because he savors the pleasure of seeing her outperform the child next door, whose father he envies and detests.

Is it necessary in the latter case to despair of the daughter's future? Since there is no controlled experiment here, it is simply unknowable whether the father would have helped the daughter absent the extraneous circumstance. It seems clear what Bell and other race theorists desperately want: a white debt to black people acknowledged and then paid off in the simplest terms possible. If white people's standing in the world rises as a result of the repayment, the victory is tainted.

As the doctor joke in chapter 4 suggests, and as a large though not necessarily conclusive literature suggests, there may, however, be a limit to selflessness. The best that those seeking power may be able to do in this world, as freedom fighters in fact did, is to make things so uncomfortable on so many fronts for those already in power that the latter ultimately yield. If a culture critic cannot enjoy these triumphs, because a multiplicity of the loser's problems are concomitantly solved, he or she may have some growing up to do.

No Holiday from Complaint

Bell's childish cynicism extends to the debate over the decision to honor the Reverend Martin Luther King Jr.—and his African American roots—with a national holiday. "The holiday," says Geneva Crenshaw, Derrick Bell's fictional interlocutor, "is just another instance— like integration—that black folks work for and white folks grant when they realize that it is mostly a symbol that won't cost them much and will keep us pacified. . . . It's an updated version of the glass trinkets and combs they used in Africa a few centuries ago to trick some tribes into selling off their brothers and sisters captured from neighboring tribes."[50] Whatever the motivation of whites—and the holiday proposal met with considerable resistance—the reality of Martin Luther King Day represents a victory for those who believe in Dr. King's vision. How, then, to explain Bell's ill temper? White people have unfairly taken away a stick that he would have had to beat them up with.

Interest convergence plays a no more enlightening role in the domain of affirmative action. Here is how Bell puts it through Crenshaw:

[A]ffirmative-action remedies have flourished because they offer more benefit to the institutions that adopt them than they do to the minorities. . . . Rather than overhaul [invalid] admissions criteria . . . officials claimed they were setting lower standards for minority candidates. This act of self-interested beneficence had unfortunate results. Affirmative action now "connotes the undertaking of remedial activity beyond what would normally be required. It sounds in *noblesse oblige*, not in legal duty, and suggests the giving of charity rather than the granting of relief."[51]

This passage also begs for deconstruction. Again, the fact that a program offers benefits to institutions that adopt it does not necessarily diminish the moral quality of the decision to do so. Whether it does or does not will depend on whether the benefit itself is immoral. The claim that white institutions gain advantage by admitting members of minority groups has even less substance. In what way are they advantaged? Because they keep down political pressure? Because they avoid a potential uprising among students? Because they so enrich the educational program for white students? But as at least one commentator has acutely asked, if "affirmative action benefited whites, why were [and are] whites so resistant"?[52]

As for admissions criteria being invalid, Bell does not tell us what criteria would be more valid. Regarding the charge that colleges are announcing that they are setting lower standards for minorities, Bell needs to listen better. Colleges that apply alternative criteria typically explain that they are doing so in order to determine academic potential, which cannot be measured well through SAT and grade point averages. With respect to the suggestion that colleges should tell minority students that they were admitted because of legislative or judicial action, it is hard to imagine how that would make them feel more welcome.

On the other side, what would Bell tell a white student who, notwithstanding top grades and board scores, cannot get into Berkeley? That he is not such a hot student after all? That a minority student has accomplished more, given his or her disadvantages? How would we go about measuring these disadvantages? By reference to family income? Family education? Age of parents? Teachers? I.Q.? Quality of parenting? Is ig-

noring mastery of subject matter a prescription for psychological and social peace? Bell does not say. Can we not conclude that Harvard Law professor Christopher Edley's position makes more sense? Edley holds that
although it is at odds with some key elements of American ideology, affirmative action should be seen as the best current solution to a horrific
social problem that needs to be resolved.[53]

Looking Free Speech in the Mouth

The most bizarre conspiracy theory promoted by race and gender theorists relates to free speech, surely among America's greatest gifts to all minority and oppressed populations. Not, however, to these theorists. In
principle, according to Delgado and Stefancic, free speech is premised on
the notion that we "can somehow control our consciousness despite limitations of time and positionality"—that is, step outside ourselves to evaluate arguments objectively. But, they claim, "modernist and postmod-
ernist insights about language and the social construction of reality show
that reliance on countervailing speech . . . is often misplaced. [O]ur ability to escape the confines of our own preconceptions is quite limited."
The notion that more speech can counter racism, they say, is appealing,
lofty, romantic—and wrong; in fact, free speech often makes matters far
worse by encouraging culture-makers to be amoral, because they believe
that racist messages can be neutralized with antiracist ones. We are left
with a "parade of Sambos, mammies, coons, uncles—bestial or happy-
go-lucky, watermelon-eating African-Americans." The problem, we are
told, is not only the effect on the majority, but that minorities internalize
the images, become demoralized, and blame themselves.[54]

The effect of free speech on race in America is much too complex a
matter to be dealt with in the short space we can give it here. Suffice it to
point out a central contradiction. If words have no consequences, if they
cannot allow us "to escape the confines of our own preconceptions," how
can the images that the authors decry have caused any damage? If words
do have consequences, if we have paid a heavy price for the imagery just
referred to, why can we not combat these images through argument and
counterimages? Why must we "deepen suspicion of remedies for deep-
seated social evils that rely on speech and exhortation" and legislate
speech codes? (ibid., 225). If restrictions were to be imposed on speech,
as is strongly suggested by race and gender critics, how would minorities

get their oppositional ideas to the majority and, on an administrative level, who would decide what could be said by and about minorities? Finally, who gets more from free speech than a group which uses language so wildly?

That there is no satisfying the race critics is evident in one final example. Consider the busloads of New York City visitors on Sundays who descend on Harlem to witness, and sometimes even participate in, religious services. The air of exuberance is palpable, as visitors anticipate an experience that, from all they have learned, will be new and uplifting. Notwithstanding the inconveniences, the churches are happy to share the Good News and bring in who knows how many tens of thousands of dollars per year, a necessary conclusion from the fact that they keep the doors open. For Patricia Williams, however, the scene smacks of racial "voyeurism." "People don't just go there for the religion. They go for the show; there's this sense of whites being on safari. All that's missing is the hats."[55] No one likes to be gawked at, but is there no middle ground here?

If the visitors Williams complains of were moved by the religious services in question, would that make her happy? More generally, how should black people feel about those who, when exposed to vibrant black culture, end up adopting its values and styles? Hard to say. "Blacks are supposed to rejoice whenever our way of life becomes mainstream," says Lena Williams. "We seldom do. For we see it as something that can be granted only by white society."[56] So, when whites are not influenced by blacks, they are displaying contempt. When they are so influenced, it only reinforces the fact that blacks are dependent on whites for affirmation. Short of leaving the country, what can whites do?

What are the consequences for the nation if so many race theorists are "lonely discontents . . . who don't know when to stop complaining, who fill in meaning when none was meant,"[57] and who "take life way too hard"?[58] Focusing exclusively on the ugliest aspects of the American legal order, says Randall Kennedy, "conceals real achievements." It "robs them of support" and renders "attractive certain subversive proposals that are, given actual conditions, foolish, counterproductive, and immoral."[59] More important, it would seem, it deprives minorities of hope; and hope, the renowned psychologist Erik Erikson wrote, is "the basic ingredient for all vitality."[60] Indeed, it is the basic ingredient, a new subfield of psychology holds, for any sense of well-being. Hope, Positive Psychology teaches, is a product of perceived power over one's environment. Mental health in this view is tied to the ability to see "the good in the world," and this ability can be taught.[61] Conversely, "learned helplessness"—which follows from the belief that one has no control over his or her environment—guarantees depression and failure.

Blaming the Media

So, is it antiblack conspiracies that are keeping African Americans down, as race theorists maintain? Or is it antiblack-conspiracy *theorizing* that is doing so? We can test race theory on this issue by evaluating the way antiblack conspiracies reputedly work. In the vanguard of the conspirators are the media. "We must begin to think . . . about the fiercely coalescing power of the media to spark mistrust," writes Patricia Williams, echoing a common theme, "to fan it into forest fires of fear and revenge."[62] But is it media reportage that is at fault and thus sparking mistrust? Or are the media just convenient bogeymen for a group that will say anything to keep from disciplining itself?

A Lebanese-born winner of France's venerable Goncourt (literary) Prize begins an answer to the media question when describing what he finds "irritating" about American television. "Nine times out of ten," he writes, "the rapist in a police series has fair hair and blue eyes, so as to avoid giving a negative impression of any minorities. And if the delinquent is black," he continues, "and the detective pursuing him is white, the police chief has to be black too."[63] The print media are no different in underplaying black crime.[64] As for the movies, a recent study shows that a substantially smaller percentage of black males on screen "committed physical violence" than white males.[65]

We will let a media insider have the last word on the media's responsibility for the black image in the white mind. "I know what all you black people think," says black comedian Chris Rock, anticipating his audiences' questions. " 'Man, why you got to say that? Man, why you got to say that? It isn't us, it's the media. The media has distorted our image to make us look bad. Why must you come down on us like that, brother? It's not us, it's the media.' " Rock answers the questions he has just posed: "Please cut the s——t. When I go to the money machine at night, I'm not looking over my shoulder for the media."[66]

Which leaves us with a final question. The princes and princesses of darkness preach that up is down and down is up; that bad (ba-aad) is good and good is bad; that weakness is power and power is weakness; that white Americans' gifts to minority populations are but Trojan horses designed to abet their murderous work; and above all, that every African American is potentially "the bomb" and "collectively, we are a nuclear explosion of beauty."[67] Whom should all Americans fear more than the race theorists?

6

Pink and Blue

After scurrying about his especially busy station, a waiter finally attends the three women who have just finished their entrees: "Is *anything* all right, ladies?"

—Anonymous

When things are not going well, according to new research, "women tend to blame themselves and men tend to blame others."[1] Going against type, gender theorists have, since the 1970s, enthusiastically blamed white men for a legal system that allegedly impairs women's lives in every way. Inspired by race theorists who have driven whites to exhaustion and self-doubt, gender theorists now move in for the kill.

Much like the charge that whites have created a facially neutral but distorted jurisprudence, the fundamental feminist charge against men is that they have loaded the legal system in their own favor: "The idea that the law is male is the core of feminist jurisprudence."[2] What precisely is the female disadvantage? The "quantity of pain and pleasure enjoyed or suffered by the two genders is different," says Georgetown University law professor Robin West; "women suffer more than men."[3] In particular, family law, criminal law, and employment law are land mines camouflaged as shelters, whose aim is maiming women when they feel most secure. This chapter provides an overview of common gender theory charges along with some basic responses thereto. In the next three chapters I examine three areas of gender theory complaint in detail.

For gender theorists, the male-dominated legal system conspires against women by systematically undercompensating them for the economic harm they suffer in marriage. Not only does the law fail to properly recognize women's household and child-rearing labor during or after marriage, but it also ensures that when the marriage fails, women are not compensated for the lack of skills that prevent them from competing in the marketplace.

The claimed emotional toll on women is even greater. Suffering "greater emotional harms of *separation* and isolation than do men," women are penalized by a no-fault divorce system that refuses to compensate them for the loss of community, which the marriage has caused, or for other psychological abuse during the marriage.[4] Women's emotional well-being is of no greater concern to the law in custody cases, says Judith Baer, where fathers win in 35 percent to 70 percent of the cases.[5] She concludes, "It would be difficult to find a clearer example of male bias in the law."[6]

The law's failure to respond to women's needs at the end of marriage is bad enough. Worse yet is the day-to-day emotional toll on women resulting from failure to recognize that sex is inherently coercive. Indeed, says West, the woman defines herself as "a being who 'gives' sex, so she will not become a being from whom sex is taken."[7] What does this mean as a practical matter? Rape within marriage "is criminal in name only, and even then generally to a lesser degree than rape outside marriage." But even outside the context of rape, a harsh outcome is likely: "If a man wants to have sex and his female partner doesn't," says West, "they more often will than won't."[8]

The availability of abortion, says University of Michigan and University of Chicago law professor Catharine MacKinnon, only increases the coercive pressure because it "removes the one remaining legitimized reason that women have had for refusing sex."[9] If the story were not so sad, the ironic implications could be savored: *Roe v. Wade*,[10] that monument to the women's movement, is no more the glorious victory for women's autonomy than it is a triumph of home rule for men.

Husbands injure their wives not only by having sex with them but also by having sex with others. To remedy the wife's hurt from the extramarital affair, and perhaps to discourage the husband from wandering, two leading feminist writers propose holding the straying spouse liable to the innocent spouse for adultery.[11]

Similar forces conspire against women outside marriage, where the law allows continual violence against women by underenforcing laws against rape when committed by lovers, dates, and strangers. The principal problem is the definition of consent. "Viewing 'yes' as a sign of true consent," says University of Southern California law professor Susan Estrich, "is misguided."[12] To ensure consent, a growing body of opinion argues that an "affirmative yes" should precede intimate access. Would a woman who begins caressing her partner's thighs be agreeing to such access? The partner cannot be sure. Nothing less than "unequivocal consent" will do. "Silence and ambiguity would be construed against the intruder."[13]

The law is no better at protecting women from assault, battery, and harassment than it is from rape. "The same law of self-defense that remains impervious to battered women who kill their abusers yields," in ordinary settings, "to the claims of men who use deadly force against trespassing and harassment." Women are, moreover, no safer in public places. "[I]t is extremely damaging to be . . . yelled at, jeered at or worse on the street."[14]

The Gender That Can't Say No

In an ideal world, women might just give men up. For gender theorists, however, they cannot do so because they still need men for physical protection. As if this were not coercive enough, the legal and economic systems reduce women's ability to pay their own way. The resulting "physical and financial pressures," we have seen Frug charge, "encourage unmarried women to yield to the sexual demands of escorts or companions they have turned to."[15]

The law, the feminist critique holds, fails to protect women at work. To show the extent of women's hurt at being treated as sex objects in the workplace, New York University law professor Stephen Schulhofer reports that when asked to have sex by a co-worker, 67 percent of the men but only 17 percent of women said they would feel flattered; indeed, 67 percent of the women said they would feel insulted.[16]

Conversely, abusing and misusing "knowledge, power and theory," the law reportedly offers *too much* protection against fetal injury by trying to preclude women from working at their jobs of choice.[17] Meanwhile, the law favors men over women by providing unfair employment advantages for veterans in civil service and other jobs.[18]

The savvy reader will note the parallels between race and gender attacks. In both cases victims sustain deep and long-term injury to their persons, their property, and their sexuality. If men are not inflicting even greater injury on women, it is presumably because such action would conflict with their predatory sexual objectives.

Ignoring women's complaints is the wrong approach, according to co-director of the Wellesley College Stone Center and Harvard Medical School assistant professor Judith Jordan: "we need to listen carefully to women's complaints." Women, in turn, "*need* to complain" because "[c]omplaining is one of the most important human capacities we can exercise to name injustice. . . . With encouragement from others complaints become protest." This then turns into "social action" and then "social revolution."[19]

A man who truly listens to women should have trouble restraining himself from speaking up, or even striking back. And yet, notwithstanding a reported instinct for domination, men have remained silent. Is it any wonder that gender theorists hold American males in such contempt? "Why men should have responded with so much timidity in the face of so violent an assault on them," notes well-known writer Midge Decter, "I could not understand then and . . . do not understand it to this day."[20] In sum, what we have, at the level of rhetoric, if not in other ways, is a good thrashing. Hence a crude, but no less apt, alternate heading for this section: "P---- Whipped."

The Taming of the Shrews

Should men of even average courage be laying themselves bare to the pack of gender theorists? The answer should be obvious: no more Mr. Yes, Ma'am. Black and white men must set aside whatever differences they may have and come together as brothers.

Nothing said below can detract from splendid feminist achievements in the 1970s and 1980s in such areas as equitable distribution, insurance coverage for pregnancy, equal pay for equal work, family leave, and sexual harassment. One example: in 1981 Lenore Weitzman published a landmark article that reported that, in the first year after divorce, women and children experienced a 73 percent decline in their living standard while men improved theirs by 42 percent. In the wake of this reportage, feminists were able to induce non-community-property states to redefine "marital property" so as to ignore formal title. The result is that property accumulated during the marriage is now split roughly fifty-fifty.

But the *succès fou* of earlier feminists, it will become readily apparent, went to their heads. Feminists, for starters, now blame men for not supporting improvements in alimony policy. But is the charge fair? The

Movement, Betty Friedan herself conceded, was so anxious to drive would-be homemakers out of the house into the marketplace, and to establish that "equality of opportunity had to mean equality of responsibility, [that] alimony was out."[21]

Women's claim to higher sensibilities (and thus to damages flowing therefrom) is as ironic as the attack on *Roe v. Wade*. In the lifetimes of many readers, an oft-heard male view was that a woman could not be an airline pilot or an academic, much less president of the United States. The claimed obstacle was rarely an inadequacy of mind. Rather, according to a long-standing tradition beginning perhaps with Aristotle, it was because women were slaves to their emotions; their thinking was not rational.[22] Thus, when gender theorists today wax on about women's deeper feelings, they support the historical case for inequality.

Be that as it may, is there anything to the idea that women suffer greater emotional harm from "separation and isolation" than do men, so that divorce causes them greater harm? Apparently not. Two-thirds of divorce actions are brought by women.[23] That may not prove that divorce is less harmful to women, but it would seem to show that the "greater" harm to women is not in the "separation," as claimed. Moreover, as Weitzman herself reports, long-married "housewives who suffer the greatest financial hardships after divorce," and who are the most angry, "say that they are 'personally' better off than they were during the marriage."[24]

A broader answer to the charge that women suffer greater emotional damage requires an excursion into contemporary feminist philosophy and some empirical studies. In 1982, Harvard professor Carol Gilligan (now at New York University Law School) wrote a book, *In a Different Voice*, which laid the foundation for what is now called "relational feminism." Responding to a male researcher who found that boys developed universal principles of justice before girls did, Gilligan concluded that while boys were working out their abstract principles, girls were developing a no less important "ethic of care."

Feminism Means Peace

Unlike men, whose lives are lived in the pursuit of power, Gilligan suggested, women pursue interpersonal harmony. Relational or *difference* feminism—bedrock doctrine in the six hundred women's studies pro-

grams[25]—is now supported by perhaps the best-known relational feminist, Deborah Tannen. Having overheard hundreds of conversations between and among men and women, Tannen found that men seek to establish hierarchy over their interlocutors; women, by contrast, seek to
bond with their conversational partners. The relational spirit is nicely
captured by the title of columnist Ellen Goodman and Patricia O'Brien's
recent valentine to one another, *I Know Just What You Mean: The Power
of Friendship in Women's Lives.*

The ethic of care, according to Robin West, also a well-known propo-
nent of relational feminism, originates in women's biological relationship
to life through childbirth and nursing.[26] Regardless of its origin, she
holds, "men are simply incapable of empathetic knowledge regarding the
subjective well-being of others."[27] The "central insight of feminist theory
of the last decade has been that women are 'essentially connected,' not
'essentially separate' from the rest of human life, both materially . . . and
existentially, through the moral and practical life."[28]

Gilligan's work has been enormously influential. If relational feminism
is sound theory, then women should be compensated for the extra harm
they incur from divorce because separation is so much harder for them.
Catharine MacKinnon, among many others, however, has raised a fundamental issue with it. However aesthetically and morally gratifying relational theory may be to them, women, in her view, are no more em-
pathically oriented than are men. Men have secluded women in the home,
deprived them of the opportunity to be independent and creative, and
then deluded them into thinking that that is what they really want.

Being products of a culture controlled overwhelmingly by men, contemporary notions of essential womanhood, MacKinnon urges, are but a
mirage. "Take your foot off our necks," she famously writes, "then we
will hear in what tongue women speak."[29] This putdown administered to
relational feminism effectively serves as the motto for MacKinnon's
school of "dominance feminism."

The issue of the essential (or not-essential) nature of women, a subject
of fierce debate among feminists, will not be resolved here either. There
are a few observations, however, that need to be made if MacKinnon et
al. are right that caring for family is no labor of love for women. Women
would still, of course, be entitled to compensation for services rendered
to the family. But how could women reasonably claim compensation for
the greater emotional damage that they suffer? In any event, as we have
seen, women already receive about half the marital assets.

Compensating emotional harm brought about by divorce would bring serious practical problems. How to measure the harm? How exactly does divorce separate the wife more than the husband from the larger community? And what if the greater emotional harm suffered by one party in a divorce resulted from some behavior on his or her own part? Which leads to the question, Do feminists want to go back to the old system by unwinding no-fault divorce? The legal system may not be perfect, but if feminists offer no better alternatives, there is little to talk about.

As for child custody, can anyone with any empirical sensibility advance a case of bias on the supposed strength of data, previously noted, showing that men win custody in 35 to 70 percent of cases? Quite apart from the huge range that hides essential information, is it not important to know something about the fraction of all cases in which men seek custody? It seems likely that men bring actions only in unusually favorable situations for them. Assuming they did so only 10 percent of the time and won, say, 40 percent of these actions, it would mean that men get custody in only 4 percent of cases. This is, presumably, nothing for feminists to worry about. In sum, if there is no "clearer example of male bias in law," the feminist cause is lost.

Nor should sex be assumed to offer a greater payoff to men, suggests classicist, philosopher of the emotions, and University of Chicago chaired law professor Martha Nussbaum. "It simply is not true that the state of arousal and desire in a human being is a function only of biology." For Nussbaum, a "pull" factor operates, under which arousal takes place where there is a perception of special value.[30] That is, with the right person, the woman's sex drive is no less powerful than the man's. Not being driven to have sex for its own sake, the woman, one could suppose, would normally assign that special sexual value to her husband. This position recalls the Lord's curse upon Eve: "Your desire shall be for your husband."[31] In Nussbaum's and Genesis's view, upon divorce the wife would have no credible claim for compensation on the theory that she gave more than she got.

An Excess of Sex

Which brings us to *Roe v. Wade* and marital sex more generally. Defended tooth and nail by many feminists—and others—*Roe v. Wade* has been the linchpin of the women's movement for the past thirty years. Should gender theorists be mocking men for their support? Should they not instead be grateful? According to a recent feminist study, 51 percent of women believe that abortion should either be banned or limited to cases of rape, incest, and mortal risk to the mother.[32]

If more marital sex is taking place than in West's and MacKinnon's ideal world, is that cause for alarm? Hard to say. Before drawing a conclusion on such a loaded subject, someone who was "basically an empiricist" would have engaged in a careful study of who initiated sexual activity, what the response was, and the ultimate result. Looking at one's own experience is hardly sufficient. Assuming, however, that more marital sex is taking place than in Catharine MacKinnon's and Robin West's paradise, does justice require that the imbalance be compensable? Is the woman injured by accommodating her husband when sex is not on her front burner? Not, it would appear, according to author Carolyn Graglia, who summarizes her experience of "four decades' enjoyment of marital sex." "Normally," she writes, a woman "who is married to a minimally competent lover should rarely find a sexual encounter anything less than pleasant. It not only will do no violence to her nature but will contribute to her enjoyment if she tries to think of herself as being always available for sex."[33]

But even if marital sex is uncongenial, nothing changes. As feminists themselves have noted, marriage requires negotiation.[34] One would have to suppose that in return for the sex, husbands are doing more than they would if they had their druthers. Thus, if women are to be rewarded for booty calls beyond the call of duty, the law will have to compensate men for any extra vacuuming, garbage-removal, house-painting, shopping, or for pilgrimages to Mother-in-law's on Super Bowl Sunday.

Not all sex is marital; a widening of the discussion is thus needed. Should the law strengthen the female's bargaining power by requiring an "affirmative yes" from her before the male is off the hook for rape? Simply asking the question would seem to answer it. However well motivated, the proposal envisions a world in which requests for sex will be met with a yes or a no. The sophisticated copulator knows that things are more complex than described in feminist dualisms.

A recent experiment highlights the point. Asked if they had ever said no when they meant yes with a potential new partner, 37 percent of women said they had. Of these, 36 percent went ahead and had sex anyway. As psychologist Linda Mealey concedes, "sometimes 'no' really does mean 'try a little harder.'"[35] Such a notion would be consistent with a practice, in effect for centuries, according to which a woman was required to reject a marriage proposal several times to test the man's resolve.

In any event, a response that is ambiguous may, more generally, be consistent with the volitional valence of many decisions in this world: "Do I have to?" This kind of response would seem particularly useful to a woman who seeks to distance herself from the sexual act because she is unhappy with her partner, because she feels fat or otherwise unattractive, because she feels constrained by traditional sexual morality according to which marriage should precede sex, or because she wants to use her ambivalence to negotiate for something she wants more than sex. Caring men and women alike will be repelled by the idea that criminal prosecution is condign treatment for a loving man whose partner's objective is to avoid feeling like a "slut."

The New Puritans

Even an "affirmative yes" is not enough to satisfy many gender theorists. A number of universities have adopted sex codes which, on a theory of imbalance of power, ban relationships between faculty and their students. Employers now frequently control, if not prohibit, sexual relationships between supervisors and employees. We need not concern ourselves here with whether these intrusions into what used to be thought of as private life are right or wrong; the point—for the moment, at least—is only that regulating sex was unthinkable a generation ago.

Picking up the scent of tainted sex, the American Bar Association now recommends extending sexual controls to the legal marketplace through a ban on new sexual unions between lawyers and their clients.[36] Adopted by many states, the rule requires an attorney who begins a sexual relationship with a client to renounce the professional relationship. What next? Criminalizing sexual relationships between landlords and tenants? Tenants and cleaning ladies? Even corporate salesmen and purchasing agents? Do lawyers demand sex more than do landlords, tenants, and salesmen? There is no end to what the law can do when it tries to protect people from themselves.

"In seeking to drive power relations out of sex," says Camille Paglia, who helps explain what is going on, feminists "have set themselves against nature. Sex, she insists, "*is* power. Identity is power. In Western culture," she concludes, "there are no nonexploitative relationships."[37]

Who is to say where power lies in a relationship? Professional power is only one form of power. Beauty is power, muscles are power, vulnerability is power, a sense of humor is power, a poetic sensibility is power, cooking is power, youth is power, maturity is power. Not only are power differences endemic in human relationships, but they are also protean; the person in the saddle regularly gets thrown off. A rule that prohibited sexual relationships that were unequal would be one that, arguably, would preclude all relationships. Paglia's conclusion follows naturally: "Leaving sex to the feminists is like letting your dog vacation at the taxidermist."[38]

It is hard to resist yet another irony here. In the 1960s, a shift in sexual theory and practice began in this country that continues to this day. Abortion rights are premised on the notion that a woman should have power over her own body; no private or public figure has the right to second-guess her. Yet the American Bar Association—in a case where no fetus is being extinguished—wants to prevent the grown woman from exercising her body the way she wants because she cannot distinguish between business and pleasure.

How to understand this reversal? Safe now in the cocoons of their presumably comfortable and sexually quiescent middle-aged marriages, one imagines, feminists are organizing to pull the revolutionary curtain down on their daughters' heads, on the theory that finding a mate and enjoying sexual freedom are not so important after all. One has to wonder how the younger and single lawyers voted on the ban issue.

As for physical abuse by lovers, courts are issuing orders of protection every hour of every day. And violations of these orders are regularly prosecuted when women cooperate with prosecutors, which they often refuse to do, because many batterees want their men making love and money rather than dissipating their energies in jail.[39] One winces at the prospect of battered wives being dragged into court in handcuffs, forced to testify against their victimizers.

Is male street rowdiness not only annoying but also "extremely damaging" for women? A recent study reveals that women do not consider "comments or whistles intended as compliments" to be sexual harassment.[40] Nor are heart-rending accounts of the financial pressures on single women persuasive. Women now make up more than half of America's college graduates and are to be found in all fields. If some women cannot resist the sexual pressures generated by a man picking up the dinner tab, they really should not eat with the man. And if that means the women cannot go to Europe or to the opera, because they cannot afford it on their own, what would Frug have suggested? That America socialize the cost of European vacations and the opera for single women?

The Professor Who Did Not Know How to Ask

Does the fact that women disproportionately take offense when asked for sex at work prove a hostile workplace environment? Schulhofer's evidence can be evaluated by recasting the invitation to one for coffee. A brief investigation would teach that such an invitation can easily elicit a different response—even though the inviter is after the same thing in the two cases. That is to say, it might be the style not the substance of the proposition that offends the woman. Only someone with a tin ear for seduction language would confuse the two, a point that even pointy-heads would seem to understand. "If avoiding sex is vaguely a part of your complex set of desires," says Michigan law professor William Ian Miller, "there is probably no better way of accomplishing it than by coming on with 'Hey, wanna f***?' "[41]

More on seduction strategies later. For now, we turn to legislative and corporate efforts to prohibit women from working in certain dangerous occupations. Is charging discrimination the proper response to what is likely, at least in part, the same kind of chivalry that leads men to oppose a draft for women? To evaluate the position that the driving force here is to protect men from competition rather than to protect mothers and the fetuses they may be carrying, do we not at least have to examine the votes of women legislators on the issue? And finally, the charge that providing veterans' benefits unfairly disadvantages women is easily countered even without reference to the growing number of women in the armed forces. Veterans give up significant portions of their careers and risk their lives for their country. What patriotic activity qualifies feminists for affirmative action benefits? To begrudge a veteran a few points in civil service employment at the end of his or her tour of duty is crude and *infra dignitatem*.

How then should we understand the foregoing nuttiness and ill temper? Feminist theory, it is suggested here, has led to the absence of an internal dialogue, which might, in turn, have disciplined feminist attacks against men.

Women's Ways of Knowing

To understand how women may have painted themselves into a corner of victimhood requires an excursion to another movement that Carol Gilligan helped launch. Several years after the appearance of *In a Different Voice*, four academic women got together to produce *Women's Ways of Knowing: The Development of Self, Voice, and Mind.* Sponsored by the Fund for the Improvement of Post-Secondary Education and the Stone Center of Wellesley College and the winner of the 1987 Distinguished Publications Award from the Association of Women in Psychology, this highly influential work introduced the idea that women's different emotional development leads them to learn differently from men. Women's epistemology was born.

Women's Ways of Knowing highlights the comments of two college sophomores who speak of their approach to school. Here is Naomi:

> I never take anything someone says for granted. I just tend to see the contrary. I like playing devil's advocate, arguing the opposite of what someone is saying, thinking of exceptions to what the person has said, or thinking of a different train of logic.

The authors contrast Naomi's view with that of Patti:

> When I have an idea about something, and it differs from the way another person is thinking about it, I'll usually try to look at it from that person's point of view, see how they could say that, why they think that they're right, why it makes sense.[42]

Naomi's thinking is characterized as male-like. Reading a poem would prompt the question in her, "What standards can I use to analyze it?" Borrowing a term from Gilligan, the authors refer to Naomi's epistemology as "separate knowing." Patti, by contrast, would respond to the poem by asking, "What is this poet saying to me?" Patti exemplifies "connected knowing," which is more characteristic of women.

Naomi wants to put distance between herself and the object; she wants to analyze. This supposedly male point of view is reflected in the practice of placing a text and an interpretation on the table and asking students to "start ripping" at them. Patti, on the other hand, seeks intimacy and equality between self and object. She seeks not so much knowledge as "understanding," which "precludes evaluation, because evaluation puts objects at a distance, places the self above it, and quantifies a response to the object that should remain qualitative." Connected knowers "consider others as [they wish] to be considered" (ibid., 101).

The noted anthropologist Helen Fisher calls women's ways of knowing "web thinking" and contrasts this with men's "step" or "linear" thinking.[43] When analyzing problems, according to Fisher, women tend to see the complexities brought about by interrelationships. As a consequence, women have come to focus on the long term. Because men tend to analyze problems by simplifying them, that is, by ignoring matters that can be discarded as extraneous, men can make judgments faster than women. In raising this matter, Fisher, of course, is describing the very heart of Western scientific genius: peeling away matters that are less important so as to allow a focus on deeper, more fundamental relationships.

But, says Fisher, faster is not necessarily better. Because the world is increasingly and inexorably becoming more complex, women's contextual thinking destines them to become "the first sex," which is also the title of her book.

I Know, Therefore I Am a Woman

Women's Ways of Knowing works out the implications of these views. At the heart of separate knowing is critical thinking, or doubting. For separate knowers, again, principally men, doubting is a game in which it is assumed "that everyone—including themselves—may be wrong." Women are more likely to find it hard to accept doubting or being doubted; taking doubting personally, "women find it easier to believe than to doubt." They assume that the people they come into contact with have something good to say. They exhibit "generous thinking," that is, they "seek to understand other people's ideas in other people's terms rather than in their own terms."[44] (Men obviously do not qualify as "other people" in this formulation.)

In any case, whether one agrees entirely with *Women's Ways* or not, as adjusted, it is surely on to something. A asks B, "Do you like my haircut?" or "Does this new suit make me look fat?" These are not real questions for connected knowers; a woman must respond with oohs and ahs. If A and B are male, however, the response might well take a different form. Someone seeking dominance, not empathic connection, might well rebuke A by asking where he found the demon barber or tailor.

Connected knowing is not just different, it is likely better for women. The doubting model, concludes *Women's Ways,* "may be peculiarly inappropriate for women, although we are not convinced that it is appropriate for men, either" (ibid., 228). The authors highlight the point with a story of first-year college science class. The professor entered class one day carrying a jar of beans and asked the students to guess how many beans were in the jar. After hearing numerous wildly inaccurate estimates, the professor revealed the correct answer, declaring, "You have just learned an important lesson about science. Never trust the evidence of your own senses" (ibid., 191).

According to *Women's Ways,* it is not the students who needed a lesson, but the professor. Specifically, he did not understand that the sense of security of many of his female students was based precisely on trust of their senses, and thus the professor was pulling the rug of intellectual self-confidence out from under them. The result of the teacher's insensitivity was entirely predictable and appropriate, the authors report. "I remember feeling small and scared," says one female student, "and I did the only thing I could do. I dropped the course that afternoon, and I haven't gone near science since" (ibid.). The solution to the problem of women's living in the shadows of science apparently lies in their hearing that the sun revolves around them, and not vice versa. Here it is again, a brief for teaching as therapy.

A similar phenomenon drives black kids away from whites. "Why are all the black kids sitting together in the cafeteria?" asks dean and professor Beverly Tatum in her best-selling book of the same title. Tatum tells the story of a black girl who was asked by her white teacher whether she was going to the prom. When the girl said no, the teacher tried to reason with her: "Oh come on, I know you people love to dance."[45]

In this comment lies the answer to Tatum's question. If the reluctant dancer shares her concern with a white girl, she may hear a defense of the white teacher. He probably meant well, she will be told, and therefore should be given the benefit of the doubt, a response that, of course, tends to contradict relational theory. But, argues Tatum (who is happy to objectivize the white teacher), human beings need affirmation of their feelings. The girl will now move on to the black girls' table; they will know where she is coming from.

Hairbrained Thinking

If girls and young women are not discouraged from pursuing such hermetic self-affirmation, what will happen when they grow up? Lena Williams tells the story of a white woman who, while in a Macy's elevator, threw back her head and proceeded to run her fingers through her long flaxen hair. Williams first heard the story from her brother-in-law, who told Williams that he "hated it" when white women do that and that if she did it again, "I'm going to tell her about it!" Williams's reaction was no less critical of the white woman, as the tortured history of race relations unfolded before her. "All our lives we've been bombarded with images of white movie stars, models and other beauty icons with long flowing hair, which has been beyond our reach," she writes. "For that moment we both saw a white woman flaunting a symbol of preference. . . . We knew the woman meant no harm," Williams concedes, and "that it wasn't just about hair. There's a history of suspicion, distrust, and to a degree, envy between black and white women."[46]

Should white women be required to wear headdresses to avoid giving offense to black women? If so, American women would be indistinguishable in appearance from their Talibanese counterparts. And from one another; for the relentless pursuit of equality—and damnation of difference—offers endless possibilities. To level the sexual playing field, good etiquette could require long-legged women to wear flats when out in public and full-figured women to be corseted. Behaired men could similarly be induced to shave it off to avoid giving offense to the rest of us.

The problem facing women comes into focus. To the extent that, as is said, a feminist is "someone who believes women," women need fewer feminists around and more agnostics, so that they can be doubted. Knowledge, if Kant and many others are right, is formed through judgments, and the practice of judging requires an instinct for doubt. Thus, to the extent that women instinctively "find it easier to believe than to doubt," should they not, instead of celebrating that instict, suppress it? Is it not absolutely clear that any epistemology that does not encourage this "male" response of "prove it!" or even "baloney!" risks creating an intellectual trap? For if the basic building blocks of a structure are not rock solid, and if they are not regularly and rigorously tested, how can any superstructure, no matter how elaborate, stand secure?

Thinking outside the Box

To respond more specifically to the authors just cited, must we not agree that the science teacher's opinion is more valuable than the student's? That, more directly, women need to learn that their feelings about the number of beans in the jar are less important for a science class than the actual number—even if that notion currently reflects a male sensibility? And that the teenage girl is doing herself no favor by running away from an opinion that conflicts with her own?

As for the Lena Williams matter, should not black women be teaching black girls to find charm in their own hair? Race theorists, instead, have made hair the symbol of 350 years of white supremacy. America, bell hooks complains, "is in the middle of a blond backlash to the multicultural beauty ethos."[47] "I want to know my hair again, to own it and delight in it again," begins one of the most elegiac passages in the entire legal academic canon. "I want to know my hair again," continues New York University law professor Paulette Caldwell, "the way I knew it before I knew that the hair is me . . . before I knew that the burden of beauty —or lack of it—for an entire race of people could be tied up with my hair and me."[48]

If black women such as Caldwell and Lena Williams do not believe that black is beautiful, may a white man not remind them? Complementing this message is another one that a white man can usefully provide. As long as the white woman's hair-slinging is not being done in black women's faces—and as long as the white woman does not have cooties— a black woman has no more standing to tell white women what to do with their hair than whether to cover up their freckles. Long in use in cases of alcohol addiction, the Serenity Prayer would seem equally valuable to temper Williams's black rage: "God, grant me the serenity to accept the things I cannot change, the courage to change the things I can, and the wisdom to know the difference."

In short, more important than whether the world knows where a woman is coming from is whether it helps her figure out where she should be going. By concentrating on the latter, women can sort out those problems that can be fairly laid at the doorstep of the patriarchy, those for which they themselves are responsible, those for which everyone is at fault, and those for which there is no solution.

But are women looking for solutions? It seems not. "Just as a man is fulfilled through working out the intricate details of solving a problem," says John Gray, author of *Men Are from Mars, Women Are from Venus,* "a woman is fulfilled through talking about the details of her problems."[49] A woman does not need a man to tell her this. According to Carrie Paechter, gender specialist senior lecturer at Goldsmiths College, University of London, women use "troubles talk" "as a way of reinforcing interpersonal connection; the conversation, as an expression of solidarity in adversity, is more important than solving the problem."[50] On the other hand, Paechter says, men "prioritize coming to a solution," finding it "puzzling that when a woman says she is troubled by something[,] she does not necessarily want to be told what to do about it."[51]

Why Can't a Woman Be More Like a Man?

If women are not solving their problems and are then taking out the resulting frustrations on men, the responsibility of men, again, is clear. Finding solutions is not some secondary human function. If the woman is concerned that she looks like hell or that her outfit makes her look fat, she is better off hearing it so she can do something about it; that's what friends are for. What women really need, in other words, is not the traditional relationalism, which provides a rush of self-esteem, but a response that helps to fix more deep-rooted problems. *Toxic Diversity* may be the highest expression of a much-needed New Relationalism.

In this view, women have been blind to the real source of male power, which is not muscle or misogyny. Women will not get to their desired destinations until, taking inspiration from Carl Douglas's response to Johnnie Cochran, they can comfortably say to their women friends, "No, I don't know what you mean," or, yes, "Janie, that's bulls—t."

Phyllis Chesler, professor of psychology and author of the encyclopedic and provocatively titled *Woman's Inhumanity to Woman,* sums up the problem for women. Most obviously, the feminist movement has failed women by not encouraging a vigorous internal dialogue about their condition. The deeper problem, says Chesler, lies in women's culture. Women are not accustomed to having their thinking challenged, especially by other women. As a result, they are not comfortable maintaining relationships with those they disagree with or those who disagree with them. Unlike men, who are trained not to take difference personally, many women take criticism as "disconnection and abandonment, the transformation of the Other as Good Mother into the Other as Evil Step-mother." Being too ready to hear criticism where none is intended, women who could offer useful criticism are trained to "smile and agree . . . even if they secretly disagree."[52]

Women, in other words, are not receptive to, or exposed to, a real diversity of views from other women. They also do not get a chance to openly express aggressive instincts to one another, as do men. The result is that the aggression gets transformed into backbiting, but because the woman pretends to herself that she is relational, "she will have no reason to learn to control her own normal, but emotionally primitive, human inclinations" (ibid., 473). Hence, the sharp title to Chesler's book. Women's relationalism, in this view, is only a cover for behavior that is less out in the open but perhaps even more vicious than men's.

Chesler's message to women in short: "Asking another woman what she really thinks is not the same as asking her to support you, right or wrong, or to falsely flatter you. A woman has to be able to endure opposing views without collapsing and without feeling personally betrayed" (ibid., 480).

Out of the Mouth of Babes

Until gender theorists understand that the issues they raise are trickier than they think, that the white-black and the man-woman matrices are not analogous (i.e., that even on its face, the case that men hate women is preposterous), women will be vulnerable to pleas by the likes of Robin West. West urges women to shuck off the protective coating of culture and accumulated self-knowledge so that they can experience the world raw. More specifically, women must "give voice to the hurting self, even when that hurting sounds like a child rather than an adult; even," she emphasizes, "when that hurting self voices 'trivial' complaints."[53] "And a little child shall lead them."[54]

PART II

The Vagina Monologues

I find women more interesting; on the one hand, they are oppressed, but on the other, they aren't; rather, they use oppression as
a means of terrorism.
    —Rainer Werner Fassbinder, *Cinema Arts Centre Folio*, 2003

7

Chicken Little
Goes to Law School

There can be no doubt that law schools . . . favor men over women
in almost every way imaginable.   —Morrison Torrey et al.

A year after President Clinton abruptly withdrew his nomination for Assistant Attorney General for Civil Rights following a public
outcry that Lani Guinier was promoting a "minority veto," Guinier made
headlines again with a stunning announcement that the venerable University of Pennsylvania Law School was "stratified deeply along gender
lines." Indeed, in their landmark article "Becoming Gentlemen: Women's
Experience at One Ivy League Law School," Guinier and her co-authors
(henceforth the "Penn Researchers") charged the University of Pennsylvania Law School with fostering a "hostile learning environment for a
disproportionate number of its female students."[1] The characterization is
important. A "hostile learning environment" suggests a "hostile environment" which, in employment and educational settings, can be action-
able.

A Giant Leap for Women

Having made a splash with the article, the Penn Researchers got cocky.
Without evaluating the learning environment at any other law school,
they republished the article, together with a short essay, as a book, keeping the main title but subtitling their work "Women, Law School, and Institutional Change."[2]

129

"Becoming Gentlemen" has inspired extensive commentary on law school gender climate. Seeing law school as a painful and endless trial for women, feminists have turned the Penn Researchers' jeremiad against male-dominated law schools into a literary genre. A few feminists have, to be sure, tried to qualify the Penn Researchers' findings in one way or another. No one, however, has scrutinized the Penn Researchers' methods and interpretations for consistency, cultural logic, or even sincerity. Why? The conversation-stopping effects of "I hurt" have previously been noted. For well-brought-up men, no amount of provocation can justify striking back at women. As for women, to the extent that they are inclined by nature or culture to bond with other women, they will be no more disposed to question heart-rending stories of women's oppression and pain.

Reading "Becoming Gentlemen," one starts to wonder, do male professors ever perform acts of kindness for their female students? If so, do these occur in spite of contempt for women or on account of normal male fondness for them? Would it upset a central feminist plan—and would he not earn respect and maybe secret admiration—if a male professor stood up to defend himself, for once, like a man? *And ain't I a man?*

After presenting the Penn Researchers' findings, this chapter proceeds to evaluate those findings in light of cultural norms, the related gender-climate literature, and a recent survey of gender climate I conducted at my own law school. The last part of the chapter takes a broader sociological and psychological look at the "Becoming Gentlemen" phenomenon. Because no study, however well conceived, can neatly evaluate something as intangible and protean as the gender climate at even one school, a major objective will be to examine the biases, contradictions, and other limitations of previous studies. I conclude that the evidence fails to support the Penn Researchers' charges. If I am right, the smugness, *tua culpa*s, breast-beating, and self-abasement should stop.

The Ladies of Continuing Sorrows

From beginning to end, according to the stories female students told the Penn Researchers, law school is a harrowing experience. First year "was like a frightening out-of-body experience," a student reported. "[F]or me the damage is done," reported another, "*it's in me*. I will never be the same. I feel so defeated."[3] Female students complained that their "voices were 'stolen' from them" by instructors who had allowed classroom discourse to be dominated by male students who, in turn, failed to use gender-neutral language or control other sexist impulses. The resulting alienation of these women, the Penn Researchers argue, was related to the distinctly lower grades they earned relative to men, a phenomenon inconsistent with their comparable entering credentials.

Upper-division female students complained about male professors favoring male students not only by encouraging them to speak more often but also by giving them more positive feedback. As evidence of women's distress, the study pointed out that far more women than men were seeking "professional help" at the law school and reporting behavior such as crying.

By the end of the third year, readers learn, law school has obliterated much of the women's former selves. Women came to law school with public service dreams only to leave as servants of capitalism. Initially unhappy with their level of class participation, they ended up participating no more frequently but with greater acceptance of their silence. Incidents that were earlier condemned as offensive displays of sexism came to be seen as jokes. Law school taught them to be "less emotional" and "more objective," to stop caring about others; so destructive of women's identities was the law school experience that by the end of their studies, women were expressing fewer complaints than men about their law school experience.

Accepting relational theory, the Penn Researchers report that the Socratic method, which calls for student "performance," is distasteful and intimidating to women because it emphasizes hierarchy and conflict. In short, the problem with law school is the male model at its heart. Hence the Penn Researchers' opening epigraph: "Am I to be cursed forever with becoming somebody else on the way to myself?"[4]

If women's sense of self is so fragile, the function of law schools cannot be to train women to operate in a world historically shaped by men. "Although some have said in response to our data that perhaps women are not well suited to law school or should simply learn to adapt better to its rigors, we are inclined to believe that it is the law school—not the women—that should change." What should be done? Beyond admitting and hiring more women students and faculty, law schools must dismantle "the hierarchy itself" by a "reinvention of law school" and effect "a fundamental change in . . . teaching practices, institutional policies, and social organization."[5]

Skirting the Issues

"Becoming Gentlemen" leaves unanswered a host of important questions that it provokes. Among them: How did the men they studied respond to the questionnaire? If in fact men expressed less distress in law school, is that perhaps only because they are socialized to grin and bear burdens more than women? Do women find nothing of value in their legal education? Are law schools responsible for the malaise among female students when a sense of insecurity is pervasive among young women in American society, as Gilligan and others report? A number of studies have shown that significantly more first-year college women than men feel overwhelmed by school. Other studies have shown consistently lower class-participation rates of women students in their earlier schooling[6] and, on average, 50 percent greater use by women than men of psychotherapeutic sevices.[7]

A woman professor puts the problem sensitive students present in perspective: "If you call on them, you're imposing hierarchy; if you don't call on them, you're overlooking them."[8] A comment by a first-year female Harvard law student seems especially revealing: "When I get called on," the student says, "I really think about rape. It's sudden. You're exposed. You can't move. You can't say no. And there's this man in control who is telling you exactly what to do."[9] Would calling on women not implicate even the most sensitive instructors in such violation?

Rape is hardly the only issue for women where the Socratic method is concerned. Interrogating women in class may be oppressive to women to the extent, as reported, that their words have a special meaning, a notion perhaps grounded in the idea that women like to think things through before expressing a view. Such a theory is promoted in *Women's Ways.* "An opinion," a woman is quoted therein as saying, "is more than an exercise of the intellect. It is a commitment; it is something to live by." "I don't take on an opinion as my own unless I have really thought about it and believe in it."[10] A policy that favors calling on women under these circumstances would produce inauthentic women and undermine women's culture.

Finally, complaints about the Socratic method are not new; nor are they made only by women. Indeed, the intense intrusion of the method on students' lives led Harvard Law's Duncan Kennedy to urge all students to refuse to participate when called on in class.[11]

The Penn Researchers report only that men dominate class discussions; they never claim that female *volunteers* are disproportionately ignored. We have a problem here. Assuming that male law students volunteer more frequently than do female students, if the professor recognizes volunteers proportionately, will men not end up dominating the discussion? On the other hand, if the professor favors women volunteers to achieve gender balance, would that be fair to individual men who have questions?

As for the public service aspirations of women entering law school, a subject on which the evidence is mixed,[12] maybe women's shift into corporate practice results from an increased sense of financial responsibility —not wanting to saddle themselves, their actual or potential spouses, or their parents with $100,000 in school debt—and the realization that with the obligation to pay back that debt, they cannot live in a major metropolitan area on a $40,000 public service salary. To the extent that they promote conflicting goals—that is, equality and the preservation of women's culture—feminists create a major dilemma for law schools as well as for women students. Assume that female law students do enter law school motivated by public service. Now suppose that they hold on to these values throughout their law school years. Given how gender theorists operate, would they not charge schools with *steering* women into low-paying jobs?

Did You Ever See a Lassie . . . ?

If women students bear witness to pain in the first year but not in the third, is this *bad* news for women? Would it be *good* news if women had been miserable throughout? A more benign explanation than brutalization into acquiescence can surely be offered. Perhaps, by the end, women law graduates have concluded that the gender atmosphere at law school was not so bad and that their initial reactions were more pre-feminist than feminist. Education should lead to changes in thinking, and the more rigorous the education the greater the change. But change involves loss as well as gain, and focusing only on loss surely obscures the gain. In this light, let us evaluate the argument that the law graduate who changes has sacrificed her identity. Consider Myra Bradwell, who more than a century ago sought the right to practice law in Illinois. In rejecting her petition, the Illinois Supreme Court wondered whether a woman could "engage in the hot strifes of the bar, in the presence of the public, and with momentous verdicts the prizes of the struggle."[13] If women are essentially conflict averse and relational, as the Penn Researchers believe, a victory for Bradwell in that sensational case might have led to a giant step backward for the culture of women.

Heads, I Win; Tails, You Lose

What would happen if law schools, respecting alleged differences, shifted to a female pedagogy that promoted expression of emotion, a pedagogy that was less adversarial? In the long run, the world might be a better place. But the practice of law currently requires channeling emotion into acceptable ratiocinative form. Surely, it would be throwing women to the lions—and women would experience a real hostile climate—if law schools did not teach them to go for the kill and, even, to enjoy the process. How else would a woman student learn to deal with a witness who was not properly cooperative or relational? This suggests that, rather than interviewing current law students, researchers should be interviewing law graduates, say, five years after graduation, at which time they could better evaluate the law school experience. The alternative is to put law schools into a position where, because women pursue mutually exclusive goals, law schools can't win.

One might think that MacKinnon's dominance feminism would lead her to support at least some practices challenged by the Penn Researchers. After all, if it is domination rather than stylistic difference that lies at the heart of the lived effect of gender, mastering the master's tools would seem especially useful. But MacKinnon is no less critical of legal education than Guinier. Focusing on the number of women lawyers who choose to defend pornographers, she places the blame squarely on law schools, whose methods produce what a sociologist of the legal profession calls "moral eunuchs."[14]

Ignoring the possibility that all serious enterprises require some sacrifice of sexuality, MacKinnon explains that law schools effectively tell women students that "to become a lawyer means to forget your feelings, forget your community, most of all, if you are a woman, forget your experience. Become a maze-bright rat. Women lawyers as a group," she adds, "go dead in the eyes like ghetto children, unlike the men, who come out of law school glowing in the dark."[15] Once again, the moral gender turns into the suffering and, even, the insufferable gender.

MacKinnon may be explaining more than she realizes—or wants. What rational employer will want to hire people who are "dead in the eyes"?

Finally, there are technical questions. Did the Penn Researchers rely too much on leading questions? Consider their survey's final question: "Please use this space to describe any acts or comments made by a professor or fellow student you have witnessed or experienced at the law school that made you uncomfortable for gender-based reasons."[16] A more appropriate question would surely have been: "Has any professor or colleague ever made a statement . . . ?" Most unsettling, what was the *frequency* of the gender-climate complaints that the Penn Researchers describe? Offering not even a brief discussion of these matters, the report is hopelessly flawed.

The Cult of Hostile Gender Climate

What led up to the Penn Researchers' attack on legal education? How should readers understand the provocative finding in the most recent major study of women in the legal profession that at "many if not most law schools, blatant discrimination against women is still the order of the day"?[17]

Exploring what they called the "four faces of alienation" in law school, "from ourselves, from the law school community, from the classroom, and from the content of legal education," two young women Yale Law graduates in 1988 found that students were "silenced in the classroom" by (1) a flood of grandstanding male voices; (2) the acontextuality of discourse "in which feelings and personal beliefs are rigorously excluded"; (3) the almost exclusive use of male pronouns; and (4) the fact that women were not "important enough" for most after-class discussions with the professor.[18]

Exploring another face of women's alienation the next year, Mari Matsuda hypothesized a first-year woman student of color in a criminal-law class who wants to talk about the race of the defendant or victim, about police brutality, and about the experience and fear of rape but suppresses the impulse. If the class is taught by a woman, the student would feel invited to talk about her consciousness as a woman. If the teacher is not a member of a historically disadvantaged group, however, a student of color will suppress "her nationalist anger at white privilege and her perception that the dominant white conception of violence excludes the daily violence of ghetto poverty."[19] Since, for therapeutic jurisprudes, a suppressed impulse is oppressive, so too will be criminal law and, by extension, any law school class taught by a white male teacher, that is, someone not like Matsuda herself. The more practical point is that if the student cannot train herself to speak her mind to a male professor, she will likely be unable to properly represent her clients before a male judge.

At the same time that the Penn report was being disseminated, the American Bar Association was engaging in a large-scale study, *Elusive Equality*.[20] Among its findings: "many women still experience debilitating instances of gender bias" (ibid., 2); young white men seem "more threatened by women classmates today then [*sic*] in the past" (ibid., 4); men speak more than women in class; and women underachieve relative to men at "some" law schools.

There has never been a scintilla of evidence that women are graded more harshly than men, and *Elusive Equality* found that "women seem to do better than men on conventional measures of success such as grades and membership on law reviews" (ibid., 8). Nevertheless, *Elusive Equality* wildly recommends that professors consider take-home exams to allow students to type their answers because "handwritten exams can reveal gender to some readers" (ibid., 13). It further recommends creation of a National Committee on Gender Issues in Law Schools and the establishment at all law schools of a Standing Committee on Gender. The study influenced an ABA committee to create an elaborate questionnaire and to urge its use in every law school to evaluate the gender climate.

Two years after "Becoming Gentlemen" appeared, a woman-authored Law School Admission Council report portrayed an improving, if still not ideal, law school environment for women. Women's grades in the first year were lower than those of men to a statistically significant degree, but the disparity was not large enough to be of "practical significance"; the perceptions of male and female students differed little concerning their instructors' supportiveness and concerning issues of justice; and the lower self-image of women compared to men at the end of the first year was proportionate to the gap existing upon entrance. The report warns that exaggerating differences "perpetuates myths and distorts reality, allowing significant achievement by women to go unrecognized or to become lost among concerns of underachievement and alienation."[21]

"A Simpering, Whimpering Child Again"

One might expect that this last report would have tempered opinions on the subject of a hostile gender climate. One would be wrong. A 1997 graduate of Yale Law School provides details of the contemporary environment for women law students in a 110-page whine against the law school. Here are a few student comments: unlike men, women "want to say something intelligent, whereas the men just spout off"; the men were "intimidating and so focused on speaking in class, on learning the rules of the game . . . to get the kinds of jobs they wanted"; "I just felt inhibited, and I probably should have spoken up more"; when "a woman says something that's more visceral, or more emotional . . . it tends to be . . . debunked by other people."[22] Very few women reported approaching professors after class or during office hours. Here is the problem in a nutshell. The author of the Yale study complains that women law students are not speaking up in class but snivels at the same time that they are being silenced. When students do speak up and are not ignored, they complain about being challenged. Women do not reach out to their professors yet feel free to complain about their invisibility. Is this not another dilemma which, because there is no escape, is not worth talking about?

Of two women who spoke frequently: "they were really quite pathologized in the sense that—I would see the looks on people's faces, like, 'Oh God, she's talking again.'" About a small group: "There were only about three women who said anything. . . . I mean it was horrible, it was just absolutely horrible."[23]

The testimony is excruciating: "I thought I was the stupidest person here. . . . I just felt like I was a fraud." Incremental change is not the answer, the author insists, echoing the Penn Researchers: "in some sense it's like a microcosm of society, you'd have to dismantle the entire structure . . . it's so bad here."[24]

In the last analysis, the Yale author is searching for a male experience at her school. Men, she says, "are better at not internalizing their failures." She ends her article with a haunting lament by an interviewee who wishes she could "have had a great experience, like it is for most of the first-year guys I talk to now, who are like, 'It's wonderful, I love it here!'

I so envy them. I so wish my experience had been like that."[25] This assessment requires some context. In twenty years of teaching, I have never heard *any* student characterize law school study so rapturously.

A few years later, things reportedly got even worse for women. "There can be no doubt that law schools . . . favor men over women in almost every way imaginable," concluded "What Every First-Year Female Law Student Should Know."[26] Authored by Professor Morrison Torrey and student assistants, the report complains about "walls covered with portraits of distinguished alumni and jurists, all of whom are white and male";[27] too few women teachers as authority figures and role models; and rampant sexual harassment by both peers and professors. Proposed solutions are frightening: (1) exclude men from some courses so as to provide safe havens for women; (2) eliminate or reduce the influence of the Socratic method; (3) require students to take one course focusing on women; and (4) withhold accreditation from those schools unwilling to go along with the program and eliminate gender bias. Professor Jennifer Brown takes the foregoing opinions to their natural conclusion: Because law school is such "an alienating experience for women," America needs a women's law school.[28]

Among the latest chapters in this story is *A Woman's Guide to Law School,* in which Professor Linda Hirshman rates 158 law schools with a *Femscore* by applying such factors as percentage of the faculty and student body made up of women and percentage of women honors students. Finding dramatic differences in law school gender climate, the author urges prospective students to "[m]ake demands" when their leverage is greatest. "[B]efore you accept the offer," she urges, "ask for a schedule that has at least one woman teacher," one "that doesn't include teachers your research has revealed will demand that you become your own worst enemy."[29] And, presumably, one that includes people exactly like Hirshman herself.

The Numbers Speak

To determine whether male teachers turn women students into their own worst enemies, I have engaged in a study of my own, using end-of-semester evaluations of individual law faculty members sorted by gender of the student evaluator on a class-by-class basis, the approach recommended by *Elusive Equality.* The benefits of asking student evaluators to self-identify by gender should now be clear. If, in fact, women "go dead in the eyes like ghetto children," and if "[w]omen are given the feeling that if they speak out of their own experiences or their own ideas, or express ideas that are not fully developed, they will be dismissed," those sentiments should be reflected in differences in the way they evaluate their teachers. The results should be helpful in determining whether the legal academy should be more attentive to the needs of female students.

The questionnaire set forth in Appendix I was administered in all Touro Law School classes in the fall of 1999 and contained no leading questions on the subject of gender. Giving students the opportunity to talk about gender, without requiring them to do so, allowed for measurement of the strength of any gender-based responses to law school life at Touro. (Responses to teacher's gender are analyzed in chapter 8.) Because Touro is not an Ivy League institution, the results of this study should be more representative of the average American law school than those produced by the Penn Researchers.

Here is a summary of the initial results obtained by studying means and T-scores of the data. In three of five categories carefully evaluated— "overall teaching ability," "openness to consultation," and "presents material clearly"—there was no statistically significant difference between the reactions of male and female students. In the remaining two categories—"sustains student interest" and "treatment of students"—differences were statistically significant (meaning that they were unlikely to have arisen by chance), with female students giving less favorable evaluations. Breaking down results by year of study quickly reveals that this male-female gap appears only in the first year of law school. In years two and three, male and female student opinion was about the same, with both groups giving weaker evaluations in year two and higher evaluations in year three, as students were ready to graduate. These results replicate the Penn Researchers' findings.

Statistically significant differences in year one, however, are not dispositive. What also has to be evaluated is the "effect size," or relative magnitude, of the difference. In this case, the effect size of the disparities for the two items in question is quite small, .13 and .15, respectively, on a five-point scale. Moreover, a "hostile learning environment for a disproportionate number" of women students is simply not indicated when the mean score for both men and women is between excellent and very good and when, again, there is no appreciable difference in the *overall* evaluation of their teachers by male and female students.

The evaluation used in the above study did not test all the important charges leveled by the Penn Researchers. Therefore, I prepared and, a few days later, administered the more comprehensive questionnaire in Appendix II to the same Touro law classes.

Here again, the conclusions affirm contemporary legal education. There are no statistically significant differences between the means of male and female responses for eight of the twelve variables, including "calling on students without regard to gender" and "offense taken to gender-insensitive language." The remaining four variables resulted in statistically significant differences to varying degrees. With respect to the complaint about "too much black letter law," women disagreed slightly more than men; women wanted more, not less, black letter law. As for "this class is a more difficult, less satisfying experience for me" than for the opposite sex, women disagreed appreciably more than did men.

With respect to comfort with the Socratic method, women respondents were only marginally more likely than men to think that men were more at ease with that method. Regarding reluctance to speak, perhaps the most salient finding is that of 214 women respondents, only 9 felt silenced because of disrespect shown by the opposite sex. By comparison, 7 men of 222 felt silenced by the women in the class.

In terms of tests for gender bias discussed in this study, male and female student comments about their professors proved to be indistinguishable. To be sure, six female students—out of about a hundred students who offered comments—did complain about domination of class discussion by men. Too much should not be read into this finding, however. All six complaints were about one male instructor in one class.

Marginal Chic

How have so many women law academics managed to believe that law school oppresses women students? Todd Gitlin, a prominent left-leaning social critic, frames the question broadly in a 1995 book. "Why," he wonders, "are so many people attached to their marginality? . . . Why insist on difference with such rigidity, rancor and blindness?"[30]

The question is implicit in Katie Roiphe's observation that women "vie for the position of being silenced."[31] Gitlin argues that America is a "vertiginous . . . society founded on rootlessness, devoted to self-creation, worshipping evanescence, stuffing its spiritual voids with the latest gadgets." It is this unsettledness, according to Gitlin, that leads to the cant of identity politics with its attendant binary thinking: "This is a person of Type X, not Type Y."[32] If Gitlin is right, it is, once again, not white men but race and gender critics who are guilty of binary thinking. As insightful as Gitlin is, however, the culture wars in recent years have hardly been limited to the United States, so there must be more to the gender-climate story than American rootlessness or even moral bragging rights.

We have already noted a connection between identity politics and tenure. This link may also be evidenced by Lani Guinier's appointment at Harvard as the first tenured black woman law professor. At a press conference announcing her appointment, then-dean Robert Clark introduced her as a "first-rate scholar" who has produced extremely important work" and as "one, who by her presence, will help the school attract other top scholars, including more women of color."[33]

Gender Defender

However solid Guinier's record of scholarship, if the Penn Researchers had concluded that all was well with women in law school, Guinier would have been a much less valuable prize for Harvard. As will become clear in chapter 9, Harvard was under great pressure to hire a black woman. But a finding by the Penn Researchers that women did not need a defender would have meant that Guinier could not have been billed as a champion for women. We need not believe that the Penn Researchers cooked the books or that they were insincere, only that law schools, no less than the rest of us, can be taken in by tabloid-style headlines: "Law Professors Found Terrorizing Philadelphia Coeds." Identity scholars who want to play the diversity card in the job market must embrace bad news.

Controlling the self-serving idealism that fuels these studies is not easy. Identity politics is different from other politics. A libertarian who argues for the abolition of tenure will quickly hear opposition from members of her own faculty. Statements of identity position are not so hospitable to challenge. Hence, it should not be surprising that, among all the authors considered here for their recent scholarship on gender climate, there have been only a handful of males.

Preaching Diversity to the Choir

One could, of course, argue that women have been dominant in this area of study because they are more interested than men in the subject of women in law school. But how to explain with respect to *Elusive Equality*, the report of the ABA Commission on Women in the Profession, an *institutional* sponsor, that the three principal writers are women, that all four people who "contributed significantly" to the project were women, and that thirteen of the fourteen commission members who provided "thoughtful feedback" were women? The topic, as it has been defined, has a built-in need for male participation. Guinier and others premise their work on notions of femaleness: women are more egalitarian, they are collaborative in nature, and they resist hierarchy. But such positions make sense only in relation to fundamental notions of maleness. And it is not only women who have a stake in the exploration of fundamental gender characteristics.

Put another way, it seems strange that women, among the strongest supporters of diversity, have failed to invite men onto commissions to study gender issues in legal education. Can any reasonable person deny that gender talk would be more productive with more inclusiveness? That the rhetoric of gender in recent years might have made such an invitation necessary should be clear to anyone who walks into a large bookstore and looks for a male author among hundreds of works devoted to "women's studies." Professor Nancy Levit provides the best solution to the problem of inbreeding, which has arguably turned gender discourse into a tempest at a tea party: "Feminists," she writes, should "try to foster men's interest in writing about gender issues and interpreting, adopting, expanding on, and reacting to feminist ideals and methodologies."[34] Accepting Levit's invitation is precisely what is being done here.

To acknowledge that women are doing quite well today in law school is not to ignore past problems. It cannot have been easy for women in the early 1970s, when Lani Guinier was in law school. But the law school experience for women was radically different by 1997, when *Becoming Gentlemen* came out as a book. For one thing, with all the law shows on television and other media attention on what lawyers do and how they do it, women students are coming to law school with a far better sense of the rigors of legal education and law practice than they previously had. It is hard to imagine that these students, even if they grew up without personally knowing any women lawyers, would nevertheless be surprised by the adversarial system. Second, as a consequence of the women's movement presumably, the academy has added women-and-the-law seminars, small sections for first-year classes, and dispute resolution and negotiation courses, while perhaps taking some of the hard edge off the Socratic method in recent years. Third, enrollment rates for women in law school have gone up from 20 percent in 1975, to 40 percent ten years later, to 50 percent today. Last, as the next chapter will show, about half of new law teachers are women. As evidence of women's engagement, to repeat (see note 21), in by far the most comprehensive of empirical studies since "Becoming Gentlemen" was first published, no gender difference of "practical significance" was found in men's and women's grades. Characterizing the contemporary law school environment for women as "hostile" under these circumstances is preposterous.

The Little Engine That Couldn't

Do women pay a price for the sententiousness and tendentiousness in the discussion of differences between men's and women's learning styles? Would a moratorium on discussion of women's essential differences from men be salutary? Consider the impact on women of hearing from relational feminists that they, more than men, learn from personal experience and not through abstract principle, from collaborative learning rather than from hierarchical teaching methods. Words having consequences, such theories could discourage women from going to law school. For those who persist, might these diagnoses of women's *mals* not have an iatrogenic effect?

In defending her brand of dominance feminism against charges that her emphasis on women's powerlessness demeans women, Catharine MacKinnon concedes the power of academic discourse to shape social consciousness, thus rejecting the argument frequently heard that academics have no influence. "Speak as though women are not victimized," she says, "and we will not be any more. . . . Speech has an almost mystical power here."[35] But if MacKinnon's position is right, it would seem to follow that the obverse—the demoralizing power of victimization claims— is also right. If so, and if the findings of "Becoming Gentlemen" are irrelevant, MacKinnon is effectively critiquing her own and the Penn Researchers' work. Indeed, is it not likely that women—who, regardless of major, already outperform men in high school, college, and graduate school—might also outshine men in law school if they were taught that law school is women's natural habitat? It seems fair to say that it is not American law schools but promoters of negative, can't-do feminism who, "allowing significant achievement in women . . . to be lost among concerns of . . . alienation," thereby creating even more alienation, have become women's worst enemies.

Backlash

A final question: How should the female reader understand this book? If she adopts an essentialist view of men's and women's natures, she will see it as hopelessly male. She will find nothing relational here, no attempt at collaboration, no synthesis of related viewpoints, but rather a bullheaded effort to undo feminist victories and reestablish the old order. In boxing terms, she might see it as one mass title bout in which an ambitious and loutish male attempts to knock out all ranking feminists so as to establish himself as champ.

Would dismissing this response to "Becoming Gentlemen" as backlash —a term used regularly in feminist literature—be useful? Not if we want to "get past the Catch-22 in which merely talking about [gender] is considered an act of war." Nor would such a reaction be right on the merits. No, if Lani Guinier is not from Venus, I am not from Mars. Its male authorship notwithstanding, this book comes not to bring the sword of patriarchy to womanhood. Much less is this project designed to bring primitive talionic pleasures to fellow male professors for the repulsive things feminists have said about them.

Unlike "Becoming Gentlemen," which purports to only report on hostile gender climate but actually serves to fuel it, this project aims at gender peace by teaching women that those whom their teachers perceive as women's enemies are really their friends. This lesson has the simple experiential logic of intuition behind it; most men like being around women and enjoy making them happy. Knowing that law school is not the unremittingly grim place that they have been led to believe, women can come with high hopes and confidence—and good will towards men.

The withdrawal of Guinier's nomination for the civil rights job led to expressions of strong support for her. Derrick Bell couldn't "imagine anybody being more qualified than Lani Guinier, . . . and suddenly, qualifications mean nothing." Wanting to force the president's hand, he encouraged other nominees to declare, "Mr. President, you may not understand her writings, but I do. And if there is no place for her in this administration, there's no place for me."[36] Yale's Stephen Carter speculates that Guinier "might have been the finest head the Civil Rights Division has ever had."[37] Are Bell and Carter right that a golden opportunity was lost for civil rights when Lani Guinier was sacrificed to the anti-quota mob? To join Bill Clinton's judgment with the analysis in this chapter, only if a qualification for America's top civil rights job is a capacity to poison its gender, as well as its race, climate.

8

The Tall Tales of
Women Teachers

[T]hat discrimination or bias can be inferred from statistical inequalities . . . is the reigning non sequitur of our times, both intellectually and politically.   —Thomas Sowell

Toward the end of his hard life, the old story goes, an embit-
tered old man finally confronts his Maker. "Lord," he complains, "my
wife is an invalid, my children have married outside the faith, I have to
beg for work, and my friends, so to speak, abandon or mock me. I know,"
he continues, "that you don't repair relationships and health, or operate
an employment agency, that we are responsible for these aspects of life
ourselves. And I respect that. But," he goes on, "couldn't I at least have
won the lottery?" Too broken to expect a response, the man is stunned to
hear a Heavenly Voice: "I hear you, my son; I will look into it." The next
day the Voice returns. "You have indeed suffered widely and deeply. But,"
the Voice continues, "couldn't you at least have bought a ticket?"

Is a hardened patriarchy dashing the dreams of women faculty, as it reportedly does those of students? Or are charges of oppression misguided
—like those of the old man in the foregoing narrative—because law faculty women are not doing the necessaries for success? A brief discussion
of law school past and present will prove helpful.

Over the past forty years, as the percentage of women law students
rose from about 3 percent to 50 percent, the growth in the proportion of
women on law school faculties has increased even more dramatically.
Comprising less than .5 percent of tenure-track faculty in 1960,[1] today
women make up 22 percent of full professors, 46 percent of associate

professors, and 48 percent of assistant professors.[2] The story of women in legal education may well be the greatest story of group professional success ever told.

Party Poopers

Is it time for celebration, or at least a cheer? Apparently not. Reviewing the history of the legal academy, a recent (male) commentator captures the cranky and widespread view of feminists that women law professors are "greeted, at best, with ambivalence."[3] Blaming male law students and male-dominated administrations for creating a hostile gender climate for female faculty, feminists have warned of a "glass ceiling" in hiring and tenure, a metaphorical charge that has been recently ramped up to a "glass house."[4] A glass ceiling or glass house is precisely what could be expected in an environment characterized a few years ago by a professor of feminist jurisprudence as "favor[ing] men over women in almost every way imaginable."[5]

Critics have eagerly spelled out the burdens endured by women law faculty beginning with the charge that students force women academics to adopt teaching personae that are alien to them—the authenticity matter again. The claim emerges from a famous experiment, conducted in 1981, in which students were asked to describe the law. They depicted it as "logical, rational, rigorous . . . intellectual . . . analytical, difficult, exacting." The researcher next asked her students to describe differences between men and women. Men were seen as "rational, strong, hierarchical, aggressive . . . efficient"; women, by contrast were "dependent, nurturing, emotive, weak, caring, . . . egalitarian."[6]

Without acknowledging that some of these characterizations emerge from bedrock relational feminist doctrine, Professor Kathleen Bean concludes that students perceive the law to be of the male gender and that this leads to an unhealthy environment for female law faculty.[7] First, women faculty will enjoy less credibility among students than will male faculty. Second, the loss of credibility generates hostility in students as they decide that they are receiving an inferior education from female professors. Third, the sense of being cheated will consume valuable energy, which will prevent students from properly focusing on their studies.

The preceding chapter showed that, at least at one school, there is likely no appreciable difference in the way that male and female students evaluate their professors today. The question to be addressed here is whether, in fact, both male and female students judge female faculty more harshly than they do male faculty.

Learning of a study suggesting that women teachers were perceived as less competent than men, Professor Christine Farley undertook her own investigation of teacher evaluations at an unspecified top-ten law school.[8] Her data, published in 1996 and presented more fully in Appendix III, are summarized here.

Women professors, Farley found, faced two criticisms: they were neither "man" enough nor "woman" enough for teaching the law. They were deemed unable to control the class, unprepared, disorganized, unclear, and confusing. In addition, they lacked objectivity and were too political. Paradoxically, they were also "too harsh, curt, or condescending" and insufficiently "supportive." Women's appearance was commented on, a sign to Farley that women were not taken seriously. Even when comments were positive, the evaluations of women professors differed from those of men. Women were "praised for being approachable, accessible, helpful, interested, concerned/committed, enthusiastic, and creating a congenial atmosphere," while men were lauded for being "masters of their subject matter." Farley's conclusion in brief: The reasoning in *Bradwell v. Illinois*—that women are not suited by character for the rude world of law practice—"is alive and well in students' course evaluations" of female faculty.[9]

To what extent can Farley's findings be extrapolated across the law school community? For this purpose I compare her results with those of the earlier-described Touro study.[10]

The study provides no evidence of a lack of respect for female faculty. Appreciable differences appeared in the evaluations of men and women in only a few categories. In this regard, results were inconsistent with those obtained by Farley. As for categories where differences did appear —"Challenging," "Professional," "Wonderful human being," "Abrasive"—far from being evaluated more harshly, Touro women faculty stand out as models for the men (see table below).

That Touro women faculty reportedly had greater difficulty controlling class than did the men may result from the women faculty's relational nature, the same factor that likely led the women faculty to be evaluated as wonderful human beings.

Another disparity strongly favoring men in the Touro study is in the humor department, a finding that will resonate strongly with readers of

Comments about Male and Female Professors

	Male Profs.	Female Profs.
Knowledgeable	102	73
Great/excellent/outstanding teacher	126	123
Very good teacher	14	18
Good/fair teacher	16	18
Well-prepared	19	33
Enthusiastic/enjoyable	50	40
Clear/understandable	40	47
Interesting/creative/intelligent	9	18
Good stories/animated/sense of humor	26	4
Approachable/accessible	26	29
Respects students	13	18
Challenging/inspiring/stimulating	2	33
Professional	2	22
Wonderful human being/very nice person/ caring/compassionate/supportive	24	54
Confusing/unclear/not helpful	66	69
Abrasive/condescending/unresponsive/ rude/impatient	43	11
Egotistical	8	0
Uncaring/miserable human being	6	0
Can't control class	0	29

this book, or students of feminism, generally. Feminist doctrine may again help us understand. To the extent that humor arises out of establishing superiority over another person, and to the extent that women are uncomfortable in that position—preferring instead to bond with their audience—women professors will perforce not be the successful entertainers that men are. Women academics thus have the choice in the foregoing areas of either swallowing hard and modeling themselves on men or resigning themselves to being uncompetitive and trying harder to make up for their "deficiencies" in other ways.

No More Students' Dirty Looks

Not a single comment among the hundreds received referred explicitly to the gender of the instructor or student, his or her physicality, or—with only a couple of exceptions, each involving a male—his appearance.[11] Because such comments about women have been reported and decried in other settings, it seems worthwhile to think about their significance. Does an anonymous end-of-the-year comment have any deep meaning?

Elusive Equality, for example, reported the following comments: "Loved your show, babe" and "I enjoyed watching her jiggle when she wrote at the chalkboard."[12] In highlighting these comments about women's appearance, the American Bar Association in effect accepts an old theory that desire and respect are mutually exclusive: "As you climb up the ladder of success," the grade-school ditty goes, "don't let the boys look under your dress." But is there a real opposition between sex and success? Power, Henry Kissinger held, is the greatest aphrodisiac for those lacking it. The opportunity to connect with their professors offers the nonpowerful, in this case students, the prospect of either triumphing over power or, if they choose, subordinating themselves to it. Whether or not Kissinger is right, surely one can both desire and admire a person, even a spouse. For what it's worth, the woman who has received the most comments about her appearance over her twenty years at my school—perhaps a half-dozen times—is also the highest rated female professor, and perhaps the highest rated professor overall. Is the dualistic and much ballyhooed Madonna/whore conundrum for women just another feminist fantasy?

But what about the distraction or blow to her self-esteem and her future career that an "I loved your show, babe" might cause an ambitious professor? A woman promoted by *Fortune* as an outstanding and tough business leader cautions women about their reactions to such comments. For "those who find the use of the word 'babe' inappropriate or even horrifying: I seriously doubt, as long as you retain this attitude, that you will ever appear on the cover of *Fortune*—or that you will accomplish enough in business to warrant this distinction."[13]

Female law faculty are allegedly kept down by law school administrations as well as by law school faculty. Sex segregation reigns in course assignments, says a chaired professor at the University of Missouri–Kansas City. Women law professors make up 58 percent of those teaching family law, 22 percent of those teaching corporate and commercial law, 13 percent of those teaching corporate finance, and 93 percent of those who have taught a course in gender and law.[14] But if women law faculty are more relational, if they are determined to raise maximum consciousness in the areas that they most care about, will they not demand to teach family law and the law of gender and seek to avoid corporate and commercial courses? The astute reader will have no trouble imagining the response of relational feminists to a dean who forces traditionally "male" courses on female faculty against their will.

Arguing with Success

Culminating a long series of law school *faculty* gender-climate studies, a comprehensive empirical study published in 2000 purports to show the second-class status of women law faculty in American law schools. Providing a raft of data on male-female differences in hiring of tenure-track law faculty, tenure rates, hiring of legal writing instructors, and decanal appointments, Richard Neumann's "Women in Legal Education: What the Statistics Show" reports, as we have seen, that women are "greeted, at best, with ambivalence."[15] Based on the data, it might just as easily have concluded that women in legal academia often do not position themselves for success.

Neumann's first specific finding is that women are not applying for tenure-track jobs at rates proportionate to their presence on graduation rolls. It is, of course, possible that a wretched law school climate for women faculty has discouraged them from buying a ticket. But surely an important part of the story is what happens to the women who do apply. It turns out that for the last seven reported years, the job success rate for female tenure-track applicants to the legal academy's hiring clearinghouse is somewhat higher than that of men, and the fact that (the fewer) women applicants are getting just about one-half of new tenure-track jobs means that many women apply through alternate channels. The fact that they are not getting precisely 50 percent of the jobs may only mean that, as has been well documented, one-half of women, as opposed to one-quarter of men, limit their job searches geographically.[16]

Neumann then adduces a study on faculty retention and tenure.

Tenure Rates for Men and Women Hired on Tenure Track in 1990 and 1991,
through the 1997–98 Academic Year[a]

	Tenured	Not tenured or no longer at an AALS law school–accredited school	Totals
Women (199)[b]	61%	39%	100%
Men (239)	72%	28%	100%

[a] Richard A. White, "Preliminary Report: The Promotion, Retention, and Tenuring of New Law School Faculty Hired in 1990 and 1991" (unpublished manuscript). White, the AALS (Association of American Law Schools) statistician, collated this data from the questionnaires law faculty fill out every spring for AALS directories.
[b] Numbers in parentheses are raw numbers.

Does the fact that 72 percent of men but only 61 percent of women achieved tenure mean that women were being forced out? If indeed women and men are similarly situated, statistical disparities favoring men would tend to show discrimination. But, as will become clear shortly, there are quite a number of potential explanations for the disparities that militate against such a gloomy view. In many cases it is women themselves who have pointed them out. We consider two of them now. First, women bear children and are their primary caretakers. The implications of these realities for women in law seem clear. Data are unavailable on why women leave law schools, but having and caring for children is the reason most frequently cited by women for leaving their law firms. Second, as suggested earlier, women are far more likely than men to follow their spouses geographically on their career paths.[17] So perhaps it should not be surprising that more women than men left law teaching before becoming tenured. If the decision to leave is the product of rational and free —if painful—choice, surely we need a more nuanced notion of institutional "ambivalence" than a mere numerical difference. We are back to Sowell's point that, having no solutions, our problems offer only trade-offs; our failure to understand this bespeaks silly sentimentalism.

There is much more. In her book *Unbending Gender: Why Family and Work Conflict and What to Do about It,* American University law professor Joan Williams, citing the burden of female domesticity, calls on the federal government to require employers to create a part-time track for parents, with full proportionality of benefits.[18] Williams points out that 90 percent of women become mothers at some point in their lives, and women provide 80 percent of the child care and do 67 percent of the housework. These data, she adds, help explain why one-third of fathers can work at least forty-nine hours per week outside the home, which makes them the "ideal workers." Two-thirds of mothers (of children under eighteen) who are themselves between the ages of twenty-five and forty-five, by contrast, work less than forty hours per week, and only 7 percent of mothers work substantial overtime,[19] a finding that, another study suggests, may explain why lesbians earn 30 percent more than do their heterosexual counterparts.[20] Relationships between spouses, Williams says, would appear to be no different in academic families.[21] Women see themselves as "co-breadwinners or committed workers" in only 20 percent of dual-career families.

Publishing and Flourishing

Williams's findings may explain a long line of research across academic disciplines showing that male professors publish considerably more than do women, often 50 percent more.[22] The law school experience is no different. A recent study found that, on average, white men published fully 40 percent more articles on average than white women, black men almost 40 percent more than black women.[23] Men also published in more prestigious places, though citation rates for men and women were comparable. Since Neumann fails to address the implications of this kind of data, we must do so here. If law school men publish 40 percent more than do women and, right or wrong, publishing is coin of the realm in academic life, that women move up at a somewhat lesser rate than men is hardly evidence that women are "greeted, at best, with ambivalence" in law schools.

Williams does not hesitate to draw lessons from these kinds of studies: "It is time to admit that women as a group do not perform the same as men as a group when jobs are designed around an ideal worker with men's . . . access to a flow of family work most women do not enjoy."[24] If, because they do not have access to child care and household help, women cannot be competitive "as a group" and thus cannot normally become "ideal workers"—which Williams defines as doing "good work" for fifty to seventy hours a week—then tenure rates for women can be expected to be somewhat lower than those for men. Unless, of course, men should be penalized for excessive devotion to work, a notion that Williams almost seems willing to embrace, or women should be subjected to lower standards for the same productivity, a notion that, for understandable reasons, Williams is reluctant to promote.

Much could be added here about Williams's intriguing proposal. Recall, however, that Williams herself conceded that "my goal is not to deliver the truth but to inspire social change."[25] Suffice to ask, then, that if women are aware that the gravity of domesticity limits their growth—and it is hard to imagine that it does not—will women, and especially mothers, not lower their professional sights accordingly? Yet here is where Neumann takes his strongest stand. He complains that women are overrepresented in low-status law school positions such as legal writing. Women do indeed represent almost 70 percent of legal-writing teachers, who are not full citizens in the legal academy. But is this a story worthy of despair? Women, we have seen, make up about half of new tenure-track faculty hires. Before women came on the scene, moreover, legal-writing courses were taught by men, whose positions were also of lower status. If, finally, regular teachers have stronger credentials than do legal-writing teachers, and if legal-writing teaching requires less commitment in time and energy (e.g., a lesser obligation to publish), might that not explain gaps in benefits?

Big "ifs," to be sure, but not necessarily insurmountable ones. To begin with, a recent study of legal-writing teachers suggests that they may not have the same elite school and law review pedigrees as tenure-track faculty.[26] Moreover, a woman director of legal writing for twenty years reports that a great number of applicants for her legal-writing slots have been women with young children who chose to leave their law firms in order to spend more time with their families.[27] Perhaps, then, a considerable part of the legal-writing benefits gap is the result of legal-writing teachers' working substantially fewer hours at their jobs than tenure-track teachers—a surmise consistent with the fact that men (and presumably single women) spend substantially more time on the job than do married women with children. If so, why is the market an inappropriate basis for determining salaries? In sum, the legal-writing issue—like the hiring and tenure problem—requires a far more subtle inquiry than male-bashing critics have given it.

The climate on the administrative side of legal education is even more baleful, according to Neumann, with women making up less than 13 percent of law school deans. But what is to be made of this datum? Women, it has been noted, currently make up only 22 percent of full professors, the group from which virtually all deans emerge. Since many of these women are fairly new in their positions, one might reasonably expect the rate of female deans to be lower. Given that women make up about 30 percent of tenured associate deans, moreover, it seems inane to hold that women are not welcome in the dean's suite.[28]

Going for the Gold

Do women in general even strive for the jobs that are the most demanding, the jobs that keep them out of the house for large blocks of time? Or do they seek a balance in their lives between family and career? A 1995 study showed that 45 percent of male executives aspired to be CEOs, compared to only 14 percent of women, and that 75 percent of women wanted to retire by age sixty-five, compared to less than 33 percent of men.[29] Women, says Stanford law professor and chair of the ABA Women in the Profession Committee Deborah Rhode, "have placed lower priority than men on objective forms of recognition in employment such as money, status and power."[30]

Looking at private law practice, where the money and prestige differences are greatest, and citing a recent ABA study, Susan Estrich rebukes young women attorneys for their unwillingness to make the sacrifices to become partners.[31] In law firms they "drop out in much higher numbers" than men; even women who could make it don't because they never signed up. And it is not only having children that causes women to do what they do; according to Estrich, too many women "simply don't want to get to the top."[32]

A *New York Times Magazine* story, "The Opt-Out Revolution," suggests that high-powered women are dropping out across the board, a conclusion supported by the fact that only 38 percent of the women in the Harvard Business School classes of 1981, 1985, and 1991 work full time.[33] One solution to this "problem" was suggested thirty years ago by feminist pioneer Simone de Beauvoir: mothers should not be given the option to stay at home with the kids, because if they were, they would take it and thereby limit women's advancement.[34] Taking a more relational line, Estrich urges young women to persevere and avoid stigmatizing the entire sex: "motherhood doesn't need a movement anywhere near as desperately as ambition does."[35]

Psychology professor Virginia Varian helps explain the problem. For Varian, male and female schemas are encoded by our culture and constantly reinforced throughout our lives. According to these schemas, which cannot come as a revelation to anyone who studies gender and which impose a heavy burden on both males and females, men dominate the outside world and women the hearth. In her 1984 book *Femininity,* the well-known journalist Susan Brownmiller fleshes out the schema when she concedes that "ambition is not a feminine trait" and that its absence "is virtuous proof of the nurturant female nature." "The single-mindedness with which a man may pursue his nonproductive goals is foreign not only to the female procreational ability, it is alien to the feminine values and emotional traits that women are expected to show."[36]

How will working women accommodate these values? Many women will avoid situations in which they are authority figures. Authority, says psychiatrist Anna Fels, "has become insidiously mixed up with dominance," a word which "makes women queasy—unless perhaps they have a penchant for whips, stilettos and leather"—because it leads to "fear of being desexualized."[37] They will underestimate their ability to do the job.[38] Even "[t]he successful woman protects her 'femininity' by denying the authenticity of her success," says psychoanalyst Ethel Person.[39]

Women who are less confident in the workplace will be "committed to thinking that they can excel in their relations with other people," says Varian, "and will be less concerned about whether they excel professionally."[40] She illustrates with a hypothetical medical student who is having trouble in school:

> Instead of trying harder she can drop out. Dropping out is not a cause of unbearable shame, because her self-esteem is not solely dependent on achieving in a masculine domain. A woman can say, "Forget medical school, I'll get married." If she doesn't say it to herself someone else will say it to her. She can very easily say, "Forget medical school, I'll be a nurse." Or, "I'll be a social worker." She might find these professions less fulfilling, and they might not meet her human aspirations, but they are available alternatives. Women with high professional ambitions have many nonprofessional and low-status alternatives.[41]

Working to Live and Living to Work

Reflecting on the essence of women's different approach to work, *New York Times* editorial-page columnist Anna Quindlen, who quit her high-powered position to raise a family and write novels, had this to offer: "many more women put on the camouflage to get by," she says, "but at a certain point they say to themselves, *Work is what I do, but it's not who I am.* Whereas men are still really invested in a work-is-everything kind of thing."[42]

A world of data supports this theory. New research out of the London School of Economics shows that men are three times as likely as women to regard themselves as "work-centered."[43] Perhaps this is why women who work part-time are reportedly happier in their jobs than those who work full-time.[44] A study of University of California at Berkeley seniors by sociologist Anne Machung provides additional empirical evidence. Men there were found to be more focused on career and money than women, who viewed work more as a vehicle for personal satisfaction.[45]

Long before they became adults, women were making choices that assured that their career would not be primary and that their incomes would be lower. They were planning only to support themselves, not families. They were "talking 'career,' but thinking 'job.'"

We need not rely on speculation to evaluate women's interest in decanal positions. Several years ago I sent out questionnaires to some twenty-five law schools identified by the ABA as having recently undergone a dean search. Presumably concerned with liability issues, most schools did not respond, and, of those that did, most responded in the vaguest terms. Only five schools responded usefully. While one school reported that women made up 30 percent of the dean candidates, the corresponding percentage at the second school was 17 percent. The three other schools reported that "far fewer women than men applied," "it is extremely difficult to attract women and minorities," and "very few women did apply." A more meaningful datum may be that a dean search at my school in 2003 enticed thirty-one male but only three female applicants.[46]

An undersupply of women applicants for dean positions is wholly consistent with either relational or dominance feminism, according to which women try to "achieve interpersonal harmony, and [to] work and play in egalitarian teams versus men's [drive] to social dominance and their need to achieve rank in real or perceived hierarchies."[47] For, regardless of whether programmed by biological or cultural forces to bond with others, if women attach special significance to "personal feelings and the quality of their relationships," as Regina Austin argued earlier, they will have less interest in straining their connection with friends through newly acquired status. Women, again, may not be positioning themselves proportionately for advancement.

Looking behind the Numbers

The refusal to think about the data reflects acceptance of the proposition that, as Thomas Sowell says in the epigraph to this chapter, "discrimination or bias can be inferred from statistical inequalities," a notion Sowell characterizes as "the reigning non sequitur of our times, both intellectually and politically." Instead of expecting equality in all things, he tells us, we should expect inequality, because diversity is the dominant condition on this planet, not sameness. "What is wholly unsubstantiated is the prevailing assumption that the world would be random or even in the absence of discrimination or bias by individuals, institutions or 'society.'"[48] To support this assertion, Sowell cites a dazzling range of esoterica. For example, more than four-fifths of the donut shops in California are owned by people of Cambodian ancestry. Presumably, few would ascribe a malignant cause to data of this kind. Yet, it is hard to deny, many supporters of diversity will insist with equal vigor, when faced with actual difference, that it is bad.

Sowell spells out a number of the factors making for difference among individuals, including intelligence, family literacy and discipline, birth order, age of population, and marital status. To illustrate the last point, he reports that, as late as twenty years ago, long before "gender equity" became a major legal issue, women who had never married and had worked continuously since high school were actually earning more than never-married continuously working men. Sowell's datum regarding earnings of single women suggests that career limitations experienced by women in the workplace are not the product of gender, per se, but of motherhood and marriage, in the context of which women have made hard choices that should be ascribed to their own agency. If Sowell is right, it would make no sense to allow the mere existence of statistical disparities in such areas as race and gender to prove discrimination.

It would be silly and ill-mannered to condemn women because, as Varian puts it, "Women value a well-rounded life, which includes work, love, friendship, and other interests."[49] There is no guide to ethical or practical living that requires aspiration to CEO status—for men any more than for women. Indeed, men might lead happier lives and we might be a healthier society if Kenneth Lay, Dennis Koslowski, and others tamped down their ambition, if fathers spent more time with their families and, particularly, with their children. Of course, wives will have to live with fewer resources for this condition to materialize.

But if Coca-Cola is looking for an executive today, it surely cannot afford to hire someone suffused with an "ethic of care," a person not inclined to obliterate Pepsi under a rallying cry of "*Pepsico delenda est*" (Pepsico must be destroyed). To be sure, there could be micro and macro advantages in a ladylike sharing of the marketplace, but such an arrangement is out of bounds on the playing fields of today's capitalism.

The setting is no different in law practice and law schools. To remain in their games, the top firms need attorneys who prefer slaughtering the competition to bonding with it, then taking the whole carcass to sharing it. Elite law schools, like other elite institutions, spare no effort in their unceasing and often quixotic quests to establish themselves as Number One, and making oneself the best almost inevitably requires seeing others as competitors, if not enemies. If things were otherwise, law schools would adopt the grade school practice of evaluating students on playing well with others. Accordingly, in intensely competitive situations, relational women will bail out.

Women's predisposition to being relational is, of course, only one of feminism's principal theories. But even accepting the teachings of the dominance school, that is, that women are relational only as a result of programing by a male culture, nothing changes for our purposes. Why a woman *on average* may be less ferocious than a man can be of only marginal interest to a law firm or a law school, which has little power to reformulate either her personality or its own competitive setting.

Gender theorists have not ignored the issue of choice. In challenging landmark cases such as *EEOC v. Sears, Roebuck & Co.*,[50] commentators have rightly observed that a company or industry culture can easily discourage women from considering choices that may be legally theirs. But with women making up such a large proportion of new faculty and associate deans, the argument that law school is an alien culture surely requires, again, more than a showing of certain disproportionalities. Unless, of course, we want to write the central liberal notion of choice right out of our social, political, and legal theories—and perhaps institute a decanal draft for women.

Production and Reproduction

Explanations for men's economic dominance that rely on social science data are vulnerable to a charge that women's choices have been limited by a hostile patriarchy. Some attention to biology is thus needed. While a vast, though often unsatisfying, literature on this subject exists, the job is made easier by our limited objective—to show that a number of theories advanced by women themselves *might* explain why women, on average, are not reaching statistical equality with men in their work lives.

We can begin with a theory put forth by America's most influential female psychoanalyst of the last century. Appalled by Freud's theory of penis envy and the influence it had, Karen Horney argued that it is not women who are envious of men, but, quite the contrary, men of women.

Working in the 1930s and 1940s, Horney tied this envy to the young boy who quickly learns that his mother has the capacity to reproduce the race, while his father does not. To offset this inadequacy—described as "womb-envy"—upon reaching adulthood, the boy throws himself into creative activities outside the sphere of reproduction.[51] His achievements, a not insubstantial literature suggests, become his babies, his legacies to the world. Camille Paglia takes this position to an extreme when announcing that if "civilization had been left in female hands, we would still be living in grass huts."[52]

Is motherhood envy so hard to imagine? Here is how Germaine Greer, one of modern feminism's mothers, describes motherhood:

> The experience of falling desperately in love with one's baby is by no means universal but it is an occupational hazard for any woman giving birth. Most of the women who find themselves engulfed in the emotional tumult of motherhood are astonished by the intensity of the bliss that invades them.[53]

Can a child fail to perceive her mother's bliss? If she does perceive it, will she not seek the same payoff for herself and make the same sacrifices as her mother? The question can be asked otherwise. Does Bill Gates experience bliss? How can being CEO of Microsoft compete with Greer's vision of motherhood?

Sexual selection offers another frame for viewing the male drive for achievement. We start here with the notion, supported by anthropologist Donald Symons, that "copulation is a female service."[54] Like any other service, it has to be paid for. Symons shows that gifts almost always pass to the woman, not from her. On what basis can a woman expect that the resources will continue to flow—*post coitum*? Psychologists have found that in all societies women place a far higher premium than men on good financial prospects of spouses.[55] To help assess these prospects, the woman looks at prior achievement in the same way that an investor looks at company history as a guide to its future revenue.

Males' achievements in the verbal arts have additional evolutionary force behind them. Researchers have looked into the question of why men "show off verbally" more than women. Because, suggests the well-known evolutionary social psychologist Geoffrey Miller, the woman wants to be dazzled by the males she consorts with. Similarly, the male knows that his reticence will only invite other men to step in with their own "public verbal displays" to take his place. The "ocean of male language that confronts modern women in bookstores, television, newspapers, classrooms, parliaments and businesses," Miller concludes, "must not be seen as part of a conspiracy to deny a voice to women" but, rather, as a development of evolutionary history, "in which the male motivation to talk was vital to their reproduction."[56] *Toxic Diversity* and other books, in this view, are not just informational; they also serve as seduction devices. If, at bottom, males are writing for sex, and women are not, is it any wonder women are not competitive *on average?*

Feminists, we have seen, have theories to explain the greater worldly success that males have enjoyed, theories that are grounded not in biology but in domestic production. For years they have argued that most highly successful men have stay-at-home spouses who allow the men to invest fully in their careers, and since few women have this spousal support, they either cannot rise as high or they must give up having children. The feminist objective in this domain is to show how unfair the world is for ambitious women, a position that cannot be quarreled with. Suffice it to say for our purposes here, however, that some of the very same data can be used to support the Horney theory that many women with children do not need the personal career success that childless women do.

Endocrinology and sociobiology supply additional frames for discussing women's relationship to worldly achievement. For Helen Fisher, testosterone and estrogen are likely implicated in the inability of women as a group to match the success of men in the corporate world.[57] Two male sociologists would seem to agree.[58] It is not altogether clear that the testosterone causes the dominance—rather than vice versa—but that hypothesis is being tested.

A central sociobiological tenet is that, unlike the female, the male can never be secure in parenthood, so his reproductive objective is to spread his seed as far and wide as possible. This might explain Midge Decter's famous observation about men's "undifferentiated lust," the desire to unite with the entire female population.[59] Bearing the burden of pregnancy, breastfeeding, and nurture generally, and being more limited in her reproductive capacities because of pregnancy, by contrast, the female must be more cautious, more protective of herself in her sexual dealings. Unlike men, who will extend their sexual orientation to the workplace, the woman has no experience in, to borrow Robin West's image, "*thrusting* herself into the world, thereby changing the world with a felt presence."[60] In so projecting himself onto life's stage, the man learns to take the consequences and to convince himself, as he must if he is to succeed, that acceptance is personal, while rejection is not. The female has no analogous essentialist experience to infuse her relationship with work. Her search is not for an exciting job but for a safe one.

"Merely to repeat this nonsense," says Neumann, "is to discredit it."[61] To which, two responses: First, maybe so, but much of it is women's nonsense. Second, the theories are hardly farfetched. If women scholars can derive women's "ethic of care" from childbirth and breastfeeding, is it absurd for a male scholar to infer a devil-may-care ethic and a competing drive for creation from the biology of men?

Work and Reward

What are the implications of this discussion for the feminist project? It depends on how that project is defined. For gender theorists, it would appear, feminists must not rest until there are as many female law firm partners as male partners, as many male secretaries as female secretaries. But is this realistic? If, for whatever reasons, women who are mothers work a standard work week while a substantial number of men put in 50 percent more hours on the job, and if work has to be rewarded in order to get done, then men will ordinarily be selected to be the managers—unless women work more efficiently than men. To test the point, readers should ask themselves if they had their life savings and economic futures tied up in a law firm, whether they would, all other things being equal, prefer a regular-timer or an overtimer to manage that investment.

As for equalizing the number of male legal secretaries, that goal will also remain elusive if it flies in the face of the male psychobiology. Under the circumstances, one wonders whether the real goal of contemporary feminism is that women should die unfulfilled and unhappy, if not crazed. (This is among the questions addressed by two intriguing books: Carolyn Graglia, *Domestic Tranquility: A Brief against Feminism,* and James Tooley, *The Miseducation of Women.*)

It should be clear by now that the foregoing issues require more illumination and less inflammation. We cannot "simply look at women's income and occupational attainment," says Professor Kingsley Browne, "without also considering what they get in return for the occupational trade-offs that they make."[62] And while it is wonderful to have opportunities drop in one's lap, to the extent that women also want equal success in the marketplace, they will simply have to openly and actively pursue them to maximize the chances of success.

If At First You Don't Succeed

A classic story, no less instructive for its grossness, highlights the point. Devoid of charm, Harry is standing on a street corner. As female prospects pass by, he addresses them: "Want a good time?" Witnessing the scene as one, two, three women shoot harsh glances at him as they walk brusquely past, a friend approaches Harry. "What's the point," he asks, "if you are so regularly rejected." "Oh, I get rejected a lot," Harry admits, "but I also get laid a lot."

Ignoring the intriguing possibility that Harry may have learned his lines from a prostitute, is Harry not on to something important? But if true equality does not mean that women should "measure [them]selves by male standards, on male terms,"[63] if fetishizing female authenticity, feminists bend their energies to reformulating the world in women's image, how will women get what they want in the competition with each other and with men, without modeling themselves on Harry? Identification with "masculine" traits "is a more powerful predictor of career success than parental expectations or maternal employment status."[64]

Happily, gender theorists do not need a white male, however well intentioned, to instruct on leading the professionally successful life. The woman, says Phyllis Chesler, "must be encouraged to put what she wants into words, to ask for it directly, not to wait for someone to guess what she wants."[65] A new self-help book for women starts out with the announcement "Women don't ask. They don't ask for raises and promotions and better job opportunities. They don't ask for more help at home."[66] A considerable literature tells women that they don't know how to ask a landlord for heat and a boyfriend for support[67] or, an older literature body of work suggests, for sexual satisfaction. A new study at Carnegie Mellon shows the extent of the price women pay in the workplace for their diffidence, an attitude the researchers tie to women's reluctance to upset delicate relationships. Women holders of master's degrees earned starting salaries that were $4,000 less than those of men. Why? Ninety-three percent of the women had accepted their initial salary level, whereas 57 percent of men had asked for more.[68] When women negotiated, by contrast, their salaries were comparable to those of men.

There are no guarantees, of course, in the asking and competing business. But if women do not ask and compete—which as a practical matter means selling themselves and bargaining—they will continue to earn thousands less for their services and to pay hundreds of dollars more for their cars.[69] And they will continue lashing out at men in frustration, a response that only serves to embitter them and everyone else.

What to do about the inevitable rejections, failures, and defeats? "If a woman does not get what she wants," Chesler continues, "she does not have to pout, blame herself, give up, disconnect, or become enraged."[70] Women must learn, as men do from sports activities, that "competing head-on for the gold is desirable; that if they lose one day, they won't die, it's not all over, they may very well win the next day; that falling down, getting bruised, getting dirty won't kill them," and that they can end up befriending their competitors.[71] Whether or not women eventually get what they want, there is an advantage in proceeding on this basis. "If women can interpret their failures as normal," says Virginia Varian, "and reinterpret rejections as par for the course, they might find work easier and more satisfying."[72]

A higher authority than the psychologist helps drive the critical point home: "Ask," Scripture announces, "and it shall be given you."[73] By asking, we place ourselves into a world of possibility. If the Woman Who Did Not Know How To Ask wants a deanship, she is simply going to have to learn to apply for one. Surely without such action on women's part, there can be neither a law school future for women nor an end to a legal literature bemoaning a "hostile gender climate." Nor, most important, will women find any joy in their lives and in their extraordinary achievements when they remain stuck at the stage of excoriating an allegedly brutish male professoriate for greeting them "at best with ambivalence" and then confining them under a glass ceiling, and lately to a glass house—from which, even if they are right, feminists should perhaps not be throwing stones.

9

Unwed Motherhood
and Apple Pie

It is time to stop demonizing single mothers or anyone else who
makes family where there was none before.   —Patricia Williams

If gender and race critics have a tendency to make molehills
into mountains—that is, to portray American institutions as insurmountable hurdles for women and minorities—do they conversely endeavor to deconstruct mountains into molehills? Are they treating the real
as unreal? Consider the following story.

Not long ago in a small city there lived a young unmarried woman
named Crystal Chambers, who worked as an arts and crafts teacher.[1] The
Omaha Girls Club, her employer, was an organization whose clientele
was 90 percent black, having as its goal to "help young girls reach their
full potential." Because "[t]eenage pregnancy often deprives young
women of educational, social and occupational opportunities, creating
serious problems for both the family and society," the club had a policy
of forcing out single staff members who became pregnant. The rule apparently did not extend to unmarried males who became fathers, but it is
not clear that any men were employed as teachers.

Time passed; Ms. Chambers became pregnant. Compelled to leave, she
sued the club, charging that its policy violated Title VII of the Civil Rights
Act because its impact would fall most heavily upon black women, whose
fertility rate was significantly higher than that of white women. She further claimed that the "role model rule" constituted per se sex discrimination banned by the Pregnancy Discrimination Act of 1978. The district
court rejected the claims, holding that the club "did not intentionally dis-

criminate against the plaintiff and that the policy is related to [its] central
purpose of fostering growth and maturity of young girls." In sum, the dis-
proportionate-effect argument was trumped by the "business necessity"
defense, a determination that was upheld on appeal.

The Road to Hell

While recognizing that the outcome in *Chambers* might be "born of sympathy for poor black youngsters and desperation about stemming 'the
epidemic' of teenage pregnancy that plagues them," Regina Austin has
condemned the decision, arguing that the club

> managed to replicate the very economic hardships and social biases that
> . . . made the role model rule necessary in the first place. [The opinion
> evinces] a theory of reproduction that can only be termed "primitive,"
> which posits that simply seeing an unmarried pregnant woman can have
> such a powerful impact on adolescent females that they will be moved to
> imitate her. . . . Surely the Club and the courts do not [really] believe that
> black teenage pregnancy is the product of social voyeurism or a female
> variant of "reckless eyeballing."

Why then did Chambers lose her job? "It is likely," Austin suggests,
"that the club sacked her in part because she resisted its effort to model
her in conformity with white and middle-class morality." Again, the
bugaboo of oppressive white cultural norms. A "black feminist jurisprudential analysis of *Chambers*," says Austin, "must seriously consider the
possibility that young, single, sexually active, fertile, and nurturing black
women are being viewed ominously because they have the temerity to attempt to break out of the rigid economic, social, and political categories
that a racist, sexist and class-stratified society would impose upon
them."

For Dorothy Roberts, Northwestern University law professor and reproductive rights expert, racism and sexism lurk in the depreciation of
single mothers. Single motherhood, she explains, "has deeper roots in the
lives of black women" and can be a "rare source of self-affirmation" for
the black teenager."[2] How can one be sure? The out-of-wedlock birth rate
is 68 percent for African Americans versus 22.5 percent for whites;[3] 92
percent of children born to black teens are nonmarital,[4] and the birth rate

for fifteen- to nineteen-year-old black girls is roughly 250 percent of that for whites (82 versus 32.5 per thousand).[5]

Race and gender critics draw only one conclusion: "We must . . . authenticate ourselves," insists Professor Joan Tarpley, and "parent without shame."[6] Discouraging black procreation, Roberts adds, is "a means of subordinating the entire race."[7] Says Patricia Williams: "It is time to stop demonizing unwed motherhood or anyone else who makes family where there was none before."[8]

"The war on illegitimacy," Williams explains, "is a way of drawing lines between children who are thought legitimate and children who are not. In terms of its civic consequences, it builds a barrier between . . . those who are all in the family and those who are deemed alien."[9] Even when unwed parenthood is discussed altogether aracially, the racial dimension rears its ugly head. During the 1992 presidential campaign, Vice President Dan Quayle leveled an attack on Murphy Brown, the fictional white newscaster on the eponymous television show, for having a non-marital child and thereby effectively legitimizing such practice. "The ingredient that so distinguished Quayle's remarks," says Williams, "was his bold equation of Ms. Brown's morals with those attributed to real women of color."[10]

Hearing this, some whites might be disconcerted, or even shocked. But they are likely to keep concerns to themselves. Arguments about black illegitimacy, suggests a *New York Times* columnist, are based on "insistent, if sometimes unconscious racism."[11] And white males have no standing to speak. "*What can the white man say to the black woman?*" asks the famed black novelist Alice Walker, when "[f]or four hundred years he ruled over the black woman's womb." "*What can the white man say to the black woman?*" after "lin[ing] up on Saturday nights, century after century, to make the black mother, who must sell her body to feed her children, go down on her knees to him." Only one thing, Walker answers herself: "I will cease trying to lead your children, for I can see I have never understood where I was going. I will agree to sit quietly for a century or so, and meditate on this."[12]

Notwithstanding the history lesson, white men have not been entirely silent. It is important to listen to their words. For Anthony Alfieri, University of Miami law professor and director of its Center for Ethics and Public Service, Austin "illustrates the continuing oppression of black women in employment as well as the diversity of black women's cultural practices in the areas of the family and reproductive freedom."[13] For Noel

Ignatiev, unwed mothers are loyal to their social group; they deliberately choose to "link their future and that of their child with the community they belong to . . . rather than to pursue the limited opportunities for upward mobility that exist. It is a decision not to rise out of the working class but with it—a display of the kind of solidarity essential to an oppressed class preparing to assert itself."[14]

Celebrating Diversity

The Chambers drama, Austin continues, takes place on a well-recognized historical stage. At bottom, she says, "unmarried black woman workers [*sic*] who have babies are being accused of carrying on like modern-day Jezebels when they should be acting like good revisionist Mammies. . . . When Crystal Chambers refused to subordinate her interest in motherhood to the supposed welfare of Club girls," Austin goes on, "she essentially rejected the Club's attempt to impose upon her the 'positive' stereotype of the black female as a repressed, self-sacrificing, nurturing woman whose heart extends to other people's children because she cannot (or should not) have kids of her own." If, as Austin holds, Chambers is a "Sapphire" for "having the temerity to break out of a . . . racist, classist" system, she is not a sucker in life's game, but a culture hero. By this logic, the Omaha Girls Club needs more, not fewer, of her, and, by extension, girls clubs should be hiring only young, single women who are visibly pregnant.

Not all young women who make families without husbands are, to be sure, like Chambers. Yet "all of them deserve a measure of freedom with regard to their sexuality that the dominant culture withholds. All of them have the potential of being guerrilla fighters." Intriguing. Premarital sex, once a sin whether or not procreation occurred, is now a virtue when it does. Every birth to a fifteen-year-old single black mother is a potential blow for racial justice and against black cultural annihilation. (The saucy oppositionist cannot help but wonder how a black law professor would react to a fifteen-year-old daughter's announcement that she was going out tonight to join the insurrection.)

And, finally, who should support these incipient Harriet Tubmans? "Economic resources," says Austin, "should be available to both black men and women who want to maintain families with children." Making no distinction between Social Security Survivor benefits and welfare,

Dorothy Roberts has bitterly attacked the motives of those who want to cut back on welfare.[15]

Austin and Roberts raise a number of questions, both broad and narrow. Suppose, for example, that the Girls Club had a rule prohibiting convicted rapists and murderers from working there because of the danger to the girls. If black males disproportionately commit such crimes (see chapter 11), so that the impact of the rule would fall most heavily on them, would such a policy also be illegal under Title VII? On another level, can black teenage pregnancy be celebrated for its protest value when 79 percent of teenage conception is apparently unintended?[16] Or do race critics need to invent the "inadvertent protest"?

The role modeling argument raises even more basic issues. If young people do not model themselves on others, what does it mean that Crystal Chambers is a culture *hero*? Defending affirmative action, a law professor suggests that the presence of minority faculty in more than token numbers provides "concrete role models for minority law students. They dispel the myth of preordained mediocrity for minorities . . . and challenge the idea of 'diversity' in law school admissions which is too often translated as the presence of interesting 'oddities' in the classroom."[17] But if these faculty members do not serve as role models, Austin subverts the case for affirmative action.

The role model argument has similarly come up in an important book by the renowned Harvard sociologist William Julius Wilson. He begins his book by pointing out that "most adults in many inner-city ghetto neighborhoods are not working in a given week" and that the consequences of this high joblessness rate are devastating, because children will model themselves on adults who are not working.[18] Would Austin dismiss an argument that ghetto children are harmed through absence of role models as founded on a "primitive" theory of "reckless eyeballing"? If not, is reckless eyeballing then just another trope to be trotted out for rhetorical advantage and otherwise quickly closeted?

Guerrillas in Our Midst

What if Chambers had been white? Though Austin does not explicitly address the issue, a "black feminist jurisprudential" defense of her behavior implies that a white teacher could legally have been terminated. But surely it is not healthy to keep expanding the notion of black exceptionalism, thereby undermining our notion of nation. More important, however manifold the blessings of multiculturalism, does any nation have an ethical obligation to feed guerrillas in its midst?

This brings us to the welfare issue, where race theorists face an interesting problem. We have heard Dorothy Roberts's argument that motherhood comes more naturally to teen black girls. The implication, spelled out clearly in other places, is that in getting pregnant, teens are not trying to abuse the welfare system. If that is the case, however, teen mothers are not guerrillas.

To avoid the inevitable attacks on unwed black teens, race and gender theorists make still another argument. Although welfare mothers are mostly unwed, they say, and notwithstanding the prevailing notion that the substantial majority of welfare recipients are black women, the majority of women on welfare are actually white. Implied is that cutting back on welfare benefits will thus affect whites more than blacks. The fact of the matter, however, is that in 1996, just before passage of the federal welfare act, of the families on welfare, 37 percent were black and 36 percent were white.[19] Race critics, furthermore, prove too much here. If welfare is not a racial problem because more whites benefit than blacks, how can trying to reduce teen pregnancy be racially motivated? Race critics solve the problem by asserting that welfare mothers are *perceived* to be black,[20] hence the political pressure on black welfare mothers. Thus, for race critics, welfare is a black problem only in the white imagination. Nothing, however, changes the underlying painful reality. Based on the ratio of black people to white people in America, black welfare recipients should represent less than one-fifth as many welfare recipients as white ones. There is no hiding the enormous race-based financial challenges posed by welfare recipients.

Madness and Method

Why, then, one wonders, are major civil rights organizations like the NAACP and Operation Push making no effort to discourage unwed parenthood in the black community? Why are Roberts and Williams working so hard to defend it and Austin to promote it? Clearly not for the pure pleasure of having more babies around to make goo-goo eyes at or to extract incremental Social Security contributions from. No, a black cultural defense of Crystal Chambers implies that critics are interested only in increasing the supply of black nonmarital babies. You don't have to be an antiwhite-conspiracy theorist to discern outlines of the game plan. For race critics, we are in a culture war—a war over the American lifestyle. Whose will prevail? More insurrectionist babies eventually means more power. If you can successfully promote black teen motherhood for "a century or so," and successfully *guilt-trip* white men to "sit quietly" for that time period, you will no longer be the subordinated minority. You win the war; the culture is yours.

Our questions thus far have been directed at the legal, financial, and political sides of the *Chambers* analysis. The psychological side will be addressed shortly. For now, however, consider that the Chambers story, while important in its own right, was part of another important drama. In 1990, when Derrick Bell was teaching at Harvard Law, Regina Austin, a visiting professor at the school, was being considered for a regular faculty position. Had she received an offer, she would have become the first tenured African American female on the Law School's faculty. Bell reports in his book *Confronting Authority* that he told the appropriate committee that she was having a "profound effect" on many of his students, and on him as well, conceding that before reading an article of hers he would have found it difficult to defend the position that Austin had taken. Now we understand why; the article in question was the very one under discussion here. And we also understand why Bell did not tell his readers anything about the specific program that Austin was promoting so it could similarly have a "profound effect" on us.

Hooray for Harvard

Playing a race *and* gender card, Bell told the Appointments Committee and confessed to the dean that while he once thought he could "both comprehend and represent the needs and interests of black women," Regina Austin's "presence and effectiveness" had shown such a notion to be "inexcusable presumptuousness" on his part. He urged the Appointments Committee to do "whatever was necessary to retain Austin" because her "views needed to be heard."[21]

Presumably unpersuaded of the great value of increasing the number of black nonmarital babies in America, the law school faculty and administration failed to offer Austin an appointment. When, in addition, the faculty recommended no other black woman for an appointment that year, Bell took a leave of absence. He subsequently tendered his resignation in a protest which attracted national attention.

None of Bell's Harvard colleagues has ever told the other side of this very hot tenure case. Why? Not, presumably, because Alan Dershowitz et al. are publicity shy. Rather, in a postmodern world where everyone defines truth in his or her own way, as a colleague quoting Gary Zukav puts it,

> The importance of nonsense hardly can be overstated. The more clearly we experience something as "nonsense," the more clearly we are experiencing the boundaries of our own self-imposed cognitive structures. "Nonsense" is that which does not fit into the prearranged patterns which we have superimposed on reality. There is no such thing as "nonsense" apart from the judgmental intellect which calls it that.[22]

Rejecting a black woman job candidate on the grounds that promoting black nonmarital children is demented could well be discriminatory in a legal environment that, following Zukav's logic, has abolished the category of nonsense. In this setting, a professor who publicly confessed repugnance to the candidate's views would be singularly inept. Such is the environment that our legal institutions have created.

Austin at least perceives the possibility that *Chambers* presents a larger issue, even if she, surprisingly, cannot imagine any damage done by her advocacy. "[D]esperation," "epidemic," "plagues"—the words she uses in recounting the Chambers story—are telling. The same cannot be said of Patricia Williams, for whom the schools are now filled only "with supposedly fatherless children," and for whom a teenager having children "makes biological sense, if not normative social sense."[23]

Devaluing "Family Values"

Writing about the issue of unwed motherhood, Williams suggests that the traditional family may not even be a desideratum. "'The family' is a complicated affair in America," she tells us. "One in three women and one in seven men have been molested by an adult before they reach the age of eighteen."[24] No evidence supports this fantastical assertion nor the implication that children are safer with daddy gone. In fact, we know what happens when "Uncle Charlie" moves in. Like male lions who regularly eat or kill the children of their mates sired by rivals, step-parents are one hundred times as likely to abuse children and eleven times as likely to kill them.[25]

For Williams, nevertheless, unwed parenthood is a decoy for social control. "There are enough children in the world already, black women are told—care to try some Norplant? . . . Yet this anxiety about population control," Williams complains, "does not extend to middle-class whites, who are encouraged to spend tens of thousands of dollars on artificial means of reproduction if necessary."[26] But Williams is being disingenuous here about the basis for the attempted intervention. The concern is not population control; nor is it race or class. It is family status. Which is the largest group seeking fertility treatments these days? Teenage singles? Or middle-aged, middle-class marrieds, black and white, at the end of their rope?

Williams's position on single parenthood is linked to views on another issue. She wonders why now, when there are so many black children of single parents around, the Horatio Alger myth is no longer in fashion. This myth,

> after all, was about captains of industry who came up the hard but noble way, the proud products of struggling widows, urban single mothers. And peaking in the 1930s there was a whole genre of Depression-inspired literature in which single mothers and their resolute sons plowed the fields and wrassled coyotes, milked their bone-dry cows with faith and patience. . . . Then a miracle would happen.[27]

But surely the reader can see—if Williams cannot—that here too racism is no part of the explanation. The Horatio Alger hero was the product of an initially intact home, not of a home that, for traditionalists, never was. In the Alger stories, it was the death or disability of a parent, the loss of a parental job that placed a crushing burden on the child. And in subscribing to the myth, society was telling him that, notwithstanding the trying circumstances, he could make it. As we shall see in a moment, the distinction is important.

To be sure, a revival of the myth would be helpful in many ways. Black children of single mothers need all the help they can get, and, because they are no more responsible for their predicament than is the Alger hero, they are entitled to it. But if someone is to breathe life back into the myth, it will not likely be Williams or any other race theorist. Harlon Dalton dislikes success stories of young, fatherless black males that involve guts, ambition, and independence: "my objection to the Alger myth," he says, "is that it serves to maintain the racial pecking order. It does so by mentally bypassing the role of race in American society."[28]

Striving for Failure

Black success obviously represents a failure of theory, living hope that maybe, just maybe, black youths can make it on their own, that maybe skin color is not the alpha and omega of human division or the ultimate determinant of all achievement. Blacks in Dalton's view must fail to succeed. The only dream Williams allows is one of a community in which "no child raised in this supposed 'man's world' should be without dozens of good men to look to for protection."[29] Of course, she is right. But why children who are of no interest to their fathers will be of interest to others, Williams does not say.

A new Alger-type myth for black boys, alas, cannot come from the majority community either. Why not? It carries too great a social risk. If a child born to a single parent is hero material merely by virtue of birth, as Austin suggests, then does not the glory reflect on the single parent him- or herself? But celebrating all "the young and teenaged single black parents over all the generations who have so heroically prevented black genocide in this republic," as black journalist Les Payne did in a Mother's Day tribute,[30] will serve to produce more single mothers. And that again raises the question of who will pay for them.

In a country as rich as ours, it is crass to address the issue of unwed parenthood only in financial terms. The Chambers matter thus needs to be evaluated at a deeper level. For this purpose, we need to find someone who actually studies family life and ask, What are the realities of single-parent families in a country with the highest rate of teen pregnancy in the Western world?[31]

First Comes Marriage . . . Then the Baby Carriage

There are a number of experts who can help us understand the implications of unwed parenthood. Here is what David Blankenhorn, perhaps the best known expert on family life today, says in his new book, *Father-*

less America, after informing readers that 40 percent of our children will go to bed in fatherless homes tonight and that never "before in this country have so many children grown up without knowing what it means to have a father":

> Fatherlessness is the most harmful demographic trend of this generation . . . the engine driving our most urgent social problems, from crime to adolescent pregnancy to child sexual abuse to domestic violence against women. . . .
>
> . . . in personal terms, the end result of this process, the final residue from what David Guttman calls the "deculturation" of paternity, is narcissism: a me-first egoism. . . . In a larger sense, the most significant result is our society's steady fragmentation into atomized individuals, isolated from one another and estranged from the aspirations and realities of common membership in a family, a community, a nation, bound by mutual commitment and shared memory.
>
> . . . the supreme test of any civilization is whether it can socialize men by teaching them to be fathers—creating a culture in which men acknowledge their paternity and willingly nurture their offspring.[32]

There are enough data supporting these observations to choke the information superhighway. According to Professors Sara McLanahan and Gary Sandefur, we may lead the world in the percentage of families headed by a single parent.[33] The authors go on to say that children who grow up with only one parent (almost always the mother) are approximately 2.5 times more likely to become teen mothers themselves, twice as likely to drop out of school, and almost 1.5 times more likely to be idle (out of school and out of work); that these outcomes are adjusted for race, sex, mother's education, father's education, number of siblings, and place of residence; and that all differences are statistically significant.

Doing What Comes Naturally

Is it more important to stay in school or to follow one's urges? "Schools must stop being holding pens to keep energetic young people off the job market and off the streets," Nobelist Toni Morrison says. "What is this business that you have to finish school at 18? . . . A body is a terrible thing to waste. . . . The body is ready to have babies, that's why [you] are in a passion to do it." As to the implications for prospective mother's career, not to worry: "when you want to be a brain surgeon, call me—I will take care of your baby."[34]

Morrison's generous invitation notwithstanding, the data say that when a teenage mother drops out of school to have a baby, her action has an impact not only on herself but also on her child, for a "mother's education is generally regarded as the single best predictor of a child's school achievement."[35] Children of single mothers who stay in school have lower grades and poorer attendance records then others with similar test scores for aptitude. Thus, it should not be surprising that a national study of 17,000 children aged seventeen and under found that "young people from single-parent families or step families were 2 to 3 times more likely to have had emotional or behavioral problems than those who had both of their biological parents present in the home."[36]

The significance of single parenthood per se on the child must not be overstated. The overall nonmarital birth rate in parts of Europe is higher than it is in America: 60 percent in Iceland, 50 percent in Sweden. But Europe does not have social problems on our scale; perhaps that is because the overriding "proportion of European nonmarital births is to two persons who are coresiding,"[37] while in the United States the rate is 50 percent. The important point is that in this country, for whatever reason, the out-of-wedlock children of our youngsters do not generally flourish. McLanahan and Sandefur point out that low income itself—including that brought about by divorce—accounts for half the single/dual parent gap and that nonmarriage is a cause of poverty, at least in the sense that it prevents parents from enjoying the economies of scale that would arise from sharing one household. Though unsure precisely of how these factors interact, the authors confidently, though sadly, conclude,

> Children who grow up in a household with only one biological parent are worse off, on average, than children who grow up in a household with both of their biological parents, regardless of the parents' race or educational background, regardless of whether the parents are married when the child is born, and regardless of whether the resident parent remarries.[38]

The authors explain why the integrity of the family is so important. For one thing, the absence of emotional and financial support undermines a child's trust in parents and increases uncertainty about the future.

"Having another parent around who cares about the child increases the likelihood that each parent will 'do the right thing,' even when otherwise inclined," they write. "[T]he two-parent family structure creates a system of checks and balances that both promotes parental responsibility and protects the child from parental neglect and, sometimes, abuse. This is an important function of social capital within the family."[39]

For another thing, the intact family is likely to make the child less vulnerable to peer pressure. A strong father can provide guidance; he can highlight in word and deed that working hard and getting a good education still pay off. His participation in the family is important to a girl's ability to form healthy relationships with men. As for his son's development, if the man treats his wife well, he provides a role model for the child in his future dealings with women. By contrast, if he shirks his responsibility to his family or, even more damaging, fails to acknowledge his child at all, the message a father gives his son is that it is easy and appropriate to do the same. Through her dating behavior, the single mother's influence on her daughter's relationships with men may be no less powerful.

Public policy analysts William Galston and Elaine Kamark have extended this work to crime. The relationship between family structure and crime is so strong, they have found, that "controlling for family configuration erases the relationship between race and crime and between low income and crime." This conclusion, the authors announce, "shows up time and again in the literature; poverty is far from the sole determinant of crime."[40] The data support them. Sixty percent of America's rapists come from fatherless homes, as do 72 percent of its adolescent murderers and 70 percent of its long-term prison population.[41]

Our discussion thus far has focused on fatherlessness generally. But if America indeed consists of two societies, as race theorists insist, specific attention must be given to the black community, *where only 20 percent of nonmarital births are to coresiding parents,*[42] where, in the lowest socioeconomic classes, a child born to a married couple can be a rare event, and where, overall, 44 percent of children are growing up in a household headed by a married couple, compared to 80 percent of white children.[43] What, then, are the psychological realities of black social life today? Limiting their focus to what whites are doing wrong, race theorists offer no vision of what blacks are doing to themselves. Orlando Patterson, however, can serve as a guide with his remarkably frank work "The Crisis of Gender Relations among African Americans."[44]

Wham Bam, Thank You, Ma'am

Insisting that in the black middle class there is not "the slightest trace of a distinctively African American 'ethnic family form,'" Patterson describes a destructive cycle of behavior resulting from black father flight (ibid., 75). It begins, Patterson suggests, because mothers, being "desperately overstressed" and "physically overburdened" in attempting to raise children alone and in poverty, cannot help but express their anger and panic in their relationships with their sons, who are the embodiment of the men who abandoned them (ibid., 67). It is the son who must then find release. As Patterson puts it, the "violence of the mother toward her son is displaced in the violence of the son toward women, which is then reproduced in the violence of these women toward the sons they begin to generate while they are still children themselves, under the powerful influence of their own mothers" (ibid., 67). In other words,

> in the ghetto the sexes are pitted against each other from an early age, and mistrust is built into the socialization process very early in a child's life [as a result of which there is] throughout the underclass today, the vicious desire to impregnate and abandon women, as if Black men were unable to shake off the one role of value (to the master) thrust upon them during slavery, that of breeders. (Ibid., 88)

Patterson reserves his greatest contempt for those who trust the black community to rally behind the children of single mothers. The prevailing dogma that "effective father substitutes exist in the network of support that poor Black women mobilize to raise their male children is pure Afrocentric myth," he says, "as is the twin dogma that father absence does not matter anyway" (ibid., 73). Chris Rock answers the proud black women who claim not to need men to keep their boys in line. "You could be the baddest mama on earth; [but] ain't nothin' more powerful to say than 'I'm gonna tell your daddy.'"[45]

Patterson works out the long-term consequences of these patterns for mother and child:

> Teenage childbearing is usually catastrophic for the life chances not only of the teenage mother, but for her own mother, who is further burdened just when she begins to look forward to relief from the trials of childrearing under poverty; [and] for younger siblings of the teenage mother,

who receive even less attention as their already burdened mother now takes on the role of grandmother.[46]

The children of teenage mothers, of course, pay the heaviest price, which Patterson catalogs: lower grades, risk of social impairment, behavioral disorders. "Worst of all," Patterson maintains, "the children of adolescent mothers are far more likely to become adolescent mothers themselves, thus perpetuating the pattern of poverty and destructive gender and parenting behavior. This may be the single most important cause of chronic poverty among Blacks" (ibid., 70).

Patterson's depictions of family life in the ghetto are sobering. One would think that gender and race theorists would urge state intervention in family life to ensure the well-being of black children. Far from it. For Dorothy Roberts, the black family suffers no crisis that requires intervention. For her, the fact that black children, who constitute less than one-fifth of the nation's children, make up one-half of the nation's foster care population proves that the foster care system is racist and bent on destroying the black family.[47] We are back to Sowell's observation about how deriving discrimination from statistical inequality is the reigning non sequitur of our time.

What if anything can be done about unwed parenthood? For Shelby Steele, responsibility for the problem lies in the welfare system which, while not providing for a luxurious lifestyle, has established

a powerful system of incentives and reinforcements in which people— particularly women—were literally paid for having children out of wedlock, for failing to finish school, for not developing job skills, for not marrying, and so on. It is not at all an exaggeration to say that welfare politics of the last thirty years . . . *created* the black underclass in America.[48]

Testing the claimed link between welfare, nonmarital children, and the truly disadvantaged is beyond the scope of this book. Suffice it to say that at least some political leaders have tried to alert their community to the problem of unwed parenthood. Indeed, for Martin Luther King, the time for action was long ago, long before the modern welfare age. Telling his black listeners in the late 1950s that "we have eight times more illegitimacy than white persons," a troubled King asked the black community to "work to improve these standards."[49] While the rate of white unwed parenthood has skyrocketed to the point that the black-white ratio is now 3:1 (68 percent versus 22.5 percent), the problem in the black community is far worse today than when Dr. King was with us.

"The obvious place to begin" the rehabilitation process, writes Hugh Price, former president of the Urban League, "is for individuals of child-bearing age not to bring children into this world until they are mature enough to love, nurture and provide for their offspring." The current situation, he continues, "undermines the viability of our community by creating households, often headed by a lone teen mother, which lack the education and earning power to escape poverty. Though there are heroic exceptions," he concludes, "this is profoundly unfair . . . because it severely handicaps the children from the outset."[50]

Perhaps only a black woman who has worked in the community has the credibility to challenge the message of black academic feminists. "My seven-plus years in public health only reinforced the view I first drew in Arkansas," says former surgeon general Joycelyn Elders, that "out-of-wedlock teen pregnancy is the key factor in perpetuating the cycle of poverty. This is especially true in the Black and Hispanic communities," she concludes, "but in the white community as well, where teenage pregnancy has also shot up wildly, with devastating social and economic results."[51]

This brings us back to the Omaha Girls Club. In dismissing Chambers, the club claimed it was trying to break the cycle of despair. Should it be condemned for imposing middle-class values? Should Crystal Chambers be revered as a black culture hero? Or is Regina Austin just "get[ting] truly hysterical" about this (see her own words, quoted on p. 57)?

Such questions are deeply troubling. Unlike nations such as China, America is not one to lightly brook interference—whether governmental or private—in procreation and its cultural environs. Efforts at control, such as those by the Girls Club, are especially disquieting if, as Patricia Williams has written, they "play dangerously against a social backdrop in which . . . white protectionism still demands black loyalty to white people and their lifestyle as a powerful symbolic precedent for deeming black social organization 'successful.'"[52] The field of black sociology reportedly functions to counter this cultural imperialism by demonstrating "that the Western European form of family organization is not necessarily superior to other types of family organization."[53]

Yet, for all the authenticity of contemporary black lifestyles, there are the problems identified above. Aggravating these problems is the ethic of cool which, say black scholars Richard Majors and Janet Billson, suppresses feelings that "might facilitate nurturant relationships" and thus helps explain "why so many black males father children they cannot support."[54] One has to wonder whether, without rejecting Chambers and "cool pose," and embracing a more traditional and, yes, middle-class family model, a black community can even exist, let alone thrive.

For those still troubled by issues of unwed parenthood and white cultural imperialism, chapter 10 examines in detail race-based performance in America's schools. It is not hard to imagine that black underperformance in this realm is devastating to race relations in our country. Lack of confidence about school can spread to other aspects of students' lives. Fear of low academic standards, of disruptive behavior in and out of class, and of rampant single parenthood itself will, perhaps understandably, promote black and white middle-class flight from schools with substantial minority populations, thus further undermining efforts at preserving academic standards and racial integration. Last—Alice Walker and her supporters notwithstanding—black girls brought up in single-parent households may find it all the harder to get off their knees to white, or even black, men on Saturday nights.

Contrary to the view of race and gender theorists, a white male who loves America would seem obliged to address the issue of unwed parenthood. On this theory anyhow, chapter 11 tries another tack to help resolve the unwed-parenthood issue. For obvious reasons, race theorists do not like to talk about crime. Perhaps you have to be from Bedford Stuyvesant, or at least far away from the ivory tower, to worry about such matters. At any rate, Crystal Chambers is no role model for Chris Rock. "It's real easy to tell whose kids are going to be f----d up," he tells audiences. "If the kid calls his grandma 'mommy' and his mama 'Pam,'" his destination is fixed; "he's goin' to jail."[55]

PART III

Black and Blue

The poisonous atmosphere surrounding any attempt to debate issues of race and ethnicity is demonstrated in . . . overheated
rhetoric [and] a fundamental disregard for truth, . . . which is beginning to creep into scholarly publications. . . . Lies out of whole
cloth are not uncommon and straw men dot the landscape.
                    —Thomas Sowell, quoted in Fein, *Race and Morality*

10

A Casino Society

[W]hat destiny awaits us if nearly 80 percent of our youngsters in
Denver fail the fourth-grade reading tests, as they did last year?

—Hugh Price

Two beggars are standing across from the university in pre–
World War II Berlin. The atmosphere is repressive, even hateful, though
not yet murderous. On one side of the street is a disheveled, beaten-down
old Jew huddling under a tattered coat and holding up a sign, "Help a
poor but proud and good Jew in distress." On the other side is a man in
his ancient, but neatly pressed, World War I uniform whose sign reads,
"Proud and loyal Son of the Fatherland fallen on hard times—please help
me get back on my feet." The Jew has little to show for his efforts, while
his counterpart is doing rather well. A distinguished and sympathetic professor stops to advise the Jew to disguise himself or to move to another
block. Uninterested, the Jew tries to shoo the professor away; the professor, however, refuses to leave, insisting that the Jew has no hope in that
competitive setting. After twenty minutes of hectoring, the Jew can bear
it no longer. Bidding the do-gooder to follow, he leads him across the
street to his competitor. "Abie," he announces, "this guy's trying to teach
us business."[1]

Weighing in with great conviction on two areas where America is the
envy of the world, and with no ostensible business experience, Lani
Guinier and Columbia Law School professor Susan Sturm are quick to
lecture our higher education and business institutions on how to do business—more precisely, on how to admit students and hire workers. The
problem they identify: standardized testing. Being "deeply problematic as
a predictor of actual job performance" and thus "underinclusive of those

185

who can actually do the job," standardized testing "does violence to fundamental principles of equity and 'functional merit' in its distribution of opportunities for admission to higher education, entry-level hiring, and job promotion." Its overall result is a "class-linked opportunity structure that credentializes a 'social oligarchy.'"[2] Sturm and Guinier would revolutionize contemporary "merit"-based admissions and hiring practice by replacing much of it—even hard-won affirmative action—with a lottery system.

The attack on testing is at center stage these days. Under pressure from Guinier, Sturm, and many like-minded critics, grade schools, high schools, and universities around the country are resisting the use of standardized tests. The vaunted SAT (Scholastic Assessment [formerly Aptitude] Test) is no longer required for admission at a number of colleges; the president of the University of California proposes to replace it with Scholastic Achievement Tests; the University of Texas now admits a significant part of its entering class based only on grades, a policy that frequently provides an advantage to the top student at weak schools over a higher-achieving but lower-ranking student at more competitive schools. In the wake of *Grutter v. Bollinger*,[3] which authorizes universities to use student diversity as an admissions criterion, tests will likely assume even less importance. No reader should be surprised at these developments. If existing standards are not neutral in the sense of yielding equality of results—if they are tailored to highlight the strengths of white males—they must be brought down.

You don't have to be a fan of standardized testing to be skeptical about the Sturm and Guinier proposal to achieve equality and, equally important, to end race consciousness in the process. The questions come fast: Is the lottery proposal another race theory smokescreen, designed in this case to obscure a wide interracial skill gap that must be eliminated if the battle for racial equality is to be truly won? Is it another mushy-headed, sentimentalist product which denies the value of discipline and self-control? If so, that would suggest that the campaign against testing in our public schools on a theory that it promotes "teaching to the test" is really founded on fear that test results would make schools and some children look bad. Is ignoring curable disparities not a short-term fix which will make it that much harder to close a performance gap?

Put differently, are current evaluation systems—including affirmative action—so fundamentally flawed that they should be replaced by a lottery? Should we disconnect input and outcome, work and achievement, and turn life into a giant crap game where no one is more than a throw of the dice away from success?

These are not trivial questions. America currently sits astride a global market. People in faraway lands are willing to do our work for one-tenth of the wages that we receive. If a lottery system precludes America's educational and economic institutions from operating efficiently, we will have little chance of maintaining our current standard of living and economic power.

Signifying and Significance

Dramatizing some of these issues for his readers, Yale Law professor Stephen Carter begins the discussion of the Sturm and Guinier proposal. He tells how when he first applied to Harvard Law School from Stanford University he was rejected.[4] Soon thereafter Harvard administrators started calling to advise him that they were reversing the decision because they had mistakenly thought that he was white. They warmly urged him to come to Harvard Law. Deeply hurt, Carter chose Yale instead.

Carter's hurt is palpable and understandable, given the university's insensitive behavior. But are any fundamental flaws revealed in Harvard Law's admissions policy? Since Carter concedes that even at Yale his admission might have been tied to his race, the problem was only that Harvard was guilty of making explicit that his "college record was too good for a black Stanford student, but not good enough for a white Harvard Law student," a message that—again, understandably—he was pained to hear (Owen, 51).

One way to avoid the problem is to abolish affirmative action. This Carter is not willing to do: "I got into law school because I am black," he says, "so what?" Another solution is for law schools to require that students identify themselves by race in bold print so that mistakes of the kind described do not happen. But that would underscore the conclusion that maybe Carter did not make it in a racially neutral competition.

Carter imagines a way out. He tells of the year when, as a member of the school's admissions committee and with time running out, he started "rating files at random: 2, 3, 4, 2, 3, 4" (ibid., 55). Without explicitly mentioning Guinier—and without conceding his own appalling behavior, given the importance he himself attaches to admissions policy—Carter refers to the Harvard professor who "suggested establishing a minimum cutoff for grades and LSAT scores, and then pulling out students at random. In that way, the student body would be exactly as diverse as the pool of qualified candidates. The idea never caught on," he suggests, "but it isn't obvious that it would be bad" (ibid.).

The lottery system is attractive because it can remove the stigma of inferiority. So why isn't Carter more enthusiastic? Two answers are suggested. First, a lottery might not be helpful at the great majority of America's educational institutions where the range of applicant credentials is far greater than that at Yale. Second, and more important, the luck of the draw would not guarantee admission at Yale or elsewhere to Carter, who needs to see himself *as* (and who is) a talent of the first order. For all the carrying on, once again, an "I hurt" story has no practical significance because there is no solution. This is not to attack Carter but only to observe that the distinguished Yale law professor is just venting.

Some race-based facts are necessary to lay the foundation for a proper evaluation of the lottery proposal. These data, which are not pretty, are inspired by James Baldwin's previously cited notion that "nothing can be changed until it is faced." As early as kindergarten, white students are already twice as likely to be in the top quarter of readers and one-half as likely to be in the bottom quarter,[5] a datum which sheds light on Hugh Price's plaint in the opening epigraph in this chapter.[6]

Test gaps continue into high school. The average black high school graduate has reading and math skills that are comparable to those of an eighth-grade white student.[7] White students earn SAT scores that are one hundred points higher in both math and verbal skills than those of black students,[8] gaps that for the most part persist even where family income and educational level of parents are equalized, gaps that indeed are increasing (albeit by minor amounts), not decreasing.[9] Under these circumstances, the cutoff point for measuring minimal competence would have to be drastically lowered to have any real impact.

Same Street, Different World

Dramatic white/black gaps appear not only in the aggregate but also within individual schools. Describing conditions reminiscent of those at Berkeley High, a recent and comprehensive study of one high school in Ohio may well illustrate what is going on at our elite schools. In one unspecified year, of roughly four hundred students who graduated from

Shaker High, half of whom were black and half white, late University of California–Berkeley professor John Ogbu reports that 78 percent, or 156, of the whites graduated with honors (GPAs of 3.0 or higher). In comparison, only 2.5 percent, or 5, of the blacks did so.[10] As if the news were not bad enough, for years 1992–95, black students made up 295 of the 325 graduates in the bottom 20 percent of their class.

Are these results tied to inadequate school funding, poorly trained or uncaring teachers, and tracking, the usual bogeymen for critics of our schools? Not according to Ogbu, who calls the Shaker Heights school system "one of the best in the nation" (ibid., xii), a conclusion that the black community reportedly shares (ibid., 219). The importance of a good education, Ogbu tells readers, is not hidden in the solidly middle- and upper-middle-class community that is home to numerous black academics, professionals, and corporate executives. This will destabilize another widely held notion, namely, that "the best predictor of educational achievements of children is the level of education attained by their parents."[11]

Nor, apparently, are Shaker Heights teachers grading black and white students differently (ibid., 131). As for tracking, black and white students often occupy different tracks based on teacher recommendations, but parents are clearly informed that they can place their kids at any level class they choose, including advanced classes (ibid., 92). In any event, there are few, if any, reports of teachers, black or white, objecting to the system in place. If the teachers, legislators, and administrators are not the problem for Ogbu, they are not the solution. As we shall see in a moment, black parents are.

The stark black/white high school performance differentials in America continue into college, where two-thirds of a letter gap between the grades of white and African American college graduates again suggests the futility of a lottery system without a radical reduction in acceptable standards.[12] On average, African American college students rank in the twenty-third percentile of their classes, the bottom quarter. And the problem is not only that, under affirmative action, poorly prepared black students are being admitted with lower SAT scores; there is also an appreciable grade difference across race within each SAT range. In fact, the highest black SAT scorers are "especially likely to underperform relative to white classmates with similar scores."[13]

Nor are grade disparities bridged among students who make it to law school. Indeed, a new study by UCLA law professor Richard Sander has found that they are greater. "In the vast majority of American law schools, median black GPAs at the end of the first year are between the 5th and 10th percentile of white GPAs"; the enormous disparity narrows slightly in the next two years, but only because the lowest performing black students drop out.[14] To deal with these disparities, law schools are, among other things, changing award structures for admission into their highly competitive and prestigious *Law Review* programs, which have traditionally been based on grades and demonstrated writing skills. To be sure, at Columbia Law, thirty-two students per year are still accepted in that manner. Seven students, or 18 percent of Columbia's *Law Review* population, are now admitted based on grades, writing, *and* diversity.[15]

Finally, performance gulfs continue on bar exams, Sander reports, citing a study showing that 88 percent of whites pass on their first tty, while only 61 percent of blacks do, which corresponds to a failure rate for blacks that is four times that of whites. In our two most populated states, New York and California, the pass rate for African Americans is less than half that for whites.[16] If we want to increase the number of black law professors, should we not be addressing this real problem instead of losing ourselves, like Derrick Bell, in nightmares such as the lost colony at Roanoke?

School and Work

The large gap in education and skills extends to the workplace as well, with equally destructive social implications. Skill differences as measured on the Air Force Qualifying Test, a recent study shows, explain what Orlando Patterson calls "nearly all of the wage gap" between blacks and whites.[17] The only "good news" in all this is Orlando Patterson's warning about despair. After what African Americans have been through, he writes, it is not surprising that they have not yet reached educational parity; what is needed now is patience. In the meantime, it would seem, we must be careful not to read racism into the lack of "willingness of employers, including African American entrepreneurs, to hire unqualified persons further burdened by poor soft skills."[18] But that, of course, is precisely what race critics continue to do.

America should be confronting the excruciating reality of race-based achievement at Shaker and elsewhere, instead of toying with a lottery system. And yet confrontation cannot happen if important racial news is not fit to print; the *New York Times* reviewer of Ogbu's book provided no detail on Ogbu's findings, referring to the problem, as did Ogbu himself, as the persistent "academic gap."[19] That characterization, the reader must agree, is misleading. At Shaker, at least, what separates students living in the same neighborhood is not a "gap" but a canyon, a feature which sheds light on white-black income gaps for graduates of the same school, arguments about the benefits to minorities of integrated schools, and claims of minority-group cognitive advantages (see chapter 2).

If the disparities were invisible, a lottery system that kept them under the radar screen might make *some* sense; it would eliminate the pain that such data might bring. But, in an environment bombarded with messages of racial identity, to imagine that students (whether honors students or not) are unaware of the disparities is absurd. Unless honors are distributed proportionately, a lottery system that did nothing to help blacks and whites to march across the school stage at graduation in equal glory would only perpetuate the complaints registered by several black Shaker Heights students that whites did not think highly of blacks. In the face of the data, what are white students—and for that matter, black students—supposed to think?

Nor will affirmative action, that magic pill for many, eliminate the grade canyon or its psychological effects. Paraphrasing the testimony of a prominent law school dean about the importance of diversity for majority students, the Supreme Court wrote "that when a critical mass of underrepresented students is present, stereotypes are weakened because nonminority students learn that there is no 'minority viewpoint,' but rather a variety of viewpoints among minority students."[20] But even a supporter of affirmative action has to admit that diversity is a problem as well as a solution. A good reason for thinking that there was a minority viewpoint is that identity-obsessed race critics have fetishized blackness in cultural terms. More important, at law schools as at Shaker, there is at least one stereotype that diversity aggravates, not eliminates—that black students are not as good.

The implications for anyone concerned with the well-being of his country are not obscure. Hendrik Hertzberg, who has served as an editor of the *New Yorker* and the *New Republic,* has written that he has never met an unbiased black man who would disagree with the proposition "If you're black, you have to be twice as good to travel the same socioeconomic distance as a white person in this country—twice as talented, twice as ambitious, twice as determined."[21] How much socioeconomic distance will black students traverse if they are only half as good?

Here are some of Ogbu's recommendations for the black community: parents need to participate in their children's education at school and supervise their work at home;[22] students must be urged to stop modeling themselves on successful black athletes and entertainers, to stop worrying about what their peers think, and to pay more attention to their studies, as white students are doing (ibid., 277, 17–20); black parents and school-children need to develop trust in the school system and to understand that while collective action was the basis for the civil rights revolution, the emphasis must now be placed at the level of the individual and the family (ibid., 275); the entire black community must concern itself with whether children are developing practical skills in school rather than worry about such things as whether children are learning to "act white" and are thereby losing their racial identities (ibid., 279, 285–86).

Whether or not Ogbu was a self-hating black man, he has company. A large-scale study of mathematics education in black communities backs him up; holding that African American students must "begin to associate the learning of mathematics not with being a 'nerd' or with attempts to 'act White,'" Professor Danny Martin places the onus not only on teachers but also on parents and especially on the black community.[23]

Ogbu's and Martin's, to be sure, are not the last words on the subject. Harvard senior research fellow Ronald Ferguson argues that blacks and whites are not socioeconomic equals in Shaker Heights because half of black students live with one parent. That, however, subverts the argument in the last chapter that single-parenthood is innocuous. Ferguson also found that black high achievers are disparaged in their communities for "acting white" *only* "because the low achievers suspect the high achievers believe they are superior." Likewise, Ferguson adds, when black students spend class time socializing or home time watching television, "they are not purposely avoiding academic success."[24]

Assuming Ferguson is right, that does not take black parents off the hook when: five times as many black as white twelfth-graders watched television five hours or more per day; black students are considerably less likely than whites to complete homework; suspension and expulsion rates are far higher for black than for white children; according to an important study, white parents provide appreciably more cognitive and emotional support than do black parents; and in San Francisco, at least, two-thirds of black high school students were absent for eighteen or more days compared to one-third of white students.[25] If the key to solving these problems is not in the hands of black parents, are we not left without alternative hypotheses to hateful biological explanations for difference? There can be no progress on that basis.

Whether Ferguson or Ogbu is closer to the mark, there is a payoff to these discussions that goes far beyond narrowing racial gaps, crucial as that is. If racial disparities, at Shaker and elsewhere, often stem from something other than bad faith on the part of this generation of whites, Ogbu has made a major contribution to America's racial climate.

Testing the Test Critic

The existence of large race-based disparities in school and in the workplace on reputed tests of ability, of course, does not necessarily mean that the attack on testing is misguided or that a lottery system cannot be productive. It may be, for example, that testing alienates black students. A look at such a critique of measurement follows. We then return to the more global charges leveled by Sturm and Guinier.

Consider Stanford professor of psychology Claude Steele (brother of Shelby Steele), whose work is widely cited but poorly understood. Studying black-white test gaps, Steele has found a phenomenon he labels "stereotype threat," according to which African Americans tend to freeze when taking standardized tests that purport to measure intellectual ability, because they know that they are stereotyped as less academically prepared than whites.[26]

The freezing manifests itself, according to Steele, when, while knowing the answers, black students invest too much time on each question and thereby become inefficient exam-takers. The gap narrows, and may disappear, Steele claims, when African American students are told that they are not in intellectual competition with whites. If Steele is right, the SAT and related score gaps are illusory and America desperately needs measurement tools which can show the true level of academic preparation of all its students. Steele's theory has attracted much attention because it solves the wrenching problem under examination.[27] But attractiveness is the very heart of a good trap, so the theory needs testing.

Steele describes what happens under the immense pressure of a stereotype threat brought on and reinforced by a white society that has long denigrated black academic talent. Minorities come to "disidentify" with school so as to reduce or even eliminate the threat. This would explain why black students' grades do not match those of whites; it would also suggest, however, that the grade gap reflects a knowledge gap which would undoubtedly show up on *reliable* tests of basic skills, a seemingly important point that Steele does not make. If the problem is freezing, moreover, the solution should be simple. Black students need to be taught how to calm down and answer questions in an efficient manner.

A good coach would try to turn the stereotype into a source of motivation. Only a few years after the Civil War, and shut out from the white world by a "vast veil," W. E. B. Du Bois found that the "sky was bluest when I could beat my mates at examination time."[28] More than a hundred years later, the best that Steele can do is to inform his students that the exam is racially fair and not designed to show them in a poor light. To get minority students into the proper frame of mind, he further tells them that they "have to learn from people who part of yourself tells you are difficult to trust."[29] Not surprisingly, Steele says nothing about his own untrustworthiness. He has, after all, assured students that they were not in intellectual competition with whites, when comparing white and minority performance was precisely the purpose of his experiment.

Steele's comments are born of his research at Stanford and the University of Michigan. If Ogbu found stereotype threat, however, he does not report it in his extensive study of the Shaker Heights school system. For all Steele's fame, moreover, the findings of his laboratory studies have not been followed up "in applied settings, such as admissions tests for higher education and employment testing."[30] The weak support for stereotype threat as an explanation for disparate performance on exams, of course, does not necessarily mean that black students do *not* disidentify with school. What is clear is that in attacking American culture as destructive to minorities, race theory is designed to undermine any level of trust minorities might develop in the educational system and therefore any level of confidence that they can succeed therein.

This brings us back to lottery proponents Sturm and Guinier and their broad-based attack on testing. Ducking the issue of equality of skills, the two critics blame liberals because, when it became apparent that minorities were not getting a proportionate share of the benefits American society offers, they should have attacked the problem head-on by subjecting the measuring rods themselves to scrutiny. Instead, liberals essentially confirmed the validity of testing by supporting affirmative action, which, rather than "challeng[ing] the overall operation of a conventional and static selection process[,] creates exceptions to that process . . . that play into existing racial stereotypes, predictably generating backlash. By implicitly legitimizing a selection process that operates in the name of merit, affirmative action programs reinforce that backlash," Sturm and Guinier explain, with white workers focusing their wrath and blame on the workers perceived as beneficiaries of affirmative action.[31]

It's Not What You Know

Would better tests of performance alleviate the problem of allocating rewards in accordance with test scores? Sturm and Guinier's answer would, at first, seem to be yes: "functional merit is a legitimate consideration in distributing jobs and educational opportunities" (ibid., 968). And yet, their final answer is really no. "We are not suggesting that the solution is to develop a new, less biased, equally universal test that more accurately predicts future performance," they write (ibid., 1003). Rather, they are "challenging the idea of prediction" (ibid., 1003). Why? Because tests do not measure "discipline, emotional intelligence, drive to succeed, and reliability" (ibid., 976)—by all accounts, vital ingredients for success. Tests measure, instead, "qualities such as willingness to guess, conformity and docility" (ibid., 977). Predicting job success, Sturm and Guinier suggest, is especially difficult, because job success correlates positively with additional features of personality that are likewise hard to measure—"empathy, cooperation, persuasion and the ability to build consensus among people" (ibid., 1036 and n. 94).

How might an educational or business institution solve the problems of school admissions and of hiring? To help us understand the kind of creativity required today, Sturm and Guinier walk us through the circumstances prevailing at Lowell High School in San Francisco, the academically prestigious alma mater of U.S. Supreme Court justice Stephen Breyer. In the wake of an ethnically charged dispute over admission, an astonishing 1993 consent decree (no longer in effect) limited the representation of any of the various ethnic groups—Asians, blacks, Latinos, whites—to 40 percent of the school population. The racial balance of the city would be kept by requiring Chinese Americans to score 66 out of 69 points for admission, while most whites and non-Chinese Asians would need only 59, and blacks and Latinos could qualify with 56.

A lottery system, Sturm and Guinier say, could allow anyone scoring over 56, the level established for *minimal* competence, to compete for admission in a random selection. In this way, the current racially imbalanced "winner-take-all" strategy would be avoided. Exactly how a lottery would provide information on maturity, empathy, or even consensus-building ability, Sturm and Guinier do not say.

For Harvard and UCLA professors Christopher Jencks and Meredith Phillips, the attack on the SAT is a distraction: "if racial equality is America's goal, reducing the black-white test score gap would probably do more to promote this goal than any other strategy that commands broad political support. Reducing the test-gap score," these affirmative action supporters explain, "is probably both necessary and sufficient for substantially reducing racial inequality in educational attainment and earnings [and probably differences] in crime, health, and family structure."[32]

But black scholars do not make it easy when they "start with the premise that blacks are as smart as whites, so if blacks are flunking[,] there must be something wrong with the test."[33] Whites, moreover, have been complicit in sabotaging this effort, according to Claude's twin brother, Shelby. "Wherever black representation is an issue," he explains, "excellence is cast as an adversary of fairness," a position which "keeps blacks (and other minorities) down by tolerating weakness at every juncture where strength is expected of others." Seeking relief—but not real redemption—from racial shame, Shelby Steele suggests, liberals "stand [only] for an engineered racial equality but not for the principles of merit, excellence, hard work, delayed gratification, individual achievement, personal responsibility and so on." He illustrates this point by citing lawsuits filed by teachers' unions in California "claiming that minority teachers are discriminated against by teacher competency examinations pitched at a mere tenth-grade level."[34] This problem can only be resolved if, as John McWhorter holds, the black community faces the problem directly and remedies the undervaluation of academic performance.[35]

An insight into the problem of reducing performance differentials, Orlando Patterson says, is to be found in the culture of the black home and, in particular, in the sophistication of the caretaker parent. Again urging patience upon Americans in these matters, and particularly relying on recent research on mixed marriages, which found that children of white women score on average ten points higher on aptitude tests than do children of black women, Patterson concludes that principal-caretaking white women in many of these cases are giving the children the benefits of their better education.[36] As educational levels increase for African Americans, one can hope, the problem will remedy itself.

If Jencks, Phillips, Shelby Steele, McWhorter, Ogbu, and Patterson are right, it is not testing that needs to be eliminated but racial disparities, and, distracting Americans from what they have to do, the lottery proposal is malignant. Sturm and Guinier's race-based challenge to testing, then, needs a comprehensive and careful examination. To facilitate such an assessment, the subject of testing in higher education is discussed first. The discussion then shifts to the business environment.

Arguing with Success

Cheryl Hopwood applied for admission to the University of Texas Law School in 1992.[37] Her Law School Admissions Test (LSAT) score and undergraduate grade point average (UGPA) gave her an admissions score that would have virtually guaranteed admission to a black or Hispanic candidate, but not to a white one. When Hopwood and three other applicants were rejected in favor of a number of minority students with lower admissions scores, they sued the State of Texas, claiming illegal discrimination. In their own terms, Sturm and Guinier see this as a prototype case in academia. Student A scores higher than student B on an entrance test and develops a sense of entitlement. When an institution does not recognize the priority of her claim, feeling put upon, she seeks redress. But, say Sturm and Guinier, A's response is wrong.

Sturm and Guinier register three basic problems with what they call "sameness-is-fairness" in the testing area. First, merit is increasingly judged on the "criterion of performance—the ability to . . . perform well on tests that are designed to assess general intelligence or inherent ability." But success on tests like these depends largely on educational achievement, and "blacks' educational opportunities had been severely limited" as a result of stereotyping. Indeed, African Americans have been specifically targeted by the SAT: the "single criterion of performance [measured] was exactly the area in which blacks had been made most vulnerable, factually, legally, and mythologically."[38]

A second objection to contemporary "testocracy" is that test performance correlates too strongly with family income. Sturm and Guinier's third and strongest objection is that the SAT does not successfully predict academic performance of students, as evidenced by a correlation between the SAT and first-year college grades ranging only from .32 to .36. This level is only slightly above .3, which Sturm and Guinier suggest is generally considered useful. They argue, moreover, that the SAT score is consistently less predictive of first-year grades than is high school grade point average (HSGPA), that high school class rank is an even better indicator than HSGPA, and that the SAT only marginally enhances predictability when added to HSGPA or rank.

Racing to Judgment

Evaluating the Sturm and Guinier claim that standardized testing in use today not only has the effect of putting black kids in a bad light but also is actually designed to do so requires some historical perspective. How did the SAT and LSAT acquire their power in educational circles? To answer these questions we must go back some seventy-five years (long before the first LSAT), to a time when distribution of benefits and higher education admissions favored those with wealth and family background, a system that would have been especially disadvantageous to minorities. It was to undo the privileges of aristocracy, to make merit the touchstone for admissions, that, after World War II, universities turned in large numbers to the SAT.[39] Was this goal the huge mistake that Sturm and Guinier suggest? Not, it would seem, to black culture critic Gerald Early. The bourgeois culture which gave rise to it, he says,

> is perhaps one of most stunning products of the Enlightenment, indeed, of all of human history. It has apotheosized merit, the measure of human effort and ambition, of ability and discipline, as a way of distributing society's goods, privileges and prestige, a way that is far more advanced, despite its obvious flaws, than any previous way we humans have gone about our business of living together.[40]

This suggests that the charge against testing is just more understandable frustration camouflaged as science. Who can deny that whites often have greater educational opportunities than do minorities[41] and that this disparity leads to differentials in test scores? The degree to which the difference is the direct or indirect consequence of racism can be debated. But the bottom line—the existence of a differential in educational achievement—is the same. This painful reality, however, is a dubious basis for abolishing standards. "The fact that some do not have the same chance to develop excellence is *not* an argument against excellence," insists Shelby Steele. "*In fact a fair standard of excellence is what both clarifies their problem and points to its solution.*"[42] As Sturm and Guinier concede, an institution can validly require applicants to perform, and, given their better preparation, whites will in general perform better than blacks. To the extent that racism is the underlying cause of the problem, traditional affirmative action is not an unreasonable response. In order to go further and limit the use of tests across-the-board, while adopting a lottery system, one has to suppose that test scores do not matter, an issue to be taken up again shortly.

Buying Success

As for the implications of the income advantage of whites, a recent study implies that the income/SAT correlation may cover up relationships that are far more important than income, such as family structure and educational background.[43] At the very least, the study suggests, it is important to think carefully about how the income edge might translate into an advantage on the SAT. Is income the cause of the SAT gap because whites can give their children benefits that minorities cannot, for example, travel to other countries, after-school programs, and test preparation? The problem with this theory is that, as Sturm and Guinier demonstrate—and other evidence strongly supports[44]—minorities perform much worse on the SAT than whites in the same income class. Is the problem that white students from high-income families go to better schools than minorities with the same family income? Sturm and Guinier do not say. In any event, that is obviously not true of students at Shaker High.

Part of the problem in assessing whether income gives children of wealthy parents an unfair SAT edge is that the acquired skills of high-income earners are likely to correlate with higher academic performance in their children. Every parent has a different mix of assets to give his or her offspring, a phenomenon alluded to in the mixed-race-couple discussion earlier. These may include reading, test-taking, budgeting time, writing, mathematics, or setting high standards. While there may be an argument for controlling the amount of money passing between generations, only the most repressive society will consider prohibiting parents from sharing their wisdom, skills, and even connections with their children. Just as

Kirk Douglas's children had a better chance of having a career in the movies than my own, my children will have a better chance of becoming academics. We could, at least theoretically, go some of the way in redressing these imbalances, possibly by precluding our offspring from careers in academia and film, but any realistic alternative to unfettered transmission is likely to fall far short of a cure and to be undesirable for another reason. For again, if one concedes that performance is a valid criterion for determining society's rewards, the fact that minority children may not reach the same educational levels as whites because of lesser parental resources—financial or otherwise—is not in itself an argument for a lottery system. As Shelby Steele insists, it is not oppressive to require individuals to work harder to achieve goals for which they have no built-in advantage.

Accepting the idea that those with the greatest skills should be rewarded, we turn to the issue of predictability. Careful evaluation has revealed that overall SAT/first-year-course-grade correlations have risen to .64 and, under some circumstances, to .75; this is far above the .3 level admitted by Sturm and Guinier to be significant.[45] The SAT now does a better job of predicting grades than does the HSGPA[46] and an even better job yet of predicting black performance. Indeed, according to a recent study, "the SAT increment in correlation over HSGPA for this group (for whom the predictive effectiveness of HSGPA was very low) was by far the largest among all ethnic groups."[47] In sum, the case that the SAT is unfair to African Americans fails the grade.

Which brings us to the LSAT, the exam that Cheryl Hopwood took. In challenging its validity, Sturm and Guinier point to the .24 correlation between LSAT scores and first-year law school GPAs of white students. Predicting minority-student performance at the University of Texas Law School, Sturm and Guinier claim, is perhaps more problematic.

Richard Sander, however, shows the fallacy of such reasoning when he says that the "individual-level correlation between smoking and longevity is only .2"; yet we strongly discourage smoking.[48] As Sturm and Guinier themselves concede, moreover, since Texas and Penn are highly selective institutions—meaning that students come from a narrow band of test-takers—a *restriction of range* problem is raised. Sturm and Guinier, however, refuse to make the appropriate adjustments that the restriction of range diagnosis requires.[49] The low correlations in Texas and Pennsylvania are, therefore, not surprising.

More significant, general data, which Sturm and Guinier ignore, undermine their argument about test invalidity. According to one important study of 167 American law schools, the average correlation between first-year law school grades and LSAT score is about .49. Though the study reports a great deal of variability in coefficients among law schools, it concludes that a "substantial amount" of this variability "is directly attributable to the amount of variation in LSAT scores and UGPAs in the data used to estimate the validity,"[50] that is, the restriction of range problem again. In his recent study, Richard Sander found correlations ranging from .45 to .65. He concludes that "indices based on the LSAT and undergraduate grades can be shown to be far more effective in predicting law school performance . . . than any other factor that has been systematically tested."[51]

Perhaps most important here, Sturm and Guinier's charges about the LSAT's predictive value for minority law school performance are groundless. A study some years ago could not speak more decisively to the point: "The validity data do not support the concern that the LSAT score or the traditional combination of LSAT score and undergraduate grade-point average are less valid for any of the minority groups than they are for the white group." (Sander did not examine this question.) As for the relative value of the LSAT and UGPA in predicting academic success for minority and white students, the results are even more damaging to Sturm and Guinier's claim. The study shows that, as a predictor, UGPA alone "seems to be significantly less valid for black students than for white students."[52] In sum, if there is a case that tests are not useful in helping to predict future academic success—of whites or minorities—Sturm and Guinier have not made it.

Cheryl Hopwood Meets Brian Gilhooly

Brian Gilhooly was a young firefighter in the City of Chicago when, with an associate's degree in fire science in hand, he applied for promotion to lieutenant. Months of study for the exam helped him emerge 175th out of 2,059 test-takers, but when scores were adjusted for race, Gilhooly, who is white, dropped to 217th and was out of contention for promotion. For Sturm and Guinier, Gilhooly's is the stock workplace story, equating as it does merit with scores on a standardized test.

But, Sturm and Guinier insist, there are a number of problems here, just as in the case of academic prediction. First, "testers have failed to develop meaningful measures of . . . worker productivity or even . . . pay."[53] Part of the problem is that tests are of a linguistic or logical-mathematical variety, and this kind of "one-size-fits-all" approach will invariably ignore attributes crucial to the job, such as adaptability and creativity. Moreover, tests do not, and by implication cannot, measure such crucial values as "honesty, courage and ability to manage anger" (ibid., 977). Even supplementing objective tests with subjective supervisor evaluations docs not solve the problem, because such evaluations "are notoriously unreliable measures [that] have been shown to be biased in ways that correlate with race and gender" (ibid., 970).

Second, test score differences frequently emerge from one-shot measures, like the SAT, that are both unreliable and statistically insignificant.[54] Third, tests are predicated on the notion that "we can predict what the job will require in the future based on how it has operated in the past," while, in reality, work takes place "in a rapidly changing, unstable, and increasingly complex marketplace."[55] Thus, tests tend to freeze modes of production, thereby excluding those who bring no less effective, but different, approaches to the job. This problem can be resolved only by recognizing that minorities lead lives that are different from those of the majority, on account of the different traditions they start with, voluntary or coercive.

Fourth, testing undermines our democracy:

> Access to work and education is rapidly becoming a fundamental attribute of citizenship at the turn of the century. Work provides an identity that is valued by others. . . . [It] organizes and shapes a citizen's sense of self. . . . [It] legitimates. Virtually every aspect of citizenship [and financial well-being] is channeled through participation in the workplace . . . [e.g.,] medical care, pensions, social insurance. . . . In these ways, work has become a proxy for citizenship. (Ibid., 1031)

If one-size-fits-all standardized tests are of limited utility in predicting performance, on what basis can employers decide whom to hire? Sturm and Guinier are explicit:

> Actual performance often correlates best with on-the-job training. Those people who do well learn their job on the job. Often those people who

have been given an opportunity to *do* a job perform because they have been given an opportunity to *learn* the job. It is the opportunity to learn a job, a craft, or a skill that often predicts successful on-the-job performance. This phenomenon tracks the way many experts "learn" their expertise. Experts become skilled as a result of the opportunity to develop their expertise by tackling actual problems.[56]

What, practically, does this mean? Sturm and Guinier tell of Bernice and the large company which was looking to promote one of its staff members to general counsel. Given an opportunity to perform on a trial basis over a nine-month period, Bernice got the job. Faced with problems, even crises, she was able to turn them to advantage through collaborative (i.e., relational) decision-making. Now comes the giant leap of logic. But "unless we are prepared to move to a lottery system, we cannot fairly and democratically avoid individual assessment that takes into account functionally [ir]relevant differences and [fails to provide] individuals the opportunity to demonstrate, in context, what they are capable of doing" (ibid., 1035).

The Fire Next Time

With their emphasis on a jobs sweepstakes, do Sturm and Guinier care about fighting fires? In the real world, individuals are rarely hired on the strength of tests without also undergoing a rigorous interview, which will likely include a review of the candidate's record as well as an evaluation of such character traits as ambition, creativity, team-playing, and emotional intelligence. Going to fire school, moreover, can send important signals to employers that may otherwise go unrecognized. "Those who attend college may *not* acquire skills that will necessarily make them a more valuable employee," says law professor Michael Selmi, "but the decision to go to college reveals characteristics such as determination and future-orientation that play an important role in one's productivity."[57] Selmi's observation also helps highlight the central contradiction in the Sturm and Guinier game plan. Even conceding that tests may be of little or no use because they do not measure such qualities as creativity, determination, and future-orientation, how the lottery can do a better job is not clear.

As for the reliability of one-shot tests, a good response would seem simple: candidates should be allowed to repeat employment tests, if they do not do well. In any case, relying on grades over a substantial period of time solves the one-shot test problem.

Regarding the importance given to minor differences in test scores, the validity question, let us consider a marathon race won by a hair's breadth. There is, it would seem, natural discomfort in knowing that a small disparity in performance creates an enormous disparity in honor and riches, and there is a natural inclination to want to narrow the gap through regulation. If only one race is to be run, it might conceivably make sense to act on this impulse. But if races are regularly scheduled, the case for such regulation is substantially vitiated. The competition for success in school and in the workplace seems not unlike the regularly scheduled races just described. With tenacity, imagination, and some skill, there are opportunities for success in the many races in which we compete all along the line.

Additional flaws in the lottery system should be apparent. Life's important decisions must frequently be hard ones. Take the decision to go to law school. Not all students who enroll in law school do so out of a single-minded commitment to the law. Law school, according to John Grisham, is a "great American babysitter for directionless postgrads."[58] Some of us, then, may have been seriously tempted by medical or business school, or a career on the stage. The precipitating factor was, perhaps, no more weighty than that the law school was down the block. And yet, however the decision to go to law school is made, it is not made randomly. Indeed, it is almost inconceivable that, of the over one hundred thousand students now in law school, a single student is currently enrolled on the basis of the functional equivalent of a lottery—a toss of a coin.

Little Things Mean a Lot

Minor differences, moreover, may not be trivial. "[I]f an employer has no other information than test scores, and no other objective than maximizing its productivity," says Selmi, "then, in the long-run, the employer would likely obtain some gains by selecting individuals in rank order."[59] Such a strategy would seem especially useful in a competitive economy like ours. In planning for the long run, then, the employer must seek every advantage. For want of a nail the entire enterprise may be lost.

Sturm and Guinier's contempt for the little things would seem bizarre, given that our jurisprudence gives them great significance. Fifty-five miles per hour may be a reasonable speed and entail no risk to the driver. If she travels faster by one epsilon, she risks losing a personal injury case and plunging into penury. Indeed, there may be no viable alternative to a somewhat arbitrary bright-line rule in this case. A law professor who denies the relevance of all small differences, as Sturm and Guinier do, has a very large project indeed on her hands.

Next, if the world is "rapidly changing, unstable, and increasingly complex," and we therefore need more creative and efficient thinking, having a multiplicity of approaches on the table can certainly help.[60] An even better solution, however, might be to force potential employees to take more, not fewer, tests, in particular, IQ tests, and to overturn the landmark *Griggs v. Duke Power Co.*[61] This case held that the employer could not require employees working as unskilled plant laborers either to have a high school diploma or to score at or above the median level of high school graduates on an IQ test, where such standards had racially disparate effects. Why overturn *Griggs*? Among other things, the IQ test measures what psychologists call "*g*," arguably "the single most powerful predictor of job success" because, at least for the many psychologists who study it, it signifies "higher trainability."[62] In fact, requiring SAT scores of job candidates as a measure of trainability is precisely what many firms are starting to do.[63] Says Bill Gates on a related subject: "It's all about IQ. You win with IQ."[64] What better approach to an environment proclaimed to be so protean? Who speaks more authoritatively on success in business, Sturm and Guinier or Bill Gates?

For Sturm and Guinier, "diversity is an independent value in generating creative solutions to problems."[65] But diversity, unlike book writing, is not a skill; difference, as race theorists argue, may not imply deficiency, but it does not, in and of itself, necessarily imply efficiency either. Evolutionary biology can offer a useful insight here. Mutations are differences. But most of them are maladaptive.

Even when a difference is adaptive, diversity other than the racial kind is available to employers. So it is important to think carefully about what precisely racial diversity might mean, in connection with a specific job, say, in microbiology. A black microbiologist may be more interested than others in AIDS research because the black community is disproportionately affected by the disease. But surely nothing in the black experience makes a black microbiologist more valuable than a white one and, therefore, compensates for what might be even a marginal disadvantage in scientific knowledge, all other things being equal. If there is, indeed, a black microbiological—and for that matter sociological—approach, it has to be spelled out.

But now let us assume the existence of a black microbiological approach and an open position on a professional research team. What happens if we do not allow an institutional need to be satisfied by a direct appointment of the highest-scoring black candidate, or even the best overall black candidate? Surely a lottery will be far less effective than traditional affirmative action in solving an individual employer's problem of achieving the benefits of a diverse perspective.

Whether or not there is a minority microbiology and sociology, or a minority microbiological and sociological *method,* or whether being a minority is itself a skill, minorities, like everyone else, have to learn something in order to achieve success.

Which brings us to perhaps the heart of this matter. Succeeding in school, as Gilhooly presumably did, shows more than determination; it shows the ability to learn. What better evidence is there that a prospective employee will be able to adjust to rapidly changing circumstances?

Appeals to democratic principles, finally, are just cant. America owes jobs to no groups. Even if our Constitution could be construed otherwise because of slavery and its legacy, the lottery proposal would likely fail because it is not "narrowly tailored" to achieve the requisite result. In the latter case, again, affirmative action may be another story. But Sturm and Guinier reject it.

The Fortune Cookie's Message

It should be clear that, in an economic world which rewards learning, a lottery system announces openly, unmistakably, and destructively, "You need not be the best, only good enough; making the extra effort may well be a waste of time." What a message to be sending to our children in the name of equality.

If job testing is jettisoned, furthermore, employees will have no objective basis for showing what they know. This may work at cross-purposes with the needs of minorities. If, because of racism, minorities are evaluated less favorably than whites for the same skills, the absence of objective measurement will give those in power greater opportunity to apply their judgments destructively. This is undoubtedly why Gerald Early celebrates the philosophy behind testing.

We come, ineluctably, to the problem that Sturm and Guinier share with the German academic who counseled the Jewish beggar: business is not their specialty. It seems fair to say that only academics could write a book seeking to revolutionize admission and hiring strategies while making only passing reference to cost. That reference is to a very rough estimate by Harvard psychologist Howard Gardner that moving to a performance-based assessment of students "might increase costs by 10 to 15 percent but probably not more."[66] But what about performance-based evaluation in the workplace? As for the employment setting, Jencks acknowledges that cost is far from a negligible problem. "The economic benefits of getting the best possible workers," he writes, "will not always exceed the cost of hiring, training and firing a lot of the less capable workers." He draws out the inevitable implications: "When the costs of hiring mistakes are high, employers may find that it pays to rely on test scores, even if doing so excludes more competent blacks than competent whites."[67]

If anything, Jencks understates the cost problem. These days, a job notice for an assistant professorship in English or history can attract hundreds of applications. "[I]f the opportunity to participate . . . offers the best evidence of capacity to perform," should these applicants be brought in and given what would effectively be adjunctships to see how they perform in the classroom?[68] Selmi himself says no: "It is simply not possible, in all but the most unusual circumstances, to hire all of the applicants on a trial basis."[69] Or, should a lottery be used to weed out applicants? Sturm and Guinier do not say.

Nor can the showcase Bernice illustration extricate the Sturm and Guinier proposal from that difficulty. The absence of outsiders suggests that they were not welcome to apply. But if this is the case, under the theory that lots of folks could do the job, the firm has just hurt itself by eliminating innumerable qualified applicants. We might also note that the civil rights movement has for many years (rightly) insisted that an important way to break up the old boys' network is to post job opportunities so that outsiders have a chance. It is inconceivable that Sturm and Guinier would want to reverse that strategy. And yet, if they did not reverse it, we would be back to our example of the advertised vacancy in the English or history department.

Talk is cheap, so perhaps the best way of thinking about the viability —and perhaps even the sincerity—of Sturm and Guinier's proposals is to ask, Do Guinier and Sturm do their own hiring, say, for research assistants through a lottery system? Would they use a lottery system to hire faculty at their schools?

The Best or the Luckiest

Whatever we imagine their responses to this last query, one thing is fairly sure. Rightly or wrongly, Harvard thought that Guinier was the best. What is not clear is Guinier's thinking about whether thousands, indeed, tens of thousands of others around the country could successfully have stood in for current faculty and students at Harvard, if only a lottery system or a giant apprenticeship program had given them a chance. To establish her good faith in this regard, perhaps she should announce publicly that she, her students, and no doubt her colleagues are nothing special—not only in an academic law review article, which the people who really count do not read, but in the *New York Times* and the *Wall Street Journal* and in a reprint of *Harvard Magazine*. And she should do her best to persuade her colleagues and students to do likewise. The 99.9 percent of Americans who have yet to be certified as Harvard material could then witness the fallout with some *Schadenfreude*.

How, in the end, should we understand Sturm and Guinier? We would seem to be back to Senator Mitchell's comment about our never-ending drive for respect (see chapter 2) and the likelihood that the lottery project is linked to the long list of scholarly gyrations identified here that were designed by race theorists to distract minorities from the pain of disrespect. But again, by not facing the "canyon," we cannot bridge it.

What is to be done to refocus the attention of minorities away from perpetuation of problems and toward solutions? Getting parents involved in their children's education, as Ogbu proposes, is a start. A recent pronouncement by the prominent educator Diane Ravitch shows what they and others can do to help. Concerned about the consistently dismal performance of American students in international evaluations, she rejects the temptation to, as Shelby Steele puts it, "demonize the very principles—rigorous intellectual effort, skill mastery, grade and test performance—by which those who compete . . . are strengthened."[70] Rather, she insists, our "[s]tudents need to know that their work in school will count in the world of work." To help put this idea into action, Ravitch suggests, "[e]mployers should insist on high school transcripts at hiring [which] should provide clear information about grades, courses taken, attendance."[71] Ravitch's emphasis on this point makes it very hard to ignore the anti-education strain in Sturm and Guinier's work.

In evaluating the lottery proposal we should keep in mind that bashing education is hardly uncommon among radical thinkers. Since cultures tend to perpetuate themselves through education, insurrectionists must, of necessity, attack education. According to Mao, "The more books you read the more stupid you become." Mao spoke even more precisely on the subject of book knowledge when justifying the cadre of "barefoot doctors" he unleashed on the country more than thirty years ago. "It is not so important to have so much formal training," he explained. Doctors "should mainly learn and raise their standard in practice."[72] These musings on the value of reading metamorphosed into the foundation of Maoist educational policy.

Who can doubt that it is more important to push white and black Brian Gilhoolys into the study of fire science—which we know now from the hardest experience is not a game—rather than to assuage potential damage to their self-esteem by making mediocrity the standard of the day? Can anyone in this fast-moving Information Age fail to see the absurdity of devaluing information—to say nothing of drive and imagination—through a lottery system? And yet race theorists continue a bias against education as we know it today when they suggest, as we have seen, that knowledge and epistemology are indissolubly tied to political power; that educational standards are created by white men to further their own interests and are therefore invalid; that the bar exam in particular is unfair to minorities because they do not do as well.

Mocked by many as an Uncle Tom, Booker T. Washington suggested a solution to the race problem a century ago that, although dated in its details, offers more insight and hope than anything offered by race critics:

When a Negro girl learns to cook, to wash dishes, to sew, to write a book, or a Negro boy learns to groom horses, or to grow sweet potatoes, or to produce butter, or to build a house, or to be able to practise medicine as well as or better than someone else, they will be rewarded regardless of race or colour. . . . No man who continues to add something to the material, intellectual, and moral well-being of the place in which he lives is long left without proper reward. This is a great human law which cannot be permanently nullified.[73]

While understating the problem of racism, Washington surely described a necessary condition for the well-being of the society in which we live. Almost one hundred years later, Shelby Steele, who is hardly a testocrat, develops the implications. Is anyone listening? "There is no full equality for any group," he writes, "that is not educationally and economically competitive." African Americans must "internalize a devotion to academic and economic excellence," he insists, "that *is not contingent on any assistance that we might or might not get from the larger society.* I do not believe that minorities will ever have true respect for a reform," he concludes, "that does not demand as much or more from them as from others."[74] If Washington and Shelby Steele are right, even if designed for the noble purpose of eliminating the stigma that affirmative action produces, Sturm and Guinier's proposal foreshadows disaster.

The Song of the Black Canary

An image evoked by Guinier highlights this destructive power of race theory in Steele's terms. Honored as the University of Kentucky Blazer Lecturer in February 1997, Guinier began her address by announcing that minorities and women were the miner's canaries of our society, a trope she reinforces through the title of her recent book, *The Miner's Canary: Enlisting Race, Resisting Power, Transforming Democracy.*[75] Just as the canary, with its fragile respiratory system, alerts miners to the dangers of asphyxiation and explosion, so the delicate condition of women and minorities testifies to the state of social well-being of the nation. Pondering the question of whether the canary should be fortified in some way against the rigors of the mine, Guinier concludes that, no, "it is not the canary that needs to be fixed; it is the . . . social environment."[76]

Let us pursue this canary metaphor promoted by Guinier—and further spread by a score of race and gender critics—for what it reveals about contemporary race and gender thinking. Operating entirely on instinct, the canary does not think; it reacts. The canary is beautiful. It sings. It is different. Indeed, it is perfect the way it is, notwithstanding that it cannot produce, even with the greatest amount of training. Above all, it performs its most useful service when caged.

Could we realistically expect more hope-inducing imagery from the desperate game of chance Sturm and Guinier market under the seductive subtitle "Reclaiming the Innovative Ideal"? Shelby Steele suggests that we run for the hills when we hear such appeals to our creativity. He summarizes his experience in four Great Society programs: "Our mission was simply to be 'innovative,' but this only meant rejecting the traditional ways of doing things, whether that way made sense or not."[77] Rather than addressing the problem at hand, an "innovative" thinker blithely throws the baby out with the bathwater.

With black academic leadership all too reluctant to change its thinking, the canary has evolved in a few short years into a potent symbol. But if we marry Guinier's lottery proposal with her canary imagery, establishing our own Cultural Revolution with the canary as its official bird, then we deliver a message that warms the hearts of hardened racists: that blacks in America today should not aspire to serious work, that their function is but to entertain and to die.

11

Crime Stories

> No data demonstrates either a general or a circumstantial correlation between race and crime.   —Professor Deborah Ramirez et al.

Notwithstanding traditionalists' arguments that storytellers forfeit their credibility because their tales are born of unvalidated and un-replicated experience, readers of this book cannot now dispute that there are certain aspects of human existence that are best captured and communicated in the form of stories and, as a result, have an educational value not to be found in a score of scholarly works by "neutral" social scientists.

White male academics do not tell their share of stories. They "do not employ the narrative, storytelling style," explains Dean Alex Johnson, "because to do so would result in their talking about their dominance and that is currently not socially acceptable discourse."[1] If white men are not well-practiced storytellers, for this or other reasons, are their (our) stories worth telling? Yes, insists Richard Delgado, who calls on everyone to pour out their stories in his "Legal Storytelling: Storytelling for Oppositionists and Others: A Plea for Narrative."[2] Here, in response to Delgado's plea, is a personal and intimate narrative that sets the stage for our discussion of crime.

It was 9:30 on a warm and clear September evening almost ten years ago, a perfect time for a walk. After a long day at work—and a morning jog of three and a half miles—I felt entitled to a treat. Most enticing following a heavy fish dinner, which left a strong aftertaste, was a ninety-nine-cent sale on Dove Bars at Cumberland Farms, the local equivalent of the 7-Eleven.

On my walk back home I noticed that my car was parked on the street. Since it was illegal to leave it there overnight, I decided to put it in the driveway straight away rather than drag myself out later to do it. I was heading for the car, maybe forty feet away, when in the shadows I made out the silhouette of a man walking in my direction. At first I ignored him. But as I crossed the street, I could see that he had changed direction and was walking straight at me. I noted something else as well. He had pulled the hood of his sweatshirt down over his head so that most of his face was covered. I could tell, however, from his movement that he was young. Part of me wanted to change direction or even run, since if I turned my back to him and fumbled with the keys at the car door, I would have no chance. At the same time, I felt committed to continuing my course, for any evasive action I took would be evidence that, without precise knowledge of his intentions, I feared the man, that I was assuming the worst about him. I kept walking toward the car.

As I pulled out the car keys, he was in my face. In an instant, he demanded my wallet and pulled up his sweatshirt to show a gun in his belt. I might have taken him—I was bigger than he—but I could not be sure I would win the fight and I had a wife and two children at home. I gave up forty dollars along with some identification and credit cards and became my mugger's lunch.

As he turned to leave, my heart started pounding. I had been ripped off, played for a sucker. When he was about thirty feet away I could no longer control myself. "YOU SON OF A B————! I'M GONNA GET YOU!" I shrieked and started after him as he started to run. I did not want to catch him, of course, but I knew he was not going to take the time to turn around and shoot at me either. And if he did, I could have ducked behind some cars. I had been violated, and, if life was fair, terror had to be requited with terror. Neighbors started looking out their windows or coming out to the street to offer consolation. Soon it was all over—or so it seemed.

The police came and took down the usual information. They asked whether I could identify the mugger, and I told them it would not be easy. They asked if I was all right, and, though visibly shaking, I said yes. They offered little hope of recovery or of what I desperately sought: justice.

Sleep did not come easily for weeks thereafter. Having terrorized my terrorizer, I wondered whether my mugger would come back for revenge, this time shooting first. I thought of my vulnerability and that of my family if he was found and I had to press charges; he knew where I lived. At the same time, I fully understood that I had not been raped, slashed, or shot, as tens of thousands are each year; I could not even imagine the hor-

214 | Crime Stories

ror they go through. Unlike them, I could howl at the absurdity of an un-armed fifty-year-old chasing a twenty-year-old carrying a gun.

I have not been able to shake the memory of my mugging in the eight years since it happened. Mostly, I have wondered about my emotional in-telligence, especially because, about a year earlier, after attending a late-night movie with a friend, I had experienced a virtual preview of the later incident. We had come out of the theater, and, except for the two of us, the wide street was deserted. All of a sudden, as I was walking toward my car, I saw a young man heading toward me. Here too I did nothing to pro-tect myself. My friend, however, less concerned with the proprieties than I, jumped into her car and flashed her brights on us to divert my would-be assailant as he brushed past me.

A Memory That Keeps on Giving

The incident comes back to me frequently at night in all kinds of ways. Six years ago, I found myself walking down the street at 1:00 a.m. when I saw my mugger twenty feet ahead waiting for me to pass. This time I would not be fool enough to play his game; I stopped. Summoning all my force, I let out a scream—"HELP!" The next thing I knew my wife was shaking me, telling me to shut up and go back to sleep. More about both the incident and my mugger a little later on. For now, a few observations: First, if I do say so myself, unlike the mewlings of race and gender theo-rists over experiences such as Patricia Williams's at the five-and-dime, *this* is a story. Second, Alex Johnson's theory about white male storytelling may be just another critical race theory that has to be respectfully junked. This story was told not to highlight a white male's dominance but, quite the contrary, a white male's vulnerability. Third, stories like this usefully remind us that even minor crime can leave deep wounds.

The Gift of Fear

Incidents like the one just described, which crime data suggest take place fifteen hundred times a day and make America among the most violent countries in the industrial world, sap the sense of personal and national well-being and raise the questions addressed in this chapter: How can we avoid victimization? Who is doing what to whom? Is crime something to worry about? Is fear by whites of black crime reasonable? If so, is it nevertheless racist? What of black fear of white crime? To what extent do and should individuals and law enforcement officials take into account racial disproportionalities in rates of offending? Is black crime to be treated as a political response to racism? What can be done to bring down the crime rate and undercut white fear of black crime?

Individuals are not powerless in crime settings, says Gavin De Becker, security expert and best-selling author of *The Gift of Fear*: "your survival instinct is a gift from nature" which must be cultivated, for it "knows a lot more about your safety" than a potential victimizer. If the would-be victimizer questions your response, De Becker concludes, "tell him that nature does not require his approval."[3] De Becker recounts dozens of stories in which individuals became victims by failing to heed their inner voices.

Intuition, however, must be disciplined. This requires stepping outside oneself and developing good information. Potential criminals must be identified. Who are they? The truth, as we shall see in greater detail in a moment, is that the incidence of victimization by blacks is far greater than that by whites and that whites make up a not insignificant share of the victims. And yet ignorance and disingenuousness pervade discussions of race and crime. In his magisterial *Race, Racism, and American Law,* which devotes more than a hundred pages to criminal law, Derrick Bell fails to raise the issue of whether blacks impose more on the justice system than vice versa.[4] Professor Deborah Ramirez announces that "[n]o data demonstrates either a general or a circumstantial correlation between race and crime."[5] "Lecturing on race and racism all over the country," says bell hooks, "I am always amazed when I hear white folks speak about their fear of black people."[6]

Was hooks listening to the "first black president"? Here is what William Jefferson Clinton had to say on the subject:

[B]lacks must understand and acknowledge the roots of white fear in America. There is a legitimate fear of violence that is too prevalent in our urban areas and often, by experience or [by] what people see on the news at night, violence for those white people too often has a black face. It isn't racist for a parent to pull his child close when walking through a high crime neighborhood. Or, to wish to stay away from neighborhoods where innocent children can be shot in school or standing at bus stops.[7]

Think Nationally, Act Locally

If Clinton had continued speaking bluntly, he might have added that in 1999 African Americans were seven times more likely to commit homicide than whites.[8] Blacks were responsible for 46.5 percent of robberies, whites for 42.4 percent,[9] though blacks represent only 13 percent of the population. Fear, of course, will be less a function of national than of local data. People live locally, where the disproportions and the resultant fear is often much greater. In 1998, for example, "blacks in New York City were thirteen times more likely than whites to commit a violent assault, according to victim reports."[10]

Do men of color also disproportionately commit crimes against women? "[C]ontrary to the popular lie," insists Mari Matsuda, "they do not."[11] The fact is, however, that the rape rate for male African American perpetrators is five times higher than for whites.[12] Disproportionate offending may be the highest price paid by African Americans for abandoning the traditional family and for having perhaps the highest rate of teen pregnancy in the industrialized world. And crime may well be another area where diversity ought not to be celebrated.

A frank discussion on what impact crime disparities should have on race relations and on law enforcement would seem to be needed. But Americans, Professor Paul Butler laments, "seem reluctant to have an open conversation about the relationship between race and crime."[13] If Abigail and Stephan Thernstrom are right, however, that "[n]o issue so poisons relations between the races as that of black crime,"[14] and if Carol Swain is right that an "honest and open dialogue about crime . . . is one of our most pressing current needs,"[15] a devotee to public service must force the discussion.

There are, of course, two principal sides to the discussion—causes and effects. If most of the rest of this chapter deals with the effects of black crime, and not its causes, it is not because the causes are unimportant. It is rather because these effects have received less honest attention and also because they can actually help explain some of the causes. Some, but by no means all; an equally comprehensive and forthright assessment of the causes of crime is also sorely needed.

What, You Worry?

"Crime, shrime," say race critics. Even if black men disproportionately offend, the danger, in the scheme of things, is small. Speaking on the subject of racial profiling, Georgetown University law professor David Cole likes to point out that in any given year "98% of African-Americans are not arrested for any crime."[16] But what to make of a datum like this when it is not the general population of black people who are committing crimes but young black males? In this class that generates fear, the relevant percentage number may not be an insignificant 2 percent, but may be 10 percent or more, a point that Cole would seem to support by reporting that one out of three black men in their twenties is under criminal justice supervision at any one time.

Holding that the fear of crime is wholly disproportionate to the actual danger, an editorial writer has pointed out that in New Orleans the odds of being killed in a traffic accident are three times higher than those of being killed by a black male.[17] But how much consolation does this provide? Is the fact that the vast majority of drivers drive safely sufficient reason for letting down our guards when entering our cars? In fact, we take precautions: we drive at reasonable speeds; we do not drink and drive; we wear seatbelts. Should we act less defensively with respect to crime? A few years back, University of Pennsylvania sociologist John DiIulio reported that we are twice as likely to be victimized by violent crime, he tells us, as to be injured in a car accident.[18]

According to a well-known black criminal justice authority, Americans need to focus their attention not only on crime statistics between groups but also on those within them. If they did this, they would quickly learn that while blacks represent a disproportionately high percentage of those arrested for violent crimes, "only 7.7 percent of black arrests are for violent crimes."[19] In other words, while African Americans are robbing and killing at rates far greater than those of whites, other Americans can take comfort from the fact that blacks are committing so many lesser offenses that crimes of violence make up a small proportion of total black lawbreaking.

Another commentator holds that race is too undefined a category to provide useful crime data;[20] whether it is too undefined for affirmative action he does not say. Frank Wu reports that blacks are arrested for 62 percent of robberies (a datum which is no longer current) but concludes that there is only a "superficial sense" in which "African Americans are slightly more likely to break the law."[21] Would 99 percent, one wonders, also be superficial? Still another writer discounts the validity of crime-victim studies with a claim that three-quarters of sexual assaults and one-third of robberies go unreported,[22] but he fails to consider the likelihood that underreporting is even greater in minority communities, where the population is more fearful and the police are less trusted.

Attempting to deflect the legal and ethical spotlight from black offenders in yet another way, a black law professor, the late Dwight Greene, invited readers to focus on Newark, New Jersey, a largely black city, during the decade of the 1980s. Conceding that Newark experienced the highest per capita car-theft rate in the nation at that time, Greene nevertheless argued that the public's fear of carjacking and joyriding was wildly disproportionate to the danger because the media treated joyriding as though it were as serious a matter as car theft and carjacking, thereby hiding the fact that it "only rarely results in physical harm to people."[23] The media, Greene charged, flashed images before us that created a sense of urgency, as these crimes were portrayed as "epidemic" and exaggerated the racial element in order to instill fear in the public.

We come back to Chris Rock's trope, "It's not us; it's the media"; that is, the media are to blame for stirring up fear of crime. But, according to what is perhaps the most systematic study of fear of crime, Americans are "fairly realistic in digesting the mountains of information regarding victimization and interpreting their risk." Although some argue that fear of crime is greater than crime itself, the study continues, "the findings of the present investigation boldly reach the opposite conclusion. . . . Fear of crime is not the problem; crime is."[24]

Nor, as we have seen, are the media guilty of exaggerating the *racial* dimensions of crime. The data are overwhelming. According to one study, only 5 percent of perpetrators of aggressive acts on crime shows are black, and only 17 percent on reality-based programs.[25] According to another, whites commit 90 percent of fictional murders but only 40 percent of the real ones on televsion.[26] A Los Angeles study of news programs shows that blacks are overrepresented as homicide victims, not as perpetrators.[27] Newspaper editors, again, bend over backward to hide the racial identities of black criminals.[28]

As for the charge against the media's treatment of the subject of joyriding, a Philip Roth depiction of early-1980s Newark should prove helpful:

A car coming the wrong way on a one-way street and they ram me. Four kids drooping out the windows. Two of them get out, laughing, joking, pointing a gun at my head. I hand them the keys and one of them takes off in my car. . . . They ram cop cars in broad daylight. Front-end collisions. To explode the airbags. Doughnuting . . . This is what they steal cars for. Top speed they slam on the brakes, yank the emergency brake, twist the steering wheel, and the car starts spinning. Wheeling the car at tremendous speeds. Killing pedestrians means nothing to them. Killing themselves means nothing to them. . . . They killed a woman right in front of my place, same week as the car was stolen. Doing a doughnut. I witnessed this. I was leaving for the day. Tremendous speed. The car groaning. Ungodly screeching. It was terrifying. It made my blood run cold. Just driving her own car out of 2nd St., and this woman, a young black woman, gets it. Mother of three kids. Two days later it's one of my own employees. A black guy. But they don't care, black, white doesn't matter to them. They'll kill anyone. Fellow named Clark Tyler, my shipping guy—all he's doing is pulling out of our lot to go home. Twelve hours of surgery, four months in a hospital. Permanent disability. Head injuries, internal injuries, broken pelvis, broken shoulder, fractured spine . . . The car thief is twelve years old.[29]

Although Roth is explicit about the race of the victims, he is silent about the race of the perpetrators.

Chris Rock administers the *coup de grâce* to media bashers: "Ted Koppel never took anything from me. Ni————s have. Do you think I've got three guns in my house because the media's outside my door trying to bust in? . . . Oh s——t. It's Mike Wallace. Run!"[30]

The few race theorists who have chosen to speak on black criminality are, by contrast, breathtakingly mealy-mouthed: Regina Austin acknowledges only that "blacks are supposedly overrepresented among lawbreakers."[31] A black colleague writes of the "perception" that blacks commit more crimes than whites.[32] And the ordinarily exacting Glenn Loury refers only to the "purported" criminality of the black population.[33]

What is to be made of the refusal of talented and ambitious race critics to get to the heart of an issue that poisons race relations? There would seem to be no greater service that they could perform than to prove that whites need not fear black crime. And if there is a problem, should it not be faced and dealt with? Jesse Jackson's tortured and oft-quoted confession in 1993 will be the last word on the subject of who is generating fear through disproportionate use of violence: "There is nothing more painful for me at this stage of my life than to walk down the street and hear footsteps and start to think about robbery and then look around and see it's somebody white and feel relieved. How humiliating."[34]

The Best Defense Is a Good Offense

Whatever the gap, black-on-white street violence is a red herring for race critics. For Richard Delgado, it obscures the damage done by white-collar crime such as embezzlement and securities fraud which, he holds, causes forty times as much financial injury as street crime.[35] This, he argues, is what rational Americans should worry about. Delgado is on to something important. White-collar crime requires much more serious attention than this society has given it. And no doubt a racial dimension helps explain disparities in punishment.

But how much does that change things for our purposes here? When walking down the street with this knowledge, a woman will still be more frightened of running into Jack the Mugger than into Kenneth Lay, former CEO of Enron. She will not experience victimization the same way by the two victimizers. The matter of physical injury aside, having your money taken stealthily from your investee companies and having it ripped out of your pocket at knifepoint are two different phenomena. In brief, at the level of lived experience, it is not the quantity but the quality of the loss that matters. A group whose ideology is based on valorizing its emotional responses should understand this.

Black-on-white street crime is a distraction for race critics in a more direct way. "Blacks," says author and *Washington Post* writer Nathan McCall, "have more reason to be afraid of whites than [whites] have to be afraid of us."[36] Patricia Williams would seem to take this position one step further. Whites, she complains, have "projected onto blacks all criminality and all of society's ills. It has become the means for keeping white criminality invisible."[37] Rather than fixating on black-on-white criminality, according to Williams, we should direct our attention to Michael Griffith and Bernhard Goetz, two individuals who, in her mind, apparently represent all blacks and whites, respectively. Griffith was the young black man chased onto a highway by a group of whites in Howard Beach,

New York, where he was killed by a passing car; Goetz is the white man who, claiming that he was under threat of robbery, shot four black teenagers on a subway car, paralyzing one of them. The implications? Black criminality directed against whites is far outweighed by white crime against blacks.

In a limited sense, McCall is right. The Bureau of Justice reports that for the year 2002 a large majority of crimes of violence were intraracial: 71.8 percent of white victims of "completed violence" were victimized by other whites, only 15.4 percent by blacks; conversely, 8.6 percent of black victims were victimized by whites, 84.6 percent by other blacks.[38] But neither McCall's nor Williams's conclusion follows. For the same data show that blacks victimize whites at a rate somewhat in excess of the black percentage of the population. Whites, by contrast, victimize blacks at a rate that is far, far *below* the percentage of the population that is white. The horrific Griffith case, that is, was anomalous.

A prominent researcher several years ago concluded that blacks are fifty times more likely to commit violent crimes against whites than whites are against blacks.[39] Black radio commentator Larry Elder reports that, of the 1.2 million interracial crimes each year, nearly 90 percent involve a black perpetrator and a white victim and that a "black man is ten times more likely to rape a white woman than a white man is likely to rape a black woman."[40]

Counting only homicides by a stranger, the black-on-white rate is four times greater than the white-on-black rate. Blacks perpetrated 30.5 percent of robberies of whites, while whites were responsible for only 7.4 percent of robberies of blacks.[41] Patricia Williams offers all that is needed to support Sowell's lament that "overheated rhetoric [and] a fundamental disregard for truth" has seeped into contemporary race scholarhip.[42]

If the overall and interracial African American crime rates are higher than white rates, are male African Americans at least innocent of hate crimes, arguably the worst type of crime, the type that cost Griffith his life and traumatized New York City? Nope. White males proportionately commit fewer violent hate crimes than do blacks.[43] There are five and a half times as many whites as blacks, but black males are suspected of more than one-third as many violent hate crimes as white males. Considering only racially (as opposed to, say, religiously) motivated hate crimes only increases the disproportion of black suspects.

First Racist

Worrying about black crime is wrong, according to University of Southern California law professor Jody Armour, author of *Negrophobia and Reasonable Racism*. Even if we do "assume—perhaps erroneously—that the rates of robbery by race are in some marginal sense 'statistically significant,'" he sermonizes, "'rational discrimination' is not reasonable; it is racist."[44] The implication is clear: when Bill Clinton defended fear of black crime, he became the "first racist." To support the charge of racism, Armour goes on to cite a study showing that one out of two Americans believe that blacks are "violence prone" (ibid., 20).

But this formulation begs for deconstruction. "Violence prone" may not refer to a biological propensity, the connotation that Armour conveniently gives it, but to a statistical probability, that is, "tending to commit more violent crimes." This is a proposition for which the evidence could not speak louder and clearer. Attributing fear of crime to racism does not work for yet another, and perhaps the most important, reason. African Americans may be more fearful of crime than are whites.[45] Whom do they fear and why? Part of the answer is suggested by the foregoing data. But blacks are also disproportionately victimized by victimizers. Indeed, blacks age twelve and over are 250 percent as likely to be robbed, and 60 percent more likely to be sexually assaulted or raped, than their white counterparts.[46] In the case of the most serious crime, murder, they are victimized at six to seven times the rate for whites.[47]

No one has captured the connection between black victimization on the streets and black public life better than the chaired, black University of Pennsylvania sociology professor Elijah Anderson, whose unsentimental and, indeed, tragic portraits highlight the urban state of nature known as the inner city. The most pressing problem in the inner city, his comprehensive study reports, is violence, against which one must always be on guard.[48] The Code of the Street is the only source of protection: "Keep your eyes and ears open at all times. Walk two steps forward and look back. Watch your back" (ibid., 23). Friends reassure one another, "I got your back" (ibid., 26). Black residents scrutinize unfamiliar black youths to decipher their intentions. Blacks and whites are both alarmed when a black youth approaches them, if only to ask for the time. The white man, by contrast, is "not taken seriously on the streets."

To avoid being victimized, it is important to gain respect, which involves displaying an ability to defend oneself. "A person's public bearing must send the unmistakable, if sometimes subtle, message that one is capable of violence, and possibly mayhem, when the situation requires it, that one can take care of oneself" (ibid., 72). This is an especially important message in light of the perception that police and other civil authorities are powerless to protect residents from violence (ibid., 109).

One sends the appropriate message to victimizers through jackets, gold jewelry, sunglasses, "gangster caps," and expensive firearms, together with a certain gait and direct talk. It is helpful to "get ignorant," to show oneself to be a street person, or to "grit," to look mean and to put one's hand in his pocket to suggest a gun (ibid., 177). These tactics announce not just the possessor's taste and power but also a determination to defend all that he displays (ibid., 73). By contrast, the man who crosses the street upon encountering a suspicious character (ibid., 171), who fails to strut, who is "nice," or who lacks the finer things will get rolled (ibid., 72). The Code, not surprisingly, is different for a woman. She does not advertise her wealth. She carries her pocketbook under her coat, not over her shoulder. And she displays no jewelry. If black people take other black people "seriously" on the streets, but *not* whites, can whites be expected to do otherwise? Whose heart will not go out to those having to endure such living conditions? Can all Americans not see why African Americans want more, not less, police protection?[49]

Here is one of the great tragedies of our age. To bring peace to the black community, a number of black commentators have called for an end to black-on-black crime. We can all hope that these urgings are having some effect. But can a white person derive any security from them? Whites can, of course, read these messages synecdochically, that is, symbolically, to stand for all crime. Chris Rock instructs his audiences to take the term literally. "There's no black-on-black crime," he says. "When you say black-on-black crime, you know what you're really saying? Crime is cool if you rob white people."[50]

What a curious world race critics live in. On a principle that antiblack-conspiracy theories are liberating for blacks, race critics ignore the issue of whether they are sound. Fear of whites is good; racial paranoia is better. When there is a statistically sound basis for fear, by contrast, fear is wrong-headed, and even racist. On the slippery slope of asymmetrism, reason takes a fall.

The Pot and the Kettle

What is going on here? Do the paranoid scenarios of race critics have their origins in the radically different rates of offending? That is to say, is it the disproportionate offending that drives Bell, Delgado, Patricia Williams, and Armour to launch their rhetorical strikes on whites in order to preempt similar charges against black victimizers?

The question is, of course, empirically unanswerable, but a subtle inquiry into the needs of those who fear crime and of those who fear being branded as criminals may help us approach the answer. Here, to begin the discussion, is another personal story not to be found in the gender or race theory storybook:

I was walking up West End Avenue in Manhattan several years ago at about 11:00 p.m. The contents of the small suitcases in my hand were jangling. Ahead of me was a young (white) woman, perhaps thirty years old, heading in the same direction, albeit at a slower pace. When I was about thirty feet behind her, she turned around, anxiously, to size me up. A few seconds later, as I gained on her, she did the same thing. Then again. I did not know what to do. I moved to the other side of the sidewalk. It did not help. I so wanted to tell her that I intended no harm, "I AM NOT A RAPIST," but I quickly realized that any attempt to defend myself would make things worse. I had come to know what the black man feels like. Finally, I passed her and returned to my life as a more or less respected member of bourgeois society. Man is to woman, I now understood, as black is to white.

"Safety First"

Not having read about Staples's "Scatter the Pigeons" game at the time, I never even considered running her down. At the time, however, like Staples, I resented being thought a criminal. It was only some time later that I came to understand that the woman in question was not trying to undermine my mental health; she was just playing the odds. How could I fairly be upset? I asked myself, when I was thinking statistically like a savvy feminist. "I need not assume that every man is a potential rapist," insists Judith Baer, "but for my own safety I must assume that any man *may* be."[51]

If extrapolating from groups to individuals is rational, is it nevertheless wrong? Suppose that 99 percent of the members of a group are known to be dangerous. Should this experience be ignored? To be sure, it is risky to base judgments of danger on membership in a group that is organized around immutable physical characteristics, whether men or, hypothetically, people nine feet tall. And, in principle, innocent members of the group should not have to pay the price exacted by the failings of other group members just because of physical characteristics over which they have no control. In particular, black people should not be targeted with suspicion because they stand out in a largely white society. In our country, we repudiate claims of group responsibility—except for some claims of racism and sexism. But in assessing danger, is there an alternative? If the quest for physical security were the goal of a parlor game, excluding relevant information from the deliberative process might make sense. But it would be fatuous to suggest that safety is other than a fundamental need.

Indeed, famed psychologist Abraham Maslow listed "safety" second in his famous hierarchy of human needs, right after the category encompassing food and shelter.[52] Maslow's landmark work can hardly be condemned as just another part of the antiblack conspiracy. Who can doubt that the quest for personal security is central to human existence? It would seem, then, that we need not make any pretense of wanting to disqualify certain kinds of rationally relevant information about safety where the risks are especially high; railing at their use is just cant.

The Metaphysics of Bums and Booze

To persuade readers of the unfairness in generalizing about risk, race theorists resort to stories. Patricia Williams, for example, tells of her visit to the New York University area on a winter day some years back. Walking down the street, she spied a sign on a store door: "Sale! Two-dollar overcoats. No Bums, No Booze." Offended, she turned away only to see a black man in the middle of a busy street who seemed to need a coat. The man, an obvious drunk, teetered from side to side, begging from passing cars whose drivers were swerving to avoid him. There were tears in his eyes as no one responded to his pleas. For Williams, the store sign was as segregationist as "whites only" signs had been. Here, writes Williams, "we risk the life-crushing disenfranchisement of an entirely owned world. Permission must be sought to walk the face of the earth."[53] This is the tragic conclusion Williams asks us to draw from "No Bums, No Booze."

In effect, Williams is arguing that it is OK to seek protection *for* the drunk but not *from* him. The proposition needs to be tested. So let us suppose that she owned the store. Would she have risked financial ruin through damage to her inventory or injury to her patrons by welcoming someone obviously out of control? Or suppose the drunk had wanted to enter a lecture hall at Columbia Law School where Williams was about to give a public address. Would she have welcomed him? If he had begun to disturb her or a member of her audience, would she have used her considerable skills to defend his right to do so? If Columbia had had a continuing problem with drunks, would she have objected to a sign disinviting them?

We cannot be sure of the answer to any of these questions, of course, but it seems reasonable to suppose that, having spent weeks preparing, she would have wanted to give her talk in peace. And yet, to be consistent, would she not have been obliged to defend the intruder? Unless, of course, the merchant's peace of mind is less valuable than hers because he is white or because he is a businessman. In life, as opposed to scholarship, then, Williams's policy may well be identical to that of the store owner, only she posts no sign.

A final question to test Williams's good faith in recounting the story of the drunk: If Williams was so concerned about the well-being of the drunk, instead of fulminating about the merchant who was making coats available at a bargain price—and so could hardly be accused of gouging the needy—why did the well-paid professor not reach into her pocket, pull out the lousy two dollars, and buy the drunk a coat?

Williams is far from alone in dismissing the needs of merchants. Regina Austin takes under her protective wing black consumers who are viewed by store owners as "potential shoplifters, thieves or deadbeats."[54] This is a painful issue. The phenomenon Austin complains of is widespread and debilitating. But Austin wholly fails to ask a few important questions: What is the relative rate of law-breaking for white and black customers? Do black store owners view black customers differently from the way white store owners do? Has shoplifting gotten to the point that it devastates businesses in black communities? These questions should not necessarily drive legal policy, but an inquiry on Austin's part would show that she was at least trying to balance the needs of all the relevant parties.

The "Black Tax"

We return to Jody Armour who, we recall, concedes the possibility of a disparity in law-breaking. Armour tries to provide a comprehensive account of what a person who is feared may be feeling. For Armour, the classic defense of the fearful, "I'd rather be snubbed than raped," cannot justify what he calls the "Black Tax," the extra burden imposed on blacks by white fear. When a woman crosses the street to avoid a suspected racist or robber, says Armour, society's focus should not be on the frightened woman but on the victimized black man. We should not think of him as merely being "snubbed"; he is being dehumanized. What the woman is thinking, Armour opines, is, "I'd rather have waves of strangers spit in my face than run the extremely remote risk that a random anonymous Black man might rape me." Meanwhile, the man explains, "I always feel like taking a bath after these encounters, but with so many to contend with every day, if I tried to bathe after every one, I'd live in a bathtub." Because of the "exclusion of Blacks from core community activities, objectification, stigmatization, and humiliation," Armour concludes, "the scales of justice tilt decidedly" in their favor when they ask whites to suppress their fear.[55]

On what basis does Armour think he can speak for women? Is Armour, moreover, tilting the scales himself? Would my mugger have woken up and screamed for help in the middle of the night because I had crossed the street to avoid him? Not likely. And thus, Armour's "tax" would seem to bring us back to Thomas Sowell's observation that race theory specializes in putting the burden of social problems on third parties.

The Democracy Card

Armour knows better than to argue the case for suspending fear solely by reference to the wounded sensibilities that fear causes. Citing Abraham Lincoln, he calls on Americans to respond to the "higher angels of our nature" (ibid., 159). (Lincoln's term was actually "better angels.") We license those with disabilities to drive because we believe "it is important that they have equal access to core community activities" (ibid., 56). We live, he urges, in an environment full of risks, with automobiles and airplanes ready to snuff us out, and we accept these risks as the price of a "comfortable, convenient, decent, and democratic way of life" (ibid., 57). Accordingly, "we must accept incremental race-based risks as the price of living in a just, humane, democratic society, as just, humane, democratic citizens" (ibid.). In a sense, then, the racial disparity in crime is just another cultural difference that must be respected.

We will come back to the "higher angels" argument. For now, must we not distinguish between licensing disabled drivers and private action? Public policy is normally produced by balancing the needs of disparate components of the community. For this reason it cannot substitute—nor obviate the need—for private action. If, for political reasons, the government feels compelled, say, to license drivers over the age of eighty-five, many of whom are marginal, should pedestrians as a result exercise less than ordinary caution in crossing the street in Miami Beach when they see an elderly driver approaching? Arguably, the opposite should be the case.

As for the airplane and the car, must we not distinguish between things over which we have no control and things over which we do—that is, our own behavior? That a person is willing to assume *some* risks to live a good life does not mean he or she is, or ought to be, willing to assume others, even if the risks are smaller. A person who drives a Harley Davidson on an icy road at 80 mph without a helmet should not be forced to play roulette against Donald Trump in one of his casinos. Wrapping the profiling issue in democratic rhetoric is no more helpful.

Actions and Reactions

Armour essentially is saying that the fact that a young black male is far more likely to be a victimizer than an old white female should have no relevance to a potential victim. But the wise person understands that much of life involves assessing probabilities and acting on the judgment accordingly. Will wearing a red tie or green tie be more likely to get me the job? Will I get to my destination faster by making a right turn here or at the next light? Should I have tackled my assailant when there was a 10 percent chance I would be killed? Someone more science-minded than Armour—one who understands that social actions produce reactions just like physical ones—would hold that a potential victim should, on average, worry six to seven times as much about being murdered by a black male as by a white male. This is, of course, an aggregate view. As a practical matter, different subsets of the black population will be perceived as more or less dangerous, depending on such things as location, time of day, sex, age, dress, and whether they are alone or in groups.

Not all minority commentators argue, like Armour, for suspending the laws of probability in dealing with potential crime. Holding that it is appropriate to try to avoid crime, and that young black men commit a "disproportionately large share of the nation's street crimes—robberies, rapes, murders, aggravated assaults," Randall Kennedy has recently drawn a conclusion that Armour calls "racist": "it makes sense for many people to engage in racial discrimination."[56] "The most lethal danger facing African Americans in their daily lives is not white, racist officials," Kennedy continues, "but private, violent criminals, typically black, who attack those most vulnerable to them without regard for racial identity."[57]

Which brings us back to the opening story. My mugger was a young black man. I now understand why, though sensing danger, I made no effort at the time to avoid him by crossing the street; I did not want to risk offending a presumably innocent black man by treating him like a criminal. I survived, perhaps through luck. Mary Jo Frug, in her walk to the store, was not so fortunate with her attacker, whoever and whatever he was. If, as Kennedy suggests, private race-based fear can be rational, it is ignoring danger, not facing up to it, that is irrational.

The Limits of Pragmatism

Kennedy's concern for potential victims of violence does not extend to cab drivers. He recounts the problems described by Michael Dyson, Clarence Page, Danny Glover, and others in trying to hail cabs at night in New York City. It is hard not to be moved by the indignity suffered by accomplished black men who have to dress to the nines to have a chance of being treated as well as the scruffiest looking white man. And yet, there is the matter of taxi violence. The U.S. Department of Labor has ranked cab driving as among the most dangerous of all occupations, with homicide victimization rates sixty times that of other occupations,[58] a datum available to Kennedy but one which he apparently did not think relevant.

Who is committing this crime? Very little data is available, though cabbies obviously have an idea. Apparently 85 percent of taxi crime in Washington, D.C., is perpetrated by black people, presumably men,[59] while blacks represent only 60 percent of the population. An inventive theory proffered by Glenn Loury in support of a hailer's right to a cab may fill in some of the blanks. After legitimate black cab hailers are regularly passed by, he suggests, they get discouraged and find alternative means of transportation. Having more determination in these matters, those with evil intentions will keep waiting for a cabbie to stop.[60] If Loury is right, blacks make up a disproportionate number of cab-crime perpetrators.

But are cab drivers worthy of our concern? Apparently not. To be sure, in conceding that "devising the means of ensuring the cabbie's safety may not be easy" to find, Frank Wu implies the need for such measures. But the relative unimportance of cab drivers' well-being is made clear when, in the absence of those measures, he concludes that the "remedy requires that taxicab drivers open their doors to African American men."[61]

"If cabbies are given a personal safety excuse for failing to abide by antidiscrimination laws," Kennedy asks, "why not employers or landlords?"[62] In a nation with a tragic history of race relations like ours, he argues, we cannot afford to give in to fear, which can be so easily manipulated by those with a toxic agenda. Maybe so, but once more, not so fast. Potential employers and landlords have ample opportunity to size up those they do business with. They can check references. Often, there are other people around to protect them in case an applicant for a job or apartment gets out of hand. The proof: employers and landlords do not assume appreciable incremental risks in urban America. The cab driver, by contrast, has no chance to self-protect. It is not irrational, therefore, to grant rights to prospective tenants and employees but not to cab hailers.

Employers and landlords, moreover, can defend themselves against charges of discrimination by showing that, although a given applicant is rejected, others are accepted. Again, the cabbie is defenseless. Would Kennedy allow as a compromise a peremptory rejection of, say, five hailers per month?

Finally, in many of our big cities, cab drivers are commonly minorities (though often not African American) and perforce the major victims of taxi crime. Must they serve as Lani Guinier's miner's canaries, her *agni dei*? Are prominent black men's lives more important than those of cab drivers? Do only men like me worry about cabbies of color? It would seem so in light of the utter lack of concern shown by race theorists for cabbies. Minorities, of course, are not automatically exempt from bigotry. Without sitting in the driver's seat, however, it is presumptuous to attribute cab drivers' behavior to racism and not to fear for their persons.

Hiding behind Race

Kennedy reserves his greatest fire not for cabbies but for law enforcement authorities who profile in their efforts to control illegal immigration and other crime. His point of departure is *U.S. v. Martinez-Fuerte*,[63] a case in which the U.S. Border Patrol stopped a car for a search thirty miles from the Mexican border. The stop, triggered in part by the driver's apparent Mexican American ancestry, turned up two illegal aliens. Upon his arrest and subsequent conviction for illegally transporting aliens, the driver appealed to the Supreme Court, claiming that the stop and search of the car, based on race, was illegal. The Court upheld the conviction on the grounds that race can be one factor in the decision to force a stop.

Even if a Mexican American is more likely to harbor illegal aliens, Kennedy protests, the authorities may no more act on that link than may cab drivers discriminate against passengers who appear dangerous; to the extent that illegal immigration is a problem, the costs of policing our borders must be borne by everyone equally. Only when the blondest, blue-eyed Scandinavian is checked at the Canadian border as often as Hispanics at the Mexican border, Kennedy suggests, will America understand the social cost imposed on our Mexican American citizens. The same standard must apply in other settings: "Do we want there to be, in effect, two lines at airports? One for non-Arab people and one for people of Arab descent? No, we should not."[64]

We will come back shortly to the problem posed by Arab descent. For now, recall Sturm and Guinier's condemnation of a one-size-fits-all solution to education and employment Here Kennedy welcomes the very same approach to border control. But do we not need more information to formulate sound social policy? Where do most illegal immigrants come from? Do some groups stay longer and use more services? Do they join criminal gangs or otherwise contribute more than their share of crime? Do they adjust to American society more readily? But risk to the nation in these areas is apparently no more relevant than risk to cab drivers. Ask not what you can do for your country, Kennedy is telling Mexican Americans, ask what your country can do for you.

What is the realistic alternative to asking Mexican Americans to bear the burden of being subjected to more border-area stops than others simply on account of their race? If the Border Patrol's jurisdiction is limited to the immediate border area, then as soon as an undocumented person gets both feet across the line, he and the *coyote* (transporter) may be effectively beyond police power—at least until they commit some new crime on this side of the border.

The real purpose of attacks on immigration law enforcement, it seems, is to secure open borders—and, perhaps beyond that again, to dilute the power of white people. Nowhere, however, does Kennedy—or many of those who explicitly call for open borders—assess the implications of such a policy. But if race critics want to change national policy, should they not do so openly, evaluating trade-offs, instead of hiding behind race? Or is it their position that Americans are either too stupid or mean-spirited to have an open debate on immigration policy? In any event, what irony! Here are race theorists who, trying to create a just society, argue *for* race neutrality. To get beyond racism, we apparently do not always first have to take account of race.

Which brings us to the issue of racial profiling in criminal law enforcement more centrally, a subject that has triggered much legal and political commentary in recent years. We stop now to define racial profiling:

> any police-initiated action that relies on the race, ethnicity, or national origin rather than on the behavior of an individual or information that leads the police to a particular individual who has been identified as being, or having been, engaged in criminal activity.[65]

The current whipping boy for racial tensions in recent years, racial profiling by police has been labeled "morally indefensible, deeply corrosive" and "the opposite of good police work," by no less a figure than President Clinton, who concluded that "it is wrong, it is offensive and it must stop."[66] This is no partisan matter. "Racial profiling is wrong," President George W. Bush affirmed recently, "and we will end it in America."[67] Scores of political leaders have gotten into line. The 9/11 devastation, of course, has reopened the issue.

DWB *on the New Jersey Turnpike*

In a landmark New Jersey drug case, the defense charged the state police with conducting a drug search of a black driver, following a pattern of disproportionate stops of African Americans on the New Jersey Turnpike for traffic infractions.[68] Civil libertarians now label the driver's putative crime "Driving While Black" (DWB). The New Jersey court threw the case out after an expert witness had testified that traffic infractions were proportionate across racial lines but that African Americans, who composed only 13.5 percent of turnpike drivers, made up 35 percent of those stopped.[69]

In his book *Profiles in Injustice,* law professor David Harris condemns racial profiling. In addition to discussing the New Jersey case, Harris reports the results of a Maryland study by the same expert witness: while making up 17 percent of the driving population, blacks represented 72 percent of all those stopped and searched by the Maryland State Police.[70] Is this the dreadful criminal justice problem that it appears to be?

Yes, says Harris, for two reasons. When the police target African Americans, they will of course find more black people using contraband. He insists, however, that this result proves nothing; its only consequence is that "*skin color itself has been criminalized.*"[71] Furthermore, "hit rates," that is, the rates at which contraband is found on drivers who were stopped, should reflect the disproportion in stop-and-search rates. But troopers in Maryland, he reports, found guns or drugs on whites 28.8 percent of the time and on blacks 28.4 percent of the time. His conclusion: the data show the key "flaw in the basic assumption underlying racial profiling" and "the opposite of what 'rational' law enforcement approach would have predicted."[72] Hence the book's subtitle: "Why Racial Profiling Cannot Work."

Not so fast, yet again. For one thing, a new Maryland study has found that black drivers were twice as likely to speed on the New Jersey Turnpike as white drivers and, even more disproportionately, to speed at reckless levels.[73] Far more important, if cars with black occupants make up 72 percent of stops and searches in Maryland and the hit rates for whites and blacks are comparable, and *if* the police are *not* searching randomly but are employing tested criteria for sniffing out contraband, the logical conclusion is that, while more black people are unfairly targeted for searches in proportion to their *driving,* they are *not* unfairly targeted in proportion to their *drug running* or *gun possession*. A big "*if*" again? Not if we confront the staggering 28 percent datum. No reader will buy the idea that 28 percent of *all* drivers on the turnike are transporting contraband. In this key respect, the Maryland police got it just right.

DWB and DWD

Indeed, one could well argue that too little police attention is given to African Americans in New Jersey, where the hit rate, which Harris never identifies, has been found to be 10 percent for white and 13.5 percent for black motorists,[74] and in Maryland, where, according to one study, drugs were found in 33 percent of searches of blacks and only 22 percent of searches of whites.[75] For all the hand-wringing about disparate enforcement, insofar as interdicting contraband is concerned, the police may be under- not overenforcing the law, and DWB can too often, if painfully, be understood as DWD, Driving with Drugs.

Similarly, a study of police "stops and frisks" (*Terry* stops) in New York City shows that, while composing 26 percent of the city's population, African Americans made up 51 percent of those searched; whites, who represented 43 percent of the population, made up 13 percent of stops.[76] But while searching six times as many blacks as whites, city police were almost as likely to charge blacks with carrying weapons, arresting one white person for every 15 searched and one black person for every 17.6 searched.[77] This again suggests that, in statistical terms, the cops have their criteria almost right. It also suggests that a lot of guns are being taken away from people who should not have been carrying them and who might well have used them for harm.

Undoubtedly, a person who has never been patted down or, worse, thrown up against a car or wall cannot understand the stress and humiliation involved. But if African Americans are searched six times more often than whites and arrested at a rate that is fairly close to that of whites, then for the same reasons as in the Maryland case, the disproportion *by itself* cannot be the basis for ending profiling. If we are to get rid of disproportionate pat-downs on some higher (constitutional) principle, we need to do so with full consciousness of what we have been doing. Harris's subtitle tells us that profiling cannot work. He is wrong. It can and has worked. The only question is whether we should continue to allow it to work.

Readers expecting a call here for reinstatement of the now abandoned stop-and-search policy on the New Jersey Turnpike will be disappointed. Drug stops on the highways are highly disruptive and offensive to the law-abiding majority of minority drivers, and a fairly small percentage, 10–13.5 percent in New Jersey, result in arrests.

I make no argument for racial profiling on the highways; neither do I support the notion that highway stops need to be proportional, racially or otherwise. I suggest only that current police policy on our highways needs honest consideration. Is it a cop-out if no such attempt is made here? I think not. My objective is more fundamental.

Consider the following story. After a reported nighttime break-in at a bank, two cars speed past the police in different directions. The first has two men in it; the second, two women. The police have a policy in such cases of pursuing the car with the males, on the theory that bank burglars are more likely to be men than women, that is, that maleness is a suspect classification. Is there a moral violation?

Statistically speaking, the answer is no. The vast majority of bank burglars are surely male, and a major purpose of the criminal law is to deter crime by punishing violators. Before they are punished, however, they have to be found; before they are found they have to be suspected; and before they are suspected they have to be scrutinized. On whom should police focus their attention? There is only one response. When notorious robber Willie Sutton was asked why he robbed banks, his famous response was "because that's where the money is."[78] If the police are to protect banks, accordingly, they will have to keep their eyes on males, because that's who the bank robbers are.

Protecting and Serving

The same argument would seem to apply to cases of robbery generally and other crimes. In this arena, as I believe Manhattan Institute policy guru Heather Mac Donald has pointed out, there is no problem of self-fulfilling prophecies. Unlike in the case of drug and gun busts, in robberies there are often nonpolice witnesses, and, except in the most unusual circumstances, there are no suggestions that they are falsely testifying on the basis of race. In sum, if young black men are, statistically speaking, far more likely than whites to murder and rob, then in relation to the need to control street crime, the first light of scrutiny must be on young black men. The motto of the Los Angeles Police Department is "To Protect and To Serve"; protection against crime is most effective if victims and police are alert before the fact, not after it.

This brings us to the difficult problem posed in America by Arabs, from whose ranks have come a large fraction of major terrorists. Criminal-procedure policies were shaped long before the development of weapons of mass destruction. Since it is now—or soon will be—possible for a handful of people to blow up, contaminate, or paralyze a large part of a city with a portable bomb, we need rules of criminal procedure that reflect our new vulnerability, that allow police the flexibility necessary to prevent detonation. That is to say, our rules of criminal procedure simply must be a function of the anticipated measure of harm. Premised on a rule of reason, our Constitution cannot be understood as standing in the way of this result. The Constitution "is not a suicide pact."[79]

An old story is relevant to understanding the approach to law enforcement promoted by race theorists. An obvious drunk is on his hands and knees under a lamppost. An inquiry by a concerned passerby elicits the information that the drunk is looking for his keys. Returning an hour later, the passerby finds the drunk in the very same place and position. "Are you sure you lost the keys here?" the passerby asks. "Not at all," answers the drunk. "If that is the case," the passerby asks gently, "why don't you retrace your steps?" "This," answers the drunk, "is where the light is." Modeling themselves on the drunk, race theorists would sap the criminal justice system through a pixilated law enforcement policy.

The Alchemy of Race and Rights

How to explain why America's law professors, of all people, are so blasé about crime? Why, as Randall Kennedy puts it, are so many people "unduly hostile to officials charged with enforcing criminal laws, insufficiently attentive to victims and potential victims of crime, and overly protective of suspects and convicted felons"?[80] Some simply perceive anticrime regimes to be antiblack because blacks are disproportionately implicated.

Taking a more aggressive posture, others see crime as a political response to racism. Dwight Greene exemplifies this view in his defense of joyriding, which he renames "protest joyriding." He explains: "Conduct is appropriately considered a protest when the acts are openly expressive of an oppositional social or political point of view."[81] It need not be verbal in nature; indeed, minorities are more likely to protest through "hidden transcripts" because of the danger of direct communication.

What is the nature of the protest in joyriding? "[C]ars play a central and defining role in American materialism." Hence a "car is not just a transport, but a speech act." Standing at the heart of American culture, then, joyriding is entitled to First Amendment protection. How should this constitutional right be vindicated? "Black youngsters should be provided what their parents cannot give them: opportunities to learn how to drive and perhaps recreational access to vehicles."[82]

What is absent from Greene's analysis, however, is as significant as what is not. Are white youths entitled to First Amendment protection for their joyriding too? If, moreover, joyriding is a form of "speech," then why not decriminalize it like other forms of speech? And, finally, what else should be socialized? Meals with friends at four-star restaurants? What could be closer to "speech" than shooting the breeze with your pals over a fully satisfying dinner?

The Irresponsibility Card

The most wide-ranging political defense of criminal behavior is offered by Regina Austin. Instead of the old "politics of distinction," wherein the community rejects the criminal element in an effort to improve social conditions, she says, in the new politics "'[t]he community' chooses to identify itself with its lawbreakers and does so as an act of defiance. Such an approach might be termed the 'politics of identification.'"[83] Drawing on "lawbreaker culture would add a bit of toughness, resilience, bluntness, and defiance to contemporary mainstream black political discourse, which evidences a marked preoccupation with civility, respectability, sentimentality, and decorum."[84]

While Austin recognizes that "[b]lack lawbreaking . . . is a form of collective economic suicide," sometimes you have to destroy a community in order to save it. Lawbreaking allows the "vicarious release of the hostility and anger" needed by the respectable elements of the black community and brings resources into marginal neighborhoods. It provides protection in such neighborhoods against even more ruthless people and "justifies the existence of anti-crime . . . social programs that employ community residents and otherwise benefit the law-abiding population.[85] "Clerks in stores cut their friends a break on merchandise, and pilfering employees spread their contraband around the neighborhood."[86] These folks can teach all "[o]ppressed people . . . when to obey the law and when to ignore it."[87]

What about the victims of such undertakings? Will they not be driven out of business and thereby wreck the very communities black people call home? Not to worry. Citing an authority on ghetto life, Austin suggests that owners can in turn redistribute the losses "through theft insurance, higher retail prices and tax deductions."[88]

Austin assures us that women are doing their part in terms of shoplifting, credit card fraud, check forgery, petty larceny, and drug dealing. "[V]ice," she insists, "must have some virtue." Indeed, the foregoing actions would provide a "wellspring of a valuable pedagogy for a vibrant black female community, if straight black women had more contact with and a better understanding of what motivates black women in street life."[89] One starts to wonder, would the heroic Rosa Parks have glued herself to her bus seat for this cause?

"Yale or Jail"

Where will Austin's advice leave those who developed no skills in school and, because they have been taught to steal from their employers, cannot be trusted with a job? Here are fragments of stories told by two such individuals:

> I didn't do s––t in school, my people ain't got no paper. I tried to join the Marines, I couldn't pass their written test. Ain't got no transportation to get a job. So what's a fella to do? You talk all that righteous s––t, but you got a job. Got one for me? So I'm going to get with somebody rolling. . . . That's the only job for fellas like me.

> [I]t's like this, if we don't sell the s––t, someone else will. Ni–––––s getting paid in full, slinging dope hard every day. So why should we take some bulls––t ass minimum wage McDonald's job? F–––, everything is illegal [laughing]. Pork is deadly, bacon can kill ni–––––s, whiskey, cigarettes, cars, guns, but ain't nobody stopping them companies from selling them![90]

Of such folks, Timothy Simone says, "They demand to be viewed as the hunters and 'savages' that the general population, preoccupied with crime and safety, is more than willing to see them as."[91] In that light, the ostensibly shocking observation that incarceration costs more than college, and its implication that inmates should be sentenced to Yale, is revealed in its full-bodied inanity. And common sense suggests that in such an environment the rest of us cannot concern ourselves with the sensibilities of predators when we cross the street to avoid them.

The Devil Made Us Do It

For Austin implicitly, and for Paul Butler explicitly, the "ugly truth" is that disproportionate criminal behavior is "often a predictable reaction to oppression" through "internalized white supremacy" and the "racial and economic subordination every African American faces every day."[92] For bell hooks, basically law-abiding black men choose violence to give effect to white people's images of them. "In actuality many black males explain their decision to become the 'beast' as a surrender to realities they cannot change. And if you are going to be seen as a beast, you may as well act like one."[93] Just when an oppositional stance would really be helpful, black men play into white stereotypes.

For Derrick Bell, the theory of black innocence is still more subtle. "[O]ur automatic reaction to white hostility is to accommodate, accommodate, accommodate," says Bell. "And then we let off our frustration by violence against one another and often unspeakable treatment of our women whom we can't respect because their very presence is a constant reminder of our inability to protect them against . . . racism."[94] White people, in sum, are responsible for black crime because black people are altogether too indulgent of whites.

In his 1972 book, *Why Blacks Kills Blacks,* the renowned Harvard psychiatrist Alvin Poussaint brings the problem back to the media. American cultural experience has taught us that crime and violence is the way to success and manhood," he wrote. "The whole frontier cowboy mentality sanctions and teaches violence. Television and movie folklore reinforce the popular conception that problems can and must be solved by violence."[95] Whites are presumably watching the same television programs but are murdering at one-sixth the black rate. Yet here they are, the old bugbears again, the media.

Constitutional strictures would make it hard to end violence on television and in the movies. Offering no constitutional impediment to the effort of discouraging black crime would be a pronouncement issued tomorrow by Derrick Bell, Regina Austin, Paul Butler, and other black academic, political, and religious leaders. Here is a script I propose for a different kind of message, one entitled "Doing Our Part":

> Brothers and sisters, we have come to a crossroads in our journey together. Our victories in recent years have been great ones. Yet much remains to be done; and this, not our success, is what I come to talk to you about today. For we have picked up some bad habits along the way that need our full attention. Among these is crime and particularly the contribution we make to the problem of violence in the country we call home. Until now, we have been unwilling to face the role that violence plays in our lives, except, occasionally, in private conversations full of despair with one another. That must change.
>
> Crime is a tricky matter, which no one fully understands. A few things, however, are clear. Liberation brings crime in its wake. It throws people into a world they are not prepared for, established patterns into disarray. For us, this was true of Emancipation, and it is true of our civil rights victories a generation ago. As our chains have come off, some of us have come to believe that we have earned a special grace through our suffering, that normal rules of behavior no longer apply to us either as a group or as individuals. There is an old word for this kind of thinking—*antinomianism*—and we African Americans are not the only ones to suffer from it. Far worse is the situation in South Africa and in other countries where liberation has unleashed crime waves of far greater intensity.
>
> Hiding from the reality of crime is, of course, understandable; people instinctively hide from things that hurt them. And let us be clear—crime hurts us in all kinds of direct and indirect ways.
>
> But not facing our problems solves nothing. Neither does lashing out at white folks. We need not absolve white people for our difficulties here. The wisest person among us cannot work out the long-term consequences of ripping four million souls from everything familiar and comforting, and then subjecting us for generations to Jim Crow, lynchings, and more genteel, but nevertheless iron-fisted, forms of discrimination. But we can never enjoy the fruits of a harmonious society if we do not

do our part to build it. And that requires, to begin with, committing ourselves to the idea that crime is not an act of resistance to white power; it is a blot on the very thing that a God-fearing people hold dearest—their souls.

I know what some of you are thinking. White supremacy was a problem for us in America long before crime spun out of control, and it will not disappear no matter what we do. I hear you. There are no guarantees that directing our attention to our own efforts, rather than to those of whites, will improve our status and condition. But if we do our part, if we take responsibility for our own actions and not assign it to others, even if white America fails to allow us into its heart, we will have triumphed. For we will never again have to fear that we do not deserve America's good will in the healthy and felicitous community we build for one another.

The "Higher Angels" Card

Instead of looking within for solutions to the crime problem, Armour has called on white Americans to act upon the "higher angels" of their nature. This will not help. Though Americans of all colors are among the most philanthropic people on earth, predators have no greater claim to our lives and resources than does anyone else. To be sure, self-serving and sanctimonious appeals to our "higher angels" will always resonate with some. But, for better or for worse, saintliness is not a part of our national character, nor perhaps even a desideratum for most of us. One of our Founding Fathers has spoken clearly here. Among our central obligations, wrote John Adams, "is self-love [and] Blackstone calls it the 'primary canon' in the law of nature. That precept of our Holy religion which commands us to love our neighbors as ourselves," Adams goes on to explain, "enjoins that our benevolence to our fellow men . . . should be as real and sincere as our affections to ourselves, not that it should be as great *in degree*."[96]

Thus, when there are too many criminals on the streets—because the laws of probability have been repealed for the police—middle-class Americans will respond with guns and gates, responses that cannot enhance communal life. A middle-class ideology of self-reliance discourages most Americans from becoming victims, let alone from wallowing in victimhood. Relying on prayers for security in this view is no more American; our "higher angels" are trumped by a God whose priority is helping those who help themselves.

The keenest black academics understand where the burden for crime fighting initially lies. The first order of business for black leaders, according to Carol Swain, is to "*[m]ake the reduction of the black crime rate America's number one issue.*" She sets no conditions for this purpose; nor does she prescribe the usual nostrums, that is, the calls for more funding for schools, after-school programs, job development. Rather, she insists, for the sake of national unity—to highlight that all Americans are on the same team—black leaders must "acknowledge the legitimacy of white fears of black criminality and . . . abandon the racial double standard that permits them to ignore heinous black-on-white and black-on-Asian crimes at the same time that they vigorously denounce white crimes perpetrated against blacks."[97]

Is there anything else that black Americans can do to lower the racial temperature? Consider a final story here.[98] This one takes place not on Brent Staples's Chicago lakefront, but on the very same latitude some 820 road miles to the east and, just maybe, on the very same day. Herb Boyd, a black man, was trekking in his jeans and khufia hat in New York's Central Park several Januarys ago when he perceived an elegantly dressed white couple walking in his direction, perhaps on their way to an evening affair. The woman became apprehensive. Central Park had been the scene of numerous crimes, including the brutal beating of a Central Park jogger. As they got closer, the woman showed even greater unease by shifting from one side of her companion to the other. Nearing the point of their fated rendezvous, the woman tightened her hold on her companion. Boyd started working out his strategy.

His first instinct was just to give the couple a good scare. But that, he quickly decided, would not have been enough. We do not know why. Was it that it was dusk, when most of the park visitors were gone and the couple would have felt most vulnerable? In any event, when the woman came within twenty feet, the middle-aged co-editor of *Brother: The Odyssey of Black Men in America* smiled and asked, "How are you doing?" At which point the couple "lit up with laughter," while Boyd laughed the loudest. When Boyd was fifty feet beyond them, he turned around and found them looking back at him. They all broke out in laughter once again. "If we laugh at each other," to quote Ellison one final time, "we won't kill each other."

Though admittedly neither Brent Staples nor Herb Boyd offers any long-range solutions to the crime problem, Staples brought terror to the couple while providing release for himself. Boyd, by contrast, brought joy to all concerned. Which of the two messages better serves all Americans?

12

Conclusion
Eyes on the Prize

[W]hite liberals who involve themselves in these matters will get a
sometimes stormy reception. . . . But if one is not always welcome,
does that mean that the moral call of America's racial problems has
become any less urgent, that one should not try to do anything or
that nothing can be done?   —Nicholas Lemann

Our racial monologues having proved so sterile, and our
racial tensions so deep, Columbia University School of Journalism dean
and culture critic Nicholas Lemann urges whites to brave the storm of
race and say their piece.[1] For parallel reasons, one might well argue,
men must strive to master fears of embroilment in matters of gender.

By calling for engagement rather than withdrawal, Lemann elicits
dreams of a better future for our troubled country. My own dream is simple; it benefits from no pyrotechnics or other special effects. If its presen-
tation is successful, it will clarify but not alter the nature of the American
experience. If it were made into a movie, this dream would be edited so
as to place its entire focus on the central core of our culture. The dream,
in brief, is of a middle-class, even if somewhat drab and clichéd, America.
So far, surely nothing about the dream intrigues you. But stay with me—
you may change your mind. For you see, unlike the race and gender critics discussed in this book, I am bullish on our country.

Bourgeois Chic

Understanding the dream requires, for starters, a good dictionary. *Middle-class,* as an adjective, connotes such traits as "a desire for stability and

a high material standard of living, a respect for convention and the proprieties, and high ideals of education, professional competence, and personal ambition."[2] Are critics right to bash these values? Not, we have
seen, according to Gerald Early, who has characterized bourgeois culture
as "one of the most stunning products of the Enlightenment, indeed, of
all of human history."[3]

It is not easy to flesh out the meaning of bourgeois or middle-class values. A search for these key-word terms in a major research library turned
up only one title, a thirty-plus-year-old book by the late James A. Michener.[4] We should not be discouraged. No self-satisfied burgher, Michener's zest for life led him to write fifty books, the last of which he completed at age eighty-seven. He brought joy to millions of readers during
his life and left millions of dollars to charity upon his death. We could do
a lot worse than to take lessons from Michener.

In the book referred to, *America vs. America,* Michener tells us a bit
about himself and his family. He was reared in "considerable poverty"
(ibid., 58). He witnessed the devastation on young adults wrought by the
Depression. His wife was the daughter of a Japanese immigrant who had
worked as a farm laborer for ten years before he could send for his
spouse. At the beginning of World War II, his wife's family was thrown
into a concentration camp, its property confiscated. Michener expresses
no nostalgia for the old days; having shared his family background with
the reader, he sets forth the middle-class values that helped him and so
many of his generation transcend the limits of their environment.

First, there is education: "Today's dropout has got to be tomorrow's
ineffectual." His explicit message to the black community: "The black
who rejects education merely condemns himself to further years of what
he today despises" (ibid., 68). Competence is next: "I find no evidence
that in the decades ahead demand for it will diminish" (ibid., 27). Then,
responsibility: "one of the foundation stones of civilized society . . . and
the core of middle-class life. . . . Not only was a man responsible for himself and his family, but groups of families were responsible for their communities" (ibid., 27, 72).

Responsibility is followed by personal and professional growth, which
Michener refers to informally as "making it" or "getting ahead" (ibid.,
22, 74–75). Finally, and most important, there is that "most ridiculed
of middle-class values"—direct from the Enlightenment—the "habit
of optimism" (ibid., 75). Highlighting the importance of this value in
his own life, Michener refers to three major airplane crashes he was

involved in, one of which stranded him in the Pacific Ocean on a raft (ibid.).

Michener is not blind to the downside of middle-class values. He strongly objects, for example, to the sexual Puritanism and the drive for unnecessary accumulation that have arisen from those values. He deeply regrets that we have not allowed our sense of responsibility to operate in the area of race relations. But, he insists, such failings do not undermine the basic case for middle-class values.

We should all be able to see what an efflorescence of these values, intelligently and humanely adjusted, would bring. Unlike the politics of identification with street culture which has generated untold trouble for our youth in school and elsewhere, a middle-class ethos would encourage people to be less concerned with doing their own thing than with doing the right thing.

People who hold true middle-class values—whatever their actual social and economic class—do not worship culture for its own sake, defined here as "the customary beliefs, social forms, and material traits . . . of a racial, religious or social group."[5] They understand that the destructive practices of a group are included as part of its culture and must not be glorified under the colors of holism or authenticity. They do not recommend having children before they can be supported financially and emotionally; in peacetime, at least, they do not maim and kill, or tolerate those who do, not only because they understand that they themselves might well become victims but also because such practices are fundamentally wrong. They do not use violence as a stick to beat up on others —"look at the terrible things you make us do"—or as an excuse for the failure of victimizers to make it into the mainstream.

People with middle-class values, moreover, respect public and private property themselves, and encourage such respect in others, because even if they are propertyless at the moment, the alternative is what is now referred to as *broken windows,* the oppression of living in ruins. Above all, people with middle-class values are prepared to do what has to be done to succeed, however trying the circumstances.

Most African Americans clearly subscribe to this last value, as well as to the other values I cite. But is there, perhaps, an appreciable part of that community which allows itself to get distracted? A look at the unskilled part of the African American population begins the discussion. According to recent studies of the fast-food industry, franchisees and other proprietors frequently favor immigrants over resident African Americans for jobs, believing that immigrants work harder.[6] Even more important to employers is attitude; immigrants are seen as having better people skills than African Americans. They do not come to work with a "chip on their shoulders" out of fear of being disrespected or other motives. Thus, they are better able to accept supervision and swallow occasional abuse at the hands of customers. One ethnographer, according to Regina Austin, links the "lack of motivation" of African Americans with "disempowerment due to [their] social conditions and the feeling—both physical and psychological—that stems from . . . the cycle that never ends."[7]

Austin does not dispute these findings. Her solution to the problem of black employment in the fast-food industry: working conditions in the industry should be improved through higher pay scales, better supervision, and real opportunities for advancement. Since it is a truism that improving pay and upward mobility in any job draws more people, including black people, Austin adds nothing useful. The problem, which Austin surely understands, is that no employer wants to pay any more than she absolutely has to in order to fill employee ranks. Other things being equal, an employer who gets what she needs from immigrants will not look elsewhere for employees. This response is due not to racism but to capitalism. To the extent that ethnographers are right, then, any solution to the problem of black employment in the fast-food industry will require some change in attitude on the part of black people toward service work.

What about African Americans at the other end of the economic spectrum, those with highly developed skills? Consider that over the past ten years, many tens of thousands of black Americans have sought middle-class lifestyles for themselves. Looking not down but up, they have set out to establish themselves in business. In so doing, Regina Austin admits, they have had to defy fear, self-pity, prejudice, plain inertia, and, perhaps above all, an anticommercial ethic ingrained in black culture that holds that money is made only through exploitation, that whites will not let blacks make money anyhow, that money weakens character, and that a steady income is preferable to the open-ended experience of entrepreneurship.[8]

Do these initiative-takers delude themselves? Is it their inescapable destiny to fail? Do race theorists have the right to try to sabotage their dreams by insisting that whites hold all the cards? Without question—

and this cannot be emphasized enough—African Americans will have a heavier burden to carry than their white counterparts. But, however much greater the difficulty, however much longer it takes them to achieve parity with the "general population," it should be clear that staking and developing a claim in the economic system is the only hope for the future. Far from being the ruination of the black community, middle-class values, especially ambition, would seem to be a key to the salvation of that part of the community that does not currently share them.

And to the salvation of that part of the female population seeking the same social and economic power as males. But again, some plain speaking is needed. If (a) 45 percent of male executives aspire to be CEOs, compared to only 14 percent of women, and 75 percent of women want to retire by age sixty-five, compared to less than 33 percent of men; (b) women see themselves as primary custodial parents, and virtually no custodial mothers work substantial overtime; (c) women lean toward such fields as education, where they earn 75 percent of the advanced degrees, while men earn 86 percent of the degrees in engineering; and (d) for reasons of nature or culture, women often do not want to risk upsetting relationships with their friends by assuming a position of authority, then one might well ask, who *should* rise to positions of power? Aspiring to a top position, working overtime, and having a hunger for power do not guarantee economic success, but they are surely a necessary condition therefor.

Anything else is just talk. No institution will succeed in inducing promising and motivated people to work seventy hours per week if others are similarly (or even proportionately) rewarded for working forty hours. No society that places a premium on economic freedom will attempt to limit individuals' labor inputs just to level the playing field for those with agendas other than to maximize status and economic success. Among other things, we share an article of faith that when Bill Gates works hundred-hour weeks everyone benefits. If wanting more than a rewarding professional life, women want a level of success that is comparable to that of men, if they are going to represent 50 percent of the CEOs, members of Congress, and law firm partners, they will need a radically new consciousness and will have to negotiate a radically new deal with their spouses and children. Whether women as a group do or should want the symbols of material success enjoyed largely by men so far, only a loutish male would presume to say.

You do not need to be a highly trained, fully certified academic to see economic ambition for the delicate flower it is. Consider the next story, which was originally told in a movie by an African American male.[9]

Do the Right Thing

It's a brutally hot summer morning in Brooklyn. The air shimmers and the streets appear as if seen through five-and-ten-cent glasses. The only air conditioner anywhere around does not work. With no relief in sight, tempers are beginning to fray. At Sal's Bedford-Stuyvesant pizza parlor, whose walls are adorned with photographs of such Italian American heroes as Frank Sinatra, Robert DeNiro, and Joe DiMaggio, Mookie arrives, late as usual. Mookie is Sal's African American delivery man, expert at stretching a ten-minute delivery into an hour. Mookie also serves as Sal's ambassador to the black community. Mookie has a family of his own, consisting of a girlfriend and a young child whom he occasionally visits. Nearby, Da Mayor, a mild-mannered old man in a sports jacket—someone who, in spite of his fondness for drink, might in another age have been called a gentleman—saunters into a small Korean grocery store and orders a Miller Hi-Life. He is told that the store does not carry that brand.

A customer now enters the pizzeria, orders a slice, and then, examining the wall, inquires as to why there are no brothers among the honorees. Customers, he explains, are black, not Italian American. Patrons, Sal tells the customer in no uncertain terms, can go hang pictures of their own heroes in their own establishments.

Hours pass. Men and women from the neighborhood are now out in the streets, playing, drinking, jiving, sweating, and listening to music. More time passes; it is night now. Shortly before closing, a young man will enter the pizza parlor with his boombox blasting, and a tragic confrontation will take place. Sal will ask him to turn the volume down, and when he absolutely refuses, Sal will level the boombox with a baseball bat. This will start a brawl that will lead to the young man's death in a shocking incident of police brutality. In reaction, Mookie will pick up a garbage can and heave it through the window, thus inciting a riot that will end only after the pizzeria has been trashed and torched and an army of cops arrives. The owner will lose his business, a black employee his job, and the community one of its major institutions. The permanent psychological damage will be incalculable.

Black and Blue

As if sensing the impending tragedy in this story, a Greek chorus of old black men is trying to sort things out and maybe avert the unhappy fate. Living on the margin, they do not worry about issues of authenticity; no, they are after something more fundamental. Choked with emotion, tears welling up in his eyes, one of them is expressing the pain of the powerless, while pointing to the Korean American grocer, who is subjecting himself to a full blast of afternoon heat by straightening out the fruit in the bins outside his store:[10]

> *Coconut, a Caribbean American*: Look at those Korean motherf——s across the street. I bet you they haven't been off the boat a year before they opened up their own place . . . in our neighborhood. . . a good business. . . . It's got to be because we're black. Ain't no other explanation.
> *Sweet Dick Willie, an African American,* is not buying it: Motherf——s, hold this s——t down. Tired of hearing old excuses. Tired of hearing that s——t.
> *Coconut*: I swear man, I would be one happy fool when we open our own business right here in our own neighborhood. I swear to God, I will be the first to buy.
> *Willie*: I'm gonna. I'm gonna do this, I'm gonna do that. You ain't gonna do a goddamned thing but sit on your monkey-ass on this corner. . . . I'll tell you what I'm gonna do. I'm gonna go over there, give them Koreans some more of my money. Get the f——out of my way. It's Miller time, mother-f——s. [A half-dozen steps later he turns around.] And Coconut, you've got a lot of damn nerve. You got off the boat, too. Damn . . . Hey, Kung Fu! Give me one of those damned beers.

We could take a cue from race theory and condemn Coconut for demeaning the Korean American grocer by addressing him stereotypically as "Kung Fu." But that would be to miss the point of telling the story, which is that spreading a range of unbaked antiblack-conspiracy theories, transforming social pathologies into new cultural paradigms, and disseminating despair at every turn, race and gender theorists must, like Coconut, get out of the way.

Misguided and misguiding, gender and race critics have "a lot of damned nerve" too. Secure in their own sinecures, they tell other blacks that "racial discrimination in the workplace is as vicious—if less obvious—than it was when employers posted signs 'no negras need apply.'"[11] Better for the brothers and sisters to rage at the "Korean mother-f——s" across the street for taking away community business and consigning African Americans to the chorus of American life, it would seem, than to try to dance at center stage to the rich music of American self-invention.

A simple question summarizes the point. Would it not have been better for all concerned if instead of drifting off to buy a beer, Sweet Dick Willie had headed to a bookstore and, when he got there, had found a book by a gender and race critic that encouraged him to set up his own business, like the Korean greengrocer, or to otherwise take control of his life?

The "Korean" strategy is hardly new. Perhaps the first black political writer, Maria Stewart, was urging precisely such a strategy for black women 170 years ago to overcome their economic powerlessness. "Do you ask what we can do?" she wrote. "Unite and build a store of your own. . . . Do you ask where the money is? We have spent more than enough for nonsense to do what building we want."[12] Radio commentator Toni Brown updates the message when he says that what is keeping blacks on the sidelines is not racism or lack of credit but lack of "economic organization."[13]

If neither Coconut nor anyone else opened a store across from Sal's Pizzeria, must the blame not be pinned on the pursuit of authenticity? Obsessing over loss of an authentic culture can only produce a continuation of the racial/gender status quo. The pursuit of authenticity for a people originating in West Africa that lacked a tradition of literacy, as John McWhorter points out, can only perpetuate illiteracy.[14] Few will set out to gain the world believing that they lose their souls thereby.

When Alex Johnson, fetishizing authenticity, insists that "African Americans should have as much influence on whites as whites have on

African Americans," the implications are no less clear. Successful implementation of that strategy will eliminate disparities in education, as well as in unwed parenthood and crime. But eliminating disparities by increasing these problems in the white community will serve only to exacerbate national problems in these areas.

An adjustment will simply have to be made by black Americans to majority practices. "We all may have come on different ships," Dr. King is widely reputed to have said, "but we're in the same boat now." The reason blacks with educated parents who attend integrated schools do not do as well in school as whites, Andrew Hacker has found, is that they "still tend to see more of their black friends and families, both of whom may reinforce cultural and educational styles that put them at disadvantage in competition with whites."[15] Similarly, there is evidence that the race gap in our schools is substantially closed only when black students are in schools that are overwhelmingly white.[16] These findings make perfect sense if Orlando Patterson is right that the key to the gap, "in a nutshell, is culture," not genetic or socioeconomic differences.[17] You don't have to be a genius to see that like the Taliban, the Amish, and the Hasidim, African Americans and, yes, women can be authentic or become president of Microsoft, but not both.

What Jesus Would Have Said

A new individual ethic is called for when, believing they have no chance of winning life's race (because the chains have just come off), too many African Americans withdraw from the competition. That kind of response was rejected two thousand years ago. "Do you not know," St. Paul asks, "that in a race all the runners compete, but only one receives the prize?" But is that reason for despair? Hardly, First Corinthians teaches, "Run that you may obtain it."[18] In his aptly titled *Losing the Race,* John McWhorter condemns the idea that blacks should compete only when the playing field is completely level.

A change in institutional mind-set is no less important. Keeping the identity of American dream-blockers in mind is the starting point; for only with this information can MacArthur grants, endowed professorships, and other leadership positions go to those whose message serves, rather than undermines, national well-being. The leaders of our major institutions need to understand (1) that the logic of diversity requires that race and gender critics make increasingly outlandish claims; (2) that Americans have no moral obligation to cater to those in the grips of Firefighter Syndrome; and (3) that America will close its race and gender gaps just as soon as it overcomes its need for masochistic rituals and starts rewarding those bringing hope and good cheer. In this respect, our institutions must learn from the long and rich history of the Catholic Church, which canonizes only those who come with good news.

Send Out the Clowns

James Baldwin may have supplied the best explanation of what is actually happening in the distribution of public honors today. Recall his conclusion that when whites treat blacks spouting "stupidities" and "absurd theses" with respect and, "at the end, overwhelm [them] with applause, there isn't the slightest doubt: they are filthy racists." According to Baldwin's logic, when, instead of writing off Guinier and Patricia Williams, Harvard and the MacArthur Foundation install them on pedestals, the action arises not out of deep commitment to multicultural ideals but rather out of white male supremacy.

No sentient reader can doubt the psychological, political, and economic insidiousness of slavery or its residue of contempt and pity. The obvious obligation for white America is to redouble its commitment to equality in the face of its systemic crimes. Whatever the responsibility of whites, however, this book hopes to have shown the risks of entrusting minority academics and their various allies with the task of implementing a program of relief for the African American community, in particular, or for American society generally. Time and again, critical race theorists, and those who tremble in their shadows, have ill served the black constituency by taking it off the hook for its own spiritual and material states of being. Derrick Bell says it all: "The racial problem in this country is not people of color but whites."[19]

In statements that are surely even more extraordinary in their frankness when read today than one hundred years ago when he made them, Du Bois spoke about the road to reconciliation. Patronizing the descendants of slaves while bashing whites would achieve nothing: "the first and greatest step toward the settlement of the friction between the races," he wrote, "lies in the correction of the immorality, crime and laziness among the Negroes themselves, which still remains as heritage from slavery. We believe that only earnest and long continuing efforts on our own part can cure these social ills. . . . *Unless we conquer our present vices they will conquer us.*"[20] Du Bois goes on: "It is not enough for the Negroes to declare that color-prejudice is the sole cause of their social condition, nor for the white South to declare that their social condition is the main cause of prejudice. They act as reciprocal cause and effect, and a change in neither alone will bring the desired effect."[21] Du Bois understood that while Scripture may teach us to love our neighbors as ourselves and to share our resources with the poor, it enjoins no one to respect anyone except fathers and mothers. The reason is obvious: self-respect and the respect of others has to be earned.

Is Du Bois's message now obsolete? Not according to *New York Times* columnist Bob Herbert, who calls on black leaders to "say, in thundering tones, that it is time to bring an end to the relentlessly self-destructive behavior that has wrecked so many African American families and caused so much suffering. . . . If ever there was a need for tough love, this is it."[22]

The Truth Shall Set Us Free

Du Bois continues:

> While the Negro Academy [Du Bois's leadership vehicle] should aim to exalt the people[,] it should aim to do so by truth—not by lies, by honesty—not by flattery. It should continually impress the fact that . . . THEY MUST DO FOR THEMSELVES; that a little less complaint and whining, and a little more dogged work and manly striving would do us more credit and benefit than a thousand . . . Civil Rights bills.[23]

There can be no doubt at this point that Du Bois is right, that Americans need more truth if it is to free itself from the curse of social subordination. But pursuing truth is not easy. Patricia Williams proves the point by insisting that we must get "beyond the stage of halting conversation filled with the superficialities of hurt feelings,"[24] while at the same time promoting the idea that minorities and women have eggshell sensibilities and thus stifling the very conversation she claims to want to encourage. Who wants to offend Patricia Williams? But if the truth hurts, a discipline striving to assuage pain is also one that necessarily distances itself from truth.

When, in the name of feminism, Joan Williams announces that her goal is "not truth" but "social action," she also loses whatever usefulness she might otherwise have. Burning accused witches is also social action.

Equally problematic for African Americans, in Du Bois's view, is giving in to and then using hardship as an excuse for failing to bear the burden. Developing this theme, Ralph Ellison invokes a different American Negro tradition from that invoked by race theorists, one "which teaches one to . . . master and contain pain. It is a tradition which abhors as obscene any trading on one's anguish for gain or sympathy."[25] Obscene may well be how Du Bois and Ellison would have characterized the race-theory ethic of coddling the black community on a principle of hear no evil, speak no evil, see no evil.

Booker T. Washington and Du Bois are often understood today as proponents of alternate strategies for black liberation, the Martin Luther King Jr. and Malcolm X of their age. Their differences on the issue of assimilation and integration, on self-help and the need for outside help, mask their agreement on one issue of interest here: the need for black achievement. Race theorists today, by contrast, promote only a vision of black self-esteem.

The two goals generally have widely different practical consequences. Indeed, self-esteem, psychologist Martin Seligman insists, works at cross-purposes with achievement. Those narcotized with self-esteem can miss signals that they are off the track. When people do not learn to "overcome sadness, anxiety, anger," they cannot have the "flow" that comes when "the highest of your abilities just matches the highest of the challenges that you face."[26] In theory, Seligman concedes, increased self-esteem can serve as a source of strength; but when unwarranted self-esteem is combined with a deep sense of victimization, the result is only learned helplessness and an inability to self-actualize.

Building self-esteem in the black community, if Orlando Patterson is right, has not served to promote black productivity where it is most needed. While enjoying self-esteem that is often higher than that of their white counterparts, the black lower classes are burdened by a sense of low "personal efficacy" or "internal control."[27] This, says Patterson, is the key to the productivity problem; the person who does not believe he has control over his environment has no chance of changing it. The tragedy and irony here for Patterson is that, with "the full support of their leaders," lower-class African Americans "have come to respect themselves because they have no autonomy."[28]

In the case of women, one can likewise surmise, building self-esteem by encouraging women to fashion grievances against a conspiratorial patriarchy is to doom many of them to failure. Women will get nowhere professionally, whatever their level of self-esteem, if they do not believe that they control their environment rather than vice versa. In rejecting "male" values on their face, moreover, gender theorists make it all that much harder for women to choose their own pathways to success.

Is there a role for whites, who laid the shameful foundation for black victimization and self-victimization, in getting America out of its racial dilemma? "[O]nly earnest efforts on the part of white people," says Du Bois, "will bring much needed reform in these matters."[29] Heeding Du Bois, whites must do everything in their power to help, while nevertheless insisting, even in the case of disempowered groups, including women, that the impetus for overcoming a paralyzing fear of failure and loss of identity can come only from within. The fact that a major focus of this book is on what African Americans and women must do for themselves should not be viewed as discharging other Americans from their own obligations.

Ogletree's Money Tree

Harvard Law professor and chairman of the Reparations Coordinating Committee Charles Ogletree has given us a dim, yet clear, view of a racial future where the hard political, cultural, and psychological work is not done. At the heart of this vision is a massive compensatory pay-out to African Americans for damage done to them over the past four centuries, beginning with slavery. We can now more fully understand the goal of the race-theory campaign to vilify whites. It is not only for the sanctity produced by suffering; it is also for the cash. Every charge against white males detailed in this book, from spreading AIDS and drugs in the ghetto to fighting teen pregnancy to employing standardized tests to racial profiling, can serve to increase the take.

That theorists' claims are self-serving does not ultimately answer the reparations question. So we need a discussion about slavery. How should Americans today understand the abomination of slavery that our ancestors not only turned into a virtue but also defended to death—their own and that of the slaves? The "present generation of [whites] are not responsible for the past, and they should not be blindly hated or blamed for it"; whites, Du Bois explained a hundred years ago—two generations after slavery's demise—"are an essentially honest-hearted and generous people."[30] You don't have to go this far to exempt today's generation of whites. Scripture establishes a clear statute of limitation for ancestral guilt. By visiting the sins of individuals no further than unto the fourth generation,[31] the Lord holds us harmless from the crimes of our great-great-great-grandparents.

Even if whites today cannot be held accountable for slavery, their sins against African Americans arguably continue, so an instrumental view of reparations is required. What will happen after billions of dollars of reparations are spent and African Americans are still disproportionately uncompetitive? Will they then be ready to take up the burden described by Du Bois? Responding to a concern that reparations will serve to take other Americans off the hook for the condition of black America once and for all, Ogletree recently reassured the questioner: "When you pay, it's not that you've paid forever." Reparations claims could be "the subject of legal action again and again."[32]

And undoubtedly not only on behalf of African Americans. For it should be evident by now that waiting in the wings for the reparations matter to play itself out are Native Americans, Hispanics, Asian Americans, handicapped people, and perhaps even women, all with timeless and deeply felt pain of their own.

Under these circumstances, clear-thinking Americans of all colors must come down hard on reparations. Dropping resources on subordinated groups gives them less incentive to become competitive—and thus make it less likely that the performance canyon separating whites and blacks at Shaker High will be bridged. Because intragroup distinctions would be impossible, moreover, the burden to pay would fall on recent immigrants who bear no responsibility for suffering. Reparations benefits, meanwhile, would go as a windfall to those with no plausible claim to a remedy. In this setting, 30 percent of Americans would be at the throats of the other 70 percent, and at each others' throats, as victim groups argue over their relative pain and thus over how to divide the spoils. In this vision, not only of tomorrow, but of the days, months, and years that follow, the American dream does not flower, it wilts.

Why, then, do race theorists say such terrible things? Could it be that describing America as a living hell yields personal as well as material payoffs to race—and to gender—theorists? In this view, each new obstacle conjured up and overcome by individuals adds glory to their triumphs.

Receiving tenure at Harvard Law is a remarkable event; but when Derrick Bell's and Lani Guinier's turn came, the glory had to be shared with some fifty scholars already on board. If, however, Bell and Guinier had successfully run the gauntlet of "No 'negras' need apply" messages (Bell's words) in reaching the finish line, then their achievement was unique. Overcoming adversity, they whupped Larry Tribe and Alan Dershowitz.

In any case, the idea that the pursuit of reparations is a garden path for black people is hardly just a white man's. Prominent among black commentators who oppose reparations is John McWhorter ("Against Reparations"). Which leads to a final, larger point. Black people don't need me to diagnose or solve their problems. This book has shown the limitless wisdom offered in recent years not only by McWhorter but also by Orlando Patterson, Shelby Steele, Thomas Sowell, Henry Louis Gates, and Stanley Crouch among others, not one of whom, notably, is a law professor. What unifies these men—without whom this book could literally not have been written—is a core of the best American values and a belief that black people hold the key to solving their own problems. Does it make sense for black academics and their liberal enablers to marginalize any of these mainstream Americans as *bêtes noires*?

The Signifying Honky

In the black-made movie *Barber Shop*, Eddie the Barber, who may never have completed sixth grade, offers a useful analysis of the community's needs.[33] Insisting that "O. J. did it" and that "Rodney King should have got his ass beat for driving drunk," he sets forth the necessary condition for remediation of the ills besetting the black community: "Black people need to stop lyin'." The therapeutic lie now prescribed for dementia patients is not appropriate for normal moral and social discourse. But if anything is clear now, it is that black critics are not alone in failing to be honest with themselves. Gender critics join them. In trying to show that white males have been stifled in our race and gender debates, I surely have too often let my fears, rascality, and melodramatic inclinations get the better of my own judgment.

Even so, the reader who has stayed the course now understands that ethnic and gender groups have important multicultural lessons for one another. By modeling themselves on race theorists, a white man can learn to signify and maybe even to outscamp the scamps. Conversely, and also through the process of signifying, the race critic has learned how much more important it was for the nation to have an unconstrained investigation into whether O. J. Simpson murdered two people, wherever that might lead, than to be distracted by a racial-profiling ploy on the subject of black speech patterns. Through their own rhetorical tradition, race critics now know something still more important—that while claiming to pursue racial justice, they have far too often and too eagerly (not to emphasize self-destructively here) attributed racial animus to whites. If the charge of racism doesn't fit, race theorists must acquit.

The Fish and the Bicycle

Men now understand that, for gender theorists, Mary Jo Frug is an icon whose memory is sacred. Meanwhile, gender theorists have learned that, while they may not require men's services as sexual partners or bread-winners, they need men to free them from the snares of their own web thinking. Gender theorists have learned, more specifically, that (1) life is not the grim and gloomy affair that they have made it out to be and that, indeed, men deserve a measure of thanks for putting them out of their misery, and (2) they are less fragile than they think and need never fear gender debate or a gender joke again.

If we have all made such progress in the face of the pontificating, signifying, and breast-beating, imagine what we can accomplish in discussions that are respectful and well balanced. Gender and race critics can, of course, reject this hard-won insight. But they should carefully consider the consequences. If this diversity lesson is unworthy of celebration, if race and gender critics treat it as an act of war, we will never "relegitimate the national discussion of racial, ethnic and gender tensions" that they claim to want so badly. If they—or you, dear Reader—go beyond ignoring the message to ridiculing it, yes, you will all get a good chuckle or two. But you should not get too smug. Laughing last, I will be the big winner. As the Signifying Monkey might put it, "For what do we live but to make sport of our colleagues and be mocked by them in our turn?"

Afterword
Final Exam

Instructions to reader: Read this passage, then answer the questions that follow.

Late Duke law professor Jerome M. Culp, who was black, was flying from Chicago to Los Angeles several years ago when he overheard a middle-aged man talking to a man and woman of retirement age. The couple had just explained that they were about to move to Illinois from Southern California. When asked why they were reversing the usual retirement pattern, they explained, "No one spoke English." In telling the story in 2003, Culp admitted that he spoke no Spanish, but he nevertheless berated the couple for "racism" and himself for the "self-hatred" he displayed in not speaking up. He went on to explain that the airplane experience turned him into a critical race theorist.[1]

Part I: (40%) Multiple Choice: Circle the Statement That Best Answers the Questions Below

1. If only the Hmong version of the *Los Angeles Times* came to be available in Culp's neighborhood, he would have:

    a. Smiled and bought walking shoes.
    b. Started getting his news from the Fox Network.
    c. Made it his business to learn Hmong.
    d. Not tried to learn Hmong, because he couldn't even learn Spanish.
    e. Bought a hair shirt—and moved.

2. Questioning Culp's judgment is racist because:

a. Culp died an untimely death at age fifty-three.
b. He is a member of a minority group, which knows oppression when it sees it.
c. Minority groups have to stick together to keep white males off-balance.
d. Culp would have wanted the last word on the subject.

Part II: (60%) Essay: Evaluate Culp's Epiphany, Self-Grading Notes

Readers of this book should be less disposed than Culp to judge the couple for leaving an area of long-term residence after a significant culture change. Accordingly, they should resist imposing an ethical obligation on residents to tough it out if, say, noisy yuppies took over an area populated by quiet-living seniors. Readers should see a language shift as even more disconcerting than a generation shift.

To weigh the charge of racism, thoughtful readers should ask themselves whether the couple would likely have reacted differently if ten million immigrants from the Czech Republic had moved into the area and thereby changed its fundamental character. Members of groups are often most comfortable living with substantial numbers of their own. Indeed, an instinct to live together may inhere in the very definition of "group." For this reason newcomers to our country are not normally labeled "racists" for gravitating toward their own group rather than dispersing themselves into heterogeneous neighborhoods and benefiting from the rich diversity that America offers.

Given the diversity and history of our country, few will want to shut fellow residents out of a place they want to live; but if we are to live in harmony with one another, we may have to allow each other some moral room to live apart. If we charge people with racism under the circumstances described by Culp, it will only make living together harder for all of us. Attentive readers should have developed a heightened caution about using the term "racism."

As for "self-hatred," another loaded term, readers should be able to find other reasons for challenging Culp. For one thing, the conversation was not meant for him. For another, "No one spoke English" may simply have functioned as a convenient way for the couple to keep the conversation short. Third, Culp relates that the couple was of "retirement age." He does not say whether that age is sixty, seventy, eighty, or more. The couple's action may be explainable in light of the fact that we all lose flexibility as we get older. If Culp does not understand this, his cultural arteries are no less hardened than those of the couple he condemns.

Is Culp right that we are required to defend ethnic groups from criticism that we deem unfair? Undoubtedly. All conceptions of justice require supporting of the cause of the righteous. No one is free until all are free. If they so conclude, of course, readers approve the purpose of this book. Wimping out in the face of the grotesque and unceasing attacks on white males by gender and race theorists would be a textbook example of cultural "self-hatred."

In short, the reader/test-taker should evidence a skeptical reading of Culp's text, which should be reflected in a calm assessment of all available data, an ability to reason fairly even when confronted with uncomfortable facts, a distaste for labeling and name-calling, and a focus on how decent, fair-minded people actually live.

Appendix I
Student Faculty Evaluation

Instructor: _____

Course: _____

Circle One: Fall   Spring   Summer   2000

Circle One: Day   Evening

Note to Students: The instructor does not see this or the Scantron sheet. The Student Affairs Office tabulates data and types student comments for administration, faculty, and students.

Please fill in the corresponding letter in pencil on the scantron sheet which best answers the following questions.

Ratings for the following are: a = Excellent; b = Very Good; c = Good; d = Fair; e = Poor.

A. Instructor's Knowledge of Course Materials

1. depth of understanding of the subject

2. level of preparation for each class

Comments:

_____

_____

_____

B. Instructor's Organization of the Semester

3. sequencing of materials

4. spacing of workload over duration of course

5. clarity of what materials will be covered during class sessions

Comments:

_____

_____

_____

C. Instructor's Choice of Course Content
6. choice of substantive content
7. integration of current developments
8. choice of casebook, texts, etc.
Comments:

_____
_____
_____

D. Instructor's In-Class Performance
9. ability to present material clearly
10. ability to respond to questions
11. ability to stimulate participation and sustain student interest
12. enthusiasm for teaching course
Comments:

_____
_____
_____

E. Instructor's Relationship with Students
13. treatment of students in class
14. openness to consultation outside of class
Comments:

_____
_____
_____

F. Did the Instructor
15. give you a syllabus?   (a = Yes; b = No)
16. follow the syllabus?   (a = Yes; b = No; c = not applicable)
17. teach the New York law or rule?   (a = Yes; b = No; c = not applicable)

G. Overall Teaching Ability
18. Without reference to any particular answer or comments already given, how would you rate the ability of the instructor to help you learn the subject matter?
Comments:

_____
_____
_____

Student Teaching Assistant Evaluation

Teaching Assistant

With respect to the teaching assistant in this course, please answer the following questions:
19. How often did you attend the TA sessions?
A = Always; B = Frequently; C = Occasionally; D = Rarely; E = Never.

For the Remaining TA Questions:
A = Excellent; B = Very Good; C = Good; D = Fair; E = Poor.
20. TA's knowledge of the material
21. TA's ability to answer questions and communicate clearly
22. TA's approachability
23. Overall rating of the Teaching Assistant

Additional comments about the teaching assistant:
24. Sex (a = male; b = female)
25. Division (a = day; b = night)
26. Year of Study (a = first; b = second; c = third; d = fourth; e = fifth)

Appendix II
Student Questionnaire

Over the last few years an ABA Commission and a number of law teachers have called for studies of the gender climate at American law schools. In this connection a few questions are presented here for your consideration. Your help would be most appreciated. TO ENSURE YOUR FULLEST COOPERATION THESE RESULTS WILL NOT BE MADE AVAILABLE TO THE FACULTY MEMBER. (Feel free to base your answer on any experience you had last semester with this instructor.)

1. Your gender: a) male; b) female (Please circle and enter on answer key.)

Unless directed otherwise answer as follows: a) strongly agree; b) agree; c) neither agree nor disagree; d) disagree; and e) strongly disagree.
2. I enjoy this class.
3. This class focuses too much on black letter law and not enough on social and psychological causes and effects of law.
4. The instructor calls on students in a fair manner without regard to gender.
5. The professor expresses ideas clearly.
6. The professor is open to discussion with students out of class.
7. The professor is in control of this class.
8. I was offended by the use of gender-insensitive language in this class.
9. As far as I can tell, this class is a more difficult, less satisfying experience for me than for most members of the opposite sex.

Please note: The next items have different response formats.

10. Did any one group dominate class discussion? a) men; b) women; c) no appreciable difference

11. To what extent, if any, is one sex more comfortable with the Socratic method? a) men much more; b) men somewhat more; c) same comfort level; d) women somewhat more; e) women much more

12. Were you reluctant to speak because of a) disrespect shown by members of the opposite sex; b) difficulty of material; c) English not your native tongue; d) other; e) you were not reluctant

13. I expect a grade of 1-A; 2-B; 3-C; 4-D, 5-F

For comments please use Answer Key (specifying question number).

Appendix III
Christine Farley's Study

Comments Overrepresented on the Evaluations of Female Professors

	Female Profs.	Male Profs.
Not suited to large class/lacks control	71	1
Not knowledgeable/unprepared	20	2
Unprofessional	13	0
Defensive	16	0
Biased/has agenda	16	0
Patient/supportive	36	18
Approachable/accessible/available	87	54
Congenial/caring	103	74
Enthusiastic	39	17
Referred to by first name	7	0
Hostile atmosphere	13	6
Harsh/acerbic/rude	26	12
Disrespectful of students/ not empathetic/not encouraging	39	9
Too tough/strict/stern	10	0

Comments Overrepresented on the Evaluations of Male Professors

	Female Profs.	Male Profs.
Knowledgeable	96	157
Demanding/challenging/rigorous	32	42
Logical/analytical	0	9
Animated, dynamic lecturer/ entertaining/good stories	19	129
Good sense of humor	28	133
Respectful of students	19	35

From Christine Haight Farley, "Confronting Expectations: Women in the Legal Academy," 8 *Yale Journal of Law and Feminism* (1996): 338.

Notes

NOTES TO THE PREFACE

1. Cicero, *De Divinatione* II, Chapter XII in *Cicero in Twenty-Eight Volumes*, trans. William Falconer (Cambridge, Mass: Harvard University Press, 1979), 401.

2. Jacob Bronowski, *The Ascent of Man* (Boston: Little, Brown, 1973), 360.

3. Jennifer M. Hecht, *Doubt, a History* (New York: HarperSanFrancisco, 2003), 317.

4. Christopher Hitchens, *Letter to a Young Contrarian* (Cambridge, Mass.: Basic Books, 2001), 29 (quoting Marx).

5. Judith Baer, *Our Lives before the Law* (Princeton: Princeton University Press, 1999), 20 (quoting Hobbes).

6. Deborah Post, in Louise Harmon and Deborah Post, *Cultivating Intelligence* (New York: NYU Press, 1996), 125.

NOTES TO CHAPTER I

1. The following account is culled from a variety of sources, including Mona Harrington, *Women Lawyers* (New York: Knopf, 1994), 64–65; Eleanor Kerlow, *Poisoned Ivy* (New York: St. Martin's, 1994); Abigail Thernstrom, "The Vile Circus at Harvard Law," *Wall Street Journal* (May 1, 1992); Rebecca Eisenberg, "A Metamorphosis of Sorts," unpublished essay, May 1993, available at http://www.carrie.org/~dom/clips/morph.html (accessed October 10, 2004); David Margolick, "In Attacking the Work of a Slain Professor, Harvard's Elite Themselves Become a Target," *New York Times* (April 17, 1992): B16; Alan Kors and Harvey Silverglate, "Harvard Law School: Postmodern Censorship, unpublished essay; Arthur Austin, *The Empire Strikes Back* (New York: NYU Press, 1998), 7.

2. Jeffrey Toobin, *The Run of His Life* (New York: Random House, 1996), 381–82 (quoting Cochran).

3. Randall Kennedy, *Nigger* (New York: Pantheon, 2002), 85 (quoting Darden).

4. Dominic Pulera, *Visible Differences: Why Race Will Matter in the Twenty-*

First Century (New York: Continuum, 2002), 187 (quoting Hacker and briefly talking about the Merriam-Webster matter).

5. R. Kennedy, *Nigger,* 86 (quoting Cochran); Johnnie Cochran Jr. (with Tim Rutten), *Journey to Justice* (New York: Ballantine Books, 1996), 282.

6. Henry Louis Gates Jr., *The Signifying Monkey* (New York: Oxford University Press, 1988), 64.

7. Ibid., 55 (quoting Roger Abrahams).

8. Ibid., 54 (quoting Roger Abrahams).

9. Elizabeth Lasch-Quinn, *Race Experts* (New York: Norton, 2001), 23 (citing Karla Holloway, *Codes of Conduct: Race Ethics and the Color of Our Character* [New Brunswick, N.J.: Rutgers University Press, 1995], 69).

10. *The American Heritage Dictionary,* 4th ed. (2000).

11. Lis Wiehl, "Sounding Black in the Courtroom: Court-Sanctioned Racial Stereotyping," 18 *Harvard Blackletter Law Journal* (spring 2002): 185, 193 n. 53 (citing research by Walt Wolfram).

12. Lawrence Schiller and James Willwerth, *American Tragedy* (New York: Random House, 1996), 509.

13. Alan Dershowitz, "Harvard Witch Hunt Burns the Incorrect at the Stake," *Los Angeles Times* (April 22, 1992).

14. Mary Jo Frug, "A Postmodern Feminist Legal Manifesto (An Unfinished Draft)," 105 *Harvard Law Review* (March 1992): 1045, 1066, 1072.

15. Mari Matsuda, Charles R. Lawrence III, Richard Delgado, and Kimberlé Crenshaw, *Words That Wound: Assaultive Speech, and the First Amendment* (Boulder, Colo.: Westview, 1993).

16. Martha Minow, "Beyond Universality," *University of Chicago Legal Forum* (1989): 115–16.

17. See, e.g., Richard Posner, *Public Intellectuals* (Cambridge, Mass.: Harvard University Press, 2001): 194–214.

18. Ernest Becker, *The Denial of Death* (New York: Free Press, 1973).

19. Todd Holm, "The Benefits of Humor," available at http://www4.cord .edu/csta/tholm/HumorCourse/benefits_of_humor.htm

20. David Morris, *The Culture of Pain* (Berkeley: University of California Press, 1991), 100 (quoting Viktor Frankl).

21. Marshall Sella, "Did You Hear the One about the Suicide Bomber?" *New York Times Magazine* (June 14, 2003): 44.

22. Paul E. McGhee, *Health, Healing, and the Amuse System: Humor as Survival Training,* 2d ed. (Dubuque, Iowa: Kendall/Hunt, 1996).

23. Morris, *Culture of Pain,* 96–97, referring to Norman Cousins, "Anatomy of an Illness (as Perceived by the Patient)," 295 *New England Journal of Medicine* #26 (December 23, 1976): 1463–85.

24. Sue Williams, "No Laughing Matter," *Sun-Herald* (Sydney, Australia) (October 5, 1997): 14.

25. Dan Subotnik and Glen Lazar, "Deconstructing the Rejection Letter: A Look at Elitism in Article Selection," 49 *Journal of Legal Education* (1999): 601.

26. Larry Elder, *Showdown: Confronting Bias* (New York: St. Martin's, 2002), 219 (quoting Schopenhauer).

27. BrainyQuote, available at http://www.brainyquote.com/quotes/quotes/m/mohandasga103630.html.

28. Frug, "Postmodern," 1047 (quoting Andrea Dworkin with approval).

29. Jane Austen, *Pride and Prejudice* (New York: Harper & Bros., 1813), 447.

30. Thomas Sowell, *The Quest for Cosmic Justice* (New York: Free Press, 1999), 137 (quoting Benjamin Rogge, *Can Capitalism Survive?* [Indianapolis: Liberty Press, 1979], 10).

31. *Morning Edition,* National Public Radio, December 15, 1995, WL 9486598.

NOTES TO CHAPTER 2

1. Becker, *Denial of Death,* xi.

2. *Jones v. Fisher,* 42 Wis. 2d 209 (1969).

3. Regina Austin, "Of False Teeth and Biting Critiques: Jones v. Fisher in Context," 15 *Touro Law Review* (1999): 389.

4. Information supplied by Larry Haukom, whose firm represented Jones, in a telephone interview with the author on December 4, 1998.

5. Orlando Patterson, *The Ordeal of Integration: Progress and Resentment in America's "Racial" Crisis* (Washington, D.C.: Civitas, 1997), 1–2.

6. K. Anthony Appiah and Amy Guttman, *Color Conscious: The Political Morality of Race* (Princeton: Princeton University Press, 1996), 182 (Appiah speaking).

7. W. E. B. Du Bois, *The Souls of Black Folk* (1903; repr., New York: Barnes & Noble Classics, 2003), 144.

8. Posner, *Public Intellectuals,* 147.

9. Merton Miller, "The Value of 'Useless' Research," *Wall Street Journal* (September 21, 1992): A12.

10. Lyn Brown and Carol Gilligan, *Meeting at the Crossroads: Women's Psychology and Girls' Development* (Cambridge, Mass.: Harvard University Press, 1992), 6.

11. Sir William Gilbert, *The Yeomen of the Guard* (1888).

12. Michael Eric Dyson, *Open Mike* (New York: Basic Civitas, 2003), 211.

13. Martha Chamallas, *Introduction to Feminist Legal Theory* (Gaithersburg, Md.: Aspen, 1999), 9.

14. Joan Williams, *Unbending Gender: Why Family and Work Conflict and What to Do about It* (New York: Oxford University Press, 2000), 244.

15. David Owen, "From Race to Chase," *New Yorker* (June 3, 2002): 57.

16. Thomas Sowell, *A Conflict of Visions: Ideological Origins of Political Struggles* (New York: Basic Books, 2001), 59 (quoting Schumpeter).

17. Catherine Wells, "The Theory and Practice of Being Trina," 81 *Minnesota Law Review* (1997): 1381, 1387.

18. Ice-T, "Cop Killer," *Body Count* (Warner Bros. Records, 1992).

19. Mari Matsuda, "Public Response to Racist Speech: Considering the Victim's Story," 87 *Michigan Law Review* (1989): 2320, 2361–62.

20. Theresa Perry, Claude Steele, and Asa Hilliard, *Young, Gifted, and Black* (Boston: Beacon, 2003), 75 (discussing black stereotypes).

21. Lasch-Quinn, *Race Experts*, 56 (quoting Norman Mailer).

22. Lena Williams, *It's the Little Things* (New York: Harcourt, 2000), 27–28.

23. John Hodgman, "Ayn Rand, in Spades," *New York Times Magazine* (June 29, 2003): 38 (quoting Rand).

24. bell hooks, *Killing Rage* (New York: Holt, 1995), 8–10.

25. Gretchen Sidhu, "Academy Blues," *Ms.* (August/September 2001): 37.

26. Sumi Cho, "Converging Stereotypes in Racialized Sexual Harassment: Where the Model Minority Meets Suzie Wong" in *Critical Race Feminism*, Adrien Wing, ed. (New York: NYU Press, 1997), 203, 204.

27. Regina Austin, "Sapphire Bound!" *Wisconsin Law Review* (1989): 539–40.

28. Derrick Bell, *And We Are Not Saved* (New York: Basic Books, 1987), 205.

29. Derrick Bell, "A Colony at Risk," 15 *Touro Law Review* (1999): 347, 349.

30. Data provided by Rick Morgan, data specialist for the ABA, on December 9, 1998.

31. For those not familiar with the story, the letters C-R-O-A-T-O-A-N carved on a tree were the only remnant of one of the first white colonies in North America.

32. Derrick Bell, *Faces at the Bottom of the Well* (New York: Basic Books, 1979), 158–94, quote from p. 194.

33. Richard Delgado, *The Coming Race War? And Other Apocalyptic Tales of America after Affirmative Action and Welfare* (New York: NYU Press, 1996), 119.

34. William Grier and Price Cobbs, *Black Rage* (New York: Basic Books, 1968), 177–78 (emphasis in original).

35. Chris Iijima, "Race as Resistance: Racial Identity as More than Ancestral Heritage," 15 *Touro Law Review* (1999): 497, 498.

36. Anthony Farley, "Thirteen Stories," 15 *Touro Law Review* (1999): 543, 627.

37. Ibid. Farley is quoting in part from postmodern theorist Julia Kristeva. Critical race theory, a radical version of race theory, is discussed in the next chapter.

38. hooks, *Killing Rage*, 18.

39. A. Farley, "Thirteen Stories," 676.

40. Patterson, *Ordeal of Integration*, 2.

41. Patricia Williams, *The Rooster's Egg* (Cambridge, Mass: Harvard University Press, 1995), 40.

42. Harlon Dalton, *Racial Healing* (New York: Doubleday, 1995), 97, 4.

43. Charles Lawrence III, "The Id, the Ego, and Equal Protection: Reckoning with Unconscious Racism," 39 *Stanford Law Review* (1987): 317, 321.

44. Christine Littleton, "Feminist Jurisprudence: The Difference Method Makes," 41 *Stanford Law Review* (1989): 751, 765 n. 72.

45. Mari Matsuda, "Pragmatism Modified and the False Consciousness Problem," 63 *Southern California Law Review* (1990): 1763, 1764.

46. Iris M. Young, *Justice and the Politics of Difference* (Princeton: Princeton University Press, 1990), 184.

47. Richard Delgado, *Critical Race Theory: An Introduction* (New York: NYU Press, 2001), 9.

48. Michael Eric Dyson, "Seeing the Simpson Verdicts in Black and White," *Newsday* (February 9, 1997): G5.

49. Patricia Williams, "Comment: Metro Broadcasting, Inc. v. FCC: Regrouping in Singular Time," 104 *Harvard Law Review* (1990): 525, 529.

50. Dyson, "Seeing the Simpson Verdicts," G5.

51. Derrick Bell, *Race, Racism, and American Law,* 4th ed. (Gaithersburg, Md.: Aspen, 2000), 136–45.

52. 426 U.S. 229 (1976).

53. Molefi Asante, *The Afrocentric Idea* (Philadelphia: Temple University Press, 1998), 78.

54. Harmon and Post, *Cultivating Intelligence*, 22–55.

55. Richard Bernstein, *Dictatorship of Virtue* (New York: Knopf, 1994), 131 (quoting Baker).

56. Derald Wing Sue, *Overcoming Our Racism* (San Francisco: Jossey-Bass, 2003), 261, 262.

57. Iijima, "Race as Resistance," 498.

58. Peter Halewood, "White Men Can't Jump: Critical Epistemologies, Embodiment, and the Praxis of Scholarship," 7 *Yale Journal of Law and Feminism* (1995): 1, 6–7, 10, 14, 25.

59. Adam Shatz, "The Way We Live," *New York Times Magazine* (October 28, 2001): 19 (quoting Naipaul).

60. Patterson, *Ordeal of Integration*, 115.

61. Katharine Mangan, "Professor's Comments on Affirmative Action Inflame a Campus," *Chronicle of Higher Education* (September 26, 1997): A33.

62. Abigail Thernstrom and Stephan Thernstrom, *No Excuses: Closing the Racial Gap in Learning* (New York: Simon and Schuster, 2003), 94.

63. Carol Swain, *The New White Nationalism in America* (Cambridge: Cambridge University Press, 2002), 6, 346.

64. Thomas Sowell, *The Vision of the Anointed* (New York: Basic Books 1995).

65. June Jordan, *Technical Difficulties* (New York: Pantheon, 1992), 178.

66. Shelby Steele, *A Dream Deferred: The Second Betrayal of Black Freedom in America* (New York: HarperCollins, 1998), 95.

67. Ibid., 120.

68. Walter Benn Michaels, "Diversity's False Solace," *New York Times Magazine* (April 11, 2004): 12, 14.

69. Trina Grillo, "Tenure and Minority Women Law Professors: Separating the Strands," 31 *University of San Francisco Law Review* (1997): 747, 754.

70. Carolyn Graglia, *Domestic Tranquility* (Dallas: Spence, 1998), 270 (quoting Disraeli).

71. Duncan Kennedy, "Legal Education as Training for Hierarchy," in *The Politics of Law,* David Kairys, ed. (New York: Pantheon, 1982), 47 (emphasis in original).

72. Sarah Willie, *Acting Black* (New York: Routledge, 2003), 5 (emphasis in original).

73. Richard Delgado, "Two Ways to Think about Race," 89 *Georgetown Law Journal* (2001): 2279, 2281.

74. Randall Kennedy, "My Race Problem—and Ours," *Atlantic Monthly* (May 1997): 65.

75. Debra Dickerson, *The End of Blackness* (New York: Pantheon, 2004), 55 (quoting Fanon).

76. Baer, *Our Lives before the Law,* 20.

77. Phyllis Chesler, *Woman's Inhumanity to Woman* (New York: Plume, 2002), 474 (quoting bell hooks).

78. Sowell, *Vision of the Anointed,* 113.

79. Lloyd Cohen, "Sexual Harassment and the Law," *Society* (May/June 1991): 11.

80. Digby Anderson and Peter Mullen, "The Idea of a Fake Society," in *Faking It: The Sentimentalisation of Modern Society,* Digby Anderson and Peter Mullen, eds. (London: Social Affairs Unit, 1998), 5.

81. Paul Butler, "Racially Based Jury Nullification: Black Power in the Criminal Justice System," 105 *Yale Law Journal* (1995): 677, 715.

82. Iijima, "Race as Resistance," 507.

83. Leslie Espinoza, "Latino/a Identity and Multi-Identity," in *The Latino/a*

Condition, Richard Delgado and Jean Stefancic, eds. (New York: NYU Press, 1998), 17 ("The politics of race in America . . . is the erasure of richness of my Mexican/Jewish/Irish mix, and a whitewashing of the colorful complexity of meaning in each of my ethnic roots," ibid., 18). See also Berta Hernandez-Truyol, "Building Bridges," in ibid., 24 ("As multiple-layered selves we are denied part of our personhood when we have to deny a part of who we are; our experience simply cannot be sanitized to fit a mold in the creation of which we were not considered.").

84. Daphne Patai and Noretta Koertge, *Professing Feminism* (Lanham, Md.: Lexington Books, 2003), 80 (quoting Baldwin).

85. Bell, *Faces*, xii.

86. Shelby Steele, *The Content of Our Character* (New York: St. Martin's, 1990), 2–3.

87. Robert Boynton, "The Professor of Connection," *New Yorker* (November 6, 1995): 100 (quoting Crouch).

88. Theodor Adorno, *Minima Moralia: Reflections from a Damaged Life*, trans. E. F. N. Jephcott (London: New Left Books, 1974), 27.

89. bell hooks, *Talking Back* (Boston: South End Press, 1989), 131.

90. hooks, *Killing Rage*, 28.

91. Jackie Wullschlager, *Hans Christian Andersen* (New York: Knopf, 2001), 177.

92. Mark Kelman, "Trashing," 36 *Stanford Law Review* (January 1984): 293 (emphasis in original).

93. Patai and Koertge, *Professing Feminism*, 80.

94. Wilbert Fordyce, "Learning Processes in Pain," in *The Psychology of Pain*, Richard Sternbach, ed., 2d ed. (New York: Raven Press, 1986), 53.

95. Ibid., 54, 55.

96. Lauren Slater, "Repress Yourself," *New York Times Magazine* (February 23, 2003): 48.

97. June Jordan, *Some of Us Did Not Die* (New York: Basic Civitas, 2002), 17 (quoting Robert Allen).

98. Christopher Kui, "Letter to the Editor," *New York Times* (June 8, 2002): A14.

99. Sowell, *Vision of the Anointed*, 129.

100. Dylan Hernandez, "Latest Curve Taken in Stride," *Boston Globe* (September 1, 2001): G7.

101. "Phillipe and Jorge's Cool, Cool World," *Providence Phoenix* (August 30, 2001): 4.

102. *Regents of the University of California v. Bakke*, 438 U.S. 265, 407 (1977) (separate opinion of Justice Blackmun).

103. Daryl Scott, *Contempt and Pity* (Chapel Hill: University of North Carolina Press, 1997), 180, 202.

104. John McWhorter, *Losing the Race: Self-Sabotage in Black America* (New York: Free Press, 2000), 161 (quoting Ellison).

105. Kenneth Lasson, "The Tintinnabulation of Bell's Letters," 36 *Washburn Law Journal* (1996): 18, 22 (quoting Cotton).

106. Shelby Steele, "Or a Childish Illusion of Justice?" *Newsweek* (August 27, 2001): 23. These numbers are not the most current. The nonmarital birth rate has dropped a little, and the black crime rate more than that. See chapters 9 and 11.

107. James Herring, "Can They Do It?" in *The Difference "Difference" Makes*, Deborah Rhode, ed. (Stanford: Stanford University Press, 2003), 76, 80 (quoting Baldwin).

108. S. Steele, "Or a Childish Illusion," 23.

109. Jack Katz, *Seductions of Crime* (New York: Basic Books, 1988), 22, 23, 26.

110. Marlene Connor, *What Is Cool?* (New York: Crown, 1995), 7, 1.

111. Ellen Goodman, "Mission: Admission," *Boston Globe* (March 30, 2003): D11 (quoting Guinier).

112. *Gratz v. Bollinger*, 123 S. Ct. 2411 (2003).

113. Bell, *Faces*, 124.

114. Molefi Asante, "Afrocentricity," in *Dispatches from the Ebony Tower*, Manning Marable, ed. (New York: Columbia University Press, 2000), 199.

115. Henry Louis Gates Jr., *Thirteen Ways of Looking at a Black Man* (New York: Random House, 1997), 137–38 (quoting Farrakhan).

116. Orlando Patterson, "Race, Gender, and Liberal Fallacies," *New York Times* (October 21, 1991): 34.

117. Swain, *New White Nationalism*, 166 (crediting Glenn Loury).

118. Clarence Page, "Sending the Right Signal to Students," *Los Angeles Times* (December 18, 1980) (quoting Washington).

119. McWhorter, *Losing the Race*, 219.

NOTES TO CHAPTER 3

1. Nancy Cook, "Outside the Tradition: Literature as Legal Scholarship," 63 *University of Cincinnati Law Review* (1994): 95, 101.

2. Richard Delgado, "Legal Storytelling: Storytelling for Oppositionists and Others: A Plea for Narrative," 87 *Michigan Law Review* (1989): 2411, 2413, 2415.

3. Charles Lawrence III, "The Word and the River: Pedagogy as Scholarship and Struggle," 65 *Southern California Law Review* (1992): 2231, 2281.

4. P. Williams, *Rooster's Egg*, book jacket (quoting West).

5. Ibid. (quoting Harvard professor Sacvan Bercovitch).

6. Jerome M. Culp Jr., "You Can Take Them to Water, but You Can't Make

Them Drink: Black Legal Scholarship and White Legal Scholars," *University of Illinois Law Review* (1992): 1021, 1034.

7. P. Williams, *Rooster's Egg*, 105 passim.

8. Sam Dillon, "Commencement Speeches," *New York Times* (June 1, 2003): sec. 4, 41 (quoting Mitchell).

9. Stanley Crouch, *The All-American Skin Game, or, The Decoy of Race* (New York: Vintage, 1995), 34.

10. *Liber Annalis* (1969 Boston Girls' Latin Yearbook), 69.

11. Dickerson, *End of Blackness*, 7 (quoting Woodson).

12. For the background of the critical race theory movement from folks inside the movement, see Kimberlé Crenshaw, Neil Gotanda, Gary Peller, and Kendall Thomas, eds., *Critical Race Theory: The Key Writings That Formed a Movement* (New York: New Press, 1995), xii–xxxii.

13. Derrick Bell, "Who's Afraid of Critical Race Theory?" *University of Illinois Law Review* (1995): 893, 901.

14. Matsuda et al., *Words That Wound*, 6, 5.

15. Richard Delgado, "The Imperial Scholar: Reflections on a Review of Civil Rights Literature," 132 *University of Pennsylvania Law Review* (1984): 561; see also Derrick Bell, "Serving Two Masters: Integration Ideals and Client Interests in School Desegregation Cases," 85 *Yale Law Journal* (1976): 470.

16. Ibid., 577.

17. Randall Kennedy, "Racial Critiques of Legal Academia," 102 *Harvard Law Review* (1989): 1745.

18. Richard Delgado, *When Equality Ends: Stories about Race and Resistance* (Boulder, Colo.: Westview, 1999), 208.

19. Patricia Williams, *The Alchemy of Race and Rights* (Cambridge, Mass.: Harvard University Press, 1991), 8.

20. Ibid., 129.

21. R. Austin, "Sapphire Bound!" 539–40, 542.

22. Ibid., 544.

23. Frank Wu, *Yellow: Race in America beyond Black and White* (New York: Basic Books, 2002), 8.

24. Ibid., 11–12.

25. Ibid., 263.

26. Robert Chang, "Toward an Asian American Legal Scholarship," 1 *Asian Law Journal* (1994): 1, 24.

27. Eric Liu, *The Accidental Asian* (New York: Random House, 1998), 158.

28. P. Williams, *Rooster's Egg*, 198–99.

29. Ibid., 200.

30. Charles Lawrence III and Mari Matsuda, *We Won't Go Back: Making the Case for Affirmative Action* (Boston: Houghton Mifflin, 1997), 30.

31. Ibid.

32. Deborah Post, "Reflections on Identity, Diversity, and Morality," 6 *Berkeley Women's Law Journal* (1990–91): 136, 163.

33. Richard Delgado, "The Inward Turn to Outsider Jurisprudence," 34 *William and Mary Law Review* (1993): 741, 766.

34. Manning Marable, *W. E. B. Du Bois: Black Radical Democrat* (Boston: Twayne, 1986), 131 (quoting Du Bois).

35. Crouch, *All-American Skin Game*, 53.

36. Ibid., 54.

37. Dickerson, *End of Blackness*, 14.

38. Glenn Loury, *The Anatomy of Racial Inequality* (Cambridge, Mass.: Harvard University Press, 2002), 145.

39. 137 *Cong. Rec.* S14, 632 (daily ed., October 15, 1991).

40. Daniel Farber and Suzanna Sherry, "Telling Stories Out of School: An Essay on Legal Narratives," 45 *Stanford Law Review* (1992): 807, 835–36.

41. Shelby Steele, "The Race Not Run," *New Republic* (October 7, 1996): 23, 26.

42. William Raspberry, "Eyes on the Problem," *Boston Globe* (January 3, 1998): A11.

43. Martin Luther King Jr., *I Have a Dream* (New York: HarperCollins, 1986), 92.

44. P. Williams, *Rooster's Egg*, 186.

45. Dickerson, *End of Blackness*, 11.

46. Richard Posner, "Beyond All Reason," *New Republic* (October 13, 1997): 42 (book review).

47. P. Williams, *Rooster's Egg*, 24.

48. Henry Louis Gates Jr., *Loose Canons: Notes on the Culture Wars* (New York: Oxford University Press, 1992), 185.

49. Robert S. Boynton, "The New Intellectuals," *Atlantic Monthly* (March 1995): 53, 66 (quoting Gitlin).

50. McWhorter, *Losing the Race*, 34.

51. Dalton, *Racial Healing*, 94.

52. Aubrey Dillon-Mallone, ed., *The Cynic's Dictionary* (Lincolnwood, Ill.: Contemporary Books, 2000), 234 (quoting Brimelow).

53. Bell, *And We Are Not Saved*, 205. I do not suggest that Bell's excesses have provoked no response. See Leroy Clark, "A Critique of Professor Derrick Bell's Thesis of the Permanence of Racism and His Strategy of Confrontation," 73 *Denver University Law Review* (1995): 23. See also Randall Kennedy, *Race, Crime, and the Law* (New York: Pantheon, 1997), 389–90 ("The most salient feature of race relations at the end of the twentieth century is its complexity—a complexity that renders unfit as a guide . . . to action . . . the claim that racial bias is as dominant now as it once was.").

54. P. Williams, *Rooster's Egg*, 227–28.

NOTES TO CHAPTER 4

1. *Regents of the University of California v. Bakke,* 438 U.S. 265, 407 (Blackmun, concurring).

2. Louise Derman-Sparks and Carol Brunson Phillips, *Teaching/Learning Anti-Racism: A Developmental Approach* (New York: Teachers College Press, 1997), 10.

3. Melvyn Fein, *Race and Morality* (New York: Kluwer, 2001), 6 (quoting Asante).

4. Judith Shulevitz, "The Close Reader: At War with the World," *New York Times Book Review* (October 21, 2001): 39 (quoting Edward Said).

5. Ex. 23:3 and Lev. 19:15.

6. Shulevitz, "Close Reader," 39.

7. Kenneth Clark, "Delusions of the White Liberal," *New York Times Magazine* (April 4, 1965): 137.

8. Frug, "Postmodern," 1047 (quoting Andrea Dworkin with approval).

9. Richard Delgado and Jean Stefancic, "Scorn," 35 *William and Mary Law Review* (1994): 1099.

10. Richard Delgado and Jean Stefancic, *Failed Revolutions: Social Reform and the Limits of Legal Imagination* (Boulder, Colo.: Westview, 1994), 129, 116.

11. P. Williams, *Rooster's Egg,* 118.

12. Ibid., 113, 114.

13. Randall Robinson, *The Debt* (New York: Dutton, 2000), 90.

14. Christie Davies, *Ethnic Humor around the World* (Bloomington: Indiana University Press, 1990), 9, 323.

15. Ibid., 285.

16. Charles Gruner, *The Game of Humor* (New Brunswick, N.J.: Transactions, 1997), 103 (quoting Davies). Other folklorists agree that groups "being mocked by ethnic jokes are the creators and best audience for those jokes." See Joseph Boskin, *Rebellious Laughter* (Syracuse, N.Y.: Syracuse University Press, 1997), 129

17. Nathan Ausubel, ed., *A Treasury of Jewish Folklore* (New York: Crown, 1948), 425.

18. Mel Watkins, *On the Real Side: Laughing, Lying, and Signifying* (New York: Simon and Schuster, 1994) (quoting Freud).

19. Lawrence Levine, *Black Culture and Black Consciousness* (New York: Oxford University Press, 1977), 320–36.

20. John Lowe, *Jump at the Sun: Zora Neale Hurston's Cosmic Comedy* (Urbana: University of Illinois Press, 1997), 156.

21. Ibid., 40 (quoting Ellison).

22. Gates, *Signifying Monkey,* 68 (quoting Hermese Roberts), 64.

23. Ibid., 76 (quoting Richard Lanham).

24. Alan Ryan, *Liberal Anxieties and Liberal Education* (New York: Hill and Wang, 1998), 159.

25. Reported in Diana Furchtgott-Roth and Christine Stolba, *The Feminist Dilemma* (Washington, D.C.: American Enterprise Institute, 2001), 101–2.

26. Watkins, *On the Real Side,* 480 (quoting Wilson).

27. Sarah Delany and Elizabeth Delany (with Amy Hill Hearth), *Having Our Say* (New York: Kodansha, 1993), 16.

28. Cheryl Bentsen, "Head Negro in Charge," *Boston Magazine* (April 1998): 104.

29. Watkins, *On the Real Side,* 31.

30. Ibid., 33.

31. Ibid., 572.

32. See chapter 1.

33. Katie Roiphe, *The Morning After: Sex, Fear, and Feminism on Campus* (Boston: Little, Brown, 1993), 6.

34. J. N. Isbister, *Freud* (Cambridge, U.K.: Polity, 1985), 141.

35. Ernest Jones, *Life and Work of Sigmund Freud,* vol. 2 (New York: Basic Books, 1955), 335.

36. Isbister, *Freud,* 141–42 (emphasis added).

37. *Complete Poems of Emily Dickinson,* T. Johnson, ed. (London: Faber, 1970), poem 1129.

38. Eccl. 7:5.

39. Anthony Lin, "Dewey Partner's E-Mail Causes Upset over Racial Insensitivity," *New York Law Journal* (January 28, 2004): 1.

40. Jonathan Glater, "Asian-Americans Take Offense at Law Firm Memo," *New York Times* (February 7, 2004): C1.

41. Julie Chao, "A Matter of Culture—and Business," *Atlanta Constitution* (September 3, 2000): 3G; Bill Savadove, "Keeping Dogs off the Dinner Table Seen as Test of Civilised City," *South China Morning Post* (May 30, 2002): 3; Julia Chao, "Is China Going to the Dogs?" *Toronto Star* (September 6, 2000): Life sec., FD04; Paula Hall, "Pet SOS Special: Caged Up and Ready to Eat," *Coventry Evening Telegraph* (October 23, 2002): 8; "China Weighs Animal Rights against Tradition, Culture, and Money," Agence France Presse (2004 Westlaw 79641587) (May 16, 2004).

42. "If love is judged by most of its effects," concluded the French epigrammatist La Rochefoucauld, "it resembles hate more than friendship." Quoted in Arnold Ludwig, *The Importance of Lying* (Springfield, Ill.: C. C. Thomas, 1965), 99.

43. Ludwig, *Importance of Lying,* 99 (quoting Durant).

44. Isaiah 11:6.

45. John Callahan, "Frequencies of Memory: A Eulogy for Ralph Waldo Ellison," 18 *Callaloo* (spring 1995): 298 (quoting Ellison).

46. Statement by Foundation for Individual Rights in Education (October 28, 2004).

47. Christopher Caldwell, "France's Native Disgrace," *New York Times Book Review* (July 15, 2001): 9 (quoting Vladimir Jenkelevich).

48. Armond Fields and L. Marc Fields, *From the Bowery to Broadway* (New York: Oxford University Press, 1993), 50.

49. Stephen Leacock, *Humor and Humanity* (New York: Holt, 1938), 219–20.

50. *Bartlett's Familiar Quotations,* 17th ed. (Boston: Little, Brown, 2002), 336 (quoting Horace Walpole, "Letters to the Countess of Upper Ossory," August 16, 1776).

NOTES TO CHAPTER 5

1. Regina Austin, "Beyond Black Demons and White Devils: Antiblack Conspiracy Theorizing and the Black Public Sphere," 22 *Florida State University Law Review* (1995): 1021.

2. Ibid., 1022, 1045, 1022, 1032, 1042, 1035.

3. Wil Haygood, "True or False, Rumors Spread," *Boston Sunday Globe* (December 15, 1996): A1 (quoting Dyson).

4. Patricia Turner, *I Heard It through the Grapevine* (Berkeley: University of California Press, 1993), 220.

5. Pascal's Wager is defined as "either God exists or not. If God does exist, the stake gained is infinite life. If God does not exist, there are no winnings. Because the potential winnings are infinite, religious belief is more rational than unbelief" because of its greater expected value. Robert Audi, ed., *Cambridge Dictionary of Philosophy* (New York: Cambridge University Press, 1995), 563.

6. Sara Rimer, "Blacks Are Urged to Act to Increase Awareness of AIDS Epidemic," *New York Times* (October 23, 1996): A16.

7. P. Williams, *Alchemy,* 8.

8. Gates, *Thirteen Ways,* xxi.

9. P. Williams, *Rooster's Egg,* 25 (see the epigraph to this chapter).

10. Gary Peller, "Toward a Critical Cultural Pluralism: Progressive Alternatives to Mainstream Civil Rights Ideology," in Crenshaw et al., *Critical Race Theory,* 135.

11. Richard Delgado, "Brewer's Plea: Critical Thoughts on Common Cause," 44 *Vanderbilt Law Review* (1991): 1, 9.

12. Peller, "Toward a Critical," 133–34.

13. Ibid.

14. Ibid., 151.

15. Gates, *Thirteen Ways,* 207.

16. Crouch, *All-American Skin Game,* xiv.

17. Stanley Crouch, *Always in Pursuit* (New York: Pantheon, 1998), 141 (emphasis in original).

18. K. Anthony Appiah, "The Multiculturalist Misunderstanding," *New York Review of Books* (October 9, 1997): 36.

19. Crouch, *All-American Skin Game*, xiv, xv, 44.

20. S. Steele, "Race Not Run," 28.

21. Derrick Bell, "Bakke, Minority Admissions, and the Usual Price of Racial Remedies," 67 *California Law Review* (1979): 1, 8.

22. Society of American Law Teachers, "Statement on the Bar Exam," July 2002.

23. The Committee on Legal Education and Admission to the Bar of the Association of the Bar of the City of New York and The Committee on Legal Education and Admission to the Bar of the New York State Bar Association, *Joint Report, Public Service Alternative Bar Examination* (June 14, 2002).

24. See chapter 2.

25. Tamar Jacoby, "Day of the Race Men," 103 *Commentary* (April 1997): 36, 37 (quoting a remark reputed to have been made by Bayard Rustin).

26. P. Williams, *Rooster's Egg*, 63, 67, 68.

27. Ibid., 66.

28. Ibid., 79–80.

29. George Bernard Shaw, *Pygmalion* (1881).

30. Alex Johnson, "Bid Whist, Tonk, and U.S. v. Fordice: Why Integration Fails African Americans Again," 81 *California Law Review* (December 1993): 1401, 1451–52.

31. Sara Rimer, "Do Black and White Children Learn the Same Way?" *New York Times* (June 24, 1988): B1 (quoting Hilliard).

32. Maria Ontiveros, "Rosa Lopez, Christopher Darden, and Me: Issues of Gender, Ethnicity, and Class in Evaluating Witness Credibility," in *Critical Race Feminism*, Adrien Wing, ed. (New York: NYU Press, 1997), 269, 273.

33. "School Colors," *Frontline* (PBS TV broadcast, October 18, 1994).

34. Ellis Cose, *Color-Blind: Seeing beyond Race in a Race-Obsessed World* (New York: HarperCollins, 1997), 45 (quoting Ogbu).

35. Available at www.nsf.gov/sbe/srs/nsf04303/pdfstart.htm (by extrapolation).

36. *USA Today* (January 5, 2004): 1.

37. *60 Minutes* (CBS television broadcast, November 24, 1996).

38. John Leland and Allison Samuels, "The New Generation Gap," *Newsweek* (March 17, 1997): 52.

39. Crouch, *All-American Skin Game*, 249, 250.

40. John McWhorter, "How Hip-Hop Holds Blacks Back," *City Journal* (summer 2003): 66, 75 (quoting Dyson).

41. Dalton, *Racial Healing*, 198.

42. P. Williams, *Rooster's Egg*, 68.

43. 8 U.S.C. § 1153(b)(5)(A) (1996).

44. Available at uscis.gov/graphics/shared/aboutus/statistics/299.htm (accessed January 26, 2004).

45. Nestor Rodriguez, "U.S. Immigration and Intergroup Relations in the Late 20th Century: African Americans and Latinos," *Social Justice* (September 1, 1996): 111. It is not clear at all that black attitudes differ from those of whites. What I offer is hardly conclusive, but recent polls have shown considerable concern by African Americans on the subject of immigration. A 1995 survey of African American residents of Houston showed that only 36 percent of them viewed "the impact of immigration" as "good" or "very good," while 54 percent rated it "bad" or "very bad." Ibid., 118. That economic factors might be at play seems irrelevant.

46. Swain, *New White Nationalism*, 438 (emphasis in original).

47. Samuel P. Huntington, "The Hispanic Challenge," *Foreign Policy* (March/April 2004).

48. Jennifer L. Hochschild, *Facing Up to the American Dream* (Princeton: Princeton University Press, 1995), 43.

49. Derrick Bell, "Brown v. Board of Education and the Interest-Convergence Dilemma," 93 *Harvard Law Review* 518 (1980).

50. Bell, *Faces*, 18.

51. Bell, *And We Are Not Saved*, 154–55.

52. Dennis Litowitz, "Some Critical Thoughts on Critical Race Theory," 72 *Notre Dame Law Review* (1997): 503, 524.

53. Christopher Edley, *Not All Black and White* (New York: Hill and Wang, 1996).

54. Richard Delgado and Jean Stefancic, "Images of the Outsider in American Law and Culture: Can Free Expression Remedy Systemic Social Ills?" 77 *Cornell Law Review* (1992): 1258, 1261.

55. Frank Bruni, "Tourists Flocking to Harlem Churches," *Houston Chronicle* (November 24, 1996): 14 (quoting P. Williams).

56. L. Williams, *It's the Little Things*, 184.

57. P. Williams, *Alchemy*, 206.

58. P. Williams, *Rooster's Egg*, 184.

59. R. Kennedy, *Race, Crime, and the Law*, 389.

60. Erik Erikson, *Gandhi's Truth: On the Origins of Militant Nonviolence* (New York: Norton, 1969), 154.

61. Jane Gillham, ed., *The Science of Optimism and Hope* (Philadelphia: Templeton Foundation Press, 2000).

62. P. Williams, *Rooster's Egg*, 108.

63. Amin Maalouf, *In the Name of Identity*, trans. Barbara Bray (New York: Arcade, 2000), 121.

64. William McGowan, *Coloring the News* (San Francisco: Encounter Books, 2001), 60–69.

65. Robert Entman and Andrew Rojecki, *The Black Image in the White Mind* (Chicago: University of Chicago Press, 2000), 197–98.

66. Chris Rock, *Rock This!* (New York: Hyperion, 1997), 19.

67. Charles Lawrence III, preface to *Crossroads, Directions, and a New Critical Race Theory,* Francisco Valdes et al., eds. (Philadelphia: Temple University Press, 2002), xix.

NOTES TO CHAPTER 6

1. Karen Lehrman, *The Lipstick Proviso: Women, Sex, and Power in the Real World* (New York: Anchor, 1997), 52.

2. Baer, *Our Lives,* 71.

3. Robin West, "The Difference in Women's Hedonic Lives: A Phenomenological Critique of Feminist Legal Theory," 15 *Wisconsin Women's Law Journal* (2000): 149.

4. Robin West, *Caring for Justice* (New York: NYU Press, 1997), 100, 148, 138.

5. Ibid., 149; Baer, *Our Lives,* 106, 107.

6. Baer, *Our Lives,* 107.

7. West, "Difference," 81, 96.

8. Ibid., 110.

9. Catharine MacKinnon, *Feminism Unmodified* (Cambridge, Mass.: Harvard University Press, 1987), 99.

10. 410 U.S. 113 (1973).

11. Linda Hirshman and Jane Larson, *Hard Bargains: The Politics of Sex* (New York: Oxford University Press, 1998), 286.

12. Robert Hughes, *The Culture of Complaint* (Malden, Mass.: Blackwell, 1993), 10 (quoting Estrich).

13. Hirshman and Larson, *Hard Bargains,* 271.

14. Baer, *Our Lives,* 19–20; West, *Caring for Justice,* 146.

15. Frug, "Postmodern," 1066.

16. Stephen Schulhofer, *Unwanted Sex: The Culture of Intimidation and the Failure of Law* (Cambridge, Mass. Harvard University Press, 1998), 169.

17. Ibid., 151–75, esp. 156.

18. Ibid., 107–9.

19. Judith Jordan, "Towards Competence and Connection," in *The Complexity of Connection,* Judith Jordan et al., eds. (New York: Guilford, 2004), 22–23 (emphasis in original).

20. Midge Decter, *An Old Wife's Tale* (New York: Regan Books, 2001), 81.

21. Graglia, *Domestic Tranquility,* 264 (quoting Friedan).

22. Elizabeth Spellman, "Aristotle and the Politicization of the Soul," in *Discovering Reality*, Sandra Harding and Merrill Hintikka, eds. (Dordrecht, Netherlands: Kluwer, 2003), 17.

23. Andrea Sachs and Judith Wallerstein, "No-Fault Divorce," *Time* (April 14, 2003): A12.

24. June Carbone, *From Parents to Partners* (New York: Columbia University Press, 2000), 18 (quoting Weitzman).

25. Patai and Koertge, *Professing Feminism*, 1–2.

26. West, *Caring for Justice*, 18, 108, 117.

27. Robin West, "Economic Man and Literary Woman: One Contrast," 39 *Mercer Law Review* (1988): 867, 869.

28. Robin West, "Jurisprudence and Gender," 55 *University of Chicago Law Review* (1988): 1, 2.

29. MacKinnon, *Feminism Unmodified*, 45.

30. Martha Nussbaum, "Only Grey Matter: Richard Posner's Cost-Benefit Analysis of Sex," 59 *University of Chicago Law Review* (1992): 1689, 1715–16.

31. Gen. 3:16.

32. Primary Sources, *Atlantic Monthly* (October 2003): 49.

33. Graglia, *Domestic Tranquility*, 211–12.

34. Hirshman and Larson, *Hard Bargains*.

35. Kingsley Browne, *Biology at Work: Rethinking Sexual Equality* (New Brunswick, N.J.: Rutgers University Press, 2002), 195.

36. ABA Model Rules of Professional Conduct R 1.8.

37. Camille Paglia, *Sexual Personae* (New York: Vintage, 1991), 2.

38. Kevin Lynch, *The Capital Times* (Madison, Wis.) (December 15, 1994): 1D (quoting Paglia).

39. Deborah Sontag, "Fierce Entanglements," *New York Times Magazine* (November 17, 2002): 52.

40. Browne, *Biology at Work*, 196.

41. William Ian Miller, *Faking It* (Cambridge: Cambridge University Press, 2003), 52.

42. Mary Belenky, Blythe McVicker Clinchy, Nancy Rule Goldberger, and Jill Mattuck Tarule, *Women's Ways of Knowing: The Development of Self, Voice, and Mind* (New York: Basic Books, 1986), 100.

43. Helen Fisher, *The First Sex* (New York: Random House, 1999), 5–28.

44. Belenky et al., *Women's Ways*, 104, 113, 123–24.

45. Beverly Tatum, *Why Are All the Black Kids Sitting Together in the Cafeteria?* (New York: Basic Books, 1997), 59.

46. L. Williams, *It's the Little Things*, 14–15.

47. Ayana Byrd and Lori Tharps, *Hair Story* (New York: St. Martin's, 2001), 176 (quoting hooks).

48. Paulette Caldwell, "A Hair Piece: Perspectives on the Intersection of Race and Gender," *Duke Law Journal* (1991): 365.

49. John Gray, *Men Are from Mars, Women Are from Venus* (New York: HarperCollins, 1992), 39.

50. James Tooley, *The Miseducation of Women* (Chicago: Ivan Dee, 2003), 36 (quoting Carrie Paechter).

51. Carrie Paechter, *Educating the Other: Gender, Power, and Schooling* (London: Falmer Press, 1998), 75.

52. Chesler, *Woman's Inhumanity to Woman*, 476, 477.

53. West, "Difference," 81, 86.

54. Isaiah 11:6.

NOTES TO CHAPTER 7

1. Lani Guinier, Michelle Fine, and Jane Balin, "Becoming Gentlemen: Women's Experience at One Ivy League Law School," 143 *University of Pennsylvania Law Review* (1994): 1, 2.

2. Lani Guinier, Michelle Fine, and Jane Balin, *Becoming Gentlemen: Women, Law School, and Institutional Change* (Boston: Beacon, 1997).

3. Ibid., 28.

4. Ibid., 27 (quoting Audre Lorde).

5. Ibid., 29, 77.

6. Myra Sadker and David Sadker, *Failing at Fairness: How America's Schools Cheat Girls* (New York: Scribner's Sons, 1994), 48; Belenky et al., *Women's Ways of Knowing*, 45.

7. David Myers, *Social Psychology*, 6th ed. (Boston: McGraw-Hill College, 1999), 581 (citing M. Olffson and H. A. Pincus).

8. Linda Hirshman, *A Woman's Guide to Law School* (New York: Penguin, 1999), 6 (quoting Arkin).

9. Scott Turow, *One L* (New York: Putnam, 1977), 245.

10. Belenky et al., *Women's Ways of Knowing*, 94, 149 (quoting an interviewee).

11. Duncan Kennedy, *Legal Education and the Reproduction of Hierarchy* (Cambridge, Mass.: Afar, 1983), 109.

12. The evidence, it turns out, is mixed as to whether women law students are more motivated to "help society." See American Bar Association Commission on Women in the Profession, *Options and Obstacles: A Survey of the Studies of the Careers of Women Lawyers* (ABA, July 1994), 6–9.

13. *In re Bradwell*, 55 Ill. 535, 542 (1869).

14. Lorraine Dusky, *Still Unequal: The Shameful Truth about Women and Justice in America* (New York: Crown, 1996), 13.

15. MacKinnon, *Feminism Unmodified*, 205.

16. Guinier, Fine, and Balin, "Becoming Gentlemen," 84.

17. Dusky, *Still Unequal*, 2.

18. Catherine Weiss and Louise Melling, "The Legal Education of Twenty Women," 40 *Stanford Law Review* (1988): 1299, 1307.

19. Mari Matsuda, "When the First Quail Calls," 14 *Women's Rights Law Reporter* 297, 298 (1992).

20. American Bar Association Commission on Women in the Profession, *Elusive Equality: The Experiences of Women in Legal Education,* Executive Summary (ABA, 1996).

21. Linda Wightman, *Women in Legal Education: A Comparison of the Law School Performance and Law School Experiences of Women and Men* (Law School Admission Council, 1996), 26. Special breakdowns for minority women were provided in the report, but they will not be analyzed here.

22. Paula Gaber, "Just Trying to Be Human in This Place: The Legal Education of Twenty Women," 10 *Yale Journal of Law and Feminism* (1998): 165, 184, 185, 196, 197.

23. Ibid., 192, 198.

24. Ibid., 180, 249.

25. Ibid., 261, 263–64.

26. Morrison Torrey, Jennifer Ries, and Elaine Spiliopoulos, "What Every First-Year Female Student Should Know," 7 *Columbia Journal of Gender and Law* (1998): 267, 309.

27. Ibid., 275.

28. Jennifer Brown, "To Give Them Countenance: The Case for a Woman's Law School," 22 *Harvard Women's Law Journal* (1999): 1, 2.

29. Hirshman, *Woman's Guide*, 272.

30. Todd Gitlin, *The Twilight of Common Dreams* (New York: Metropolitan Books, 1995), 32.

31. Roiphe, *Morning After*, 34.

32. Gitlin, *Twilight*, 32.

33. "Lani Guinier Appointed at Harvard," *Oakland Tribune* (February 11, 1998): 3.

34. Nancy Levit, *The Gender Line: Men, Women, and the Law* (New York: NYU Press, 1998), 224.

35. MacKinnon, *Feminism Unmodified*, 221.

36. Laurel Leff, "The Making of a 'Quota Queen,'" in *Feminism, Media, and the Law,* Martha Fineman and Martha McCluskey, eds. (New York: Oxford University Press, 1997), 38 (quoting Bell).

37. Stephen Carter, preface to *The Tyranny of the Majority,* by Lani Guinier (New York: Free Press, 1994), xx.

NOTES TO CHAPTER 8

1. Marina Angel, "Women in Legal Education: What It's Like to Be Part of a Perpetual First Wave or the Case of the Disappearing Women," 61 *Temple Law Review* (1988): 799, 801.

2. Richard A. White, "Association of American Law Schools Statistical Report on Law School Faculty and Candidates for Law Faculty Positions, 1999–2000," table 2, available at www.aals.org/statistics/T2A.htm. If anyone objects to these developments, he is awfully quiet about it.

3. Richard Neumann, "Women in Legal Education: What the Statistics Show," 50 *Journal of Legal Education* (2000): 313, 352.

4. Marina Angel, "Comments in Reply: It's Becoming a Glass House," 50 *Journal of Legal Education* (2000): 454.

5. Torrey, Ries, and Spiliopoulos, "What Every First-Year Female Student," 267, 309.

6. Carrie Menkel-Meadow, "Women as Law Teachers: Toward the 'Feminization' of Legal Education," in *Humanistic Education in Law: Essays on the Application of a Humanistic Perspective to Law Teaching* (New York: Columbia University Press, 1981), 16, 18.

7. Kathleen Bean, "The Gender Gap in the Law School Classroom—Beyond Survival," 14 *Vermont Law Review* (1989): 23.

8. Christine Farley, "Confronting Expectations: Women in the Legal Academy," 8 *Yale Journal of Law and Feminism* (1996): 333, 337 n. 19.

9. Ibid., 337, 339, 340.

10. Special thanks go to Dina Cangero, who was instrumental in classifying, organizing, and interpreting the data. The table is based on student responses in thirty-seven classes. The only fall 1999 class not included in this tabulation is Legal Methods, which was excluded to make conclusions more comparable to those of Farley, who, likewise, did not tabulate results for that course. Since twenty-nine of the classes were taught by men and eight by women, a factor of 3.625 (29/8) was applied to the right-hand column. Comments made fewer than four times for both males and females are omitted.

11. Comments such as "She is a nice person" are not deemed gender-based. Here is what students said about attire: "put a tie on," "I loved his colorful shirts," and "dresses like GQ Magazine."

12. C. Farley, "Confronting," 339 n. 38; ABA Commission, *Elusive Equality*, 4.

13. Larry Elder, *The Ten Things You Can't Say in America* (New York: St. Martin's Griffin, 2000), 140 (quoting Darla Moore).

14. Nancy Levit, "Keeping Feminism in Its Place: Sex Segregation and the Domestication of Female Academics," 49 *University of Kansas Law Review* (2001): 775, 781, 782.

15. Neumann, "Women in Legal Education," 313, 352.

16. Browne, *Biology at Work,* 88.

17. Joan Williams, "What Stymies Women's Academic Careers? It's Personal," *Chronicle of Higher Education* (December 15, 2000).

18. J. Williams, *Unbending Gender.*

19. Ibid., 2.

20. Primary Sources, *Atlantic Monthly* (October 2003): 48.

21. J. Williams, "What Stymies."

22. Browne, *Biology at Work,* 80.

23. Deborah Jones Merritt and Barbara Reskin, "Moving into the Legal Academy: Challenges and Achievements for Women," in Joint AALS/ABA Workshop, *Taking Stock: Women of All Colors in Law School* (2003): 29.

24. J. Williams, *Unbending Gender,* 272.

25. Ibid., 244.

26. Maureen J. Arrigo, "Hierarchy Maintained: Status and Gender Issues in Legal Writing Programs," 70 *Temple Law Review* (1997): 117, 155. The normative value to be assigned such pedigree is, of course, another question entirely and should be dealt with directly.

27. The anonymity sought by the respondent will be respected here.

28. White, "Association of American Law Schools," table 2.

29. Browne, *Biology at Work,* 40, 137.

30. Ibid., 137 (quoting Rhode).

31. Susan Estrich, *Sex and Power* (New York: Riverhead Books, 2000), 251–52.

32. Ibid., 249.

33. Lisa Belkin, "The Opt-Out Revolution," *New York Times Magazine* (October 26, 2003): 42, 44.

34. Furchtgott-Roth and Stolba, *Feminist Dilemma,* 4.

35. Estrich, *Sex and Power,* 245.

36. Susan Brownmiller, *Femininity* (New York: Linden Press, 1984), 221, 230.

37. Anna Fels, *Necessary Dreams: Ambition in Women's Changing Lives* (New York: Pantheon, 2004), 155–56.

38. Ibid., 145.

39. Ibid., 192 (quoting Person).

40. Virginia Varian, *Why So Slow?* (Cambridge, Mass.: MIT Press, 1999), 154.

41. Ibid., 159.

42. Elizabeth McKenna, *When Work Doesn't Work Anymore: Women, Work, and Identity,* 240 (New York: Delacorte Press, 1997), 240 (quoting Quindlen) (emphasis in original).

43. "Be a Man," *Economist* (June 28–July 4, 2003): 64–65 (citing the work of Catherine Hakim).

44. Browne, *Biology at Work*, 175.

45. Anne Machung, "Talking Career, Thinking Job: Gender Differences in Career and Family Expectations of Berkeley Seniors," 15 *Feminist Studies* #1 (spring 1989): 35–58.

46. I conducted the study.

47. Fisher, *First Sex*, 29.

48. Sowell, *Quest for Cosmic Justice*, 62, 63.

49. Varian, *Why So Slow?* 267.

50. 839 F.2d 302 (7th Cir. 1988) (holding that the substantial underrepresentation of women in commission-sales work was the product of their "lack of interest" and not the company's discriminatory policy).

51. Mari Jo Buhle, *Feminism and Its Discontents* (Cambridge, Mass.: Harvard University Press, 1998), 76–77, 83.

52. Paglia, *Sexual Personae*, 38.

53. Tooley, *Miseducation of Women*, 86 (quoting Greer).

54. Donald Symons, *The Evolution of Human Sexuality* (New York: Oxford University Press, 1979).

55. Ibid., 131 (citing the work of David Buss).

56. Geoffrey Miller, *The Mating Mind* (New York: Doubleday, 2000), 377.

57. Fisher, *First Sex*, 47.

58. Browne, *Biology at Work*, 113.

59. Leslie Farber, *Lying, Despair, Jealousy, Envy, Sex, Suicide, Drugs, and the Good Life* (New York: Basic Books, 1976), 170 (quoting Decter).

60. West, *Caring for Justice*, 104 (emphasis in original).

61. Richard Neumann, "Comments in Reply," 51 *Journal of Legal Education* (2001): 151, 156.

62. Browne, *Biology at Work*, 217.

63. Elizabeth Schneider, "The Dialectic of Rights and Politics: Perspectives from the Women's Movement," 61 *New York University Law Review* (1986): 589, 652.

64. Fels, *Necessary Dreams*, 150.

65. Chesler, *Woman's Inhumanity to Woman*, 479.

66. Linda Babcock and Sara Laschever, *Women Don't Ask: Negotiation and the Gender Divide* (Princeton: Princeton University Press, 2003), 1–2.

67. Lehrman, *Lipstick Proviso*, 8.

68. Babcock and Laschever, *Women Don't Ask*, 1.

69. Available at http://roadandtravel.com/businessandcareer/careers/dyk_minoritycarbuy.htm.

70. Chesler, *Woman's Inhumanity to Woman*, 479.

71. Ibid., 480.

72. Varian, *Why So Slow?* 276.
73. Matthew 7:7.

NOTES TO CHAPTER 9

1. Regina Austin tells the Crystal Chambers story in "Sapphire Bound!" 539. Chambers was the plaintiff in *Chambers v. Omaha Girls Club,* 629 F. Supp. 925 (1986) affirmed 834 F. 2d 697 (8th Cir.) 1987. Citations to pages of the article and case are not provided.

2. Dorothy Roberts, "Racism and Patriarchy in the Meaning of Mother-hood," 1 *American Journal of Gender and Law* (1993): 1, 4, 23–24.

3. Andrew Hacker, "How Are Women Doing?" *New York Review of Books* (April 11, 2002): 64.

4. Andrew Hacker, *Mismatch: The Growing Gulf between Men and Women* (New York: Scribner, 2003), 156; Dorothy Roberts, *Killing the Black Body* (New York: Pantheon, 1997), 120.

5. Leon Dash, *When Children Want Children: The Urban Crisis of Teenage Childbearing* (Urbana: University of Illinois Press, 2003), 6.

6. Joan Tarpley, "Blackwomen, Sexual Myth, and Jurisprudence," 69 *Temple Law Review* (1996): 1343, 1387.

7. Dorothy Roberts, "Crime, Race, and Reproduction," 67 *Tulane Law Review* (1993): 1945, 1977.

8. P. Williams, *Rooster's Egg,* 180.

9. Ibid., 8–9.

10. Ibid., 155–56.

11. Rosemary Bray, "So How Did I Get Here?" *New York Times Magazine* (November 8, 1992): 36, 40.

12. Alice Walker, "What Can the White Man . . . Say to the Black Woman?" *Nation* (May 22, 1989): 691–92 (emphasis in original).

13. Anthony Alfieri, "Black and White," 85 *California Law Review* (1997): 1647, 1674–75 (book review) (quoting Austin).

14. Noel Ignatiev, "The American Intifada," in *Race Traitor,* Noel Ignatiev and John Garvey, eds. (New York: Routledge, 1996), 99.

15. Roberts, *Killing the Black Body,* chap. 5.

16. Patterson, *Ordeal of Integration,* 49.

17. Leslie Espinoza, "Empowerment and Achievement in Minority Law Student Support Programs: Constructing Affirmative Action," 22 *University of Michigan Journal of Law Reform* (1989): 281, 293.

18. William J. Wilson, *When Work Disappears: The World of the New Urban Poor* (New York: Knopf, 1996), xiii.

19. Kenneth Neubeck and Noel A. Cazenave, *Welfare Racism: Playing the Race Card against America's Poor* (New York: Routledge, 2001), 5.

20. Roberts, *Killing the Black Body*, 111.

21. Derrick Bell, *Confronting Authority* (Boston: Beacon, 1994), 54.

22. Deborah Post, "Power and Morality in Grading—A Case Study and a Few Critical Thoughts on Grade Normalization," 65 *UMKC Law Review* (1997): 777, 812 (quoting Zukav's *Dancing Wu Li Masters*).

23. P. Williams, *Rooster's Egg*, 175.

24. Ibid., 156.

25. Lionel Tiger, *The Decline of Males* (New York: St. Martin's Griffin, 1999), 56.

26. P. Williams, *Rooster's Egg*, 9.

27. Ibid., 173–74.

28. Dalton, *Racial Healing*, 132.

29. P. Williams, *Rooster's Egg*, 181.

30. Les Payne, "Single Moms Keep a People Alive," *Newsday* (May 12, 1996): A42.

31. Roberts, *Killing the Black Body*, 116.

32. David Blankenhorn, *Fatherless America: Confronting Our Most Urgent Social Problem* (New York: HarperPerennial, 1995), 1, 4, 3.

33. Sara McLanahan and Gary Sandefur, *Growing Up with a Single Parent: What Hurts, What Helps* (Cambridge, Mass.: Harvard University Press, 1994), 138.

34. "The Toni Award," *New Republic* (June 19, 1989): 9.

35. McLanahan and Sandefur, *Growing Up*, 42.

36. David Popenoe, *Life without Father: Compelling New Evidence That Fatherhood and Marriage Are Indispensable for the Good of Children and Society* (New York: Free Press, 1996), 57 (repeating a finding published by the National Center for Health Statistics).

37. Lawrence Wu and Barbara Wolfe, introduction to *Out of Wedlock*, Lawrence Wu and Barbara Wolfe, eds. (New York: Russell Sage Foundation, 2001), xvii.

38. McLanahan and Sandefur, *Growing Up*, 1.

39. Ibid., 28.

40. William Galston and Elaine Kamark, *Putting Children First: A Progressive Family Policy for the 1990s* (Washington, D.C.: Progressive Policy Institute, 1990), 14–15.

41. Popenoe, *Life without Father*, 63.

42. Wu and Wolfe, *Out of Wedlock*, 17 (emphasis in original).

43. Hacker, *Mismatch*, 150.

44. Orlando Patterson, "The Crisis of Gender Relations among African Americans," in *Race, Gender, and Power in America*, Anita Hill and Emma Jordan, eds. (New York: Oxford University Press, 1995), 56.

45. Chris Rock, *Bigger and Blacker* (video, 1999).

46. Patterson, "Crisis," 69.

47. Dorothy Roberts, *Shattered Bonds: The Color of Child Welfare* (New York: Basic Books, 2002), vi.

48. S. Steele, *A Dream Deferred*, 78 (emphasis in original).

49. Joel Schwartz, "Where Dr. King Went Wrong," *City Journal* (winter 2002): 91–92.

50. Bob Herbert, "A Word to the Wise," *New York Times* (February 14, 1997): A37 (quoting Price).

51. Jocelyn Elders and David Chanoff, *Joycelyn Elders, M.D.: From Share-cropper's Daughter to Surgeon General of the United States of America* (New York: Morrow, 1996), 329–30.

52. P. Williams, *Rooster's Egg*, 221.

53. Scott, *Contempt and Pity*, 177.

54. Richard Majors and Janet Billson, *Cool Pose: The Dilemmas of Black Manhood in America* (New York: Touchstone, 2002), 12.

55. Rock, *Bigger and Blacker*.

NOTES TO CHAPTER 10

1. This story is adapted from one told in the 1980s by a recently arrived immigrant from Moscow who reported that it was circulating widely in the Jewish community there.

2. Susan Sturm and Lani Guinier, "The Future of Affirmative Action: Reclaiming the Innovative Ideal," 84 *California Law Review* (1996): 953, 957.

3. 123 S. Ct. 2325 (2003).

4. Owen, "From Race to Chase," 50.

5. Thernstrom and Thernstrom, *No Excuses*, 131.

6. Bob Herbert, "Don't Flunk the Future," *New York Times* (August 13, 1998): A23 (quoting Price, former president of the National Urban League).

7. James Comer, "Closing the Achievement Gap," *Teacher Magazine* (June 2001).

8. Gabrielle Finley, "Changes to SAT I Sparks [*sic*] Disparity Debate," *Black Issues in Higher Education* (July 18, 2002): 11.

9. Eric Hoover, "SAT Scores Rose in 2003, but Racial Gap Widened," *Chronicle of Higher Education* (August 26, 2003).

10. John Ogbu, *Black American Students in an Affluent Suburb: A Study of Academic Disengagement* (Mahwah, N.J.: Erlbaum, 2003), 6–7.

11. Marcellus Andrews, *The Political Economy of Hope and Fear* (New York: NYU Press, 1999), 42.

12. Claude Steele and Joshua Aronson, "Stereotype Threat and the Test Performance of Academically Successful African Americans," in *The Black-White*

Test Score Gap, Christopher Jencks and Meredith Phillips, eds. (Washington, D.C.: Brookings Institution Press, 1998), 402.

13. Frederick Vars and William Bowen, "Scholastic Aptitude Test Scores, Race, and Academic Performance in Selective Colleges and Universities," in Jencks, *Black-White Test Score Gap,* 470–71.

14. Page numbers are not available at the time of this writing for "A Systemic Analysis of Affirmative Action in American Law Schools," *Stanford Law Review* (forthcoming).

15. "2002 Writing Competition," pamphlet, Columbia Law School 7–8.

16. Stephan Thernstrom and Abigail Thernstrom, "Racial Preferences in Higher Education," in *One America?* Stanley Renshon, ed. (Washington, D.C.: Georgetown University Press, 2001), 195.

17. Patterson, *Ordeal of Integration,* 127 (citing Derek Neal and William Johnson, "The Role of Pre-Market Factors in Black-White wage Differences," 104 *Journal of Political Economy* [1996]: 895–96).

18. Patterson, *Ordeal of Integration,* 35.

19. Felicia Lee, "Why Are Black Students Lagging?" *New York Times* (November 30, 2002): B3.

20. *Grutter v. Bollinger,* 123 S. Ct. 2325, 2334 (quoting Kent Syverud, dean at Vanderbilt).

21. Pulera, *Visible Differences,* 122 (quoting Hertzberg).

22. Ogbu, *Black American Students,* 279.

23. Danny Martin, *Mathematics Success and Failure among African-American Youth* (Mahwah, N.J.: Erlbaum, 2000), 188.

24. This discussion is based on F. Lee, "Why Are Black Students Lagging?" B9; and Susan Goldsmith, "Rich, Black, Flunking," *East Bay Express* (May 21, 2003).

25. Thernstrom and Thernstrom, *No Excuses,* 142, 139, 134, 141.

26. Steele and Aronson, "Stereotype Threat," 401.

27. Paul Sackett, Chaitra Hardison, and Michael Cullen, "On Stereotype Threat as Accounting for African American–White Difference," *American Psychologist* (January 2004): 7.

28. Du Bois, *Souls of Black Folk,* 8.

29. Claude Steele, "Stereotype Threat and African-American Student Achievement," in *Young, Gifted, and Black,* Theresa Perry, Claude Steele, and Asa Hilliard, eds. (Boston: Beacon, 2003), 109.

30. Sackett et al., "On Stereotype Threat," 8.

31. Sturm and Guinier, "Future of Affirmative Action," 956.

32. Jencks and Phillips, introduction to *Black-White Test Score Gap,* 3–4.

33. Dorothy Brown, *Critical Race Theory* (teacher's manual) (St. Paul, Minn.: Thompson-West, 2003), 7.

34. S. Steele, *A Dream Deferred,* 53, 30, 24, 52.

35. F. Lee, "Why Are Black Students Lagging?" B9.

36. Orlando Patterson, "Taking Culture Seriously: A Framework on Afro-America," in *Culture Matters: How Values Shape Human Progress,* Lawrence Harrison and Samuel Huntington, eds. (New York: Basic Books, 2000), 202, 207 (citing the work of Richard Nisbett).

37. *Hopwood v. Texas,* 78 F. 3d 932, Reh'g en banc den., 84 F. 3d 720, cert. den., 116 S. Ct. 2581 (1996).

38. Sturm and Guinier, "Future of Affirmative Action," 957.

39. In fact, the motivation of some was—in some cases, at least—more complicated. It seems that Jews and other immigrant groups were so successful at getting into schools that administrators at institutions such as Columbia became frightened. See James Crouse and Dale Trusheim, *The Case against the SAT* (Chicago: University of Chicago Press, 1988), 19. An SAT-type test, operating ostensibly in the name of fairness, would preserve traditional values by screening out those who were perceived to be working "far beyond their native intelligence." Ibid., 21.

40. Gerald Early, "Devil in a Blue Dress," *Books and Culture* (September/October 1999): 12.

41. Jonathan Kozol, *Savage Inequalities* (New York: Crown, 1991); and Ron Suskind, *Hope in the Unseen* (New York: Broadway Books, 1998).

42. S. Steele, *A Dream Deferred,* 87 (emphasis in original).

43. Meredith Phillips, Jean Brooks-Gunn, Greg Duncan, Pamela Klebanov, and Jonathan Crane, "Family Background, Parenting Practices, and the Black-White Test Score Gap," in Jencks and Phillips, *Black-White Test Score Gap,* 118.

44. Andrew Hacker, "Saved?" *New York Review of Books* (August 14, 2003): 22, 24 (showing a black-white differential of 140 in the combined SAT scores at the $80,000–100,000 family income level).

45. Leonard Ramist, Charles Lewis, and Laura McAmley-Jenkins, "Student Group Differences in Predicting College Grades: Sex, Language, and Ethnic Groups 1 and 3" (College Board Rept. No. 93-1, 1994).

46. W. Willingham, C. Lewis, R. Morgan, and L. Ramist, *Predicting College Grades: An Analysis of Institutional Trends over Two Decades* (Princeton, N.J.: Educational Testing Service, 1990), 92. Of greater significance, a far more sophisticated study of eleven colleges and universities concludes that "controlling for gender, race, participation in varsity athletics, college and university attended, and major field of study, SAT scores are statistically significant predictors of cumulative grade point averages." Vars and Bowen, "Scholastic Aptitude Test Scores," 463.

47. Ramist et al., "Student Group Differences," 36. See also Vars and Bowen, "Scholastic Aptitude Test Scores," 466 (suggesting that the SAT overpredicts African American performance).

48. Sander, "Systemic Analysis."

49. Sturm and Guinier, "Future of Affirmative Action," 972–73.

50. Linda Wightman, "Predictive Validity of the LSAT: A National Summary of the 1990–92 Correlation Studies" (LSAC Research Report 93-05, 1993): 23, 24.

51. Sander "Systemic Analysis."

52. Linda Wightman and David Muller, "An Analysis of Differential Validity and Differential Prediction for Black, Mexican American, Hispanic, and White Law Students" (LSAC Research Report 90-03, June 1990): 23. Wightman restates this conclusion in "Threat to Legal Education," 34.

53. Michael Selmi, "Testing for Equality: Merit, Efficiency, and the Affirmative Action Debate," 42 *UCLA Law Review* (1995): 1251.

54. The one-shot point is not invalid. Interestingly, none of the critics suggests that this problem affecting the SAT and many other tests could be easily mitigated by repeating the test.

55. Selmi, "Testing for Equality," 1033, 958.

56. Sturm and Guinier, "Future of Affirmative Action," 1003–4.

57. Selmi, "Testing for Equality," 1251, 1299.

58. John Grisham, *The Runaway Jury* (New York: Doubleday, 1996), 309.

59. Selmi, "Testing for Equality," 1276.

60. Sturm and Guinier, "Future of Affirmative Action," 958.

61. 401 U.S. 421 (1971).

62. Linda Gottfredson, "Why *g* Matters: The Complexity of Everyday Life," 24 *Intelligence* (1997): 79, 83, 91.

63. Kemba Dunham, "More Employers Ask Job Seekers for SAT Scores," *Wall Street Journal* (October 28, 2003): B1.

64. Rich Karlgaard, "Microsoft's IQ Dividend," *Wall Street Journal* (July 28, 2004): A13.

65. Sturm and Guinier, "Future of Affirmative Action," 1021, n. 279.

66. Ibid.

67. Christopher Jencks, "Racial Bias in Testing," in Jencks and Phillips, *Black-White Test Score Gap,* 81.

68. Sturm and Guinier, "Future of Affirmative Action," 1010.

69. Selmi, "Testing for Equality," 1265.

70. S. Steele, *A Dream Deferred,* 134.

71. Diane Ravitch, *National Standards in American Education* (Washington, D.C.: Brookings Institution Press, 1995), 185.

72. Jung Chang, *Wild Swans* (New York: Simon and Schuster, 1991), 426.

73. Elder, *Showdown,* 149 (quoting Washington).

74. S. Steele, *A Dream Deferred,* 108 (emphasis in original).

75. Lani Guinier, "Reframing the Affirmative Action Debate," 86 *Kentucky Law Journal* (1997): 505, 506–7; and Lani Guinier and Gerald Torres, *The Miner's Canary* (Cambridge, Mass.: Harvard University Press, 2002).

76. Guinier, "Reframing," 506–7.

77. S. Steele, *A Dream Deferred,* 131.

NOTES TO CHAPTER II

1. Alex M. Johnson Jr., "The New Voice of Color," 100 *Yale Law Journal* (1993): 2007, 2047 n. 170.

2. Delgado, "Legal Storytelling."

3. Gavin De Becker, *The Gift of Fear* (Boston: Little, Brown, 1997), 65.

4. Bell, *Race, Racism, and American Law,* 461–570.

5. Deborah Ramirez, Jennifer Hoopes, and Tara Lai Quinlan, "Defining Racial Profiling in a Post–September 11 World," 40 *American Criminal Law Review* (2003): 1195, 1211.

6. hooks, *Killing Rage,* 14.

7. William Clinton, "Getting a Handle on America's 'Race Problem,'" *Chicago Tribune* (October 17, 1995): N19.

8. U.S. Department of Justice, Bureau of Justice Statistics, "Homicide Trends in the U.S., Trends by Race," available at www.ojp.usdoj.gov/bjs/homicide/race.htm.

9. Ibid., table 40.

10. Heather Mac Donald, *Are Cops Racist?* (Chicago: Ivan Dee, 2003), 25.

11. Mari Matsuda, *Where Is Your Body?* (Boston: Beacon, 1996), 40.

12. James Q. Wilson, "Crime," in *Beyond the Color Line,* Abigail Thernstrom and Stephan Thernstrom, eds. (Stanford, Calif.: Hoover Institution Press, 2002), 117.

13. Butler, "Racially Based," 681.

14. Stephan Thernstrom and Abigail Thernstrom, *America in Black and White* (New York: Simon and Schuster, 1992), 259.

15. Swain, *New White Nationalism,* 111.

16. David Cole, "Profiles in Crime," *News and Observer* (Raleigh, N.C.) (May 23, 1999): A27.

17. John Hill, "Misperceptions, Fear, Increase Racial Hostility," *New Orleans Times-Picayune* (November 17, 1993): A17.

18. John DiIulio, "Crime Truths," *Pittsburgh Post-Gazette* (January 14, 1996): B1.

19. Coramae Richey Mann, *Unequal Justice* (Bloomington: Indiana University Press, 1993), 39–44.

20. Paul Knepper, "The Alchemy of Race and Crime Research," in *The System in Black and White,* Michael Markowitz and Delores Jones-Brown, eds. (Westport, Conn.: Praeger, 2000); and see Becky L. Tatum, "Deconstructing the Association of Race and Skin Color: The Salience of Skin Color," in ibid.

21. Wu, *Yellow,* 200–201.

22. David Harris, *Profiles in Injustice* (New York: New Press, 2002), 76.

23. Dwight Greene, "Naughty by Nature: Black Male Joyriding—Is Everything Gonna Be Alright?" 4 *Columbia Journal of Gender and Law* (1994): 73.

24. Kenneth Ferraro, *Fear of Crime: Interpreting Victimization Risk* (Albany: State University of New York Press, 1995), 118–19.

25. Mary Oliver and G. Blake Armstrong, "The Color of Crime," in *Entertaining Crime*, Mark Fishman and Gary Cavender, eds. (New York: Aldine de Gruyter, 1998), 22.

26. Mark Steyn, "All Venusians Now," in *Faking It: The Sentimentalisation of Modern Society*, Digby Anderson and Peter Mullen, eds. (London: Social Affairs Unit, 1998), 169 (citing a study by David Fabianic).

27. Travis London and Daniel Linz, "Race and the Misrepresentation of Victimization on Local Television News," *Communication Research* (October 2000): 547.

28. McGowan, *Coloring the News*.

29. Philip Roth, *American Pastoral* (New York: Vintage, 1998), 25–26.

30. Rock, *Rock This!* 19.

31. Regina Austin, "A Nation of Thieves: Securing Black People's Right to Shop and to Sell in White America," *Utah Law Review* (1994): 147, 152.

32. Deborah W. Post, "Race, Riots, and the Rule of Law," 70 *Denver University Law Review* (1993): 237–39 n. 2.

33. Loury, *Anatomy of Racial Inequality*, 77.

34. John DiIulio, "My Black Crime Problem," 6 *City Journal* (1996): 14, 27 (quoting Jackson).

35. Richard Delgado, "Rodrigo's Eighth Chronicle: Black Crime, White Fears—On the Social Construction of Threat," 80 *Virginia Law Review* (1994): 503, 546.

36. Nathan McCall, *What's Going On?* (New York: Random House, 1998), 152.

37. P. Williams, *Alchemy*, 61.

38. U.S. Department of Justice, Bureau of Justice Statistics, "Criminal Victimization in the United States—Statistical Tables, 2002," table 42, available at www.ojp.usdoj.gov/bjs. Percentages do not add up to 100 percent because other victimizing groups are involved (the Bureau of Justice Statistics does not break them down) and in some cases the victimizer's racial group cannot be determined.

39. DiIulio, "My Black Crime Problem," 25.

40. Elder, *Ten Things You Can't Say*, 26.

41. Bureau of Justice Statistics, "Criminal Victimization," table 42.

42. Fein, *Race and Morality*, 23 (quoting Sowell).

43. U.S. Department of Justice, Bureau of Justice Statistics, "Hate Crimes Reported in NIBRS, 1997–99," 5, available at www.ojp.usdoj.gov/bjs.

44. Jody Armour, *Negrophobia and Reasonable Racism* (New York: NYU Press, 1997).

45. A poll taken several years ago revealed that 28 percent of blacks, as compared with 18 percent of whites, worried about being murdered. Another poll showed that 77 percent of blacks, compared to 45 percent of whites, worried about becoming crime victims. Still another study showed that blacks are four times as concerned about neighborhood crime as whites. Dan Subotnik, "What's Wrong with Critical Race Theory," 7 *Cornell Journal of Law and Public Policy* (1998): 681, 741–42 nn. 291, 292, 293.

46. Bureau of Justice Statistics, "Criminal Victimization," table 5.

47. Henry Ruth and Kevin Reitz, *The Challenge of Crime,* (Cambridge, Mass.: Harvard University Press, 2003), 37.

48. Elijah Anderson, *The Code of the Street* (New York: Norton, 1999), 32.

49. MacDonald, *Are Cops Racist?* 3–7.

50. Rock, *Rock This!* 149.

51. Baer, *Our Lives,* 59 (emphasis added).

52. Abraham Maslow, "A Theory of Human Motivation," 50 *Psychology Review* (1943): 370–84.

53. P. Williams, *Alchemy,* 42.

54. R. Austin, "Nation of Thieves," 147, 148.

55. Armour, *Negrophobia,* 55.

56. R. Kennedy, *Race, Crime, and the Law,* 146.

57. Thernstrom and Thernstrom, *America in Black and White,* 274 (quoting Kennedy).

58. Dinesh D'Souza, "The 'Rational Discrimination' of Cab Drivers," *Washington Times* (October 21, 1996); Jeff Jacoby, "Realism, Not Racism, Drives Hub's Cabbies," *Boston Globe* (July 12, 2001): A13.

59. R. Bernstein, *Dictatorship of Virtue,* 200.

60. Loury, *Anatomy of Racial Inequality,* 30–31.

61. Wu, *Yellow,* 208.

62. R. Kennedy, *Race, Crime, and the Law,* 166.

63. 428 U.S. 543 (1976).

64. Maxine Bernstein, "September 11 Alters Profiling Debate," *Oregonian* (October 29, 2001): C1.

65. U.S. Department of Justice, "A Resource Guide on Racial Profiling Data Collection Systems" (November 2000): 3.

66. Ibid., 1.

67. MacDonald, *Are Cops Racist?* 9 (quoting Bush).

68. *State of N.J. v. Pedro Soto,* 324 N.J. Super. 66 (1966).

69. Ibid., 55.

70. D. Harris, *Profiles in Injustice,* 61.

71. Ibid., 224 (emphasis in original).

72. Ibid., 80.

73. Heather Mac Donald, "The Racial Profiling Myth Debunked," *City Journal* (spring 2002): 63, 64; study by Public Service Research Institute.

74. U.S. Department of Justice, "Resource Guide on Racial Profiling," 7–8.

75. Katheryn Russell, *The Color of Crime* (New York: NYU Press, 1998): 41–42.

76. Eliot Spitzer, "The Police Department's 'Stop and Frisk' Practices: A Report to the People of New York by the Attorney General of the State of New York" (December 1, 1999): 94–95.

77. Ibid., 82.

78. Federal Bureau of Investigation Web site, "FBI History: Famous Cases— Willie Sutton," www.fbi.gov/libref/historic/famcases/sutton/sutton.htm (accessed September 9, 2004).

79. *Kennedy v. Mendoza-Martinez*, 83 S. Ct. 554, 563 (1963).

80. R. Kennedy, *Race, Crime, and the Law*, 12.

81. Greene, "Naughty by Nature," 84, 85.

82. Ibid., 90 (quoting John Fiske, in part), 120.

83. Regina Austin, "The Black Community, Its Lawbreakers, and a Politics of Identification," 65 *Southern California Law Review* (1992): 1769, 1774.

84. Ibid., 1791.

85. Ibid., 1780.

86. Ibid., 1801.

87. Ibid., 1799.

88. Ibid., 1782 n. 55.

89. Ibid., 1796.

90. Ibid., 1777, 1778 (quoting Carl S. Taylor, *Dangerous Society* [1990], 66–67).

91. Timothy Simone, *About Face: Race in Postmodern America* (Brooklyn: Autonomedia, 1989), 25.

92. Butler, "Racially Based," 677, 680.

93. bell hooks, *We Real Cool: Black Men and Masculinity* (New York: Routledge, 2004), 49.

94. Bell, *And We Are Not Saved*, 197.

95. Jewel Crawford, Wade Nobles, and Joy D. Leary, "Reparations and Health Care for African Americans: Repairing the Damage from the Legacy of Slavery," in *Should America Pay? Slavery and the Raging Debate over Reparations*, Raymond Winbush, ed. (New York: Amistad, 2003), 265–66 (quoting Puissant).

96. Alan Dershowitz, *Shouting Fire* (Boston: Little, Brown, 2002), 13 (quoting Adams) (emphasis in original).

97. Swain, *New White Nationalism*, 443–44 (emphasis in original).

98. The story is told in Kenneth Meeks, *Driving While Black* (New York: Broadway Books, 2000), 241–43.

NOTES TO CHAPTER 12

1. Nicolas Lemann, "Reply to Letter to the Editor from Morris B. Abram," *New York Review of Books* (March 6, 1997): 53.
2. *Webster's Third New International Dictionary* (1967), s.v. "middle-class."
3. Early, "Devil in a Blue Dress," 11–13.
4. James A. Michener, *America vs. America: The Revolution in Middle-Class Values* (New York: New American Library, 1969).
5. *Webster's Third New International Dictionary* (1985), s.v. "culture."
6. Regina Austin, "Bad for Business: Contextual Analysis, Race Discrimination, and Fast Food," 34 *John Marshall Law Review* (2000): 219.
7. Ibid., 207, 221.
8. R. Austin, "Nation of Thieves," 168–69.
9. Spike Lee, *Do the Right Thing* (film, 1989).
10. The following is from a personal transcription of the movie.
11. Bell, *And We Are Not Saved*, 5.
12. Patricia Hill Collins, *Black Feminist Thought*, 2d ed. (New York: Routledge, 2000), 290 (quoting Stewart).
13. Toni Brown, *Black Lies, White Lies* (New York: William Morrow, 1995), 274, 276.
14. John McWhorter, "Against Reparations," in Winbush, *Should America Pay?* 180.
15. Hacker, "Saved?" 24.
16. Thernstrom and Thernstrom, *No Excuses*, 181.
17. Patterson, "Taking Culture Seriously," 206.
18. I Cor. 9:24.
19. Derrick Bell, "Wanted: A White Leader Able to Free Whites of Racism," 33 *UC Davis Law Review* (2000): 527, 532.
20. W. E. B. Du Bois, "The Conservation of Races," in *Race,* Robert Bernasconi, ed. (Malden, Mass.: Blackwell, 2001), 90–91 (emphasis in original).
21. Du Bois, *Souls of Black Folk*, 133.
22. Swain, *New White Nationalism*, 452–53 (quoting Herbert).
23. Du Bois, "Conservation of Races," 89.
24. P. Williams, *Rooster's Egg*, 24.
25. R. Kennedy, *Nigger*, 63 (quoting Ellison).
26. Martin Seligman, "Positive Psychology," in *The Science of Optimism and Hope: Research Essays in Honor of Martin E. P. Seligman,* Jane Gillham, ed. (Philadelphia: Templeton Foundation Press, 2000), 423.

27. Patterson, *Ordeal of Integration,* 88–89.

28. Ibid., 91.

29. Du Bois, "Conservation of Races," 91.

30. Dickerson, *End of Blackness,* 254 (quoting Du Bois). .

31. Ex. 20:5 and Ex. 34:7.

32. Jack Hitt, "The Great Slave Debate," *JD Jungle* (November/December 2002): 70 (quoting Ogletree).

33. *Barber Shop* (film, 2002).

NOTES TO AFTERWORD

1. Jerome M. Culp Jr., "Seventh Aspect of Self-Hatred," 55 *Florida Law Review* (2003): 435–36.

Bibliography

Adorno, Theodor, *Minima Moralia: Reflections from a Damaged Life,* trans. E. F. N. Jephcott (London: New Left Books, 1974).

Alfieri, Anthony, "Black and White," 85 *California Law Review* (1997): 1647.

American Bar Association Commission on Women in the Profession, *Elusive Equality: The Experiences of Women in Legal Education,* Executive Summary (ABA, 1996).

——, *Options and Obstacles: A Survey of the Studies of the Careers of Women Lawyers* (ABA, July 1994), 6.

Anderson, Digby, and Peter Mullen, "The Idea of a Fake Society," in *Faking It: The Sentimentalisation of Modern Society,* Digby Anderson and Peter Mullen, eds. (London: Social Affairs Unit, 1998).

Anderson, Elijah, *The Code of the Street* (New York: Norton, 1999).

Andrews, Marcellus, *The Political Economy of Hope and Fear* (New York: NYU Press, 1999).

Angel, Marina, "Comments in Reply: It's Becoming a Glass House," 50 *Journal of Legal Education* (2000): 454.

——, "Women in Legal Education: What It's Like to Be Part of a Perpetual First Wave or the Case of the Disappearing Women," 61 *Temple Law Review* (1988): 799.

Appiah, K. Anthony, "The Multiculturalist Misunderstanding," *New York Review of Books* (October 9, 1997): 36.

Appiah, K. Anthony, and Amy Guttman, *Color Conscious: The Political Morality of Race* (Princeton: Princeton University Press, 1996).

Armour, Jody, *Negrophobia and Reasonable Racism* (New York: NYU Press, 1997).

Arrigo, Maureen J., "Hierarchy Maintained: Status and Gender Issues in Legal Writing Programs," 70 *Temple Law Review* (1997): 117.

Asante, Molefi, *The Afrocentric Idea* (Philadelphia: Temple University Press, 1998).

——, "Afrocentricity," in *Dispatches from the Ebony Tower,* Manning Marable, ed. (New York: Columbia University Press, 2000).

Audi, Robert, ed., *Cambridge Dictionary of Philosophy* (New York: Cambridge University Press, 1995).

Austen, Jane, *Pride and Prejudice* (New York: Harper & Bros., 1813).

Austin, Arthur, *The Empire Strikes Back* (New York: NYU Press, 1998).

Austin, Regina, "Bad for Business: Contextual Analysis, Race Discrimination, and Fast Food," 34 *John Marshall Law Review* (2000): 219.

———, "Beyond Black Demons and White Devils: Antiblack Conspiracy Theorizing and the Black Public Sphere," 22 *Florida State University Law Review* (1995): 1021.

———, "The Black Community, Its Lawbreakers, and a Politics of Identification," 65 *Southern California Law Review* (1992): 1769.

———, "A Nation of Thieves": Securing Black People's Right to Shop and Sell in White America," *Utah Law Review* (1994): 147.

———, "Of False Teeth and Biting Critiques: Jones v. Fisher in Context," 15 *Touro Law Review* (1999): 389.

———, "Sapphire Bound!" *Wisconsin Law Review* (1989): 539.

Ausubel, Nathan, ed., *A Treasury of Jewish Folklore* (New York: Crown, 1948).

Babcock, Linda, and Sara Laschever, *Women Don't Ask: Negotiation and the Gender Divide* (Princeton: Princeton University Press, 2003).

Baer, Judith, *Our Lives before the Law* (Princeton: Princeton University Press, 1999).

Bartlett, Katharine, "Cracking Foundations as Feminist Method," 8 *American University Journal of Social Policy and Law* (2000): 31.

Bartlett's Familiar Quotations, 16th ed. (Boston: Little, Brown, 1992).

"Be a Man," *Economist* (June 28–July 4, 2003): 64.

Bean, Kathleen, "The Gender Gap in the Law School Classroom—Beyond Survival," 14 *Vermont Law Review* (1989): 23.

Becker, Ernest, *The Denial of Death* (New York: Free Press, 1973).

Becker, Mary, American Bar Association, *Don't Just Hear It through the Grapevine: Studying Gender Questions at Your School* (1998).

Belenky, Mary, Blythe McVicker Clinchy, Nancy Rule Goldberger, and Jill Mattuck Tarule, *Women's Ways of Knowing: The Development of Self, Voice, and Mind* (New York: Basic Books, 1986).

Belkin, Lisa, "The Opt-Out Revolution," *New York Times Magazine* (October 26, 2003): 42.

Bell, Derrick, *And We Are Not Saved* (New York: Basic Books, 1987).

———, "Bakke, Minority Admissions, and the Usual Price of Racial Remedies," 67 *California Law Review* (1979): 1.

———, "Brown v. Board of Education and the Interest-Convergence Dilemma," 93 *Harvard Law Review* 518 (1980).

———, "A Colony at Risk," 15 *Touro Law Review* (1999): 347.

———, *Confronting Authority* (Boston: Beacon, 1994),

———, *Faces at the Bottom of the Well* (New York: Basic Books, 1979).

———, *Race, Racism, and American Law,* 4th ed. (Gaithersburg, Md.: Aspen, 2000).

———, "Serving Two Masters: Integration Ideals and Client Interests in School Desegregation Cases," 85 *Yale Law Journal* (1976): 470.

———, "Wanted: A White Leader Able to Free Whites of Racism," 33 *UC Davis Law Review* (2000): 527.

———, "Who's Afraid of Critical Race Theory?" *University of Illinois Law Review* (1995): 893.

Bentsen, Cheryl, "Head Negro in Charge," *Boston Magazine* (April 1998): 104.

Bernstein, Maxine, "September 11 Alters Profiling Debate," *Oregonian* (October 29, 2001): C1.

Bernstein, Richard, *Dictatorship of Virtue* (New York: Knopf, 1994).

Blankenhorn, David, *Fatherless America: Confronting Our Most Urgent Social Problem* (New York: HarperPerennial, 1995).

Boskin, Joseph, *Rebellious Laughter* (Syracuse, N.Y.: Syracuse University Press, 1997).

Boynton, Robert S., "The New Intellectuals," *Atlantic Monthly* (March 1995): 53.

———, "The Professor of Connection," *New Yorker* (November 6, 1995): 100.

Bray, Rosemary, "So How Did I Get Here?" *New York Times Magazine* (November 8, 1992).

Bronowski, Jacob, *The Ascent of Man* (Boston: Little, Brown, 1973).

Brown, Dorothy, *Critical Race Theory* (teacher's manual) (St. Paul, Minn.: Thompson-West, 2003).

Brown, Jennifer, "To Give Them Countenance: The Case for a Woman's Law School," 22 *Harvard Women's Law Journal* (1999): 1.

Brown, Lyn, and Carol Gilligan, *Meeting at the Crossroads: Women's Psychology and Girls' Development* (Cambridge, Mass.: Harvard University Press, 1992).

Brown, Toni, *Black Lies, White Lies* (New York: William Morrow, 1995).

Browne, Kingsley, *Biology at Work: Rethinking Sexual Equality* (New Brunswick, N.J.: Rutgers University Press, 2002).

Brownmiller, Susan, *Femininity* (New York: Linden Press, 1984).

Bruni, Frank, "Tourists Flocking to Harlem Churches," *Houston Chronicle* (November 24, 1996): 14.

Buhle, Mari Jo, *Feminism and Its Discontents* (Cambridge, Mass.: Harvard University Press, 1998).

Butler, Paul, "Racially Based Jury Nullification: Black Power in the Criminal Justice System," 105 *Yale Law Journal* (1995): 677.

Byrd, Ayana, and Lori Tharps, *Hair Story* (New York: St. Martin's, 2001).

Caldwell, Christopher, "France's Native Disgrace," *New York Times Book Review* (July 15, 2001): 9.

Caldwell, Paulette, "A Hair Piece: Perspectives on the Intersection of Race and Gender," *Duke Law Journal* (1991): 365.

Callahan, John, "Frequencies of Memory: A Eulogy for Ralph Waldo Ellison," 18 *Callaloo* (spring 1995): 298.

Carbone, June, *From Parents to Partners* (New York: Columbia University Press, 2000).

Carter, Stephen, Preface to *The Tyranny of the Majority,* by Lani Guinier (New York: Free Press, 1994).

Chamallas, Martha, *Introduction to Feminist Legal Theory* (Gaithersburg, Md.: Aspen, 1999).

Chang, Jung, *Wild Swans* (New York: Simon and Schuster, 1991).

Chang, Robert, "Toward an Asian American Legal Scholarship," 1 *Asian Law Journal* (1994): 1.

Chao, Julia, "Is China Going to the Dogs?" *Toronto Star* (September 6, 2000): Life sec., FD04.

———, "A Matter of Culture—and Business," *Atlanta Constitution* (September 3, 2000): 3G.

Chesler, Phyllis, *Woman's Inhumanity to Woman* (New York: Plume, 2002).

Cho, Sumi, "Converging Stereotypes in Racialized Sexual Harassment: Where the Model Minority Meets Suzie Wong," in *Critical Race Feminism,* Adrien Wing, ed. (New York: NYU Press, 1997).

Cicero, *De Divinatione* II, Chapter XII in *Cicero in Twenty-Eight Volumes,* trans. William Falconer (Cambridge, Mass.: Harvard University Press, 1979).

Clark, Kenneth, "Delusions of the White Liberal," *New York Times Magazine* (April 4, 1965): 137.

Clark, Leroy, "A Critique of Professor Derrick Bell's Thesis of the Permanence of Racism and His Strategy of Confrontation," *Denver University Law Review* (1995): 23.

Clinton, William, "Getting a Handle on America's 'Race Problem,'" *Chicago Tribune* (October 17, 1995): N19.

Cochran, Johnnie, Jr. (with Tim Rutten), *Journey to Justice* (New York: Ballantine Books, 1996).

Cohen, Lloyd, "Sexual Harassment and the Law," *Society* (May/June 1991): 11.

Cole, David, "Profiles in Crime," *News and Observer* (Raleigh, N.C.) (May 23, 1999): A27.

Collins, Patricia Hill, *Black Feminist Thought,* 2nd ed. (New York: Routledge, 2000).

Comer, James, "Closing the Achievement Gap," *Teacher Magazine* (June 2001).

The Committee on Legal Education and Admission to the Bar of the Association of the Bar of the City of New York and The Committee on Legal Education and Admission to the Bar of the New York State Bar Association, *Joint Report, Public Service Alternative Bar Examination* (June 14, 2002).

Connor, Marlene, *What Is Cool?* (New York: Crown, 1995).

Cook, Nancy, "Outside the Tradition: Literature as Legal Scholarship," 63 *University of Cincinnati Law Review* (1994): 95.

Cose, Ellis, *Color-Blind: Seeing beyond Race in a Race-Obsessed World* (New York: HarperCollins, 1997).

Cousins, Norman, "Anatomy of an Illness (as Perceived by the Patient)," 295 *New England Journal of Medicine* #26 (December 23, 1976): 1463–85.

Crawford, Jewel, Wade Nobles, and Joy Leary, "Reparations and Health Care for African Americans: Repairing the Damage from the Legacy of Slavery," in Winbush, *Should America Pay?*

Crenshaw, Kimberlé, Neil Gotanda, Gary Peller, and Kendall Thomas, eds., *Critical Race Theory: The Key Writings That Formed a Movement* (New York: New Press, 1995).

Crouch, Stanley, *The All-American Skin Game, or, The Decoy of Race* (New York: Vintage, 1995).

———, *Always in Pursuit* (New York: Pantheon, 1998).

Crouse, James, and Dale Trusheim, *The Case against the SAT* (Chicago: University of Chicago Press, 1988).

Culp, Jerome M., Jr., "Seventh Aspect of Self-Hatred," 55 *Florida Law Review* (2003): 425.

———, "You Can Take Them to Water, but You Can't Make Them Drink: Black Legal Scholarship and White Legal Scholars," *University of Illinois Law Review* (1992): 1021.

Dalton, Harlon, *Racial Healing* (New York: Doubleday, 1995).

Dash, Leon, *When Children Want Children: The Urban Crisis of Teenage Childbearing* (Urbana: University of Illinois Press, 2003).

Davies, Christie, *Ethnic Humor around the World* (Bloomington: Indiana University Press, 1990).

De Becker, Gavin, *The Gift of Fear* (Boston: Little, Brown, 1997).

Decter, Midge, *An Old Wife's Tale* (New York: Regan Books, 2001).

Delany, Sarah, and Elizabeth Delany (with Amy Hill Hearth), *Having Our Say* (New York: Kodansha, 1993).

Delgado, Richard, "Brewer's Plea: Critical Thoughts on Common Cause," 44 *Vanderbilt Law Review* (1991): 1.

———, *The Coming Race War? And Other Apocalyptic Tales of America After Affirmative Action and Welfare* (New York: NYU Press, 1996).

———, *Critical Race Theory: An Introduction* (New York: NYU Press, 2001).

———, "The Imperial Scholar: Reflections on a Review of Civil Rights Literature," 132 *University of Pennsylvania Law Review* (1984): 561.

———, "The Inward Turn to Outsider Jurisprudence," 34 *William and Mary Law Review* (1993): 741.

————, "Legal Storytelling: Storytelling for Oppositionists and Others: A Plea for Narrative," 87 *Michigan Law Review* (1989): 2411.

————, "Rodrigo's Eighth Chronicle: Black Crime, White Fears—On the Social Construction of Threat," 80 *Virginia Law Review* (1994): 503.

————, "Two Ways to Think about Race," 89 *Georgetown Law Journal* (2001): 2279.

————, *When Equality Ends: Stories about Race and Resistance* (Boulder, Colo.: Westview, 1999).

Delgado, Richard, and Jean Stefancic, *Failed Revolutions: Social Reform and the Limits of Legal Imagination* (Boulder, Colo.: Westview, 1994).

————, "Images of the Outsider in American Law and Culture: Can Free Expression Remedy Systemic Social Ills?" 77 *Cornell Law Review* (1992): 1258.

————, "Scorn," 35 *William and Mary Law Review* (1994): 1099.

Derman-Sparks, Louise, and Carol Brunson Phillips, *Teaching/Learning Anti-Racism: A Developmental Approach* (New York: Teachers College Press, 1997).

Dershowitz, Alan, "Harvard Witch Hunt Burns the Incorrect at the Stake," *Los Angeles Times* (April 22, 1992): A11.

————, *Shouting Fire* (Boston: Little, Brown, 2002).

Dickerson, Debra, *The End of Blackness* (New York: Pantheon, 2004).

Dickinson, Emily, *Complete Poems of Emily Dickinson,* T. Johnson, ed. (London: Faber, 1970).

DiIulio, John, "Crime Truths," *Pittsburgh Post-Gazette* (January 14, 1996): B1.

————, "My Black Crime Problem," 6 *City Journal* (1996): 14.

Dillon, Sam, "Commencement Speeches," *New York Times* (June 1, 2003): sec. 4, 41.

Dillon-Mallone, Aubrey, ed., *The Cynic's Dictionary,* (Lincolnwood, Ill.: Contemporary Books, 2000).

D'Souza, Dinesh, "The 'Rational Discrimination' of Cab Drivers," *Washington Times* (October 21, 1996): A19.

Du Bois, W. E. B., "The Conservation of Races," in *Race,* Robert Bernasconi, ed. (Malden, Mass.: Blackwell, 2001).

————, *The Souls of Black Folk* (1903; repr., New York: Barnes and Noble Classics, 2003).

Dunham, Kemba, "More Employers Ask Job Seekers for SAT Scores," *Wall Street Journal* (October 28, 2003): B1.

Dusky, Lorraine, *Still Unequal: The Shameful Truth about Women and Justice in America* (New York: Crown, 1996).

Dyson, Michael Eric, *Open Mike* (New York: Basic Civitas, 2003).

————, "Seeing the Simpson Verdicts in Black and White," *Newsday* (February 9, 1997): G5.

Early, Gerald, "Devil in a Blue Dress," *Books and Culture* (September/October 1999): 12.

Edley, Christopher, *Not All Black and White* (New York: Hill and Wang, 1996).

Elder, Larry, *Showdown: Confronting Bias* (New York: St. Martin's, 2003).

———, *Ten Things You Can't Say in America* (New York: St. Martin's Griffin, 2000).

Elders, Joycelyn, and David Chanoff, *Joycelyn Elders, M.D.: From Sharecropper's Daughter to Surgeon General of the United States of America* (New York: Morrow, 1996).

Entman, Robert, and Andrew Rojecki, *The Black Image in the White Mind* (Chicago: University of Chicago Press, 2000).

Erikson, Erik, *Gandhi's Truth: On the Origins of Militant Nonviolence* (New York: Norton, 1969).

Espinoza, Leslie, "Empowerment and Achievement in Minority Law Student Support Programs: Constructing Affirmative Action," 22 *University of Michigan Journal of Law Reform* (1989): 281.

———, "Latino/a Identity and Multi-Identity," in *The Latino/a Condition*, Richard Delgado and Jean Stefancic, eds. (New York: NYU Press, 1998).

Estrich, Susan, *Sex and Power* (New York: Riverhead Books, 2000).

Farber, Daniel, and Suzanna Sherry, *Beyond All Reason: The Radical Assault on Truth in American Law* (New York: Oxford University Press, 1997).

———, "Telling Stories Out of School: An Essay on Legal Narratives," 45 *Stanford Law Review* (1992): 807.

Farber, Leslie, *Lying, Despair, Jealousy, Envy, Sex, Suicide, Drugs, and the Good Life* (New York: Basic Books, 1976).

Farley, Anthony, "Thirteen Stories," 15 *Touro Law Review* (1999): 543.

Farley, Christine Haight, "Confronting Expectations: Women in the Legal Academy," 8 *Yale Journal of Law and Feminism* (1996): 333.

Fein, Melvyn, *Race and Morality* (New York: Kluwer, 2001).

Fels, Anna, *Necessary Dreams: Ambition in Women's Changing Lives* (New York: Pantheon, 2004).

Ferraro, Kenneth, *Fear of Crime: Interpreting Victimization Risk* (Albany: State University of New York Press, 1995).

Fields, Armond, and L. Marc Fields, *From the Bowery to Broadway* (New York: Oxford University Press, 1993).

Finley, Gabrielle, "Changes to SAT I Sparks [*sic*] Disparity Debate," *Black Issues in Higher Education* (July 18, 2002): 11.

Fisher, Helen, *The First Sex* (New York: Random House, 1999).

Fordyce, Wilbert, "Learning Processes in Pain," in *The Psychology of Pain*, Richard Sternbach, ed. 2d ed. (New York: Raven Press, 1986).

Frug, Mary Jo, "A Postmodern Feminist Legal Manifesto (An Unfinished Draft)," 105 *Harvard Law Review* (March 1992): 1045.

Furchtgott-Roth, Diana, and Christine Stolba, *The Feminist Dilemma* (Washington, D.C.: American Enterprise Institute, 2001).

Gaber, Paula, "Just Trying to Be Human in This Place: The Legal Education of Twenty Women," 10 *Yale Journal of Law and Feminism* (1998): 165.

Galston, William, and Elaine Kamark, *Putting Children First: A Progressive Family Policy for the 1990s* (Washington, D.C.: Progressive Policy Institute, 1990).

Gates, Henry Louis, Jr., *Loose Canons: Notes on the Culture Wars* (New York: Oxford University Press, 1992).

———, *The Signifying Monkey* (New York: Oxford University Press, 1988).

———, *Thirteen Ways of Looking at a Black Man* (New York: Random House, 1997).

Gillham, Jane, ed. *The Science of Optimism and Hope* (Philadelphia: Templeton Foundation Press, 2000).

Gilligan, Carol, *In a Different Voice* (Cambridge, Mass.: Harvard University Press).

Gitlin, Todd, *The Twilight of Common Dreams* (New York: Metropolitan Books, 1995).

Glater, Jonathan, "Asian-Americans Take Offense at Law Firm Memo," *New York Times* (February 7, 2004): C1.

Goldsmith, Susan, "Rich, Black, Flunking," *East Bay Express* (May 21, 2003).

Goodman, Ellen, "Mission: Admission," *Boston Globe* (March 30, 2003): D11.

Goodman, Ellen, and Patricia O'Brien, *I Know Just What You Mean: The Power of Friendship in Women's Lives* (New York: Simon and Schuster, 2000).

Gottfredson, Linda, "Why g Matters: The Complexity of Everyday Life," 24 *Intelligence* (1997): 79.

Graglia, Carolyn, *Domestic Tranquility* (Dallas: Spence, 1998).

Gray, John, *Men Are from Mars, Women Are from Venus* (New York: Harper-Collins, 1992).

Greene, Dwight, "Naughty by Nature: Black Male Joyriding—Is Everything Gonna Be Alright?" 4 *Columbia Journal of Gender and Law* (1994): 73.

Grier, William, and Price Cobbs, *Black Rage* (New York: Basic Books, 1968).

Grillo, Trina, "Tenure and Minority Women Law Professors: Separating the Strands," 31 *University of San Francisco Law Review* (1997): 747.

Grisham, John, *The Runaway Jury* (New York: Doubleday, 1996).

Gruner, Charles, *The Game of Humor* (New Brunswick, N.J.: Transactions, 1997).

Guinier, Lani, "Reframing the Affirmative Action Debate," 86 *Kentucky Law Journal* (1997): 505.

Guinier, Lani, Michelle Fine, and Jane Balin, *Becoming Gentlemen: Women, Law School, and Institutional Change* (Boston: Beacon, 1997).

————, "Becoming Gentlemen: Women's Experience at One Ivy League Law School," 143 *University of Pennsylvania Law Review* (1994): 1.

Guinier, Lani, and Gerald Torres, *The Miner's Canary* (Cambridge, Mass.: Harvard University Press, 2002).

Hacker, Andrew, "How Are Women Doing?" *New York Review of Books* (April 11, 2002): 64.

————, *Mismatch: The Growing Gulf between Men and Women* (New York: Scribner, 2003).

————, "Saved?" *New York Review of Books* (August 14, 2003): 22.

Halewood, Peter, "White Men Can't Jump: Critical Epistemologies, Embodiment, and the Praxis of Scholarship," 7 *Yale Journal of Law and Feminism* (1995): 1.

Hall, Paula, "Pet SOS Special: Caged Up and Ready to Eat," *Coventry Evening Telegraph* (October 23, 2002): 8.

Harmon, Louise, and Deborah W. Post, *Cultivating Intelligence* (New York: NYU Press, 1996).

Harrington, Mona, *Women Lawyers* (New York: Knopf, 1994).

Harris, Angela, "Race and Essentialism in Feminist Legal Theory," 42 *Stanford Law Review* (1990): 581.

Harris, David, *Profiles in Injustice* (New York: New Press, 2002).

Haygood, Wil, "True or False, Rumors Spread," *Boston Sunday Globe* (December 15, 1996): A1.

Hecht, Jennifer M., *Doubt, a History* (New York: HarperSanFrancisco, 2003).

Herbert, Bob, "Don't Flunk the Future," *New York Times* (August 13, 1998): A23.

————, "A Word to the Wise," *New York Times* (February 14, 1997): A37.

Hernandez, Dylan, "Latest Curve Taken in Stride," *Boston Globe* (September 1, 2001): G7.

Hernandez-Truyol, Berta, "Building Bridges," in *The Latino/a Condition,* Richard Delgado and Jean Stefancic, eds. (New York: NYU Press, 1998).

Herring, James, "Can They Do It?" in *The Difference "Difference" Makes,* Deborah Rhode, ed. (Stanford: Stanford University Press, 2003).

Hill, John, "Misperceptions, Fear, Increase Racial Hostility," *New Orleans Times-Picayune* (November 17, 1993): A17.

Hirshman, Linda, *A Woman's Guide to Law School.* (New York: Penguin, 1999).

Hirshman, Linda, and Jane Larson, *Hard Bargains: The Politics of Sex* (New York: Oxford University Press, 1998).

Hitchens, Christopher, *Letter to a Young Contrarian* (Cambridge, Mass.: Basic Books, 2001).

Hitt, Jack, "The Great Slave Debate," *JD Jungle* (November/December 2002): 70.

Hochschild, Jennifer L., *Facing Up to the American Dream* (Princeton: Princeton University Press, 1995).

Hodgman, John, "Ayn Rand, in Spades," *New York Times Magazine* (June 29, 2003): 38.

hooks, bell, *Killing Rage* (New York: Holt, 1995).

———, *Talking Back* (Boston: South End Press, 1989).

———, *We Real Cool: Black Men and Masculinity* (New York: Routledge, 2004).

Hoover, Eric, "SAT Scores Rose in 2003, but Racial Gap Widened," *Chronicle of Higher Education* (August 26, 2003).

Hughes, Robert, *The Culture of Complaint* (Malden, Mass.: Blackwell, 1993).

Huntington, Samuel P., "The Hispanic Challenge," *Foreign Policy* (March/ April 2004).

Ignatiev, Noel, "The American Intifada," in *Race Traitor,* Noel Ignatiev and John Garvey, eds. (New York: Routledge, 1996).

Iijima, Chris, "Race as Resistance: Racial Identity as More than Ancestral Heritage," 15 *Touro Law Review* (1999): 497.

Isbister, J. N., *Freud* (Cambridge, U.K.: Polity, 1985).

Jacoby, Jeff, "Realism, Not Racism, Drives Hub's Cabbies," *Boston Globe* (July 12, 2001): A13.

Jacoby, Tamar, "Day of the Race Men," 103 *Commentary* (April 1997): 36.

Jencks, Christopher, "Racial Bias in Testing," in Jencks and Phillips, *Black-White Test Score Gap.*

Jencks, Christopher, and Meredith Phillips, eds., *The Black-White Test Score Gap* (Washington, D.C.: Brookings Institution Press, 1998).

Johnson, Alex M., Jr., "Bid Whist, Tonk, and U.S. v. Fordice: Why Integration Fails African Americans Again," 81 *California Law Review* (December 1993): 1401.

———, "The New Voice of Color," 100 *Yale Law Journal* (1993): 2007.

Jones, Ernest, *Life and Work of Sigmund Freud,* vol. 2 (New York: Basic Books, 1955).

Jordan, Judith, "Towards Competence and Connection," in *The Complexity of Connection,* Judith Jordan et al., eds. (New York: Guilford, 2004).

Jordan, June, *Some of Us Did Not Die* (New York: Basic Civitas, 2002).

———, *Technical Difficulties* (New York: Pantheon, 1992).

Karlgaard, Rich, "Microsoft's IQ Dividend," *Wall Street Journal* (July 28, 2004): A13.

Katz, Jack, *Seductions of Crime* (New York: Basic Books, 1988).

Kelman, Mark, "Trashing," 36 *Stanford Law Review* (January 1984): 293.

Kennedy, Duncan, *Legal Education and the Reproduction of Hierarchy* (Cambridge, Mass.: Afar, 1983).

————, "Legal Education as Training for Hierarchy," in *The Politics of Law,* David Kairys, ed. (New York: Pantheon, 1982).

Kennedy, Randall, "My Race Problem—and Ours," *Atlantic Monthly* (May 1997): 65.

————, *Nigger* (New York: Pantheon, 2002).

————, *Race, Crime, and the Law* (New York: Pantheon, 1997).

————, "Racial Critiques of Legal Academia," 102 *Harvard Law Review* (1989): 1745.

Kerlow, Eleanor, *Poisoned Ivy* (New York: St. Martin's, 1994).

King, Martin Luther, Jr., *I Have a Dream* (New York: HarperCollins, 1986).

Knepper, Paul, "The Alchemy of Race and Crime Research," in *The System in Black and White,* Michael Markowitz and Delores Jones-Brown, eds. (Westport, Conn.: Praeger, 2000).

Kors, Alan, and Harvey Silverglate, "Harvard Law School: Postmodern Censorship," unpublished essay.

Kozol, Jonathan, *Savage Inequalities* (New York: Crown, 1991).

Kui, Christopher, "Letter to the Editor," *New York Times* (June 8, 2002): A14.

Lasch-Quinn, Elizabeth, *Race Experts* (New York: Norton, 2001).

Lawrence, Charles, III, "The Id, the Ego, and Equal Protection: Reckoning with Unconscious Racism," 39 *Stanford Law Review* (1987): 317.

————, Preface to *Crossroads, Directions, and a New Critical Race Theory,* Francisco Valdes et al., eds. (Philadelphia: Temple University Press, 2002).

————, "The Word and the River: Pedagogy as Scholarship and Struggle," 65 *Southern California Law Review* (1992): 2231.

Lawrence, Charles, III, and Mari Matsuda, *We Won't Go Back: Making the Case for Affirmative Action* (Boston: Houghton Mifflin, 1997).

Leacock, Stephen *Humor and Humanity* (New York: Holt, 1938).

Lee, Felicia, "Why Are Black Students Lagging?" *New York Times* (November 30, 2002): B3.

Lee, Spike, *Do the Right Thing* (film, 1989).

Leff, Laurel, "The Making of a 'Quota Queen,'" in *Feminism, Media, and the Law,* Martha Fineman and Martha McCluskey, eds. (New York: Oxford University Press, 1997).

Lehrman, Karen, *The Lipstick Proviso: Women, Sex, and Power in the Real World* (New York: Anchor, 1997).

Leland, John, and Allison Samuels, "The New Generation Gap," *Newsweek* (March 17, 1997): 52.

Lemann, Nicolas, "Reply to Letter to the Editor from Morris B. Abram," *New York Review of Books* (March 6, 1997): 53.

Levine, Lawrence, *Black Culture and Black Consciousness* (New York: Oxford University Press, 1977).

Levit, Nancy, *The Gender Line: Men, Women, and the Law* (New York: NYU Press, 1998).

———, "Keeping Feminism in Its Place: Sex Segregation and the Domestication of Female Academics," 49 *University of Kansas Law Review* (2001): 775.

Lin, Anthony, "Dewey Partner's E-Mail Causes Upset over Racial Insensitivity," *New York Law Journal* (January 28, 2004): 1.

Litowitz, Dennis, "Some Critical Thoughts on Critical Race Theory," 72 *Notre Dame Law Review* (1997): 503.

Littleton, Christine, "Feminist Jurisprudence: The Difference Method Makes," 41 *Stanford Law Review* (1989): 751.

Liu, Eric, *The Accidental Asian* (New York: Random House, 1998).

London, Travis, and Daniel Linz, "Race and the Misrepresentation of Victimization on Local Television News," *Communication Research* (October 2000): 547.

Loury, Glenn, *The Anatomy of Racial Inequality* (Cambridge, Mass.: Harvard University Press, 2002).

Lowe, John, *Jump at the Sun: Zora Neale Hurston's Cosmic Comedy* (Urbana: University of Illinois Press, 1997).

Ludwig, Arnold, *The Importance of Lying* (Springfield, Ill.: C. C. Thomas, 1965).

Maalouf, Amin, *In the Name of Identity*, trans. Barbara Bray (New York: Arcade, 2000).

Mac Donald, Heather, *Are Cops Racist?* (Chicago: Ivan Dee, 2003).

———, "The Racial Profiling Myth Debunked," *City Journal* (spring 2002): 63.

Machung, Anne, "Talking Career, Thinking Job: Gender Differences in Career and Family Expectations of Berkeley Seniors," 15 *Feminist Studies* #1 (spring 1989): 35.

MacKinnon, Catharine, "Feminism, Marxism, and the State: Towards a Feminist Jurisprudence," in *Feminist Legal Theory: Readings in Law and Gender*, Katharine Bartlett and Rosanne Kennedy, eds. (Boulder, Colo.: Westview, 1991).

———, *Feminism Unmodified* (Cambridge, Mass.: Harvard University Press, 1987).

Majors, Richard, and Janet Billson, *Cool Pose: The Dilemmas of Black Manhood in America* (New York: Touchstone, 2002).

Mangan, Katharine, "Professor's Comments on Affirmative Action Inflame a Campus," *Chronicle of Higher Education* (September 26, 1997): A33.

Mann, Coramae Richey, *Unequal Justice* (Bloomington: Indiana University Press, 1993).

Marable, Manning, *W. E. B. Du Bois: Black Radical Democrat* (Boston: Twayne, 1986).

Margolick, David, "In Attacking the Work of a Slain Professor, Harvard's Elite Themselves Become a Target," *New York Times* (April 17, 1992): B16.

Martin, Danny, *Mathematics Success and Failure among African-American Youth* (Mahwah, N.J.: Erlbaum, 2000).

Maslow, Abraham, "A Theory of Human Motivation," 50 *Psychology Review* (1943): 370–84.

Matsuda, Mari, "Pragmatism Modified and the False Consciousness Problem," 63 *Southern California Law Review* (1990): 1763.

———, "Public Response to Racist Speech: Considering the Victim's Story," 87 *Michigan Law Review* (1989): 2320.

———, "When the First Quail Calls," 14 *Women's Rights Law Reporter* (1992): 297.

———, *Where Is Your Body?* (Boston: Beacon, 1996).

Matsuda, Mari, Charles R. Lawrence III, Richard Delgado, and Kimberlé Crenshaw, *Words That Wound: Assaultive Speech, and the First Amendment* (Boulder, Colo.: Westview, 1993).

McCall, Nathan, *What's Going On?* (New York: Random House, 1998).

McGhee, Paul E., *Health, Healing, and the Amuse System: Humor as Survival Training*, 2d ed. (Dubuque, Iowa: Kendall/Hunt, 1996).

McGowan, William, *Coloring the News* (San Francisco: Encounter Books, 2001).

McKenna, Elizabeth, *When Work Doesn't Work Anymore: Women, Work, and Identity* (New York: Delacorte Press, 1997).

McLanahan, Sara, and Gary Sandefur, *Growing Up with a Single Parent: What Hurts, What Helps* (Cambridge, Mass.: Harvard University Press, 1994).

McWhorter, John, "Against Reparations," in *Should America Pay? Slavery and the Raging Debate over Reparations*, Raymond Winbush, ed. (New York: Amistad, 2003).

———, "How Hip-Hop Holds Blacks Back," *City Journal* (summer 2003): 66.

———, *Losing the Race: Self-Sabotage in Black America* (New York: Free Press, 2000).

———, "Toward a Usable Black History," *City Journal* (summer 2001).

Meeks, Kenneth, *Driving While Black* (New York: Broadway Books, 2000).

Menkel-Meadow, Carrie, "Women as Law Teachers: Toward the 'Feminization' of Legal Education," in *Humanistic Education in Law: Essays on the Application of a Humanistic Perspective to Law Teaching* (New York: Columbia University Press, 1981).

Merritt, Deborah Jones, and Barbara Reskin, "Moving into the Legal Academy: Challenges and Achievements for Women," in Joint AALS/ABA Workshop, *Taking Stock: Women of All Colors in Law School* (2003).

Michaels, Walter Benn, "Diversity's False Solace," *New York Times Magazine* (April 11, 2004): sec. 6, p. 12.

Michener, James A., *America vs. America: The Revolution in Middle-Class Values* (New York: New American Library, 1969).

Miller, Geoffrey, *The Mating Mind* (New York: Doubleday, 2000).

Miller, Merton, "The Value of 'Useless' Research," *Wall Street Journal* (September 21, 1992): A12.

Miller, William Ian, *Faking It* (Cambridge: Cambridge University Press, 2003).

Minow, Martha, "Beyond Universality," *University of Chicago Legal Forum* (1989): 115–16.

Morris, David, *The Culture of Pain* (Berkeley: University of California Press, 1991).

Myers, David, *Social Psychology*, 6th ed. (Boston: McGraw-Hill College, 1999).

Neal, Derek, and William Johnson, "The Role of Pre-Market Factors in Black-White Wage Differences," 104 *Journal of Political Economy* (1996): 896.

Neubeck, Kenneth, and Noel A. Cazenave, *Welfare Racism: Playing the Race Card against America's Poor* (New York: Routledge, 2001).

Neumann, Richard, "Comments in Reply," 51 *Journal of Legal Education* (2001): 151.

———, "Women in Legal Education: What the Statistics Show," 50 *Journal of Legal Education* (2000): 313.

Nussbaum, Martha, "Only Grey Matter: Richard Posner's Cost-Benefit Analysis of Sex," 59 *University of Chicago Law Review* (1992): 1689.

Ogbu, John, *Black American Students in an Affluent Suburb: A Study of Academic Disengagement* (Mahwah, N.J.: Erlbaum, 2003).

Okin, Susan, "Thinking Like a Woman," in *Theoretical Perspectives on Sexual Difference*, Deborah Rhode, ed. (New Haven: Yale University Press, 1990).

Oliver, Mary, and G. Blake Armstrong, "The Color of Crime," in *Entertaining Crime*, Mark Fishman and Gary Cavender, eds. (New York: Aldine de Gruyter, 1998).

Ontiveros, Maria, "Rosa Lopez, Christopher Darden, and Me: Issues of Gender, Ethnicity, and Class in Evaluating Witness Credibility," in *Critical Race Feminism*, Adrien Wing, ed. (New York: NYU Press, 1997).

Owen, David, "From Race to Chase," *New Yorker* (June 3, 2002): 57.

Page, Clarence, "Sending the Right Signal to Students," *Los Angeles Times* (December 18, 1980): 2.

Paglia, Camille, *Sexual Personae* (New York: Vintage, 1991).

Patai, Daphne, and Noretta Koertge, *Professing Feminism* (Lanham, Md.: Lexington Books, 2003).

Patterson, Orlando, "The Crisis of Gender Relations among African Americans," in *Race, Gender, and Power in America*, Anita Hill and Emma Jordan, eds. (New York: Oxford University Press, 1995).

———, *The Ordeal of Integration: Progress and Resentment in America's "Racial" Crisis* (Washington, D.C.: Civitas, 1997).

———, "Race, Gender, and Liberal Fallacies," *New York Times* (October 21, 1991): 34.

———, "Taking Culture Seriously: A Framework on Afro-America," in *Culture Matters: How Values Shape Human Progress,* Lawrence Harrison and Samuel Huntington, eds. (New York: Basic Books, 2000).

Payne, Les, "Single Moms Keep a People Alive," *Newsday* (May 12, 1996): A42.

Peller, Gary, "Toward a Critical Cultural Pluralism: Progressive Alternatives to Mainstream Civil Rights Ideology," in Kimberlé Crenshaw et al., *Critical Race Theory.*

Perry, Theresa, Claude Steele, and Asa Hilliard III, *Young, Gifted and Black* (Boston: Beacon, 2003).

"Phillipe and Jorge's Cool, Cool World," *Providence Phoenix* (August 30, 2001): 4.

Phillips, Meredith, Jean Brooks-Gunn, Greg Duncan, Pamela Klebanov, and Jonathan Crane, "Family Background, Parenting Practices, and the Black-White Test Score Gap," in Jencks and Phillips, *Black-White Test Score Gap,* 118.

Popenoe, David, *Life without Father: Compelling New Evidence That Fatherhood and Marriage Are Indispensable for the Good of Children and Society* (New York: Free Press, 1996).

Posner, Richard, "Beyond All Reason," *New Republic* (October 13, 1997): 42.

———, *Public Intellectuals* (Cambridge, Mass.: Harvard University Press, 2001).

Post, Deborah, "Power and Morality in Grading—A Case Study and a Few Critical Thoughts on Grade Normalization," *65 UMKC Law Review* (1997): 777.

——— "Race, Riots, and the Rule of Law," *70 Denver University Law Review* (1993): 237.

———, "Reflections on Identity, Diversity, and Morality," *6 Berkeley Women's Law Journal* (1990–91): 136.

Primary Sources, *Atlantic Monthly* (October 2003): 48.

Pulera, Dominic, *Visible Differences: Why Race Will Matter in the Twenty-First Century* (New York: Continuum, 2002).

Ramirez, Deborah, Jennifer Hoopes, and Tara Lai Quinlan, "Defining Racial Profiling in a Post–September 11 World," *40 American Criminal Law Review* (2003): 1195.

Ramist, Leonard, Charles Lewis, and Laura McAmley-Jenkins, "Student Group Differences in Predicting College Grades: Sex, Language, and Ethnic Groups 1 and 3" (College Board Rept. No. 93-1, 1994).

Raspberry, William, "Eyes on the Problem," *Boston Globe* (January 3, 1998): A11.

Ravitch, Diane, *National Standards in American Education* (Washington, D.C.: Brookings Institution Press, 1995).

Rimer, Sara, "Blacks Are Urged to Act to Increase Awareness of AIDS Epidemic," *New York Times* (October 23, 1996): A16.

———, "Do Black and White Children Learn the Same Way?" *New York Times* (June 24, 1988): B1.

Roberts, Dorothy, "Crime, Race, and Reproduction," 67 *Tulane Law Review* (1993): 1945.

———, *Killing the Black Body* (New York: Pantheon, 1997).

———, "Racism and Patriarchy in the Meaning of Motherhood," 1 *American Journal of Gender and Law* (1993): 1.

———, *Shattered Bonds: The Color of Child Welfare* (New York: Basic Books, 2002).

Robinson, Randall, *The Debt* (New York: Dutton, 2000).

Rock, Chris, *Bigger and Blacker* (video, 1999).

———, *Rock This!* (New York: Hyperion, 1997).

Rodriguez, Nestor, "U.S. Immigration and Intergroup Relations in the Late 20th Century: African Americans and Latinos," *Social Justice* (September 1, 1996): 111.

Roiphe, Katie, *The Morning After: Sex, Fear, and Feminism* (Boston: Little, Brown, 1993).

Roth, Philip, *American Pastoral* (New York: Vintage, 1998).

Russell, Katheryn, *The Color of Crime* (New York: NYU Press, 1998).

Ruth, Henry, and Kevin Reitz, *The Challenge of Crime* (Cambridge, Mass.: Harvard University Press, 2003).

Ryan, Alan, *Liberal Anxieties and Liberal Education* (New York: Hill and Wang, 1998).

Sachs, Andrea, and Judith Wallerstein, "No-Fault Divorce," *Time* (April 14, 2003): A12.

Sackett, Paul, Chaitra Hardison, and Michael Cullen, "On Stereotype Threat as Accounting for African American–White Difference," *American Psychologist* (January 2004): 7.

Sadker, Myra, and David Sadker, *Failing at Fairness: How America's Schools Cheat Girls* (New York: Scribner's Sons, 1994).

Sander, Richard, "A Systemic Analysis of Affirmative Action in American Law Schools," *Stanford Law Review* (forthcoming).

Savadove, Bill, "Keeping Dogs off the Dinner Table Seen as Test of Civilised City," *South China Morning Post* (May 30, 2002): 3.

Schiller, Lawrence, and James Willwerth, *American Tragedy* (New York: Random House, 1996).

Schneider, Elizabeth, "The Dialectic of Rights and Politics: Perspectives from the Women's Movement," 61 *New York University Law Review* (1986): 589.

Schulhofer, Stephen, *Unwanted Sex: The Culture of Intimidation and the Failure of Law* (Cambridge, Mass.: Harvard University Press, 1998).

Schwartz, Joel, "Where Dr. King Went Wrong," *City Journal* (winter 2002): 91.

Scott, Daryl, *Contempt and Pity* (Chapel Hill: University of North Carolina Press, 1997).

Seligman, Martin, "Positive Psychology," in *The Science of Optimism and Hope: Research Essays in Honor of Martin E. P. Seligman,* Jane Gillham, ed. (Philadelphia: Templeton Foundation Press, 2000).

Sella, Marshall, "Did You Hear the One about the Suicide Bomber?" *New York Times Magazine* (June 14, 2003): 44.

Selmi, Michael, "Testing for Equality: Merit, Efficiency, and the Affirmative Action Debate," 42 *UCLA Law Review* (1995): 1251.

Shatz, Adam, "The Way We Live," *New York Times Magazine* (October 28, 2001): 19.

Shulevitz, Judith, "The Close Reader: At War with the World," *New York Times Book Review* (October 21, 2001): 39.

Sidhu, Gretchen, "Academy Blues," *Ms.* (August/September 2001): 37.

Simone, Timothy, *About Face: Race in Postmodern America* (Brooklyn: Autonomedia, 1989).

Slater, Lauren, "Repress Yourself," *New York Times Magazine* (February 23, 2003): 48.

Society of American Law Teachers, "Statement on the Bar Exam," July 2002.

Sontag, Deborah, "Fierce Entanglements," *New York Times Magazine* (November 17, 2002): 52.

Sowell, Thomas, *A Conflict of Visions: Ideological Origins of Political Struggles* (New York: Basic Books, 2001).

———, *The Quest for Cosmic Justice* (New York: Free Press, 1999).

———, *The Vision of the Anointed* (New York: Basic Books, 1995).

Spellman, Elizabeth, "Aristotle and the Politicization of the Soul," in *Discovering Reality,* Sandra Harding and Merrill Hintikka, eds. (Dordrecht, Netherlands: Kluwer, 2003).

Spitzer, Eliot, "The Police Department's 'Stop and Frisk' Practices: A Report to the People of New York by the Attorney General of the State of New York" (December 1, 1999): 14.

Steele, Claude, "Stereotype Threat and African-American Student Achievement," in Perry, Steele, and Hilliard, *Young, Gifted, and Black.*

Steele, Claude, and Joshua Aronson, "Stereotype Threat and the Test Performance of Academically Successful African Americans," in Jencks and Phillips, *Black-White Test Score Gap.*

Steele, Shelby, *The Content of Our Character* (New York: St. Martin's, 1990).

———, *A Dream Deferred: The Second Betrayal of Black Freedom in America* (New York: HarperCollins, 1998).

———, "Or a Childish Illusion of Justice?" *Newsweek* (August 27, 2001): 23.

———, "The Race Not Run," *New Republic* (October 7, 1996): 23.

Steyn, Mark, "All Venusians Now," in *Faking It: The Sentimentalisation of Modern Society,* Digby Anderson and Peter Mullen, eds. (London: Social Affairs Unit, 1998).

Sturm, Susan, and Lani Guinier, "The Future of Affirmative Action: Reclaiming the Innovative Ideal," 84 *California Law Review* (1996): 953.

Subotnik, Dan, "What's Wrong with Critical Race Theory," 7 *Cornell Journal of Law and Public Policy* (1998): 681.

Subotnik, Dan, and Glen Lazar, "Deconstructing the Rejection Letter: A Look at Elitism in Article Selection," 49 *Journal of Legal Education* (1999): 601.

Sue, Derald Wing, *Overcoming Our Racism* (San Francisco: Jossey-Bass, 2003).

Suskind, Ron, *Hope in the Unseen* (New York: Broadway Books, 1998).

Swain, Carol, *The New White Nationalism in America* (Cambridge: Cambridge University Press, 2002).

Symons, Donald, *The Evolution of Human Sexuality* (New York: Oxford University Press, 1979).

Tannen, Deborah, *You Just Don't Understand: Women and Men in Conversation* (New York: Morrow, 1990).

Tarpley, Joan, "Blackwomen, Sexual Myth, and Jurisprudence," 69 *Temple Law Review* (1996): 1343.

Tatum, Becky L., "Deconstructing the Association of Race and Skin Color: The Salience of Skin Color," in *The System in Black and White,* Michael Markowitz and Delores Jones-Brown, eds. (Westport, Conn.: Praeger, 2000).

Tatum, Beverly, *Why Are All the Black Kids Sitting Together in the Cafeteria?* (New York: Basic Books, 1997).

Thernstrom, Abigail, "The Vile Circus at Harvard Law," *Wall Street Journal* (May 1, 1992): A14.

Thernstrom, Abigail, and Stephan Thernstrom, *No Excuses: Closing the Racial Gap in Learning* (New York: Simon and Schuster, 2003).

Thernstrom, Stephan, and Abigail Thernstrom, *America in Black and White* (New York: Simon and Schuster, 1992).

———, "Racial Preferences in Higher Education," in *One America?* Stanley Renshon, ed. (Washington, D.C.: Georgetown University Press, 2001).

Tiger, Lionel, *The Decline of Males* (New York: St. Martin's Griffin, 1999).

"The Toni Award," *New Republic* (June 19, 1989): 9.

Toobin, Jeffrey, *The Run of His Life* (New York: Random House, 1996).

Tooley, James, *The Miseducation of Women* (Chicago: Ivan Dee, 2003).

Torrey, Morrison, Jennifer Ries, and Elaine Spiliopoulos, "What Every First-Year Female Student Should Know," 7 *Columbia Journal of Gender and Law* (1998): 267.

Turner, Patricia, *I Heard It through the Grapevine* (Berkeley: University of California Press, 1993).

Turow, Scott, *One L* (New York: Putnam, 1977).

"2002 Writing Competition," pamphlet, Columbia Law School.

U.S. Department of Justice, Bureau of Justice Statistics, "Criminal Victimization in the United States—Statistical Tables, 2002," available at www.ojp.usdoj .gov/bjs.

———, Bureau of Justice Statistics, "Hate Crimes Reported in NIBRS, 1997–99," available at www.ojp.usdoj.gov/bjs.

———, Bureau of Justice Statistics, "Homicide Trends in the U.S., Trends by Race," available at www.ojp.usdoj.gov/bjs/homicide/race.htm.

———, "A Resource Guide on Racial Profiling Data Collection Systems" (November 2000).

Valencia, Reynaldo, et al., *Mexican Americans and the Law: ¡El Pueblo Unido Jamás Será Vencido!* (Tucson: University of Arizona Press, 2004).

Varian, Virginia, *Why So Slow?* (Cambridge, Mass.: MIT Press, 1999).

Vars, Frederick, and William Bowen, "Scholastic Aptitude Test Scores, Race, and Academic Performance in Selective Colleges and Universities," in Jencks and Phillips, *Black-White Test Score Gap.*

Walker, Alice, "What Can the White Man . . . Say to the Black Woman?" *Nation* (May 22, 1989): 691–92.

Watkins, Mel, *On the Real Side: Laughing, Lying, and Signifying* (New York: Simon and Schuster, 1994).

Weiss, Catherine, and Louise Melling, "The Legal Education of Twenty Women," 40 *Stanford Law Review* (1988): 1299.

Weitzman, Lenore, "The Economics of Divorce: Social and Economic Consequences of Property, Alimony, and Child Support Awards," 28 *UCLA Law Review* (1981): 1126.

Wells, Catherine, "The Theory and Practice of Being Trina," 81 *Minnesota Law Review* (1997): 1381.

West, Robin, *Caring for Justice* (New York: NYU Press, 1997).

———, "The Difference in Women's Hedonic Lives: A Phenomenological Critique of Feminist Legal Theory," 15 *Wisconsin Women's Law Journal* (2000): 149.

———, "Economic Man and Literary Woman: One Contrast," 39 *Mercer Law Review* (1988): 867.

———, "Jurisprudence and Gender," 55 *University of Chicago Law Review* (1988): 1.

White, Richard A., "Association of American Law Schools Statistical Report on Law School Faculty and Candidates for Law Faculty Positions, 1999–2000," table 2, available at www.aals.org/statistics/T2A.htm.

Wiehl, Lis, "Sounding Black in the Courtroom: Court-Sanctioned Racial Stereotyping," 18 *Harvard Blackletter Law Journal* (spring 2002): 185.

Wightman, Linda, "Predictive Validity of the LSAT: A National Summary of the 1990–92 Correlation Studies" (LSAC Research Report 93-05, 1993).

———, "The Threat to Legal Education: An Empirical Analysis of the Consequences of Race as a Factor in Law School Admissions," 72 *New York University Law Review* (1997): 1.

———, *Women in Legal Education: A Comparison of the Law School Performance and Law School Experience of Women and Men* ([Newtown, Pa.]: Law School Admission Council, 1996).

Wightman, Linda, and David Muller, "An Analysis of Differential Validity and Differential Prediction for Black, Mexican American, Hispanic, and White Law Students" (LSAC Research Report 90-03, June 1990).

Williams, Joan, *Unbending Gender: Why Family and Work Conflict and What to Do about It* (New York: Oxford University Press, 2000).

———, "What Stymies Women's Academic Careers? It's Personal," *Chronicle of Higher Education* (December 15, 2000): B10.

Williams, Lena, *It's the Little Things* (New York: Harcourt, 2000).

Williams, Patricia, *The Alchemy of Race and Rights* (Cambridge, Mass.: Harvard University Press, 1991).

———, "Comment: Metro Broadcasting, Inc. v. FCC: Regrouping in Singular Time," 104 *Harvard Law Review* (1990): 525.

———, *The Rooster's Egg* (Cambridge, Mass.: Harvard University Press, 1995).

Williams, Sue, "No Laughing Matter," *Sun Herald* (Sydney, Australia) (October 5, 1997): 14.

Willie, Sarah, *Acting Black* (New York: Routledge, 2003).

Willingham, W., C. Lewis, R. Morgan, and L. Ramist, *Predicting College Grades: An Analysis of Institutional Trends over Two Decades* (Princeton, N.J.: Educational Testing Service, 1990).

Wilson, James Q., "Crime," in *Beyond the Color Line*, Abigail Thernstrom and Stephan Thernstrom, eds. (Stanford, Calif.: Hoover Institution Press, 2002).

Wilson, William J., *When Work Disappears: The World of the New Urban Poor* (New York: Knopf, 1996).

Winbush, Raymond, ed., *Should America Pay? Slavery and the Raging Debate over Reparations* (New York: Amistad, 2003).

Wu, Frank, *Yellow: Race in America beyond Black and White* (New York: Basic Books, 2002).

Wu, Lawrence, and Barbara Wolfe, Introduction to *Out of Wedlock*, Lawrence Wu and Barbara Wolfe, eds. (New York: Russell Sage Foundation, 2001).

Wullschlager, Jackie, *Hans Christian Andersen* (New York: Knopf, 2001).

Young, Iris M., *Justice and the Politics of Difference* (Princeton: Princeton University Press, 1990).

Name Index

Subject Index

About the Author

Dan Subotnik is Professor of Law at Touro College, Jacob D. Fuchsberg Law Center, in Huntington, New York. Along the way he has taught at Northwestern University Law School, the University of Chicago Graduate School of Business, the University of California at Berkeley Law School, and Seton Hall Law School. In the fall of 2003, he created a seminar, "Contemporary Issues in Race and Gender," at Touro Law School.